# BECOMING  AMERICAN

# BECOMING AMERICAN

*An Ethnic History*

Thomas J. Archdeacon

THE FREE PRESS
*A Division of Macmillan, Inc.*
NEW YORK

Collier Macmillan Publishers
LONDON

The Free Press
A Division of Macmillan, Inc.
866 Third Avenue, New York, N.Y. 10022

Collier Macmillan Canada, Inc.

First Free Press Paperback Edition 1984

Printed in the United States of America

printing number paperback

2  3  4  5  6  7  8  9  10

printing number hardcover

1  2  3  4  5  6  7  8  9  10


**Library of Congress Cataloging in Publication Data**

Archdeacon, Thomas J.
   Becoming American.

   Bibliography: p.
   Includes index.
   1. Minorities—United States—History.   2. United
States—Emigration and immigration.   3. United States—
Foreign population.   I. Title.
E184.A1A75   1983          973 '.04          82-48691
ISBN 0-02-900830-1
ISBN 0-02-900980-4 pbk.

To
Marilyn Lavin

# Contents

# Acknowledgments

EVERY AUTHOR ACCUMULATES a number of unpayable debts that should
be acknowledged. I am no exception. As senior editor at The Free Press
Colin Jones provided important encouragement from the first stages of
the project. Joyce Seltzer worked hard and creatively to bring the work
to completion after Colin's departure to become the director of the New
York University Press. Robert Harrington, as editorial supervisor, and
Madeleine Birns, as copy editor, made many helpful suggestions that
improved the manuscript.

Professor Andrew M. Greeley of the University of Arizona and the
National Opinion Research Center and Professor James P. Shenton of
Columbia University made cogent critiques of the manuscript. In addition, Professors David S. Lovejoy, Jurgen F. H.Herbst, and Pekka K.
Hamalainen helped me considerably by their close readings of it. So
many other members of the University of Wisconsin faculty aided me in
smaller ways that I dare not try to list their names. I thank all these people for improving this book and, in keeping with the demands of justice
and tradition, absolve them of responsibility for its shortcomings.

The staffs of Memorial Library at the University of Wisconsin and
of the State Historical Society of Wisconsin helped me to exploit effi-
ciently the resources of their institutions. George Pasdirtz, Alvin B.
Schubert, Alice R. Robbin, and Thomas S. Flory of the Social Science
Data and Computation Center helped me master the university's data
libraries and computing systems. The secretarial staff of Wisconsin's
history department skillfully prepared the manuscript.

My late father, Daniel, and my mother, Elizabeth, taught me with
their lives the many meanings of immigration to the United States. The

hospitality of my in-laws, John and Helene Lavin, allowed me to work on several chapters of this book in congenial summer surroundings at Lake Pleasant, New York. My wife, Marilyn Lavin, took time from her own full schedule to offer valuable advice and welcome support. Our children, Meghan, Patrick, and Caitlin tolerated my irregular schedule and are the people for whom I wanted to tell the story.

THOMAS J. ARCHDEACON
*Madison, Wisconsin*

# Prologue

THE HISTORIAN WHO UNDERTAKES to describe how people have come from all over the world to North America and how they have formed the population and society of the United States must answer several basic questions. Who came, and why did they leave their native lands? When did the various immigrant groups come, and where did they go after arriving? What was the attitude of the government of the United States toward this great movement of human beings? How were the newcomers received by the people whose families had come to America in earlier years or even centuries? How did the immigrants respond to the foreign environment in which they suddenly found themselves? To what extent did the immigrants and their children become part of the mainstream of American society? Which of their Old World practices and values, if any, have survived in the New World? The questions seem simple and straightforward, but beneath their appearance lies a reality that involves serious and complicated problems of definition, measurement, and judgment.

Immigration to the Western Hemisphere has involved so many peoples and taken place over such a long period of time that making generalizations about the phenomenon is risky. The groups that crossed from Siberia to North America ages before the era of modern discovery, the Europeans and the Africans who settled the North American continent in the seventeenth and eighteenth centuries, the people who helped fill the continent from the Atlantic to the Pacific in the nineteenth and twentieth centuries, and the citizens of Asia and Latin America who have joined the immigrant stream to the United States in the most recent decades are all part of the story. Each of these movements took place under radically different circumstances. The first Americans, who will be identified throughout this work as Indians, encountered a virgin land; the colonists were able to put their cultural stamp on a new nation modeled on the states of Europe; the immigrants of the nineteenth century entered an America whose rural, agricultural economy was giving way to an urban, industrial order; and the newest arrivals have come as a postscript to the great age of migration. Even within a single era, the experiences of incoming groups often varied dramatically, as the case of the colonists from Africa illustrates. They came to America involuntarily, almost without exception passed the stigma of slavery to their descendants, and, because their distinguishing feature was a dark skin, were unable to follow other immigrants in the practice of shedding their obviously foreign attributes.

Any examination of American immigration must contend with the self-images of the United States as a nation of immigrants and as the world's refuge for the oppressed. This mythology carries an important element of truth, but it also encourages a narrow perspective. The United States is only one of several nations of immigrants: Argentina, Australia, and Canada, for example, can also claim the designation. The United States, though it has drawn people from a greater variety of sources than have most other receiving nations, cannot even boast the highest number of immigrants in proportion to the total population. The age of immigration, particularly at its apex in the nineteenth and early twentieth centuries, was a worldwide phenomenon, and the United States was but one of several New World destinations. In the Western Hemisphere between 1821 and 1924, Argentina, Brazil, and Canada welcomed relatively greater numbers of immigrants. Moreover, the movement to North and South America was just an extension of the migrations taking place between and within European and Asian nations. The Irish went to England, as well as to Canada and the United States; the Chinese made their presence felt in Indochina, as well as on the American frontier; and rural Swedes went to Stockholm, as well as to Chicago. Crossing the Atlantic Ocean was the last in a series of steps that took European peasants from their cottages to nearby market towns, to industrial centers, and to the great port cities. The old image of Europeans casting off the shackles of political tyranny and economic exploitation in their native lands in favor of liberty and opportunity in America still has validity but this view must be tempered. A host of factors made Europeans emigrants, and sometimes very mundane considerations determined the roads they followed and the destinations they reached.

Describing the immigrant experience is a difficult assignment because once the newcomers crossed the borders of the United States their foreign origin became only one of the influences in their lives. Immigrants of the same European or Asian background were likely to share many social traits, but the variations within a single group could be as great as those between nationalities. Some spoke English as their native tongue and shared to greater or lesser degrees in the British culture that was the ancestor of the American; others not only brought non-English tongues and habits but also were determined to preserve them. Immigrants often settled in the cities of the East Coast, but many of them made their way into rural America. The former were likely to have frequent contacts, however superficial, with persons of different ethnic backgrounds; the latter might live in villages as homogeneous as any in their homelands. Europe's wealthy, highly educated, and professionally trained tended to stay at home, but the people who came to America nevertheless occupied a wide range of life's stations. Some were desperately poor, others moderately prosperous; some were illiterate, others schooled; some could do only manual labor, others were experienced farmers or skilled craftsmen. All of these attributes affected the immigrants' expectations, their ability to take advantage of opportunities, and, indeed, their definition of becoming an American. The Norwegian farmer living in a Wisconsin village dominated by his countrymen must have had an image of America different from that held by the Italian factory worker residing in a Rhode Island industrial city, where he competed with Irishmen for jobs and was expected to accept as his social norms the values of descendants of the colonists.

Likewise, the people of America did not formulate a single attitude toward immigration. They approached the issue from different points of view, altered their attitudes with changing circumstances, and sometimes reacted in ways that belied their actual experiences with the problem. Blueblood racists feared immigration as a threat to Anglo-Saxon purity, but other well-born Americans saw the immigrants as pitiful, rather than threatening, and sought to help them. Trade unionists, who might be sympathetic to the immigrants at times, scorned them as competitors for jobs when the economy turned sour. People who had admired their German neighbors denounced them when America became involved in World War I. Some city dwellers who encountered daily the turmoil caused by the immigrants' presence merely moved to the suburbs, while numbers of rural folk who rarely dealt with foreigners became convinced that continued immigration would destroy the United States. Americans, moreover, differentiated among ethnic groups. Anglo-Protestants were aghast at the coming of the Irish in the 1840s and 1850s, but their descendants found the Latin and Slavic Catholics who arrived at the end of the nineteenth century a greater menace than the familiar Celts. Irish-Americans shared some of the disdain felt by their Protestant antagonists for the peoples of southern and eastern Europe regardless of shared religious affiliations. Whites of all nationalities worried about the so-called Yellow Peril posed by the Chinese and the Japanese, and Christians from every denomination would have rested more easily had Jewish immigrants from Europe not appeared on the scene on the eve of the twentieth century.

Even if the historian avoids excessive generalization, the challenge remains to put the immigrant and ethnic experiences into a suitable context and to establish appropriate criteria for judging how well the nation has absorbed its newcomers. The temptation is great to focus on the tragic incidents in the story. Recounting the riots between native-born Americans and immigrants, the clashes between rival ethnic groups, the episodes of political mistreatment and discrimination, and the repeated and eventually successful efforts to restrict entry into the United States has the advantages of being dramatic and of balancing the prevailing view that American history has been characterized by an unusually high degree of amity and consensus. But should such dark moments, however integral they may be to the tale, be allowed to outweigh the less exciting efforts of the society to incorporate strangers and the signs of gradual progress being made by people learning to live together? In a similar manner, it is easiest to measure the economic success of the immigrants and their offspring against the standards of the nation's stated commitment to equal opportunity and its implicit goal of unlimited social mobility. This approach can reveal much about American values, but expecting newcomers immediately to reach almost mythic norms is naive. Unfortunately, if the ideal cannot serve as the gauge, the task of estimating how much progress should be expected becomes difficult. How much mobility into prestigious or lucrative occupations must occur before a society can be described as open? How long can low levels of achievement in educational or professional attainment continue before they become prima facie evidence of purposeful discrimination, unconscious prejudice, or cultural and institutional impediments impinging on the affected groups?

Judging how well the nation has assimilated the descendants of the immigrants into its social networks is at least as hard as evaluating how fairly it has treated the strangers on its shores and as estimating how much economic opportunity it has afforded them. For many years the goal was assumed to be a situation in which ethnic identities would wane and would become unimportant in determining political affiliations, neighborhood preferences, marital partners, and other personal choices. Indeed, a substantial amount of evidence pointed toward the gradual achievement of that objective. Much research, however, has suggested that Americans continue tenaciously to maintain their ethnic and religious identities, and many commentators have argued that the nation's diversity is its greatest asset. At present it is no longer clear whether the United States should be a melting pot or an experiment in cultural pluralism, nor is it certain in which direction the country is heading. An abysmal lack of information, especially about the descendants of those later immigrants whom the Anglo-Saxons thought most unlike themselves, aggravates the confusion. The government simply assumes that ethnic groups become absorbed into the society after two generations in the United States. The census therefore defines the grandchildren of immigrants as "native of native parentage." The authorities decline to ask additional questions that might reveal the persistence of ethnic identities; refuse, out of a fear of violating the First Amendment, to gather data about religious affiliations; and forbid, out of respect for the privacy of persons who may still be alive, to allow the scholarly analysis of the more informative manuscript reports for the federal censuses taken after 1910.

The final problem in discussing assimilation involves determining whether American ethnic groups have preserved distinctive attitudes and values that affect their behavior and their integration into the broader society. Ethnic characteristics are an elusive item. Almost unconsciously each generation passes subtle cultural patterns to the next, but the mechanisms of this process, particularly over the course of several generations, are vague. Precisely because they are unarticulated, many of these ethnic assumptions and attitudes are hard to identify accurately. For past eras historians must seek clues from contemporary commentators, some of whom were neither perspicacious nor sympathetic to the people they observed. For more recent times they can turn to data gathered in interviews and surveys, but the sociologists responsible for these studies often neglect to put their findings in a historical perspective and sometimes design their questions to test important theses in their discipline rather than to collect general information about the ethnic and religious groups under study. As a result, historians discussing ethnic characteristics find themselves on a thin line between analyzing a legitimate subject and propagating stereotypes, including some unfavorable ones. Even when historians are confident that they have succeeded in identifying an ethnic trait or behavior pattern, isolating its impact from the effects of coincidental social circumstances is not easy. Investigators frequently argue, for example, whether the lifestyles found in some urban neighborhoods are the product of the cultural norms of the ethnic groups predominant there or reflect the values of the economic class to which most of the residents belong.

Despite the danger of these pitfalls, *Becoming American* tries to present an up-to-date account of the history of immigration to the United States and of the assimilation of foreign-born and foreign-stock Americans into the general society. Its approach is inclusive. The book examines assimilation along with immigration, inasmuch as they are two sides of a single phenomenon—the creation of the American people. It discusses Indians and Africans, as well as Europeans and Asians, because their stories are related and because intergroup differences help define the nation's alternatives for dealing with alien peoples. The book begins with the colonial period out of recognition that the assumptions governing intergroup relations in the United States were established then and concludes with an effort to make sense of what has happened to America's ethnic groups since the end of the era of mass migration. The book balances respect for the specific and unique with the desire to organize information in instructive categories and to analyze data in a theoretical framework. It shows the variety of causes that drove people from their homelands, the range of conditions that they met in the New World, and the diversity of reactions to the problems associated with the commingling of peoples. But it also makes limited generalizations about individual ethnic groups and combinations of them. In making judgments, the study relies on a comparative method. Wherever the tactic seems appropriate, it measures the experiences of ethnic, racial, and religious groups against each other rather than against an arbitrary standard. Finally, *Becoming American* puts the history of immigration and assimilation in perspective by comparing the American record in dealing with a heterogeneous population with the records of other nations.

*Becoming American* is divided into this prologue, eight core chapters, and an epilogue. Chapter I examines the establishment of English domination in North America. In the provinces, the English, whose racially conscious culture and long history of antagonism toward neighboring Celts predisposed them to dealing harshly with less advanced peoples, joined other whites in eliminating Indian competitors and in forcing blacks into subordination. Though the English constituted only 60 percent of the European population in the mainland colonies from Massachusetts to Georgia, they managed to set the standards to which settlers of other national origins had to adhere. They had to make significant concessions only in Quebec, which they conquered in 1763; there, the French, who maintained a large numerical advantage, had to be placated. The American Revolution substituted allegiance to a set of political beliefs for acceptance of English superiority as the criterion of full membership in the society, but the Anglo-American culture that developed in the postrevolutionary years intensified the association of foreign values with radicalism and subversion. Nevertheless, as Chapter II demonstrates, the rapidly developing new nation became a magnet for the large surplus population being created in Europe by changing demographic patterns and the decline of small-scale agriculture. From the 1840s forward emigrants from western Europe swarmed into the port cities of America.

Chapters III and IV treat the reactions of native-stock Americans to the newcomers and the attitudes of the immigrants toward adopting the dominant culture and seeking assimilation into the general society. Protestant America had an ingrained fear of European corruption and of the Roman Catholicism practiced by many of the mid-nineteenth-century immigrants. Respectable citizens were appalled by the conditions in which many of the foreigners lived and worked, but they were inclined to see these unfortunates as social inferiors responsible for their own plight. Feelings against the immigrants ran high, especially in the 1850s, when the daily number of arrivals increased steadily and society sought a scapegoat in a climate of sectional tensions. Though nativism became less virulent after the Civil War, it remained a staple of the culture, capable of flaring during moments of political and economic crisis. Faced with this situation, some immigrant leaders advocated programs of Americanization, but others sought to maintain the independence and integrity of their ethnic groups. The former helped make western Europeans and the Catholic church seem less sinister to the more liberal members of the American elite. The latter, however, by creating a set of ethnic and religious institutions parallel in function to those of the host community, managed to limit the absorption of the immigrants and their offspring into the mainstream of society.

Chapter V discusses the shift in the principal source of immigrants to the United States from western Europe to the southern and eastern sections of that continent. It ties the coming of these later arrivals to changes in the American economy that also brought Asians to the United States and spurred the movement of blacks from the rural South to the urban North. The chapter argues that the new immigrants were faced with the necessity of adjusting not only to Anglo-Saxon norms but also to the ethnic institutions, like the Catholic church and the Democratic party of the cities, that the old immigrants had shaped. As Chapter VI shows, the advent of southern and eastern Europeans rekindled nativism. It locates the origins of the immigration restriction movement in the American aversion to Catholics and Jews, the fear of job competition from the newcomers, the identification of foreigners with social evils of major concern in the Progressive era, the rise of a pseudoscientific theory of Anglo-Saxon superiority, and the reassertion of small-town and rural values after World War I. The chapter traces the story of restriction from the exclusion of the Chinese in the 1880s, through the gradual extension of federal control over immigration and congressional efforts to establish a literacy test for would-be immigrants, to the eventual adoption of quota laws in the 1920s.

The final chapters analyze the history of America's ethnic groups since the end of the age of mass migration. Chapter VII traces the federal government's reaffirmation of basically restrictive immigration policies during the Great Depression, World War II, and the opening years of the Cold War. It also examines the process of Americanization experienced by the nation's foreign-stock communities during the decades after congressional action deprived them of substantial, continuing reinforcement from abroad. By 1950 America's ethnic groups were becoming composed of English-speaking members of the second generation who were busily ridding themselves of the vestiges of Old World cultures. Ethnicity still counted in the lives of these people, but with each passing year they were increasingly being drawn by their shared interests into political, economic, and social contacts that transcended the boundaries of individual nationalities. Indeed, even the religious divisions that had generated so much bitterness in the past became muted as the various creeds combined in opposition to the common danger posed by the officially atheistic philosophy of the Communist bloc. Chapter VIII opens with an analysis of the 1950s image of the United States as a triple melting pot in which citizens from Protestant, Catholic, and Jewish backgrounds retained their own beliefs but managed to live in mutual respect. By the mid-1960s this optimistic view of the United States made possible the symbolically important abolition of the ethnically discriminatory facets of America's immigration policies. That decade, however, also witnessed the rising by the nation's most disadvantaged racial and ethnic minorities in protests that showed grave inadequacies in the triple melting pot analogy and sparked a new ethnic consciousness. Blacks, Chicanos, and Indians belatedly asserted pride in their heritages, and Americans of other origins responded in kind. The renaissance of ethnicity among the nation's better established immigrant groups may have begun as a negative reaction to demands for special treatment by less successful minorities, but it also entailed an honest appreciation of roots and a protest against lingering discrimination. The development had the beneficial effect of leading scholars to a greater understanding of the continuing role of ethnic and religious differences in American life. The epilogue of *Becoming American* attempts to provide some insights into these variations by describing the demographic, economic, political, and social characteristics of America's ethnic and religious groups today.

# BECOMING AMERICAN

# CHAPTER I

# The Formative Period, 1607–1790

In April 1607 Captain Christopher Newport brought three vessels, the *Sarah Constant,* the *Goodspeed,* and the *Discovery,* to the mouth of the James River in present-day Virginia. The 104 survivors of the transatlantic crossing from England soon began building a settlement thirty miles upriver. They were not the first Europeans to establish a colony in the New World: the Spanish had conquered Mexico, Central America, and South America almost a century earlier and had founded the city of St. Augustine in Florida in 1565. Nor were they the first Englishmen to try to settle in North America: in 1585 and in 1587 Sir Walter Raleigh had set up short-lived communities on Roanoke Island, off the North Carolina coast. What distinguished the founders of Jamestown was that they were the first Europeans to establish a permanent settlement in the region that was to embrace the original thirteen states of the American union. Their achievement marked England's full-fledged entry into the race for New World possessions and set the course that European colonization in America would take. Unlike their competitors—the Dutch, French, Portuguese, Spanish, and Swedes—the English did not retain as their goal the maintenance of outposts through which to exert control over native populations or to conduct trade with them. They learned instead to fill the land with self-sustaining communities that replicated, as far as possible, their English prototypes. To the extent that these settlers succeeded, they gave their language and much of their culture to a new

1

society. Insofar as they fell short, they contributed to the creation of a
new people, the Americans.

England's promoters of New World exploration hoped to duplicate
the success of the Spanish, who had found wealthy, advanced native
civilizations in America. Having killed or subjugated the leaders of
these centralized societies and captured their capital cities, the
Spaniards were able both to force the native peoples to work for them
and to expropriate their wealth. But the tribal societies of North
America were vastly different from those to the south. There were fewer
natives in the regions explored by the English, though these territories
were hardly empty or unused. Perhaps 500,000 Indians, descendants of
the pioneers who had crossed the land bridge from Siberia as early as
30,000 years before Christ, lived in eastern North America when the
Europeans arrived. More than a century of settlement would pass
before the population of the English colonies reached this total. Three
decentralized cultural groups divided the eastern woodlands. The
Algonquians—including such important tribes as the Abnaki, Penob-
scot, Wampanoag, Pequot, and Narragansett—were centered in the
section the Europeans called New England but also incorporated peoples farther south, like the Delaware of the Hudson River basin and the
Powhatan Confederacy of Virginia. The Iroquois nations of the
Cayuga, Mohawk, Oneida, Onondaga, and Seneca tribes were dominant from the Adirondack Mountains in present-day New York State
into Pennsylvania and were represented by the Cherokee and the Tuscarora in the South. The Muskhogeans, composed primarily of the
Apalachee, Chickasaw, Choctaw, Creek, Natchez, and Seminole
tribes, lived in the Southeast. The social organization of the Indian
peoples varied in sophistication, with the Iroquois having a strong
political confederacy and the Muskhogeans an elaborate caste structure.
Customs and economic practices also differed, but most Indians pursued a semisedentary way of life not far removed from that of some
Europeans. The nations of the northeastern woodlands inhabited villages that rivaled European communities in size and sometimes boasted
fortifications. These peoples hunted, fished, gathered wild foods, and
farmed, growing, among other things, beans, maize, pumpkins, and
tobacco. They weaved, made pottery, turned animal skins into finished
clothing, and—using swift birch-bark canoes and a network of overland
trails—conducted long-distance trade.

When the English came, few in number and inept at sustaining
themselves from the local resources, the natives stood their ground.
They adopted European goods, like cloth and guns, that seemed useful
and sought the newcomers' military assistance in intertribal wars, but
they rejected foreign religious beliefs and social mores and resisted subjugation. The English who came to Virginia and who settled Plymouth

in 1620 and Massachusetts Bay in 1630 found themselves dealing with people who possessed a desirable land and yet seemed different and, therefore, inferior. For the English the situation was not new: they had faced similar circumstances in Ireland for several centuries. To be sure, the Irish were fair-skinned and Christian, but more attributes distinguished them from the English than joined them. Irish society was pastoral. In the summer, the bulk of the population left behind settled communities to tend their animals in pasturing areas. Agriculture in large measure was devoted to growing oats for winter cattle feed. The ownership of land was not as precisely defined in Ireland as in England, where full-time farming was the natural order. In Ireland the family as a unit held land, and individual members could not alienate property. Political authority was diffused, with each leader having effective control over an area of no more than 300–400 square miles. The Irish strongly fought English efforts to assume the government of the island and to replace the natives' Catholicism with Protestantism. Frustrated, the English developed an extremely negative opinion of the Irish. They called the Irish savage and wild, described them as licentious and debauched, dismissed their religious beliefs as devil worship, lamented the filthiness of their primitive living conditions and habits, and criticized their diet. In this climate, English armies conducted virtual wars of extermination on the island during the last half of Elizabeth I's reign. Ideally, the English hoped to settle Ireland with more suitable inhabitants, and men like Sir Walter Raleigh and Sir Humphrey Gilbert were active in ventures to establish colonies in Ireland at the same time that they were laying plans for an American empire.

In the first decades of settlement in America, the English frequently compared the native peoples and the Irish, finding them similar in dress, dwellings, food, land tenure, and even in the mourning of their dead. Like the Irish, the Indians were considered barbarians who followed heathen religions and mated indiscriminately. When the Indians, angered by incursions into their territories, attacked the colonists, they showed cunning and perfidy. What the English found alike they treated alike, and the leadership soon decided on a policy to replace the natives with white settlers. Although the English preferred, whenever possible, to purchase the natives' lands, they were also willing to take territory by force.

Any violence by the natives brought awful retribution. After the Powhatan Confederacy, under Opechancanough, killed about one-third of Virginia's whites in an attack in 1622, the colonists adopted a policy of annihilation. In 1637, the residents of Massachusetts Bay and a party of Narragansett Indians attacked the fortifications of the Pequot, their mutual enemy, on Connecticut's Mystic River. More than 500 Pequots fell in an hour's battle; the survivors were sold as slaves. The story continued throughout the colonial era: New Englanders destroyed the Wampanoag and the Narragansett tribes, their former allies, during King Philip's War of 1675–1676; Virginians elimininated the Susquehanna, perceived as an obstacle to settlement in the Piedmont, during Bacon's Rebellion of 1676; and the whites of the Carolinas removed the natives from their path in the Tuscarora War of 1711–1712 and the Yamasee War of 1715–1728.

English bullets killed many Indians, but perhaps the settlers' greatest weapon against the natives was disease. In Spanish America as much as 90 percent of the native population had been eliminated, in most cases by natural causes, within a century after the arrival of the Europeans. Though the statistical data that would allow a definite judgment are absent, a calamity of equal seriousness seems to have taken place among the aboriginal peoples of the North. At any rate, it became clear within two generations of the appearance of the English on the Atlantic coast that the natives would be relegated to a peripheral role in the emerging society of the New World.

The absence of an exploitable indigenous civilization was the first of three conditions that directed English policy on the path of large-scale colonization. The second was the existence of a great pool of potential immigrants. No other contemporary people was so struck by wanderlust as the English in the first half of the seventeenth century. Between 1620 and 1642 almost 80,000 persons, or 2 percent of the total population, left the island nation. In addition to those who emigrated to the transatlantic colonies, several thousand went to the various nations of the European continent, and by 1642 about 20,000 were living in the northern Irish province of Ulster. Deteriorating economic, political, and religious circumstances drove many English from their homes. Landlords desiring to convert their fields to sheep pastures evicted peasants from their small holdings; periodic economic crises put clothmakers out of work; and the expanding metropolis of London was a strong attraction for displaced Britons in search of opportunity. Since the middle of the sixteenth century, Englishmen had noticed the large number of people on the move in the realm. Some observers concluded that England was overpopulated, and even those who disagreed with this hypothesis admitted that the government had failed to keep the people at work. Moreover, the reigns of James I and Charles I were difficult for people who found too many Catholic remnants in the rituals of the Anglican church, an emphasis on outward behavior to the neglect of inner conversion in Anglican theology, and a deviation from the simplicity of early Christianity in the episcopal structure of the established church. As the official head of the English church, the monarch regarded such criticism with distrust, and William Laud, archbishop of Canterbury, resorted to fines and other measures to enforce conformity to Anglican practices. Emigration provided an answer for those suffering from economic or spiritual hardship, and the motives often combined to form an almost irresistible inducement.

England's relative flexibility in establishing policies for peopling and nurturing its colonies was the third condition affecting the course of their development. The English programs differed, at least in degree, from those of France and the Netherlands, the other main colonizing powers in eastern North America. The English were able to take advantage of the pool of potential emigrants at home because the nation trusted in the essential loyalty of its dissidents. Apparently, the government hoped to relieve tensions at home and to retain the allegiance of dissatisfied citizens by allowing them to seek relief elsewhere in English domains. Even as the storm clouds gathered before the Civil War, London was sending hordes of Puritans to the New World. The English, moreover, learned that the colonies would attract settlers only insofar as they offered the prospect of improved conditions. When the Virginia Company, the joint-stock organization responsible for that colony, turned its hopes from gold and silver to tobacco, the company discovered that it could not obtain employees to grow the crop without promising them land. A large number of self-sufficient and self-interested settlers established themselves on these grants, and in 1624 the king took direct control of the province; the company had become superfluous as an agency of colonization. Though the English government occasionally devised colonial charters that seemed designed to restrict the fruits of America to narrow groups of political favorites or to reconstruct the unequal social ranks of the Old World in the New, in practice the founders usually recognized the necessity of encouraging opportunity and individual enterprise.

French policy contrasted sharply with the English approach. The French regime refused to permit Protestant emigration to Quebec for fear that the presence of Huguenots there would lead to revolution. And, despite evidence that the effort was futile, the French never fully abandoned the hope of duplicating France's almost feudal social structure in Canada. Other factors had an impact, but the insistence of Versailles on regulating almost every phase of colonial life to maintain a familiar stability goes far toward explaining why only 10,000 Frenchmen emigrated to Canada between 1608 and 1760.

A less extreme situation existed in the colony established by the Dutch along the Hudson River in the 1620s. There, throughout the four decades of New Netherland's existence, the Dutch West India Company held sway. The merchants in control tried at first to limit settlement so as not to disturb the fur trade with the Indians; they tried later to enlarge the population by offering large land grants to patroons, who in exchange would bring over tenants; and at all times they made sure that a substantial portion of the colony's wealth went to the coffers of the company. Peaceful and prosperous conditions at home discouraged emigration from the Netherlands, but the failure of the Dutch government to curb the company and to appeal to the private ambitions of ordinary citizens also stayed New Netherland's growth.

Reflecting the motives behind its colonization and the nature of its economy, each English settlement in the New World developed distinctive demographic characteristics at the outset. Only in New England, as the Puritan colonies became known, did the population soon approach a normal demographic appearance. Over 20,000 people came to New England during its first decade, most of them for a combination of religious and economic reasons. They migrated from heavily populated areas of England in which Puritanism was strong and the cloth trade in decline. Men and women came in approximately equal numbers, traveling in nuclear units of father, mother, and children; the majority of family heads were in their thirties. These colonists often brought a few servants with them, for the most part men between eighteen and twenty-two. Though many of England's male emigrants may have been urban artisans at home, most eventually entered small-scale agriculture in the New World. The patterns were quite different to the south. Virginia's immigrants tended to be young bachelors. The Virginia Company's policy of populating its colony with employees encouraged such a pattern. The early years of bitter failure, the frightening massacres, and the emergence of a labor-intensive economy based on tobacco further discouraged a demographically balanced migration. The situation was similar in Antigua, Barbados, Bermuda, Montserrat, Nevis, and St. Christopher, the island colonies that the English had founded by 1640 in the Atlantic Ocean and the Caribbean. In 1635, for example, eight ships brought 985 immigrants from London to Barbados; 91 percent of the migrants were between the ages of ten and twenty-nine, few were married, and only 6 percent were women.

Lacking demographically balanced immigrant populations and perhaps not needing them for their staple-crop economies, Virginia and the island colonies depended for their labor on the importation of bound servants. In 1619 the Virginia Company provided that any person who paid for the transportation of a servant to the colony would receive a grant of fifty acres. In addition, English merchants saw that the tobacco colonies were prime markets for selling servants. Male bondsmen were more numerous, perhaps simply because they were more available, but females were also in demand, particularly as the permanence of the settlements became evident. The merchants procured servants from the ranks of those who wanted to go to America but could not afford the passage. Through the use of promotional tracts, popular songs, and reports of the riches to be found across the sea, the merchants and their agents sought recruits in the cities, towns, and villages of the British Isles. The prospective immigrants signed indentures, or contracts, that bound them to serve temporarily the persons who paid their fares. Those who committed themselves to go were brought to London or another port, where they were kept in seclusion until their vessel was ready to sail. Once the ship reached America, the captain either sold these people to the highest bidders or, in prearranged cases, simply delivered them to their masters.

Indentured servitude became a favored way to populate America. By 1625 almost 42 percent of Virginia's residents were servants and, during the entire colonial era, more than half of the European immigrants to the provinces south of New England entered as temporary bound laborers. The practice had several advantages. On the one hand, it allowed the American colonists to obtain workers at a more modest price than they would have had to pay for scarce free labor. On the other, it permitted people who otherwise could not have left Europe to seek new opportunities in America. The immigrants received food, lodging, and clothing during their service, and some obtained grants of money, tools, and, sometimes, land at the expiration of their contracts. The ultimate fate of the typical indentured servant is a matter of debate. Individual success stories abound, but so do tales of woe, and the mistreatment of bound servants was commonly litigated in colonial courts. The best available evidence is mixed, but it suggests the commonsensical conclusion that the prospects for freed indentured servants declined with the passage of time. As the settlements matured and grew, the possibility of rapid mobility decreased.

Popular though it was, indentured servitude had shortcomings, especially in the colonies that had the greatest need for labor. Indentured servants were bound for only four or five years, and supply never managed to keep pace with demand. As a result, another form of bound labor—black slavery—came to the fore. In the English colonies, slavery apparently began as an extension of indentured servitude. In 1619 a Dutch ship brought twenty black Africans to Virginia, where they were sold. The status of these laborers may have been no different initially from that of the numerous Europeans sold in the same period. Within a generation, however, it became understood that blacks were to remain servants for life and that their subordinate status would pass to their children. In the tobacco provinces of Virginia and Maryland, chattel slavery soon became widespread. Mid-seventeenth-century accounts of property holdings set the values of blacks far above those of temporary white servants; purchasers of Africans bought not only the blacks on the auction block but also the title to their potential offspring; courts imposed on recaptured black runaways corporal punishments rather than the extensions of service terms usually meted out to white ones; and, finally, planter society took special pains to condemn both licit and illicit sexual contacts between whites and blacks, which could have produced children of an indeterminate social position.

Slavery entrenched itself in those colonies in which a rapidly expanding economy demanded a large pool of agricultural laborers in order to produce a staple crop. When England's island colonies turned in the 1640s from tobacco to the much more lucrative sugar crop, the importation of slaves soared and blacks soon outnumbered whites in the population. By 1655, Barbados had 23,000 whites and 20,000 blacks; eighteen years later, the numbers were 21,309 and 33,184, respectively. Perhaps more surprising, the enslavement of blacks also took root in the northern colonies, where the economy made no demand for this system. This fact suggests that factors besides the hunger for labor underlay the subjugation of the black immigrants.

A century of experience told the English that Africans were not their equals and could be tolerated in white society only as bondsmen. Their predecessors in exploration and colonization, the Spanish and the Portuguese, had been enslaving blacks since the sixteenth century. The blacks, moreover, were captives taken in war and, though English law did not recognize slavery, Western society had long accepted the right of victors to exact service from vanquished peoples in exchange for their lives. Most important, the Africans seemed abysmally inferior. Their dark hue so struck the English that they described it as black, a color that in the culture of northern Europe conveyed thoughts of evil and foulness, in stark contrast with the images of grace and purity associated with white. Had skin color been the Africans' only fault, however, the implications of this attribute might have been forgotten; unfortunately, the perceived behavior of the blacks told willing believers that their character conformed to their color. In an age that frowned upon diversity in the Christian community, Africans had the misfortune to fall entirely outside the bounds of approved religion. Some blacks were Moslems, which was bad enough, but most seemed to be devil worshipers and idolators. Their sexual mores and, indeed, their whole sexual being seemed bizarre. According to the English, blacks were essentially libidinous: the men had genital organs so large as to be burdensome and the women were so lascivious that they freely offered themselves to whites. Perhaps, the English rationalized, the Africans were the damned offspring of Ham, who had committed the sexual sin described in the Bible as looking upon the nakedness of his father, Noah. Perhaps they were not fully human; in the eyes of many whites, Africans bore a strong resemblance to chimpanzees, the man-monkeys with whom black women were reputed to copulate.

Had the Africans been as debased as their detractors charged, they would not have been fit candidates for importation to America. African slaves came primarily from the western coast of the continent, from the areas known as Angola, the Bights of Benin and Biafra, the Gold Coast, Senegambia, Sierra Leone, and the Windward Coast. They were most likely to be members of ethnic groups like the Bambara, Ewe, Ibibio, Igbo, and Serer. Sedentary and coastal peoples, they were prey not only to European raiders but also to the warlike nations of the interior. Well-organized and militarily strong interior peoples like the Asante, Hausa, Mandinka, and Yoruba were able to defend themselves against the Europeans and quickly discovered that profits could be made by capturing and selling their neighbors. In reality, the vulnerable tribes had much in common with the Europeans. The religions of these peoples recognized a single supreme being and their beliefs could be syncretized with Christian teachings. Their economies likewise resembled those of Europe. In the kingdom of Benin, which lies today in eastern Nigeria, the Igbo produced a variety of crops that would become common in America, including corn, cotton, tobacco, and yams. This people raised cattle, goats, and poultry; their men made metal agricultural tools and weapons; their women wove cloth and made earthenware. The Igbo had an organized marketing system, used coined money, and traded for beads, fish, and guns. When Africans from backgrounds like this came to America, they fit easily into the economic routines of Western life, replacing the great aboriginal civilizations that the English had failed to find.

By the time of the Restoration, the English had established three types of colonial society. In the aptly named area of New England, they created a world whose demographic characteristics were like those of Old England. The white population was ethnically homogeneous, the native population was kept more or less outside the bounds of the community, and the proportion of African slaves remained small, hovering around 2 percent. Colonization followed a radically different course in the island colonies. There the English came closest to duplicating the New World societies established by the Spanish and the Portuguese. A core population of whites controlled the production of sugar, which was the islands' source of wealth, and managed the labor of an increasingly large proportion of permanently bound workers, who were, in this case, black. The situation differed in several critical respects in the main slaveholding colonies of the southern mainland. There the whites constituted a much larger proportion of the population; only in South Carolina did blacks ever gain even a temporary majority. The continental English, moreover, tended to remain resident in America, providing their colonies with an important indigenous political and social leadership. Perhaps because the sugar economy allowed them greater wealth and, with it, flexibility, many of the leading West Indian planters transferred their fortunes to England, where they assumed the lifestyle of the gentry. The conditions of slavery also differed between the continental and the island colonies. Though slaves in North America suffered the same legal indignities that their brothers and sisters endured in the sugar plantations, prospects for a normal life span were greater on the mainland. Because the chance to make great wealth in sugar encouraged overexploitation of labor and because Caribbean diseases were more virulent than maladies found to the north, the African population of the islands suffered a terrible mortality rate. Though 264,000 blacks came to the sugar plantations between 1640 and 1700, only 100,000 were alive there by the latter year. By the end of the eighteenth century, the continental settlements, which imported only one-fifth as many Africans as did the islands, had twice as many blacks.

The two colonial patterns based on slavery continued to flourish after the 1660s, as the importation of Africans increased rapidly. The British brought approximately 1.75 million blacks to their colonies in the eighteenth century. As stated earlier, 80 percent went to the islands. The proportion of whites in the population of the West Indies continued to fall: by 1713 there were 32,000 Europeans and 130,000 Africans in Barbados, the Leeward Islands, and Jamaica, which the English had seized from the Spanish in 1655. As large-scale sugar planters took over the economy of the islands, ordinary whites made their exits. The white population of the Leeward Islands of Antigua, Montserrat, Nevis, and St. Christopher declined from 10,408 in 1678 to 7,311 in 1708. Many whites left the West Indies to return to England; others migrated to the mainland provinces. The plantation colonies of the continent also grew in this period, and the proportion of blacks rose from 6 percent in 1670 to 28 percent in 1730. Nevertheless, the white population managed to maintain most of its strength in comparison with the black.

The population pattern that had distinguished New England from the islands and the southern colonies failed to continue. Migration from England, especially the exodus of families and skilled workers, ebbed after the middle of the seventeenth century. The religious and civil strife responsible for the departure of thousands in the 1630s abated, and the interregnum dissipated much of the utopian energy that had inspired the Puritan hegira. After the Glorious Revolution of 1688, the lot of Dissenters improved greatly. In addition, anti-emigration attitudes became common in England. At a time in which economic theorists were arguing that a large population was vital to agricultural and industrial production and consumption, the loss of people to the colonies, the London fire of 1666, and the ravages of the plague made many Englishmen fearful that the nation was being emptied. Writers deplored the loss of craftsmen and farmers and argued in behalf of measures, such as greater religious toleration, that would encourage Englishmen to stay at home. Nevertheless, no one suggested curtailing the growth of the American colonies, which increased in number with the acquisition of New York in 1664 and the founding of the Carolinas in the late 1660s and of Pennsylvania in 1682. Commentators viewed the provinces as valuable sources of raw materials and as markets for finished English goods. Thus, they could only hope that America would grow without diminishing England's economic potential.

Englishmen eventually found the answer to the problem of settling their colonies in a fourth approach, one that originally had been pursued in New Netherland. Like the English who established Virginia, the Dutch came to the Hudson Valley under the auspices of a commercial company eager to exploit the resources of the area. The Dutch fared well in the fur trade, but they gradually learned that they would have to foster a permanent, populous agricultural colony. They met the same frustrations as the English in dealing with the Indians and followed parallel policies toward them. The Dutch bought whatever lands they could but, when the natives resisted further encroachments, the Dutch were capable of launching exterminating attacks: the slaughters perpetrated by Director-General William Kieft in the early 1640s matched any English operation in ferocity. Plagued by a labor shortage, the Dutch also resorted to African slavery; they kept more blacks than did their English neighbors to the north but fewer than those to the south. Yet the white population of the Dutch colony grew in a distinctive way: from the earliest days New Netherland was a mixture of almost every European nationality group. By 1643, Isaac Jogues, a French Jesuit who visited New Amsterdam after escaping from the Mohawks, was able to make his well-known remark that eighteen languages were spoken on the streets of the small port. The protests of the established Dutch Reformed church that only persons of orthodox religious views be allowed in the colony were to no avail. After the Portuguese seized Brazil from the Dutch in 1652 and ordered Jewish colonists to leave, the West India Company, which was cognizant of the contributions of Amsterdam's Jewish investors to the organization's coffers, permitted these refugees to establish a home in New Netherland.

The experience of diversity seems at least occasionally to have encouraged tolerance. In 1657 the residents of Flushing, Long Island, a Dutch village with a number of migrants from New England in its population, rejected Director-General Peter Stuyvesant's demand that they ban Quakers from their community. The colonists told the angry governor that they would not condemn others for fear that God would condemn them. (In the same period, the Puritans of Massachusetts hanged two Quakers who refused to quit their province.)

Englishmen had been part of the society developing in New Netherland since the 1640s. At that time, New Englanders came into conflict with Dutch settlers on Long Island over territory claimed by the latter. But England's bloodless military conquest of New Netherland in 1664 brought about a novel situation in which people from two major, competing European nations found themselves members of a single American colony. Even in relatively homogeneous, Puritan New England towns like Sudbury and Hingham, Massachusetts, there had been tension between colonists from different regions of England over matters of agricultural technique or religious enthusiasm. So it is not surprising that the period of adjustment in New York, as New Netherland was renamed, included flashes of bitterness and conflict. The English were conciliatory, but they were also firm, especially after Dutch residents helped their countrymen gain temporary control of the colony in 1673 during the Third Anglo-Dutch War. The English established their laws and language as standard and required the colony's Dutch inhabitants to swear allegiance to King Charles II. They accepted the Dutch as partners, but the absorption of New York into the English colonial network was to the disadvantage of the large majority of Dutch settlers, who lacked the capital and influence to establish in England the business connections necessary for success in America. As the outcome of the uneven competition became apparent, especially in New York City, where members of the English minority took over the key economic, political, and social positions, ordinary Dutch citizens became discontented. Many of them supported the rebels who ousted Lieutenant Governor Francis Nicholson in 1689 in the wake of the overthrow of King James II. They apparently thought that the new king, William of Orange, himself a Dutch prince, would install an administration more sympathetic to them. Unfortunately for the Dutch, William and his wife, Queen Mary, the daughter of James II, aligned with Nicholson's former adherents. The monarchs dispatched William Sloughter to New York as its new governor and, after momentary resistance, the insurgents reluctantly yielded control to him. Sloughter ordered the leaders of the uprising, Jacob Leisler and his son-in-law Jacob Milborne, executed, and the process of Anglicization resumed.

The New York experience established a model for the growth of the other English colonies in the eighteenth century. America continued to call to England for immigrants, but the provinces depended increasingly on non-English sources for their white population. Germans, French, Scots, and Scotch-Irish made the transatlantic voyage in unprecedented numbers. For the most part they, like so many of their predecessors, arrived as indentured servants. They entered an English based culture and they were expected to operate within it. Members of foreign ethnic groups were entitled to citizenship and the full range of civic privileges, but English political forms and economic practices remained the norm, and success fell to those best able to conform to them. Naturally, members of white minority groups who lived near Englishmen in ethnically mixed communities were the most likely to be criticized for failing to adapt to the prevailing standards, but they were also the most likely to learn the ways of the dominant culture. Like the Dutch of New York City, this group was welcome to become Anglicized. But it was also possible in eighteenth-century America for people to live in communities isolated from frequent intercourse with the English and from the benefits and burdens of life in the mainstream. Like the Dutch of the upper Hudson Valley, where English culture penetrated only slowly, such people could easily preserve their own customs, languages, and religious practices for many decades.

Pennsylvania, founded in 1682, quickly joined New York as an English colony with a multi-ethnic population. Indeed, as Philadelphia became the leading colonial city, Pennsylvania became the main point of entry for immigrants to America. The colony came into being when King Charles II satisfied a long-standing debt to his loyal supporter Admiral Sir William Penn by allowing his son William a sizable chunk of American wilderness. Young Penn hoped to establish a refuge in the New World for members of the Society of Friends, which he had joined. Charles's decision to permit an unorthodox band of Christians to establish an American colony was not unusual. Puritans had settled Massachusetts and Catholics, Maryland. The novelty of Pennsylvania was the proprietor's willingness to welcome all forms of Christianity in the home set aside for his Quaker brothers and sisters. The Puritans of Massachusetts were intolerant, and a growing population of Protestants soon restricted the rights of Maryland's Catholics. During his years as a Friend, including time spent in prison for his religious views, Penn had developed a philosophy that exalted individual freedom and identified suppressions of difference as criminal. His attitude resembled that of Roger Williams, the Puritan exile from Massachusetts who had opened Rhode Island to all believers, but Penn's stance became more significant historically because of the large size of his colony and of the great numbers of people who took advantage of his liberalism.

The establishment of Pennsylvania coincided with the beginning of a half century during which a mixed band of European religious and political refugees turned to America for asylum. By 1685 about 8,000 persons had come to Pennsylvania. The great majority were English, Irish, and Welsh members of the Society of Friends, but perhaps the most notable group was a small contingent of Germans from Crefeld, a weaving center on the lower Rhine. These people were former Mennonites drawn to the Quakers by Penn during his tour of Germany in 1677. Their leader, Daniel Francis Pastorius, arrived in Philadelphia in August 1683 with a small following; 33 more Crefelders came in October. Like the Welsh, the Germans demanded a separate district in which to establish themselves. Penn, though he would not allow the erection of virtually independent ethnic enclaves, did give both groups land near Philadelphia. The settlement of the Crefelders began a tradition in Pennsylvania of welcoming Pietists and sectaries. In 1710 a group of Swiss Mennonites accepted a grant of 10,000 acres in what later became Lancaster County. The Mennonites were like the Quakers in theology. They insisted on a simple lifestyle, most rigorously exemplified by the behavior and dress of their Amish subsect. In 1719 the Dunkards, another Anabaptist group, began the migration that gradually transferred their whole membership from Westphalia to Pennsylvania. The Schwenkfelders made their way to Pennsylvania in 1734. Finally, over 700 members of the United Brethren, or Moravians, came to the Pennsylvania towns of Bethlehem and Nazareth in the years after 1741.

French Protestants joined the trek to America in the 1680s. Since the proclamation of the Edict of Nantes in 1598, the Huguenots had enjoyed a large measure of religious liberty and political autonomy in the communities in which they were concentrated. But in 1685 King Louis XIV, believing that the Huguenots were losing strength and were vulnerable, revoked the edict. His decision turned many Huguenots into exiles and, as Protestants and enemies of the French king, they gained the sympathy of the English. Charles II and Parliament offered the Huguenots a refuge in England and promised to aid them in migrations elsewhere. Soon Frenchmen were on their way across the Atlantic to a variety of colonial locations. Even Massachusetts was willing to allow thirty Huguenot families to settle in the frontier town of Oxford in 1687. When native attacks dispersed the community in 1696, some of the survivors joined other Huguenots in Boston. Most of the French chose points farther south. Some went to New York City, where they formed about 10 percent of the identifiable white population at the beginning of the eighteenth century; others founded the towns of New Rochelle, outside the city, and of New Paltz in present Ulster County. In South Carolina, about 1,000 Huguenots established themselves in Charleston and along the Santee and Cooper rivers.

During the War of the Spanish Succession, the government of Queen Anne allowed at least 10,000 Protestant refugees from the Rhenish Palatinate and from neighboring territories on the Rhine, Neckar, and Main rivers to come to England. These Germans had suffered a French military attack because they were allied with the English. Because of prevailing sympathies, approximately 3,500 Roman Catholic Palatines who also escaped from the mainland were sent home. The largesse of the government and private charity supported the Protestant Palatines in temporary camps around London, but the situation was not easy. The conditions in which the Palatines lived stirred fears of disease, and the aid given the foreigners provoked needy native-born Englishmen to the point of riot and attack upon the camps. London looked to the colonies for relief. Over 3,800 of the Palatines were sent to Ireland; another 600, to North Carolina. But the main focus of the Palatines' American immigration became New York, to which colony some 3,000 sailed in April 1710. Roughly one-fourth of this contingent died either en route or shortly after landing. The survivors settled largely in the Hudson Valley where the provincial governor, Robert Hunter, hoped to employ them in the production of naval stores. When that experiment collapsed in 1712, many of the Germans began to move west along paths that ultimately took them or their descendants into northeastern Pennsylvania and into New York's Mohawk Valley.

After the first two decades of the eighteenth century, the numbers of immigrant Pietists and of refugees sponsored by the English government diminished. The years remaining before the Revolution foreshadowed the great influx of non-English Europeans in the nineteenth century. The various German states probably supplied the largest number of newcomers, with Ireland and Scotland not far behind. Whatever their origins, the migrants had much in common. Almost every person who left the Old World had a combination of motives, but economic considerations seem to have predominated. In search of a better life, most of the immigrants, like their predecessors in the seventeenth century, bound themselves as servants. Many of these "redemptioners" were responding to tales of a land of milk and honey like those told German peasants by "newlanders," who represented merchants engaged in the servant trade. For some, the price of a few years' labor was small when measured against the opportunities gained. For others, their period of indentured labor meant the destruction of family and the shattering of hopes.

The eighteenth-century immigrants shunned New England; its inhabitants were reputed to be unfriendly to non-English people and, more important, the region was declining. Constricted geographically, New England lacked land for expansion. In addition, New England bore much of the cost in men, money, and economic disruption of the frequent wars that pitted the English and French colonies against each other in the eighteenth century. The newcomers likewise avoided the plantation districts; slavery discouraged both free laborers and workers who expected to become free. Their destination was the middle colonies and, inasmuch as landlords were said to control the best lands along the Hudson, the newcomers favored Pennsylvania over New York. Philadelphia offered access to fertile lands stretching west to the Alleghenies and, if that did not satisfy the immigrants, they could proceed down the mountain line into the Back Country of the southern colonies, an area that had not been appropriated by the plantations.

Germans arrived at the rate of 2,000 a year in Pennsylvania in the eighteenth century. They spread across the colonies from New York to Georgia, often settling in frontier areas, where land was cheapest. By the time of the Revolution, Germans were well represented in the most fertile areas of the colonies, most notably in central Pennsylvania, the heart of American grain production. The aptitude of the Germans for farming amazed many observers, who used their practices as criteria against which to evaluate the techniques of other nationalities. The Germans chose limestone areas over land along navigable rivers, cleared the ground thoroughly, remained on their homesteads while others constantly pushed toward the frontier, used stoves rather than fireplaces in order to conserve wood, gardened extensively, and took excellent care of their horses and cattle. To some extent, the attributes ascribed to the Germans were simply proof of peasant conservatism and of the newcomers' unfamiliarity with the American economy. Farms near water may have been less fertile, but they had better access to markets, and moving occasionally to new ground may have been as economically rational as painstakingly maintaining old fields in a world of cheap land and expensive labor. But the behavior of the Germans also suggests that they had more familiarity than other European immigrant groups with sophisticated agriculture.

Migration was not a new experience for the Presbyterians who left northern Ireland for America in the eighteenth century. With the encouragement of their countryman King James I of England, they had gone from their homes in Scotland to colonize Ulster in the first part of the seventeenth century. By the beginning of the eighteenth century, this group constituted about one-third of the 600,000 persons in northern Ireland. In comparison with Ireland's Catholics, the Scotch-Irish (as they became known in the United States) fared well; nevertheless, they were not free from problems. As Presbyterians they suffered from the liabilities imposed by the English on Dissenters. Most annoying, the Scotch-Irish had to contribute to the support of the established Anglican church and they were barred from holding public office. As residents of a colony belonging to a mercantilist state, they also had to work within economic strictures; the Wool Act of 1699, for example, severely curtailed Ulster's manufacturing by forbidding the export of finished woolen products that might compete with goods crafted in England. Finally, as residents of Ireland, the Ulstermen suffered under rising rents, the bane of all inhabitants of the island. Ulster's linen industry, which the English allowed because it did not compete with any business in the home state, helped drive up rents by creating a heavy demand for land on which to grow flax. Thus, emigration was an attractive solution to residents of Ulster laboring under these disabilities.

The era of heavy Scotch-Irish emigration began roughly in 1715. In

Ireland, the years 1715–1720 saw a drought drive up food prices and a sharp increase in rents. Estimating the total number that came in these years is difficult, but about 1,000 Scotch-Irish landed in Boston in 1718, one of the years of heavier immigration. Altogether the 1720s saw an influx of some 15,000, driven abroad by the same factors that had sparked the movement: food scarcity and high rents. The majority of these immigrants made Philadelphia their destination, and in the following decades their successors followed them to the hospitable Quaker port. From there the Scotch-Irish headed to the Back Country, where they usually established themselves in communities located to the west of those settled by the Germans. Emigration continued steadily during the years before 1770: between 50,000 and 70,000 Ulster men and women made the transatlantic crossing. The passage of time brought Ireland a new round of rent increases in the late 1760s and early 1770s. Farmers sharply raised the price of their food products in the hope of meeting their increased costs and, on top of these shocks, northern Ireland faced a depression in the linen industry in 1771 and 1772. The inevitable results were starvation and emigration, with the flow of Scotch-Irish across the Atlantic reaching a crescendo between 1770 and 1775, when as many as 40,000 left for America.

Some striking parallels exist between the emigration of the Scotch-Irish to America and the exodus of their Scottish cousins to the colonies, but the two stories are, at least in part, distinct. In the eighteenth century, Scotland was divided into two geographic and social areas, the Lowlands and the Highlands. The former lay south and east of the mountain line running from the Clyde Valley through Perthshire and Angus and then turning north along the east coast of Scotland to the Pentland Firth; the latter lay north and west of this line. The Lowlands were closer to England, had adopted the language of the stronger nation, and were the center of both commerce and linen manufacture. Though England and Scotland had been made one by the Act of Union of 1708, the Highlands managed to resist the cultural grasp of the former and were in 1715 and 1745 the center of rebellions that vainly tried to restore the Scottish House of Stuart to the English throne. Scottish emigration, unlike Scotch-Irish, was consistently low during the first half of the eighteenth century. Contrary to popular lore, the failures of the rebellions of 1715 and 1745 did not lead to a massive displacement of people. No more than 1,000 Scottish prisoners reached the mainland or island colonies as a result of the deportations carried out after both uprisings. Following the suppression of the 1745 revolt, however, the English confiscated the estates of the rebel leaders, curbed the powers of the clan chiefs, upset the pattern of feudal relations, forbade the wearing of the traditional kilt, and sent Presbyterian ministers from the Lowlands to convert the Highlanders from Roman Catholicism. The English program shattered the social structure of the Highlands and changed its economy, setting the stage for a great rise in Scottish emigration in the third quarter of the century.

Statistics relating to the boom in Scottish emigration are incomplete, but the best estimates indicate that approximately 25,000 Scotsmen went to America between 1763 and 1775. In the Lowlands, the source of as much as 40 percent of the total, the causes for emigration resembled those at work in Ulster: rising rents drove farmers from their lands, and the economic depression of the early 1770s put weavers out of work. In the Highlands, the familiar causes of overpopulation and crop failure were also at work, but there other pressures increased the desire to emigrate. The destruction of the feudal bonds between lords and tenants after 1745 fostered capitalistic agricultural practices that hastened the enclosure of lands and displaced many peasants. The same changes also undermined the position of the Scottish tacksman, an intermediary between lord and tenant. Before 1745 the tacksmen, who held their lands by lease, paid only nominal rents; their primary obligations to their overlords were to organize agricultural labor in peacetime and, more important, to lead tenant soldiers in war. The decline of the clan system after 1745 took away the tacksmen's martial role. After that they had to pay higher rents, which they were able only occasionally to pass on to the hard-pressed peasants. Dissatisfied with their increasingly marginal status, many tacksmen looked to America as a place in which they could re-create or even surpass their lost social position. Trusting that the old clan ties would hold, they and other members of the lesser gentry hoped to lead their subtenants to the colonies, where they could establish themselves as landowners and lords. The prospect was especially attractive to those Scots who earned claims to land on the colonial frontier for their military service as British officers during the French and Indian War. As a result, the emigration of the Highlanders took a peculiar twist, with group movement and settlement frequent. Between 1769 and 1773, for example, the lesser tacksmen of the Isle of Skye led about 5,000 persons, over one-fifth of the population, to the Cape Fear Valley of North Carolina. The Macdonnels of Glengarry brought 300 of their clansmen to the Mohawk Valley, and Captain John Macdonald of Glenaladale brought 300 Roman Catholics from Boisdale to Prince Edward Island in Canada.

American colonists and their leaders accepted the changes in immigration that took place in the eighteenth century without unpredictable alarm. The servile condition in which many of the newcomers arrived, the proclivity of those who came independently to slip into the Back Country and to form isolated ethnic settlements, and the seemingly insatiable appetite of the New World for labor reduced the potential for conflict and eased the misgivings of the earlier arrivals. For the most part, the colonists' response to the surge of immigration was to extend the practices inherited from the seventeenth century. But there were special areas of concern. The control of the black population always required attention. In addition, there was doubt about the suitability of some of the European servants who were imported. And, as tensions heightened between England and France, the Protestant provincials' terror of Roman Catholics flared.

African immigrants posed a unique problem for the white population. They came involuntarily and, as bound servants, they lived in the midst of a free community. In some urban areas blacks formed a sizable minority, approaching 18 percent in New York in 1749 and 9 percent in Philadelphia in 1767. Their numbers were even greater in the plantation colonies, where by 1770 Africans formed 42 percent of the population in Virginia and actually constituted a majority of 60 percent in South Carolina. In the cities, where the typical slaveholder had only one or two blacks, and on the farms of less affluent planters, slaves lived in close contact with their masters, usually sharing their houses. On larger plantations, the field hands had separate quarters; only the house servants lived in relatively close contact with whites. Each arrangement had advantages and shortcomings. The intimacy of the small unit could soften the master-slave relationship, but this situation also offered the unhappy servant great opportunities to lash out. The impersonality of the larger plantation insulated the master and his family from their slaves, but the privacy of the workers' quarters gave refuge to plotters and the presence of a black majority allowed the rebellious to dream of successful uprisings.

Despite the injustice being done to the Africans, the amount of overt, violent resistance to slavery during the colonial era was minimal. The absence of large-scale revolts is a mark of the caution of the whites and of the control exerted over the blacks. Colonists in areas with fewer slaves were able to purchase most of their laborers from the West Indies, where they had been inured to their lot and acculturated. Buyers in the plantation colonies had to count on the large black population's being able to absorb new Africans quickly. All the English colonies established codes for dealing with blacks, and these tended to vary in severity in proportion to the number of slaves in the population. In general, slaves were not allowed either to be abroad without a pass or to congregate; masters were required to take part in supervisory patrols and to punish runaways, and they were granted compensation if any of their slaves were executed for crimes. The lack of rebellion is also a measure of the severity with which whites reacted to even suspected plots. When a band of blacks set fire to a building in New York City in 1712 and killed 9 Europeans who came to put out the flames, the courts ordered almost a score of slaves executed by hanging, burning, and breaking on the wheel. Three decades later, in 1741, the city responded hysterically to a series of possible arsons, burning 13 blacks, hanging 18 others, shipping 70 more out of the province, and hanging 4 whites believed to have abetted the alleged plot. In 1739, the militia of South Carolina put down a group of 50–100 blacks who killed several whites near Stono, and in the following year the colony executed several dozen slaves implicated in another conspiracy.

European immigrant groups caused much less concern. Pennsylvania authorities worried about potential public charges among Scotch-Irish who failed to respect the proprietor's land titles and who clashed unnecessarily with the Indians on the frontier, and Benjamin Franklin in 1751 protested that "Palatine boors" were trying to "Germanize" the province and would not adopt the English language. The main objection that existed, however, was to the deportation of English convicts to the colonies. The practice was present from the beginning of settlement but increased with the decline of voluntary emigration after 1660 and became common in the eighteenth century. As many as 50,000 convicts reached the mainland and the West Indian provinces before the Revolution. In Maryland, which received 20,000 of the total, convicts constituted one-half of the population of white servants. Sending prisoners to the colonies had beneficial effects. The people of England were absolved from the necessity of supporting some convicts and they were able to put the Atlantic Ocean between themselves and a variety of undesirables. American employers were able to add to their supply of bound labor. The convicts, in return for seven or fourteen years of service in the colonies (depending on the seriousness of the offense), escaped worse punishments, including the death penalty. Indeed, for those who had committed only minor wrongs, exile was certainly more constructive than the Draconian penalties then sanctioned by the English criminal law. But, from the colonial point of view, the program of transportation had obvious shortcomings as well. Many of the convicts were serious felons, guilty of arson, murder, rape, and other vile deeds. The colonists blamed any perceived increase in crime on their presence, and several provinces tried to curb the traffic. In 1722 Pennsylvania imposed a duty of £5 on each convict imported and required the ship captains bringing prisoners to post a £50 bond for each as a guarantee of their good behavior for one year. In 1754 Maryland levied a 20s. duty on each servant having seven years or longer to serve. The London government occasionally allowed such taxes to stand, but England overturned any laws that attempted to ban importation. As a result, contractors continued to ship convicts as long as there was a market for them.

Only one group of potential European immigrants created near panic among the American colonists, and the objection to them was not based primarily on ethnic grounds. The prospect of the arrival of Roman Catholics of any nationality curdled the blood of most provincials. Protestant colonists thought of Catholicism as a religious and political threat. The English Reformation was less than a century old when settlement began in America, and for more vigorous Protestants like the Puritans the work of cleansing the church had just begun. The Huguenots and some of the German sectaries had actually experienced persecution under Catholic rulers. And all the colonists were conscious that the gravest threat to their security was the French Catholics of Quebec and their tribal allies. The Americans' fear, however, was exaggerated. Roman Catholics represented only about 1 percent of the population and half of them lived in a single colony, Maryland. Anti-Catholicism's importance, therefore, was not its impact on residents of the colonies but its role in identifying America as Protestant territory and in creating a bond among Protestant inhabitants of all denominations.

No colony specifically forbade Roman Catholics to settle, but all of them passed laws that restricted the practice of the Roman faith or limited Catholics' political liberties. As early as 1647 Massachusetts banned priests from its jurisdiction on pain of death if they were caught in the colony twice. Virginia in the early 1640s banned Catholics from political office and authorized the governor to expel priests. In neighboring Maryland, in 1654, the growing Protestant majority revoked the Toleration Act passed five years earlier to protect the Catholic minority. During the turmoil that followed the news in America of the Glorious Revolution, New York's insurgent leader Jacob Leisler made venomous accusations against Catholics and stirred fears of a French invasion; in Maryland, John Coode led an uprising that destroyed the last vestiges of Catholic influence exercised by old settlers closely associated with the proprietor, Lord Baltimore. By the end of the seventeenth century, Catholics were free to worship only in Rhode Island and Pennsylvania, and even there their rights were circumscribed or endangered. The situation became worse in the eighteenth century. After the outbreak of the French and Indian War in 1754, Maryland imposed a double land tax on Catholics and ordered county officials to report on their activities. Pennsylvania likewise imposed heavier taxes on Catholics, disarmed them, and banned them from sensitive settlements along the frontier. The anti-Catholic animus of the colonists culminated in the years before the Revolution. Annual celebrations of Guy Fawkes Day, which was known in America as Pope's Day, combined mockery of the Roman church with denunciations of the king's government. Linking these two supposed despotisms did not seem unreasonable to the colonists, especially after the royal government promulgated the Quebec Act in 1774. The measure was the product of a decade's effort by the

English to devise a workable plan for governing the 65,000 Frenchmen who had come under their control after the cession of Quebec in 1763. But the law appeared contemporaneously with the Coercive Acts passed to punish Boston for the Tea Party, and its grant of religious liberty to Quebec's Catholics seemed, along with other provisions, most notably a southward expansion of the colony's boundary to the Ohio River, a maneuver to enlist the Canadians against the patriot cause.

The Declaration of Independence and the Revolutionary War brought to an end the colonial phase of America's immigration history and profoundly affected the assumptions that would shape this land in the future. Though the implications of independence may not have been immediately realized, the separation from England infused the definition of nationality in the United States with a distinctive political ideology. What would distinguish America was not the acceptance of immigrants as citizens; Parliament had made provisions for naturalizing newcomers to the colonies and the mother country. What would make the United States different was its demand that citizens give their allegiance to a set of political principles, as well as to a government. The Revolution, moreover, deprived English culture of much of its claim to a natural position of superiority in America. The necessity of opposing England forced the colonists to widen their perspective. From defending themselves on the basis of the rights of Englishmen, the Americans stepped forward to justify their cause in terms of the rights of humanity. The Second Continental Congress told the Canadians in May 1775 that the fates of Catholic and Protestant Americans were linked and invited them to join in the struggle against the British. The Quebecers were not persuaded by this appeal, which was written by John Jay, a staunch anti-Catholic of Huguenot descent, but the American gesture was a first step. During the warfare that followed, military cooperation and not religious affiliation was the proof of friendship, and the Americans gladly accepted the assistance of Frenchmen, whom they had previously excoriated as papists.

Participation in the Revolution legitimized the claim of non-English Europeans to a full share in the new nation. But no ethnic groups unanimously supported independence, and many colonists, regardless of their origin, aligned with or against the rebels as much out of an evaluation of their immediate interests as from a commitment to political principle. Scotch-Irish on Pennsylvania's frontier resented English efforts to prevent further settlement in the interior and the lenient Indian policies of the loyal proprietary government; thus, this group produced ardent revolutionaries. Many Scotch-Irish on the North and South Carolina frontiers, however, cooperated with the English; they saw the Revolution as an opportunity to even old political scores with the rebel elite of the coastal settlements. The Germans in the Mohawk Valley took up arms against unpopular Tory landlords; those on the Georgia frontier were unwilling to risk losing English protection against the Indians; and those who lived in isolated communities or belonged to pacifist sects sought simply to remain neutral. The Scots are probably the only immigrants about whom generalizations can be safely made: with one voice patriots and loyalists commented on the unswerving fealty of both Lowlanders and Highlanders to the crown. The Scottish merchants who had a pivotal role in the economy of the tobacco colonies were primarily responsible for the impression of Lowland loyalism. As with other persons whose fates depended on preserving the ties of empire, the reasons for their decision were obvious. Explaining the loyalism of the Highlanders, who had fought recent and bitter wars against the English, is more difficult. In part, their behavior matched that of other late arrivals who were not yet secure enough in their new environment to risk the changes that a revolution would entail. But the Highlanders were also acting as they had in Scotland, in loyalty to their tacksmen, who had recently received land grants from the crown or from Tory grandees.

The War of Independence had tangible, as well as intangible, effects on American immigration. The exigencies of war interrupted transatlantic traffic of all kinds. More important, the political turmoil created one of the few instances of large-scale migration out of the American states. Between 80,000 and 100,000 colonists left rather than disavow allegiance to England. Some of the loyalists, including many of the most well-to-do, made their way to England, where they unexpectedly found themselves snubbed as provincials. A much larger number sought refuge in the territories that would be merged into Canada. Approximately 28,000 went to Nova Scotia and dispersed from there in search of cheaper lands to Cape Breton, Prince Edward Island, and the St. John Valley. Others moved into Quebec and pushed Canadian settlement westward. Scottish Highlanders from New York's Mohawk Valley, who had fought as British soldiers during the Revolution, established Glengarry County in Ontario. Members of other ethnic groups, including Scottish Presbyterians, Dutch, and Germans, were also rewarded with Canadian lands after fighting in behalf of the crown. They established themselves in homogeneous ethnic communities along the St. Lawrence River and Lake Ontario. The migration of these peoples helped guarantee that Canada and the United States would follow different courses. The presence of these foes of the Revolution insured that there would be strong resistance whenever the American nation cast covetous eyes northward and that Canada's politics and social values would remain more conservative than those of America for a long time.

Moreover, this migration helped create an Anglicized Canada, which would serve as an alternative destination to the United States for British emigrants of later eras.

As the United States entered its first full decade under the Constitution, almost 4 million persons lived in the lands that would eventually comprise the forty-eight contiguous states. The first federal census, taken in 1790, reported that 3,172,444 whites and 757,208 blacks resided in the original states and in Vermont, Kentucky, and Tennessee; 92.1 percent of the blacks were slaves. There were 10,500 people in the Northwest Territory, 20,000 in the future Louisiana Territory, and 24,000 in the Spanish settlements to the west. The government took the census as part of the procedure for apportioning congressional seats. Except for identifying blacks and especially black slaves, each of whom counted as only three-fifths of a person in determining representation, the authorities were uninterested in the ethnic background of the nation's inhabitants. Nevertheless, through careful statistical examination of the surname patterns that appear in the records of the census, scholars have been able to create a reasonably accurate description of the presence and geographical distribution of national groups in the infant country.

Two centuries of immigration had made the former English colonies a mosaic of peoples. The English had impregnated the new nation with their laws and with important elements of their political traditions and had made their language the standard. English-stock Americans, however, accounted for only 49.2 percent of the total population and 60.9 percent of the white inhabitants of the enumerated area (Table I–1). The English were proportionately most numerous in the New England states; in Massachusetts, for instance, they accounted for 76.5 percent of the population. They also formed a majority of the white population in the South, but the presence of large numbers of blacks significantly reduced the percentage of English in the whole population. Whites did not consider Africans, especially enslaved ones, as fully part of the American people, but in point of fact they were the second largest identifiable group. Blacks constituted 19.3 percent of the people of the Unites States, and in the South, where 89.3 percent of them lived, blacks represented impressive minorities: 40.9 percent of the population of Virginia and 43.7 percent of that of South Carolina. The Africans were 2.7 times as numerous as the Germans, the second largest white ethnic group in the nation. The 276,940 Germans were concentrated in the areas that this group had settled initially. They formed almost a third of Pennsylvania's population and were barely outnumbered by the English in that state. Germans accounted for 7.6 percent of the people in New York and for 8.5 percent of those in New Jersey. The Scots formed the third-ranking white element in the thirteen states and in Vermont,

# TABLE I-1
## Proportional Representation of National, Racial and Linguistic Groups in the U.S. Population, 1790[1]

| STATE | TOTAL | WHITE (%) | BLACK (%) | ENGLISH (%) | SCOTCH (%) | IRISH Ulster (%) | IRISH Eire (%) | GERMAN (%) | DUTCH (%) | FRENCH (%) | SWEDISH (%) | UNASSIGNED WHITE (%) |
|---|---|---|---|---|---|---|---|---|---|---|---|---|
| New Hampshire | 141,900 | 99.4 | 0.6 | 60.7 | 6.1 | 4.6 | 2.9 | 0.4 | 0.1 | 0.7 | 0.0 | 23.9 |
| Massachusetts | 475,295 | 98.7 | 1.3 | 76.5 | 4.4 | 3.6 | 1.8 | 0.5 | 0.1 | 0.9 | 0.0 | 10.9 |
| Rhode Island | 69,025 | 93.7 | 6.3 | 66.5 | 5.4 | 1.9 | 0.7 | 0.5 | 0.4 | 0.7 | 0.1 | 17.5 |
| Connecticut | 237,808 | 97.7 | 2.3 | 65.4 | 2.1 | 1.8 | 1.1 | 0.3 | 0.3 | 0.9 | 0.0 | 25.8 |
| New York | 340,344 | 92.4 | 7.6 | 48.0 | 6.5 | 4.7 | 2.8 | 7.6 | 16.2 | 3.5 | 0.4 | 2.7 |
| New Jersey | 184,139 | 92.3 | 7.7 | 43.4 | 7.1 | 5.8 | 3.0 | 8.5 | 15.3 | 2.2 | 3.6 | 3.4 |
| Pennsylvania | 433,647 | 97.6 | 2.4 | 34.5 | 8.4 | 10.7 | 3.4 | 32.5 | 1.7 | 1.7 | 0.8 | 3.9 |
| Delaware | 59,096 | 78.4 | 21.6 | 47.0 | 6.3 | 4.9 | 4.2 | 0.9 | 3.4 | 1.3 | 0.8 | 3.5 |
| Maryland | 319,728 | 65.3 | 34.7 | 42.1 | 5.0 | 3.8 | 4.2 | 7.6 | 0.3 | 0.8 | 6.9 | 1.2 |
| Virginia | 747,610 | 59.1 | 40.9 | 40.5 | 6.0 | 3.7 | 3.3 | 3.7 | 0.2 | 0.9 | 0.3 | 0.5 |
| North Carolina | 394,728 | 73.3 | 26.7 | 48.4 | 10.8 | 4.2 | 4.0 | 3.4 | 0.2 | 1.2 | 0.2 | 0.9 |
| South Carolina | 249,073 | 56.3 | 43.7 | 33.9 | 8.5 | 5.3 | 2.5 | 2.8 | 0.2 | 2.2 | 0.1 | 0.8 |
| Georgia | 82,548 | 64.1 | 35.9 | 36.8 | 9.9 | 7.4 | 2.4 | 4.9 | 0.1 | 1.4 | 0.4 | 0.8 |
| Vermont | 85,343 | 99.7 | 0.3 | 75.7 | 5.1 | 3.2 | 1.9 | 0.2 | 0.6 | 0.4 | 0.0 | 12.6 |
| Kentucky/Tennessee | 109,368 | 85.1 | 14.9 | 49.3 | 8.5 | 6.0 | 4.4 | 11.9 | 1.1 | 1.8 | 0.5 | 1.6 |
| Total | 3,929,652 | 80.7 | 19.3 | 49.2 | 6.6 | 4.8 | 3.0 | 7.0 | 2.6 | 1.4 | 0.5 | 5.6 |

SOURCE: Computed by Thomas J. Archdeacon from data in American Council of Learned Societies, "Report of the Committee on Linguistic and National Stocks in the United States," *Annual Report of the American Historical Association for the Year 1931* (Washington, D.C.: Government Printing Office, 1932), I: table 13 and U.S. Census Office. Ninth Census, 1870, *A Compendium of the Ninth Census* (1872; reprint ed. New York: Arno, 1976), table 3.

[1]The lack of data and their peripheral position in the society forced the omission of the Indians from this table of estimates.

Kentucky, and Tennessee. They, too, were located close to their areas of initial settlement, most notably in North Carolina, South Carolina, and Georgia.

Estimating the size of the Irish contingent in America is a problem. Perhaps 7.8 percent of the U.S. population in 1790 had their origins in Ireland. But three distinct cultural and ethnic traditions—the Scotch-Irish, the English Irish, and the Celtic Irish—were represented among these immigrants. The Scotch-Irish were the largest element, accounting for 4.8 percent of the total U.S. population. Following a geographic distribution similar to that of the Germans, the Scotch-Irish were best known as frontier people. Less information is available about the two other Irish groups. The concentration in Virginia and Maryland of Irish names native to the southern provinces of Leinster and Munster suggests that these Irishmen may have been among the servant population brought to the plantations before black slavery became widespread. And, recognizing the paucity of Catholics in the United States in 1790, it seems likely that many of the Irish emigrants were English Protestants who had been colonists in Ireland for 200 or 300 years before migrating to America and that a good percentage of the Catholics who came surrendered their faith under the pressures of life in the Protestant provinces of the New World.

In 1790 the major chapters of American immigration history were yet to be written, but the outline of the story was already drafted. Anglo-American culture, though still evolving, had achieved dominance. The Native Americans of the East had been defeated and the imported African population subjugated. Potential competitors had been overcome; the heirs of New Netherland and of New Sweden (which had enjoyed a brief existence in the Delaware Valley between the colony's establishment in 1638 and its fall to the Dutch in 1655) formed identifiable minorities in three states, New York, New Jersey, and Delaware. Waves of non-English European immigrants had successfully entered the society, though the extent to which they were integrated into it remains in doubt. The future would tell a similar story. To the west, there were French, Spaniards, and still unconquered Native Americans; they or their descendants would be living in U.S. territory before the mid-nineteenth century. And, across the Atlantic and Pacific oceans, forces were building that would bring new influxes of immigrants in search of refuge and opportunity.

# CHAPTER II

# The Old Immigration, 1790–1890

AMAZING CHANGES TOOK PLACE in the United States between the first federal census in 1790 and the eleventh in 1890. At the end of the eighteenth century, the United States was a struggling nation composed of mutually wary political communities stretched along the Atlantic seaboard. Transportation and communication were primitive, and the American economy revolved around agriculture and the simple commercial networks that got farm products to market. More than 90 percent of the citizens lived in the countryside, and the nation's largest city, Philadelphia, had only 42,444 inhabitants. By the final decade of the nineteenth century, the United States stretched from the Atlantic to the Pacific and constituted the leading industrial nation on earth. Train rails and telegraph wires bound together the farthest points of the continent. New York, the largest city, had 1,515,301 residents on Manhattan Island; fifteen other cities had surpassed the 200,000 mark; and about 23.3 percent of the population lived in communities with more than 25,000 inhabitants. The growth of the total population was equally impressive: a nation of 3,929,652 in 1790, the United States held 62,947,714 within its bounds in 1890. The increase was the product not only of the fertility and health of the first American citizens and their descendants but also of the arrival and incorporation of more than 15 million foreign-born persons and their offspring in the United States over the course of the century. Their coming was part of one of the great

27

population movements of human history and marked the beginning of the most important era of American immigration.

Before the 1840s immigration to the United States proceeded at a modest rate, more in keeping with the earlier era of American history than with the age to follow. Until 1819 the U.S. Congress did not even think it necessary to publish statistics on immigration, and most responsible observers agreed that only about 4,000 foreigners entered the country annually between 1800 and 1810. Indeed, low estimates such as these probably best describe the flow of immigrants during the entire Napoleonic era. The almost constant involvement of the nations of Europe in war between the 1790s and 1815 mangled the normal patterns of communication and commerce that were of fundamental importance to the transatlantic traffic in peoples. In addition, European governments were especially unwilling to lose parts of their populations when the military situation demanded substantial manpower. As early as 1788 the English government extended to Ireland its long-standing ban on the emigration of skilled artisans. In 1803 Parliament imposed the first restrictions on the carrying of passengers from the British Isles to points in America outside Newfoundland and Labrador. British ships were allowed to carry one traveler or crew member for each two tons that they weighed unladen; foreign vessels could ferry one person for every five unladen tons. The former measure aimed to protect England against the loss of able workers, including those who might take with them the secrets of England's new industrial enterprises. The latter restriction sought to achieve several purposes. Improving conditions on board ships and giving English vessels a competitive advantage were the most obvious goals, but the Passenger Act of 1803 also was an attempt to discourage emigration to the United States by driving up the costs of ocean transportation. It is commonly conceded that the law effectively ruined the business of importing servants to the new republic.

Though the French Revolution may have inhibited the normal pattern of immigration to the United States, it created a new one in the form of a wave of political refugees. The lack of statistical records for the period prohibits an exact determination of the number of persons who escaped to America from France in the 1790s, but an estimate of 10,000 is an understatement and one of 25,000 an exaggeration. The majority of refugees from France arrived after 1792 and, unlike their compatriots who fled to England and Germany after the fall of the Bastille in 1789, they had sympathized with the revolution in its early phases. Those who came to the United States either objected to the increasing radicalism of the movement, made manifest in the execution of King Louis XVI in 1793, or belonged to political factions that at some point fell from power. The political underpinnings of the French migration gave it two special qualities. In the first place, a group of distinguished persons leavened the influx of French citizens. Three Orleanist princes; aristocrats like the duc de La Rochefoucauld-Liancourt and the vicomte de Noailles; the scholar Médéric Louis-Elie Moreau de St. Méry; army officers who had served in the American War of Independence; the businessman Pierre Samuel Du Pont de Nemours, whose family reestablished its fortune in the United States; and twenty-four priests, including John Lefebure de Cheverus (the future bishop of Boston), were among the notable. In the second place, for an unknown number, migration to America was only a temporary exile; when the conservative First Directory came to power in 1795, they returned home.

Hordes of colonists from the Caribbean island of Saint-Domingue, or Santo Domingo, also contributed to the French immigration of the 1790s. They were the victims of an insurrection that tore apart a society of 40,000 whites, 28,000 mulattoes and freed blacks, and 500,000 slaves. The Creoles of Saint-Domingue had welcomed the prospects of greater autonomy offered by the French Revolution and in 1789 sent delegates to the Estates General for the first time. They resented, however, the decision of the Jacobin government on April 4, 1792, to give mulattoes and free blacks the same political liberties as whites, and they objected to the appointment of three civil commissioners to enforce the policy. The situation came to a head in June 1793. When the forces of a new governor, who sympathized with the whites, clashed with mulatto troops loyal to the commissioners, the latter called on black rebels for assistance. The Africans pillaged the port of Cap Français (now Cap Haïtien) and, in the wake of their rampage, as many as 10,000 Creoles, mulattoes, freedmen, and slaves fled to North America. The large majority arrived in Norfolk, but many eventually made their way to other cities. The refugees represented a cross-section of the membership of Saint-Domingue's social and economic classes, yet they often arrived destitute and were temporarily dependent on private charity, the contributions of state and local governments, and a $15,000 appropriation made by Congress in 1794 for their relief.

The French Revolution also played a role in stimulating emigration from England and its political dependencies. English radicals who sympathized with the French cause occasionally became victims of political and popular harassment so strong as to drive them into a transatlantic exile. Joseph Priestley, the renowned scientist who lost his house to a Birmingham mob, was probably the most famous of these refugees; he fled England in 1794 and spent the remainder of his days in Pennsylvania. In Ireland the spirit of the French Revolution infected the members of the United Irishmen, an organization devoted to achieving political independence for the island. The leaders of the United Irishmen were predominantly Protestant, but they enjoyed substantial support among the large Catholic population. By the mid-1790s English resistance to

the dissidents' often clandestine efforts to spread their message and even
to seek French assistance drove several of the cause's spokesmen to
America. Some, like Dr. James Reynolds of Ulster, who became
Thomas Jefferson's political ally, reestablished themselves perma-
nently. Others, like Wolfe Tone and Napper Tandy, remained in the
United States only briefly and then returned to their work in Europe.
Emigration on a larger scale followed the arrests of prominent United
Irish leaders in the spring of 1798 and the collapse and crushing in June
of short-lived uprisings inspired in Ulster and Leinster by the movement. But accurately estimating the size of the emigration and
distinguishing the political refugees from those ordinary folk leaving
Ireland in search of economic opportunity is almost impossible. Suffice
it to say that the movement accelerated moderately the continuous flow
of Ulster natives to the United States in the thirty years after 1783 and
fostered an exodus of men and women from Leinster that historians
have failed to appreciate.

The United States experienced an increase in immigration following
the restoration of peace in Europe in 1815. Most of the newcomers came
from familiar sources. As many as 6,000 Irishmen reached port in the
United States in 1816; 2,500 more followed in 1817; and another 6,500
came in 1818. About two-thirds of the Irish came from Protestant
Ulster. Middle-class people, including farmers, weavers, and artisans
who evaded the poorly enforced injunction against their departure, were
predominant among the early emigrants, but after a crop failure in 1817
the Irish migration drew from a broader social base. About 20,000 Germans, suffering the consequences of the weather conditions that virtually deprived 1816 of a summer, joined the trek to the United States in
that year and the next. The states of Baden and Württemberg experienced the largest losses, and the Bavarian Palatinate, Rhenish
Prussia, the Duchy of Nassau, and French Alsace also suffered emigration. The agricultural crisis soon eased, and reports filtered back to Germany of the hardships suffered by *Auswanderer* who ran out of money
before reaching their destinations. Prospective migrants became more
inclined to heed the proclamations issued by the authorities discourag-
ing departure, and some governments barred indigent travelers from
entering or crossing their territories. As a result, the surge in continental
emigration came to a sudden halt in 1817.

A number of push and pull conditions had to combine before immigration from Europe to the United States could emerge as one of the
great phenomena of nineteenth-century history. The sine qua non was
the population explosion that occurred in Europe between the mid-
points of the eighteenth and nineteenth centuries. Between 1750 and
1845 Europe's population grew from 140 to 250 million. This 80 percent
increment was more than twice as large as the previous record for long-

term population growth, a rate of 36 percent observed in the twelfth century. A dramatic drop in mortality rates was the key to the boom. The decline in the frequency of death, in turn, seems to have been the product of several causes whose relative timing and importance are debatable. The killer pandemics of earlier eras, such as the black plague, disappeared or became dormant, though epidemic diseases like cholera continued to take a heavy toll from time to time. The increased cultivation of the potato, which feeds more people per acre than does grain, and the introduction of other root crops and of clovers, which made possible the maintenance of large livestock herds through winter months, improved nutrition. Better tillage techniques, including the rotation of crops and the use of fertilizer, along with the invention of new farm machinery, made agriculture more effective. Finally, developments in transportation and communication helped prevent local harvest failures from turning into famines. The various improvements especially benefited children by giving them the strength to resist the infectious maladies that previously had carried off a sizable proportion of youngsters under the age of five years. Enough were able to survive and reproduce so that they and their offspring more than offset the demographic effects of the decline in the birth rate that became evident in the leading European nations as the century passed.

Europe's demographic transformation combined with another grand phenomenon of the nineteenth century, the industrial revolution, to create a population too large to be supported within the bounds of traditional economic structures. The growing number of people put unprecedented pressure on the available land. Many farm families did not have enough property to give each of their male children a plot adequate to support a family. At the same time, the amount of fresh land that could be brought under cultivation was limited, so that the purchase price of tillable acres rose with the increased demand for them. The industrial revolution had contradictory effects. On the one hand, the increase in enterprises based on processing mineral resources and on manufacturing finished goods pushed productivity past the limits imposed by an agricultural economy. On the other, the rise in production and the accompanying improvement in the standard of living were part of the network of causes underlying the population boom. Moreover, the industrial revolution had a devastating impact on the demand for certain kinds of workers. In agriculture, the introduction of scientific techniques and mechanization made larger holdings more efficient, put smaller operators in a disadvantageous economic position, and rendered many peasant tenants and farm laborers superfluous. In manufacturing, the adoption of machinery either made the skills of certain craftsmen obsolete or significantly reduced the demand for them.

As the people of Europe continued to multiply at a record pace, statesmen and economic theorists revised their earlier ideas about the value of a large population. The thinkers of the sixteenth and seventeenth centuries who had concerned themselves with demographic problems had argued that prosperity and population increased in unison. As subjects of labor-intensive agricultural nations, they had been interested more in increasing production than in raising beyond the minimum the level of consumption and the standard of living. Moreover, these views had been influenced by the biblical injunction identifying human reproduction with the fulfillment of God's plan for the world and by awareness of the difficulties that Europe had experienced during the Middle Ages in maintaining even small-scale growth. Such attitudes became less common after the middle of the eighteenth century. Leading writers, most notably Thomas R. Malthus in England, argued that the population expanded geometrically, while increments in agricultural production were arithmetic; a demographic disaster would be inevitable once the number of people finally exceeded the ability of Europe's resources to support them. Malthus had as many detractors as disciples, particularly after improvements in agriculture increased the production of food and the development of industry dislodged farming from its central place in the economy. But in those areas in which the pressure of population on the land increased more rapidly than did industry and technological innovation, Malthusian thinking made considerable sense.

The surplus population created in Europe through natural increase, the consolidation of small farms into larger, more efficient units, and the impact of industrialization on handicrafts became the raw material of the great migration that began in the middle of the nineteenth century. Once again, the absence of adequate statistics makes precise judgment difficult, but much of the phenomenon apparently took the form of short-distance moves within national boundaries. People often simply left the countryside for a nearby urban community likely to need workers. Some relocated several times, going at each step to a larger settlement; others, who lived within the sphere of influence of a great city, often went there directly. In the nineteenth century, the cities of Europe usually grew more from in-migration than from natural increase. Between 1861 and 1864, for example, the twenty-five leading cities of Germany grew by more than one-third, and 77 percent of that increase came from in-migration. In France, 83 percent of the urban population gain between 1861 and 1865 was produced by in-migration.

Going to the city did not answer everyone's needs. A large proportion of Europe's population, especially in the less developed nations, lived beyond the orbit of urban and industrial centers. Moreover, some of those who went to the cities failed to find the opportunity and security they had been seeking. In such circumstances, more distant spots, either in the other nations of Europe or across the ocean, were likely to be attractive. By the middle of the nineteenth century, governments were no longer inclined to stand in the way of would-be emigrants though staunch nationalists and some religious leaders strongly objected to emigration. The former feared that the loss of population might weaken a nation militarily or, as in the case of Ireland, undermine a struggle for independence or autonomy. The latter foresaw a loss of faith and culture in foreign lands. These complaints were not strong enough to overcome the tenet of mid-nineteenth-century political liberalism that freedom to move was a fundamental human right and the recognition that emigration offered at least a temporary partial solution to the perceived problem of overpopulation. Thus, in most countries, laws restricting travel were repealed or forgotten.

Persons ready to leave their native lands selected their destinations on the basis of several considerations that, especially in the early decades of the nineteenth century, did not always work in favor of the United States. Migrants usually traveled to points connected with their homes by well-established transportation and commercial networks. During the intensive migration of 1816–1817, when people from the southern and western German states followed paths leading them to the Low Countries and eventually to the United States, 15,000 of their compatriots in other locales found it easier to go east toward Russia. Emigrants were also sensitive to the economic opportunities available to them in different foreign destinations and to transportation costs. The Panic of 1819 weakened the magnetism exerted by the United States immediately after the Napoleonic wars and kept immigration to the republic low in the following decade. From 1820 to 1825, American authorities reported that, on the average, fewer than 6,000 Europeans arrived annually. Irishmen trying to escape an outbreak of famine and disease in those years found England, where prosperity had made wages competitive with those in the United States, a preferable refuge. In addition, the introduction of steamboat travel across the Irish Sea had reduced the cost of travel from Ireland to England to 4d. at a time when the cheapest fare to America was £3.10. Between 1823 and 1830, when 6,230 Germans went to the United States, as many as 10,000 left for the newly independent empire of Brazil. Most were responding to a promise of free transportation across the Atlantic, while many discounted the seriousness of the requirement of military service that was attached to their passage and others wrongly expected to receive free land.

British North America, as the component parts of modern Canada were known before their unification, was the chief competitor of the United States for Europe's overseas emigrants in those decades. English laws making transportation to the United States more expensive explain part of Canada's success. In 1816, when England temporarily allowed

American and British ships to operate on equal terms, 92 percent of the emigrants leaving Ireland set sail for ports in the United States. When the English resumed their discriminatory practices, the Irish traffic was redirected. In 1818 and 1819, 67 percent of all Irish emigrants landed in New Brunswick, Nova Scotia, and Quebec; the imbalance continued in the 1820s. Observers claimed that many people who landed to the north eventually made their way to the United States, but precise measurement of the southward movement is impossible. As time passed, Canada certainly lost people to the United States, but in the last decades of the eighteenth century it had begun to attract settlers from the new republic. After Quebec was divided into Lower and Upper Canada in 1791, many citizens of the United States followed natural lines of expansion, communication, and economic intercourse into these districts. By 1812 most of the 12,000 people in the region of Lower Canada known as the Eastern Townships of Quebec were Americans who had moved north through the valleys of New York and Vermont. In the same year, about 80 percent of the 100,000 residents of Upper Canada were Americans, drawn there by the lure of land cheaper than that available in the United States. Though only about one-quarter of the Americans in Canada were loyalists or their descendants, the vast majority were neutral in deed, if not also in desire, during the War of 1812. Nevertheless, after the conflict, the worried British authorities sought to discourage further immigration from the United States. Of course, the flow of people continued; the newly opened Erie Canal brought many Americans through Canada on their way to Michigan and points west, and inevitably some of these migrants decided to settle in British territory.

By the 1830s, however, conditions were right for the United States to establish clear supremacy as the goal of European emigrants. Survival for more than half a century as an independent, democratic nation inhabited primarily by the descendants of Europeans gave America an advantage over its competitors. British North America, with its ill-matched population of English and French settlers, was a colonial possession in the midst of a struggle to find for itself an autonomous position within the empire. The major states of Latin America had only recently achieved independence, and their peoples, though Hispanicized, were mainly aboriginal Americans, Africans, or of mixed race. But the principal attractiveness of the United States was economic. Migrants followed the routes of commerce, and the republic's trade with Europe was growing rapidly. Ships that bore American products east across the Atlantic carried passengers west to Boston, New York, Philadelphia, Baltimore, New Orleans, and lesser ports. Once here, the early immigrants themselves became part of the pulling force of the United States, especially when they wrote home favorable reports of the opportunities available in America. Before 1860 the people of the nation were filling the lands east of the Mississippi; after the Civil War they spread westward across the river. America's vast Middle West offered possibilities for farming that Canada, with its Laurentian Shield—a rugged plateau stretching between the St. Lawrence and Ottawa valleys and the Manitoba Basin—could not match. At the same time, the United States was turning to industry and would in a few decades become the world leader in this area. Immigration made available the cheap labor on which the growth of factories was based, and the hopes of obtaining jobs in industry encouraged additional immigration.

Changes in the rates of immigration were, in part, the effect of improvements in transportation. Crossing the Atlantic was not an easy matter in the nineteenth century, particularly for the 95 percent of the passengers who traveled in the steerage. The ships were crowded, despite the intent of the series of passenger acts passed by both the United States and Britain. Ship operators could easily evade restrictions. Basing computations on a vessel's loaded rather than unloaded weight vitiated the rule limiting the number of passengers to two for every five tons of burden. Counting children as half persons and not counting infants undermined the requirement that each person on board have fourteen to fifteen square feet of space. The journey took approximately thirty-five days, depending on luck or the lack of it, and provisions often ran out on longer crossings. Privacy was nonexistent—passengers slept several to a bunk—and before the Passenger Act of 1849 no law forbade the involuntary assignment of men and women to the same berth. Sanitary facilities were minimal, and the mortality rate among passengers hovered around 1 percent in normal years. In desperate times, however, sick and poor refugees could turn the vessels into floating coffins. Conditions were probably best on American ships. As the importance of the immigrant trade became evident, American shipowners obtained vessels specifically designed for passenger traffic, and by the 1850s they were transporting twice as many people as were their British competitors. The American vessels were watertight rather than fast, in contrast to the more famous clipper ships of the era, and were much larger than British bottoms. In addition, American ships were noted for the ability and civility of their crews.

The introduction of the steamship brought great improvements in the transportation of immigrants. The paddle-wheeled steamers of the Englishman Samuel Cunard ferried mail, cargo, and cabin passengers across the Atlantic through the 1840s, but in 1850 William Inman of Philadelphia began to use in the immigrant trade iron-hulled steamships driven by screw propellers. Inman hoped to attract more well-to-do passengers by offering good services at a high price, but those who duplicated his innovation in the following years tried to make steamship passage available to all economic classes. The steamships cut the time of crossing by more than half, to approximately two weeks. Moreover, the use of fire and steam made possible the preparation of cooked meals on board. Conditions were still far from perfect, the food was usually poor, the crews on many vessels were rude, and putting as many people as possible in the steerage remained the goal. The steamers, which achieved gross tonnages as large as 5,000 in the 1870s and 10,000 in the following decades, could carry as many as 300 passengers in the cabin class and 1,500 in the steerage. In 1865 steamships brought 127,322 people to the port of New York; sailing vessels delivered another 84,431. Four years later, the steamers brought 258,661 passengers, or 90 percent of the immigrants arriving there.

Steamship lines encouraged emigration from Europe not only by making travel easier but also by employing agents in the major cities of the continent to promote travel. These representatives received commissions on the tickets sold, and they often made money as the operators of general stores catering to the needs of prospective passengers. The emissaries of the steamship lines employed subagents to spread their message even to the most remote villages, and their efforts at least made more people aware of the possibility of going to America. Some succumbed to the temptation of stimulating business by exaggerating the attractions of the New World, but most acted responsibly. The records of the Larsson Agency, which handled the Swedish business of the Guion Line, a medium-sized operation, indicate that steamship company representatives responded with a simple printed information sheet to the large majority of people requesting advice. When asked more detailed questions about the United States, agents tried to supply accurate information but avoided going beyond promises to make the voyage as smooth and economical as possible.

On the western side of the Atlantic, promoters of other interest groups supplemented the efforts of the steamship agents. The governments of America's frontier states lured prospective immigrants to their open and underpopulated fields and cities. As early as 1852 Wisconsin appointed a commissioner of emigration, who took up his post in New York, where he advised newcomers of the benefits of his state. The commissioner soon decided that the real work of publicizing Wisconsin had to be done in Europe through newspaper advertisements and pamphlets. The task of attracting foreign settlers to the Middle West became widespread and intensive after the Civil War; Iowa and Minnesota especially followed Wisconsin's initiative. In those years the railroad companies that were spanning the nation with their tracks took an even greater role than the government in calling Europeans to the New World. Attracting passengers for their trains was the least of the operators' hopes. Most of all, the railroaders wanted buyers for the almost 500,000 acres of land that the federal government had granted them along the rights-of-way. The immigrant purchasers represented more than a source of immediate revenue; once settled as farmers, they would produce crops and livestock to be carried to market on the trains. Jay Cooke was notably active in this endeavor, and in 1871 he chose Colonel Hans Mattson, onetime secretary of Minnesota's state board of immigration, to recruit immigrants in Scandinavia. The work of the colonel, a Swede who had earned his title serving in the Union army, bore fruit in the heavy concentration of his countrymen in Minnesota along the tracks of Cooke's two lines, the Northern Pacific and the Lake Superior and Mississippi.

Once started, the flow of immigration contributed to its own maintenance. The early immigrants themselves attracted relatives and friends from their old to their new land. For example, studies based on the Scandinavian experience suggest that specific communities or districts developed traditions of migration, sending off their sons and daughters at greater rates than social and economic conditions can explain. The phenomenon was the cumulative effect of several causes. Reports about America dispatched by early arrivals were a stimulus to those who had remained at home. Personal letters read by families and friends of the pioneers replaced the private promotional literature of the first half of the century and at least supplemented the state endorsed pamphlets of the second. The knowledge that friendly and familiar faces promised to make the New World less strange gave the timid the incentive they needed to take the great step of departure. Most important, the efforts of earlier immigrants made it economically possible for later ones to come. Soon after arriving in the United States, newcomers began sending home money in quantities that represented sizable portions of their incomes. As early as 1848, approximately $2.3 million was remitted from North America to the United Kingdom. Between 1877 and 1890, the new U.S. postal money order system transferred a net average of $2,269,998 annually to the British Isles. The money was used for many purposes, but by 1872 about 44 percent of it took the form of prepaid passage tickets. The sum was large enough to pay for three-quarters of the emigration from the United Kingdom in that year.

Nearly 15 million people made their way to the United States between the fiscal years of 1820, the first in which the government recorded immigration data, and 1890, the centennial of the first federal census. The official statistics, which were derived from customshouse reports, have a variety of imperfections but they give at least a good approximation of the volume, timing, and origins of the immigrant flow. According to these records, 128,502 people came in the 1820s and 538,381 in the 1830s. Immigration increased rapidly in the next two decades, with 1,427,337 people arriving in the 1840s and 2,814,554 in

the 1850s. The numbers of newcomers slumped in the 1860s to
2,081,261, probably on account of the American Civil War, and strug-
gled back to 2,742,137 in the 1870s, when a depression gripped the
United States. The 1880s saw the greatest boom of the entire era, with
5,248,568 people reaching American shores. Persons from almost every
point on the globe took part in the great migration to the United States
in these decades, but over 80 percent of them came from a handful of
western European nations, most of which had been important in providing settlers for the American colonies. The states of Germany yielded
the greatest number of immigrants, approximately 4,403,369 between
1820 and 1890. Ireland sent 3,431,654 but, in contrast with the past, the
vast majority came from the Catholic sections of the island. England,
Scotland, and Wales contributed 2,686,883, including an undetermined number of Irishmen who had temporarily made homes in Britain. Iceland and the Scandinavian countries of Norway, Sweden, and
Denmark sent 1,017,203; the remaining western European countries,
662,361. Almost all these nations sent people to the United States
throughout the period from 1820 to 1890, but significant variations existed in the specific causes, timing, and social patterns of emigration
operating in them. Two non-European countries, Canada and China,
were also important in the story of American growth in this era.
Canada's experience will be discussed as a subcategory of Europe's
emigration, with which process it was intertwined. China's will be examined later in a context that allows analysis of the distinctive impact of
Chinese immigration on the United States (Figure II–1).

   Ireland in the nineteenth century was a nation locked in an uneasy
political and economic embrace with England. After the failure of the
uprising of 1798, the English Parliament, through the Act of Union of
1800, abolished the Irish legislature. Great Britain and Ireland became
the United Kingdom, and the Irish were allowed to send 100 members
to the House of Commons in London and 28 peers and 4 bishops to the
House of Lords. Though only the most prescient recognized the varied
implications of the act, it proved over time to have a combination of
benefits and penalties for the inhabitants of Ireland. The act deprived
the Protestant minority that had dominated the Irish Parliament of the
limited legislative autonomy won in the 1780s and early 1790s under the
leadership of Henry Grattan. In return, the Protestants, who had to
contend with an increasingly militant Catholic majority, received an
implicit but important assurance that the ultimate political questions
concerning Ireland would be determined by a body in which Catholic
pressure was minimal. Union made Catholic hopes of national independence and majority rule more farfetched than ever. But the act's
apparent guarantee of Protestant ascendancy prevented the formation
of insurmountable opposition to the ongoing process of removing

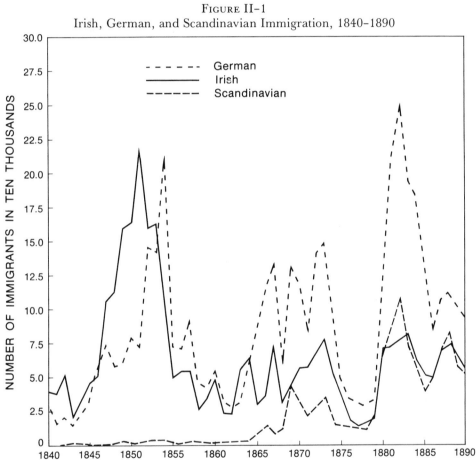

FIGURE II-1
Irish, German, and Scandinavian Immigration, 1840–1890

Source: Figure created by Thomas J. Archdeacon from data in U.S. Bureau of the Census, *Historical Statistics of the United States: Colonial Times to 1970* (Washington, D.C.: Government Printing Office, 1975), series C89–119.

political and economic disabilities from Catholics. In 1782, under Gardiner's Second Relief Act, Catholics willing to swear temporal allegiance to England won the right to purchase and bequeath freehold lands on the same terms that applied to Protestants. Ten years later, Hobart's Relief Act made a variety of concessions, including enfranchisement of Catholics with freeholds worth at least 40s. Finally, in 1829, after a protracted period of Irish agitation, in which Daniel O'Connell had played the central role, London allowed the Emancipation Act, enabling Catholics to sit in Parliament and to hold any office except those of lord lieutenant of Ireland and lord chancellor of England.

Whatever slight progress Ireland made politically was counterbalanced by the increasingly precarious condition of Irish agriculture. The structure of this crucial sector of the economy was a product of English rule. Since the beginning of the eighteenth century, a small group of Protestant landowners had gotten possession of most of the island's arable land. The typical Irishman, especially in the Catholic population, was a tenant farmer. Ireland's soil was as productive as that of France, and during the era of the Napoleonic wars, when England opened its markets to Irish grain, both landlords and tenants enjoyed prosperity. The former, of whom about one-third lived abroad and managed their estates through agents, were able to raise rents considerably. The latter were able to enjoy a better standard of living, to marry younger, and to have larger families. Ireland's population jumped from an estimated 4,753,000 in 1791 to 8,175,124 in 1841. The rapid growth of population, however, endangered the prosperity that had spawned it. Ireland lacked an industrial sector capable of absorbing the increasing numbers of people, and so the land had to take on the burden. Tenants, looking for ways to pay high rents, divided their lands among subtenants. The creation of such small units was inefficient, but landlords allowed it in expectation of a quick profit. By 1841, of the 691,202 agricultural holdings above one acre in Ireland, 310,436, or 45 percent, were under five acres. Four years later, there were approximately 65,000 holdings below one acre. A class of colliers and laborers who worked these tiny parcels formed the economic mudsill of Irish society. The colliers paid with either their work or part of their harvest for the land on which they grew their subsistence crops; even worse off, the laborers took lands in *conacre*, paying high cash rents, which they had to earn through hard-to-find wage work.

Living on the edge of demographic disaster, the Irish poor came to rely on the lowly potato. One-third of them ate almost nothing else, and an even larger proportion made the potato the mainstay of their diets. A family of six equipped with the most rudimentary knowledge of farming and a spade could draw food for a year from 1.5 acres of potatoes. The fare was as filling as the bread and cheese diet of contemporary English laborers. Had they depended on food grains, the Irish would have needed six times as much land, a better understanding of agriculture, and more tools. Unfortunately, the potato was as vulnerable as it was valuable: the fungus *Phytophthoro infestans*, which multiplies rapidly in moist and muggy conditions, had reduced the crop to rot twenty times between 1728 and 1844. When the blight appeared again in October 1845, the authorities were not especially alarmed: the damage was restricted to isolated areas and the people had already harvested about one-sixth of the crop. Moreover, hunger and disease were familiar in Ireland. Nevertheless, 1846 brought a different story. The disaster in the potato fields was complete, and some 10 million tons of the crop, the produce of 1.5 million acres, were lost. The failure disrupted the normal pattern of Irish agriculture and forced people to eat potatoes that would otherwise have been kept for seed. Only 284,116 acres of the crop were cultivated in 1847 and, as a result, a remission in the blight brought no relief. A famine of unprecedented severity continued to grip the island, and the weakened inhabitants fell prey to a variety of epidemic maladies, most notably typhus and relapsing fever, before the end of the blight in 1850.

England's leaders were unable to cope with the Irish catastrophe. Sir Robert Peel, the Tory who was prime minister at the onset of the crisis, and Lord John Russell, the Whig who succeeded him in 1846, shared a laissez-faire philosophy that precluded extensive government interference in the economy. They were fearful of undermining the principle of free trade in grain that Peel had convinced a reluctant Parliament to endorse in 1846 and they dared not jeopardize the food supply of English workers. Accordingly, neither man was willing to prohibit the exportation of Irish wheat and oats. Such an action would not have averted calamity but might have alleviated suffering and minimized later bitterness among the Irish. Peel at least ordered the purchase of £100,000 worth of American corn which he used as a weapon against persons who attempted to corner the grain market and raise prices in Ireland. Russell was less flexible: he restricted sales of food by the authorities to the west of Ireland, where the suffering was greatest, and refused to use government grain to keep down prices. Both men believed the solution to Ireland's problem lay in putting the people to work so that they could earn money to buy goods in the world market. In 1846 Peel instituted a public works program, half of which was funded from the central treasury. The effort collapsed under Russell, who despite a deteriorating situation demanded that the Irish economy bear the whole cost of public improvements on the island. By the middle of 1847, many Irish were dependent on soup kitchens funded through private charity and the poor law. Faced with an impossible situation, the operators of the kitchens did a creditable job, though some, especially ministers of the established Church of Ireland, blackened the reputation of this corps by using the promise of food to tempt starving Irishmen to disavow Catholicism.

Death and emigration took a dreadful toll on the Irish population between 1841 and 1851. The census taken in the latter year counted 6,552,385 people, approximately 2.5 million fewer than might have been expected had normal growth prevailed in the decade. Precise numbers are impossible to reckon, but about 1 million died from starvation and disease and another 1.5 million emigrated. England became the destination of many: in the first five months of 1847, 300,000 Irishmen descended on Liverpool, a city of about 250,000 inhabitants. Some could afford to go no farther, but most used England's ports as embarkation points for longer journeys. According to Irish census figures, 1,732,000 Irishmen went overseas between 1846 and 1854, and the estimate is probably 5 percent low. Of this number, 54,000, or 3 percent, went to Australia; in about 14,000 cases the British government, desirous of populating its faraway southern colony, paid the expense of the passage. At least 309,000, or 18 percent, made their way to British North America. Fares on the British vessels that dominated the route to Quebec and its neighbors were, at a minimum, 30–40 percent cheaper than those on American vessels, which were subject to stricter health and safety regulations. As a result, the poorest of the paying transatlantic travelers set off for British North America. Likewise, landlords seeking to unburden themselves and their estates by shipping off their surplus and undesirable tenants put them on bottoms bound there. Tragedy ensued. In 1847, about 17,000 of the 100,000 men and women headed for British North America died at sea; another 20,000 expired of illness in overcrowded and inadequate quarantine stations along the St. Lawrence River. The vast majority of Irishmen, however, chose the United States as their new home. Approximately 1,374,000, or 79 percent of the total, came directly from ports in the British Isles to the American republic; an undetermined, but apparently large, proportion of those who landed in the future dominion of Canada eventually crossed the border, too.

The beginning of German emigration coincided with that of the Irish, but this movement peaked several years later. The product of similar social processes, the German exodus lacked the desperate quality that characterized the flight from the Emerald Isle. While large numbers of German Catholics and poor people reached America's ports, this migration also encompassed Protestants and drew strength from a broad spectrum of social and economic classes. Most important, the Germans constituted the first sizable influx of a non-British group since the colonial era.

To speak of Germany in the 1830s and 1840s is to ignore an obvious fact while recognizing a deeper truth. Germany, in the mid-nineteenth century, was a collection of contiguous kingdoms, principalities, and duchies. These units shared a common culture but diverged along economic, political, and religious lines. Even after reaching the United States, Germans identified themselves as Bavarians, Prussians, or natives of other major districts. At the same time, however, pressures toward unification were mounting as the nineteenth century progressed. Like the rest of the Western world, the various German divisions were being pulled together by the transportation revolution, and as travel became easier and commerce more natural the artificial barriers of taxation and tariff faded.

Southern and western Germany first felt the effects of the long-term process of change. In the provinces of Württemberg, Baden, and the Palatinate, the practice of *Realteilungserbrecht*, the equal division of estates among descendants, predated the French Revolution. The system expanded under Napoleon's Code Civil to the Rhineland and the Rhine-Hesse. Thus, in these areas a trend toward smaller holdings appeared at the same time that the reforms of the French revolutionary era were commuting labor duties owed by peasants under a feudal system to simple cash payments. The constant need to raise money put the peasant farmers in a bind, while landlords in receiving these payments were in a better position to purchase more acres, consolidate their holdings, and adopt improved agricultural methods. At the same time, the artisans and small craftsmen of the region suffered. These workers felt the impact of the deteriorating conditions in agriculture: farmers no longer had the wherewithal to purchase their services. They also fell prey to the extension of economic contacts, which allowed English linen to enter the German market, and to the establishment in 1819 of a *Zollverein*, or customs union, which brought competition from Prussian factories. Nevertheless, the number of independent handicraft workers continued to grow. The increasing supply in the face of a declining demand reflected, in part, the breakdown of the guild system, which had regulated the number of persons who could become master craftsmen and marry. Even more, this trend testified to the growth of the population beyond the ability of the economy to support it.

The authorities of various German states attempted to handle the problem of overpopulation through legislation. Between the 1820s and the 1850s, Württemberg, Hanover, Bavaria, Thuringia, and other districts required men requesting permission to marry to submit proof of their ability to support themselves and a family. Such measures were ineffective; indeed, their main outcome was to encourage irregular unions and illegitimate births. The answer ultimately came in the form of emigration from the affected areas. During the 1830s and early 1840s many of the migrants stayed within the bounds of Germany. Between 1823 and 1844 a total of 256,000 men and women abandoned Germany for destinations abroad. Many of those going overseas were in danger of losing the middle-class lifestyle they had known. They were taking the final opportunity to sell their few remaining acres and translate the proceeds into larger American farms, or they simply thought that their skills could bring better livelihoods in the New World.

Germany's pattern of emigration changed somewhat in the hectic decade between 1845 and 1854, when short-term difficulties combined with long-standing problems to raise the total number of departures to 1,036,500. The potato crisis touched continental Europe, too. The situation was not so serious as that in Ireland, but the blight struck hard at those German peasants who had turned to the cultivation of the potato in the hope of eking as much food as possible from their dwindling holdings. Moreover, the potato failure drove up the price of German grain crops, which had found a new lucrative market in England following the repeal of the Corn Laws. Several German states prohibited the export of grain and the portion of the potato crop that survived, but they could only alleviate and not cure the problem. Emigration gained popularity among members of the lower economic classes; 40 percent of the emigrants in 1846 were day laborers, rather than independent farmers or artisans, and observers were sure this proportion far exceeded previous records. The call to new lands also reached districts theretofore immune: between 1844 and 1848 Prussia experienced more emigration than immigration for the first time in history. The geographic spread might be evidence that the other major contemporary disturbance of Germany's peace, the Revolutions of 1848, caused large-scale emigration, but actually only a few thousand political refugees, who became known as Forty-eighters, joined this outward movement.

By the time German emigration increased substantially, the United States had become the favored destination of a large majority of the *Auswanderer*. Of the 816,885 men and women leaving Bremen or Hamburg for foreign ports between 1847 and 1860, 83 percent were headed for the American republic. The provinces of British North America drew 36,252 (4.4 percent); Australia, another 23,510 (2.8 percent); and Brazil, some 19,000 (2.3 percent). Bremen was the most important point of embarkation in Germany. The city had negotiated a commercial treaty with the United States in 1827 and had opened a new port at Bremerhaven in 1830. In the ensuing years, Bremen captured half of America's tobacco exports by offering southern planters ready cash for their crops. For the merchants whose vessels carried the tobacco to Bremen, emigrants became an important cargo on the westward journey. Bremen sent forth 606,257 passengers between 1845 and 1860, more than twice as many as its nearest German competitor. Hamburg, the second-ranking city, feared that migrants might become a burden and did not seek to take advantage of the increasing traffic until Bremen began to overtake Hamburg economically in the 1840s. Moreover, Hamburg conducted little direct trade with the United States, and emigrants leaving there usually had to land at Hull, traverse England to Liverpool, and then board a vessel for New York. Bremen and Hamburg together accounted for about 47 percent of the passengers leaving Germany.

Immigrants generally followed well-established sea routes. The intersection between human traffic and the flow of general commerce was most obvious in the early years, when transatlantic travelers either found space on packets or other vessels engaged in mercantile communication or filled temporary bunks in the holds of cargo ships crossing the ocean to pick up raw materials in North America. But this convergence also continued in later years, when specialized passenger ships naturally gravitated to America's major ports. As the leading American port, New York was consistently the main point of entry for immigrants: the city absorbed 66 percent of the traffic between 1840 and 1844, 71 percent in the next decade, and even greater shares after 1860.

The flow of foreigners into New York reflected the overall ethnic composition of U.S. immigration; thus, during the prewar peaks of Irish and German arrivals, the city received sizable numbers of people from both countries. From the fourth quarter of 1846 through the third of 1847, at the height of the Irish crisis, New York greeted 83,146 British immigrants, about 90 percent of whom must have been Irish. During the same period, 49,962 Germans came. In 1854, when Germans immigrants arrived in record numbers, 164,538 of them touched shore in Manhattan, along with 70,393 Irishmen.

No other American port came remotely close to New York in the number of arrivals. New Orleans, which was seen by many contemporaries as the chief rival of the eastern metropolis, took in 10,035 Irishmen and 11,581 Germans in 1852; two years later the city received 6,194 of the former and 29,092 of the latter. Several other ports, however, had such distinctive patterns of use that even their limited contributions had important effects. Boston, with close ties to Liverpool, the British lumber trade, and Canada became a magnet for Irish immigrants almost to the exclusion of other groups. In 1847–1848, Boston received 13,235 Irishmen but only 208 Germans; the respective totals for 1854 were 14,779 and 544. Baltimore, an important link between the United States and Bremen, had almost the opposite experience: in 1847–1848 the Maryland port welcomed 6,171 Germans and 2,237 Irishmen; the discrepancy was even greater in 1854, when 12,002 Germans and 850 Irishmen entered.

The ports of entry were of major importance in determining the ultimate geographic distribution of the immigrant population. America's coastal cities became the initial and often the permanent homes of newcomers whose meager financial resources made simply reaching the U.S. coast an accomplishment. The ports at least occasionally became temporary stopping points for immigrants who planned to go farther but were stripped of their cash and possessions soon after landing. Though the pathos of the problem has probably caused historians to exaggerate its dimensions, contemporary observers did regularly report that confidence men, unscrupulous rooming-house keepers, and other miscreants preyed on gullible immigrants. The most vicious, without a doubt, were former immigrants who used their recently acquired knowledge of the New World and the English language to defraud their green countrymen. Immigrants did not have to be desperate to stay in the coastal cities. The ports had their own magnetic powers, which middle-class Americans, with their anti–big city bias, underestimate. They offered jobs that, however arduous, promised livelihoods no worse than those left behind by Europe's population of marginal farmers, farm laborers, and unskilled workers. Difficult working and living conditions were probably no surprise to many of the immigrants, who had already spent time in the factory towns and urban centers of the Old World on their long journey from the European countryside to the United States. Moreover, America's cities presented immediate opportunities for the body of newcomers who wanted to stay among their compatriots. The ports, of course, were important even for immigrants who passed beyond them. The factory towns emerging in their hinterlands offered additional chances for employment. Finally, the networks of waterways and railroads emanating from the coastal centers dictated the routes and destinations of those immigrants with the desire and the resources to plunge on toward the frontier of settlement.

In 1860, the main port cities—New York, Boston, Philadelphia, Baltimore, New Orleans, and San Francisco—were home to 18.4 percent of the immigrants; they sheltered only 4.8 percent of native-stock American whites. Another thirty-seven cities, ranging in size from Brooklyn, New York, with 250,000 whites, to Montgomery, Alabama, with under 4,500, accounted for an additional 17.3 percent of the foreign born and 4.8 percent of the natives. The states that served as the hinterlands of the ports held the large majority of the newcomers. New England, the middle Atlantic coast, the east north central region, Iowa, and Minnesota contained 81.1 percent of the immigrant group, compared to 63.5 percent of the native white population. California had another 3.5 percent; Louisiana, 1.9 percent; and Missouri, thanks to its Mississippi River depot at St. Louis, 3.8 percent. The number of foreign-born people in the slave states of the South was uniformly low. The immigrants' presence was most striking in those states that actually held within their borders a larger proportion of the total immigrant population than of the native white. New York was preeminent among these, with 24.1 percent of the former, compared with only 12.3 percent of the latter; however, Massachusetts, Wisconsin, Illinois, Michigan, Minnesota, and California were also notable in this respect (Table II-1).

The uneven distribution of the major immigrant groups among the ports of entry had a lasting impact. The preponderance of Irish arrivals in Boston, nearby coastal communities, and St. Lawrence River locations made the word "immigrant" virtually synonymous in New England with Irishman. About 20 percent of the Irish-born residents of the United States lived there; the comparable figure for the German born was only 2 percent. New York, New Jersey, and Pennsylvania contained 48 percent of the Irish immigrants and 34 percent of the German. The better balance in these middle Atlantic states was undoubtedly a by-product of New York City's unmatched role as a reception point. The five states of the old Northwest Territory—Ohio, Indiana, Illinois, Michigan, and Wisconsin—and the adjacent state of Missouri formed the center of German immigration. They accounted for 47 percent of the German-born population, compared with only 20 percent of the Irish born. The longtime dominance of the Germans at Baltimore, which offered quick access to the Ohio Valley, and their gradually increasing edge at New Orleans, which was linked to the northern farm belt by the Mississippi, explain part of this pattern. A consideration of the relative resources of the Irish and German immigrants goes far toward clarifying the rest of the picture. The minute size of the typical land parcel in Ireland and the limited agricultural expertise involved in digging and harvesting potatoes meant that only a small number of Irishmen would have had the experience necessary to make larger scale farming appealing or feasible. Most important, few of the Irish could afford to go directly to the Middle West, purchase land and equipment, and start a farm. An investigation of the Wisconsin population of 1850 shows that the average Irish-born resident, even before the famine, spent seven years in the East before reaching the state. The Irish had to save their money or work their way across the nation constructing railroads before they could strike roots in the Middle West.

To focus on Irish and German immigrants is reasonable: they dominated immigration to the United States in the pre–Civil War years. According to the census of 1860, the 1,611,304 Irishmen in the nation accounted for 39 percent of the 4,136,175 males and females in the foreign-born population; the 1,276,075 Germans formed another 31 percent. The other countries of the world lagged far behind. Their con-

TABLE II-1

Percentage of America's Total Foreign-Born and Total Native-Born Free
Populations Resident in Each of the Major Political Units, in 1860

| Political Unit | Foreign Born (%) | Native Born (%) | Index[1] |
|---|---|---|---|
| Alabama | 0.30 | 2.21 | 0.1 |
| Arkansas | 0.09 | 1.37 | 0.1 |
| California | 3.54 | 1.00 | 3.5 |
| Connecticut | 1.95 | 1.62 | 1.2 |
| Delaware | 0.22 | 0.43 | 0.5 |
| District of Columbia | 0.30 | 0.25 | 1.2 |
| Florida | 0.08 | 0.32 | 0.2 |
| Georgia | 0.28 | 2.50 | 0.1 |
| Illinois | 7.85 | 5.94 | 1.3 |
| Indiana | 2.86 | 5.28 | 0.5 |
| Iowa | 2.56 | 2.44 | 1.1 |
| Kansas | 0.31 | 0.40 | 0.8 |
| Kentucky | 1.45 | 3.73 | 0.4 |
| Louisiana | 1.96 | 1.26 | 1.5 |
| Maine | 0.91 | 2.53 | 0.4 |
| Maryland | 1.87 | 2.24 | 0.8 |
| Massachusetts | 6.29 | 4.16 | 1.5 |
| Michigan | 3.60 | 2.57 | 1.4 |
| Minnesota | 1.42 | 0.49 | 2.9 |
| Mississippi | 0.21 | 1.48 | 0.1 |
| Missouri | 3.88 | 3.88 | 1.0 |
| New Hampshire | 0.51 | 1.31 | 0.4 |
| New Jersey | 2.97 | 2.35 | 1.3 |
| New York | 24.14 | 12.34 | 2.0 |
| North Carolina | 0.08 | 2.82 | 0.0 |
| Ohio | 7.94 | 8.61 | 0.9 |
| Oregon | 0.12 | 0.20 | 0.6 |
| Pennsylvania | 10.41 | 10.60 | 1.0 |
| Rhode Island | 0.90 | 0.59 | 1.5 |
| South Carolina | 0.24 | 1.25 | 0.2 |
| Tennessee | 0.51 | 3.48 | 0.1 |
| Texas | 1.05 | 1.62 | 0.6 |
| Vermont | 0.79 | 1.21 | 0.7 |
| Virginia | 0.85 | 4.58 | 0.2 |
| Wisconsin | 6.70 | 2.14 | 3.1 |
| | | | |
| Colorado Territory | 0.06 | 0.14 | 0.5 |
| Dakota Territory | 0.04 | 0.01 | 3.3 |
| Nebraska Territory | 0.15 | 0.10 | 1.6 |
| Nevada Territory | 0.05 | 0.02 | 2.4 |
| New Mexico Territory | 0.16 | 0.37 | 0.4 |
| Utah Territory | 0.31 | 0.12 | 2.6 |
| Washington Territory | 0.08 | 0.04 | 2.1 |

Source: Derived by Thomas J. Archdeacon from U.S. Census Office, Eighth Census, 1860,
*Statistics of the United States in 1860* (1866; reprint ed. New York: Arno, 1976), table II.

[1] The index was determined by dividing the percentage of foreign-born residents by the
percentage of native-born Americans. Foreign-born persons were overrepresented in areas
with indexes over 1.0 and underrepresented in areas with indexes below 1.0. The index was computed from unrounded numbers.

tributions, however, ought also to be recognized. The 585,973 natives of England, Scotland, and Wales contributed 14 percent; the 249,970 former inhabitants of British North American, 6 percent. France was the only other nation to send more than 100,000 people to the United States; 109,870 of its sons and daughters had found new homes across the Atlantic by 1860. Immigration records show that the 1840s and 1850s, when 153,620 Frenchmen arrived, were the highpoint of their movement to the United States. Little is known about the causes of French emigration, but France was suffering from a depressed economy in the latter decade. In addition, the California gold strike seems to have exerted a strong pull on the French; there were 8,462 Frenchmen in the West Coast state in 1860, compared with the 24,215 and 21,826 in their largest settlements in Louisiana and New York, respectively.

In the years after 1860, Ireland and Germany continued to produce remarkable numbers of emigrants. Ireland sent 1,523,734 people to the United States between 1860 and 1890, and the 1880s ranked second to the 1850s as the decade of heaviest emigration from the beleaguered island. Germany saw 2,919,384 of its citizens go to America in the same thirty years; that nation suffered its peak period of loss in the 1880s, when 1,445,181 left home. Nevertheless, change was present in the midst of this continuity. Within Ireland and Germany, the geographic patterns of emigration shifted. As time passed, America's siren call penetrated farther into Munster and Connaught, the more remote and less Anglicized provinces of Ireland's south and west. In Germany the center of emigration shifted from the southwest, as the pressure of population against land built in the northeast at a pace that outraced the ability of the growing Prussian industrial cities to absorb excess labor. Moreover, migration became an important phenomenon in countries beyond Ireland and Germany. Scandinavia experienced its most intense period of emigration between 1860 and 1889, when 976,347 Norwegians, Swedes, and Danes went to the United States. The British replaced the Irish as the second largest immigrant group: 1,922,303 Englishmen, Scotsmen, and Welshmen entered the American republic during the same thirty-year period. Finally, the newly established dominion of Canada suffered unprecedented losses when 934,084 people from both the English and the French populations crossed the border in 1860–1885.

Scandinavian emigration to America long predated the Civil War. In the 1630s Swedes became the first Europeans to establish settlements along the Delaware River. The Norwegians dated their first contribution to the mass migration of the nineteenth century to 1825, when a small group of religious dissidents, most of whom were Quakers, set sail from Stavanger on the sloop *Restauration* bound for New York. However interesting, such early episodes had minimal impact on the course of American history. Between 1820 and 1860, only 41,669 Scandinavians entered the United States; they accounted for only .8 percent of the 5,062,414 newcomers to American shores in those decades. Scandinavian immigrants made their first major impression in the years between 1865 and 1883, with their most sustained period of arrival occurring between 1880 and 1883. In those four years, 324,559 Scandinavians accounted for 17 percent of the 1,915,680 immigrants entering the United States. The story of their coming is multifaceted. The three main Scandinavian nations—Norway, Sweden, and Denmark—each experienced its own peculiar emigration in the last half of the nineteenth century.

Norway between 1865 and 1915 passed through an era of strikingly intense emigration. Only Ireland over the whole course of the nineteenth century and Italy after 1890 lost larger proportions of their populations. The rapid exodus was the product of a combination of causes, among which an unusual cycle of population growth was fundamental. A great excess of births over deaths in the 1790s had produced an unexpectedly large increase in the Norwegian population in that decade. The numerous babies of the 1790s began their own families in the 1820s, causing the bulge to reappear in that decade. Their children repeated the process in the next generation. By the late 1870s, the products of Norway's baby boom of the 1850s were ready for employment, and the nation needed 10,000 more jobs for men between the ages of eighteen and twenty-two than had been available a decade earlier. Such a task would have been difficult under good circumstances but, beginning in 1879, Norway's industry, agriculture, and shipping entered a long depression. As a result, 263,676 Norwegians went overseas between 1879 and 1893; 104,767 of them left between 1879 and 1883. These emigrants represented more than two-thirds of the excess of births over deaths in Norway over the longer period and 77 percent of the difference in the shorter one. Almost all of these emigrants headed for the United States.

Sweden, which sent forth 714,886 of its sons and daughters between 1869 and 1893, produced the largest number of Scandinavia's emigrants. Crop failures in 1867 and 1868 set off a wave of movement that saw 106,012 people leave the nation between 1869 and 1873, with 76,133 going to the United States. It is interesting that the level of migration was highest neither in the northern areas most affected by famine nor in the districts close to the cities of Uppsala and Stockholm. Those who departed were most often from the south central and southwestern regions, where the tradition of emigration was strongest. Northern Småland, southwestern Östergötland, the Karlskoga mining district, and sections of Hälsingland were areas most affected. But the sources of the emigrant stream were multiplying, and the increase continued when economic problems broke out in 1879. Troubles in the timber exporting business of northern Sweden introduced emigration to

Västernnorland. Competition from the Krupps works of Germany, to which the Swedish military turned for its cannons, adversely affected the iron industry and especially the Finspång foundry of northern Östergötland. Emigration increased from there and spread among the metalworkers of Stockholm and other districts. The penetration of the Swedish market by American and Russian wheat, a development made possible by improved transportation, underlay the major crisis. The price of rye, Sweden's most important farm product, fell 50 percent between 1881 and 1887; this drop uprooted more people. From 1879 to 1883, 187,521 men, women, and children abandoned Sweden, and more than 99 percent of them went to the United States. The number of departures reached its single-year peak in 1887, when 46,265 Swedes left for the American republic. Emigration slackened in the following years, particularly after Sweden in 1888 introduced a protective tariff for agriculture, but industrial unemployment set off a final burst of departures between 1891 and 1893, when 117,097 left for the United States.

Denmark suffered less from emigration, in terms of absolute and proportional population losses, then did either Norway or Sweden. The difference was the product of several factors. Danish farmers survived the agricultural crisis of the late nineteenth century in better shape than did their fellow Scandinavians. The Danes quickly adjusted to the new realities of the international grain trade and switched their main efforts to dairy farming. They also managed to maintain adequately large holdings and did not fall victim to ever decreasing acreage. In the last three decades of the century, only 4 percent of Danish landowners emigrated; in Sweden the rate was 25 percent. This good fortune reflected the fact that Denmark was more urbanized and industrialized than its neighbors were. Those who had to leave farming were not forced to become expatriates; they were likely to find new work in the cities and factories of the homeland. Finally, Denmark lacked a history of migration to America. The cumulative pressure of a migration psychology, which accepts uprooting as normal, and of a network of transatlantic contacts to facilitate departure and reestablishment across the sea was missing.

Though somewhat limited, migration from Denmark was noticeable. More than 158,000 Danes left their homeland between 1869 and 1893. The exodus crested twice, with 33,623 leaving from 1880 to 1883 and 66,679 going from 1887 to 1893. Over 92 percent of Danish emigrants headed for America, compared with 95 percent of Norwegian and 98 percent of Swedish. The Danes most likely to cross the Atlantic came from the poor region of north Jutland and the relatively prosperous southwestern areas of Zealand and Lolland-Falster. The majority of emigrants came from rural areas, with ranks filled with farm servants and laborers, who had the fewest prospects for advancement. Almost 93 percent of those leaving from the countryside between 1868 and 1900 fell into this category. In terms of proportions, however, Danish emigration had a stronger urban character than either Swedish or Norwegian emigration had. About 342 of every 100,000 town residents departed; the comparable figure for rural inhabitants was 181. The high number reflected the deteriorating position of urban craftsmen. After 1862 they no longer enjoyed legal protection from rural competitors, and in the following years they also suffered the onslaughts of cheaper factory goods. The Danes who left north Schleswig for America after the Germans took over the province constituted a separate and final category of emigrants. Their desire to escape foreign domination and service in the German army was an important motivation. Because these immigrants were often incorrectly listed as Germans in the American records, north Schleswig may actually have sent 50,000 Danes to the United States.

The men and women who left England, Scotland, and Wales to come to the United States in the last decades of the nineteenth century are for several reasons the forgotten immigrants of American history. They were the last chapter in the well-known story of the British settlement of North America; their ancestors had founded the colonies and left their cultural impress on them. The British immigrants of later years resembled native-stock white Americans in language, religion, and political heritage; they did not bring with them overwhelming social problems; and they were few in number relative to the earlier influx of Irish and Germans and the subsequent wave of Italians, Slavs, and Jews. Unfortunately, concentrating on the lack of disruption caused by the British immigrants leads to an underestimation of their special characteristics and of their role in the immigration story. America and England had both changed in the century after the Revolution. By 1876 the American character was unique, not simply a colonial reflection of the English, and the denizens of the major industrial nation of western Europe were no longer the yeomen and artisans who had shaped the early history of the future United States.

Immigration to the United States from England, Scotland, and Wales was a continuous phenomenon in the nineteenth century. Before the Civil War, newcomers from the British Isles joined the search for farmlands, panned for gold, and made a niche for themselves in the infant industrial centers of the United States. The 693,631 Britons reaching American shores from 1840 to 1860 accounted for 15.7 percent of the total immigration to the United States in those years. The movement from England, Scotland, and Wales achieved its highpoint, in terms of both absolute numbers and proportional contribution to the immigrant stream, in the next three decades. Official American statistics show that 1,962,296 British immigrants entered the United

States between 1861 and 1890. They accounted for 18.9 percent of the foreign arrivals in those years and outnumbered contemporary Scandinavian immigrants by more than 90 percent. These figures, however, are only approximations, distorted by omissions and unwarranted inclusions. British passengers were more likely than other travelers to cross in better accommodations, and thus some escaped the tally of the customs inspectors, who counted only steerage arrivals as immigrants. On the other hand, an unknown portion of those identified as British immigrants were actually Irishmen who had migrated first to England and then decided to try their luck in the United States.

The ebb and flow of migration from Britain to the United States seems to have been the product of a symbiosis between the English and the American economies, but the precise process of the interaction remains unclear. Times of prosperity and investment growth in the United States, especially in the building sector, coincided roughly with periods of economic constriction in England, where Americans obtained much of their capital. At such moments, immigration to the United States from Britain reached peak points. In contrast, emigration sagged when prosperity and investment opportunities reappeared in England, Scotland, and Wales. Both British workers and their unions apparently were aware of the complementary nature of the economies of their homeland and the United States. Until the end of the nineteenth century, the unions fostered emigration, which they accepted as an answer to the twin problems of overpopulation and overproduction. Organizations like the textile workers' union earmarked part of their dues to assist members desiring to leave the country. Even in hard times, when the unions could not sustain such funds, they at least provided information about emigration to their members. The workers' leaders hoped to keep the supply of labor low while increasing the markets for industrial output. As a result, they tried to convince excess workers to seek farmlands, especially in underpopulated districts of the British empire. They discouraged emigration to the United States; in the short run an influx of British workers would depress the wages of brother workers there; in the long run this movement would provide American industries with the cheap and skilled labor needed to undercut British competitors. Rank-and-file workers, however, often ignored their leaders' advice. They preferred the United States, which took England's place as the leading manufacturing nation of the world in the 1880s, as a destination. Between 1881 and 1890, the period of greatest movement, two out of three British emigrants set out for the American republic.

Part of the attraction of the United States lay in the similarity of its occupational structure to that of the British Isles. According to studies conducted between 1907 and 1910 by the federal Immigration Commission, only 15 percent of the immigrants in American industry had pursued similar work in Europe; the comparable percentages for English-men, Scotsmen, and Welshmen were 50, 36, and 58. When cotton workers in Lancashire faced unemployment, wage cuts, and strikes in the 1860s, they were able to take their skills to the mills of southern Massachusetts. With the opening of fresh copper mines, the United States put the old diggings of Cornwall, England, at a disadvantage; Cornishmen transferred their operations to the New World and particularly to the sites of the rich ore deposits in northern Michigan. The miners of the British Isles became the backbone of both anthracite and bituminous operations in the United States after the Civil War. Of the British in the bituminous fields of America at the start of the twentieth century, 83 percent of the English and 88 percent of the Scots and Welsh had been miners back home. The story in the iron and steel industry was the same. Moreover, the experience of the British workers enabled them to win promotions and to make good money; over all the American industries Britons earned the highest average daily wages.

Some comments about the Canadian-American nexus must accompany any discussion of emigration from Europe to the United States. As has been seen, Canada was a nation of immigrants. Between 1851 and 1891 America's northern neighbor received over 1.6 million newcomers. But Canada was also a spawner of emigrants to the United States. Prominent in their ranks were persons who should properly be classified European rather than Canadian. These newcomers used British North America as a way station on the road to destinations in the United States. The imperfections of the statistics make it impossible to determine accurately how many people traveled to the United States via Canada for reasons of economy or convenience. The United States did not enumerate immigrants entering by overland routes before 1908, and between 1886 and 1893 American authorities did not record immigration from Canada at all. But Canadians were always among those headed south across the border, and the stream became constant after the mid-1830s.

Economic factors, with some subsidiary political considerations, were the stimuli for Canadian emigration. The provinces of Upper and Lower Canada, into which Quebec had been divided in 1791, were harder hit than the American states by the economic depression that started in 1837. Unsuccessful rebellions that occurred in both provinces in 1837 and 1838 against the powerful executive arm of the government —identified with English interests—increased feelings of uneasiness. In the 1840s the reduction of English tariffs on timber produced in the Baltic hurt the New Brunswick lumbering industry, a series of bad crops caused problems in Nova Scotia, and Frenchmen in Quebec became convinced that land was either unavailable there or in the hands of Anglo-Canadian proprietors. For some of the disgruntled, the United

States offered land or the prospect of jobs in the new factories of nearby New England. For others, the emerging lumber industry in states like Wisconsin promised work in a familiar occupation, and the opening of copper mines in Upper Michigan created additional job opportunities. Between 1835 and 1860 an annual average of 4,244 immigrants entered American ports from Canada, but the yearly number never exceeded 9,500. Even the American Civil War presented a chance to those who were willing either to volunteer or to replace natives caught by the conscription; more than 50,000 men born in British America eventually served in the Union forces, but it is not known how many of them emigrated specifically for this purpose.

Similar, but more serious, economic conditions intensified the wave of Canadian emigration after the American Civil War. Residents of the Maritime Provinces lost access to free markets for their products in American ports and cities when the United States in 1866 abrogated the Reciprocity Treaty of 1854. Canadian fishermen faced stiff competition in northern waters as the Yankees returned from battle armed with new techniques and equipment. Nova Scotia miners suffered after the production of coal resumed in Pennsylvania; at the same time, America's growing transportation network could now distribute domestic output more widely. The people of Quebec felt the shortage of land more acutely than ever before, and would-be migrants to the interior encountered the Laurentian Shield, which deprives Canada of the equivalent of America's Middle West. As a result, thousands of Canadians headed south. Recorded immigration to the United States from its neighbor first reached a five-digit annual total in 1865, when 21,586 Canadians entered the nation. From then until 1885, the yearly average was 43,720. The highest totals came between 1880 and 1882, when 325,560 people entered. American census records confirm that the 1880s was the decade in which the number of Canadian-born persons living in the United States rose the most: the 263,781 men, women, and children added to the tally in those years surpassed the increments of 243,494 and 223,693 in the 1860s and the 1870s, respectively.

By 1890, 20,645,542 residents of the United States were either immigrants or the children of at least one immigrant parent. This group— the people defined by the Census Bureau as having "foreign origins"— formed 32.7 percent of the overall American population of 62,947,714 and 37.4 percent of the 55,101,258 white inhabitants of the nation. Members of the European national groups whose coming has been the focus of this chapter accounted for 84.5 percent of the foreign born and the foreign stock in America. Undoubtedly, they also provided a very large proportion of the 922,268 Americans of mixed foreign blood, who constituted 4.4 percent of the 20,645,542. The remainder of the foreign population consisted of 6,851,564 males and females of German stock,

4,913,238 Irish, 2,683,957 British, and 1,535,597 Scandinavians. In addition, there were 1,453,174 Canadians, including 513,428 of French descent. As the following chapters will show, these immigrant groups had survived a period of adjustment that in some cases was almost traumatic and had established niches for themselves in the American economy and society. But, by 1890, the initial part of their history in America was coming to a close. Another phase in the peopling of the nation had begun. For every Irish-born person in the United States, there were 1.47 second-generation Irish-Americans; for every native German, 1.46 German-Americans. The comparable figures for Canadians and British were 1.24 and 1.21. There were only 2 Scandinavians born in America for every 3 from Europe, but their immigration had come late in the period, and the former would outnumber the latter by 1900. Future episodes in the story of these groups in the United States would concern primarily the experiences of their American-born members. And the next phase in the history of U.S. immigration would involve peoples whose contribution to the population was barely discernible as the nation entered the last decade of the nineteenth century.

# CHAPTER III

# Natives and Newcomers: Confrontation

WHEN THE DELEGATES to the Constitutional Convention gathered in Philadelphia in May 1787, the Declaration of Independence was barely a decade old. The former colonies had yet to establish a unique national and cultural identity, and the new nation's attitude toward immigration was an amalgam of experience, idealistic theory, and insecurity. In 1776 the Continental Congress had considered including symbols of the population's six major European sources—England, Scotland, Ireland, France, Germany, and Holland—in the Great Seal of the United States. Indeed, the members associated the motto E Pluribus Unum as much with the joining of different peoples as with the alliance of formerly separate colonies. A few years later, the Founding Fathers no longer thought it appropriate to emphasize America's ethnic diversity, but they still saw no reason to restrict the familiar influx of Europeans, whose presence contributed to the prosperity of the nation. Some leaders, like Alexander Hamilton, were willing even to offer inducements to prospective settlers with needed skills. Thomas Jefferson at times wondered whether the small increment to growth provided by newcomers was worth the risk of social disruption inherent in a heterogeneous population, but most American politicians did not envision the dramatic changes that were to occur in the volume and character of the European immigration. Their lack of concern was reflected in the Constitution, which devoted only one paragraph to the subject of immigration. The vaguely worded ninth section of Article I was obviously a compromise between proponents and opponents of the slave trade and was probably also a warning against the dumping of British convicts in the United States. It forbade Congress to stop before 1808 the migration or importation of persons currently being accepted by any of the thirteen states. Commentators expected that Congress would halt the slave trade when the period of grace expired, and in the meantime federal authorities had the power to impose a $10 levy on each imported person.

Attitudes toward the political position of the immigrants were ambivalent. The Founding Fathers, from their experience with foreign volunteers during the War of Independence, knew that the United States was vulnerable to invasion by Europeans of high ambitions and varying abilities who believed their continental background and training entitled them to immediate preferment. American leaders also worried that popular foreign newcomers might lead the people down paths alien to republican goals. Some were even concerned that advocates of reunification with England might infiltrate the country. These fears surfaced in the framers' adoption of constitutional provisions limiting the access of foreign-born Americans to elected federal offices. Article I stipulated that would-be U.S. representatives and senators had to be citizens for at least seven and nine years, respectively, prior to taking office, and Article II decreed that no immigrant naturalized after the adoption of the Constitution could become president or vice-president.

Within these limits, the framers generally were sympathetic to extending political rights to the foreign born. They were especially lenient in regard to criteria for naturalization, the sine qua non of the franchise and eligibility for office. The Naturalization Act of 1790, which was based on colonial practices, made immigrants eligible for citizenship after only two years' residence in the United States. The Founding Fathers had moved far toward accepting the idea that citizenship was a voluntary contract, rather than a perpetual and immutable relationship between subject and king that was based on the laws of nature. After all, they had justified the Revolution in terms of a contract theory of government. The argument implied the wisdom of acting quickly both to integrate willing newcomers into the political community and to make formal their allegiance to their new country. Moreover, the Americans readily accepted the image, which European liberals were busily promoting, of their nation as a land of liberty and political refuge.

From almost noncontroversial beginnings, immigration and naturalization became hotly debated matters by the end of the 1790s. Frenchmen and Irishmen, the most notable newcomers of the decade, were neither so numerous as to inundate the communities they entered nor so poor as to become an unbearable burden. As persons whose migration was directly or indirectly the consequence of the French Revolution, however, they were a center of political controversy. Many Americans saw them as a threat to extend to the New World the turmoil of the Old and as advocates of unnecessary involvement by the United States in the affairs of Europe. This fear was not without foundation. Edmund Genêt was initially an envoy of the French government, rather than an immigrant, but his appeals over the head of the U.S. government for popular support against the English underscored the dangers aliens in America posed to neutrality. Genêt's French compatriots were, by and large, reserved in their behavior, but Irish refugees carried their struggle to American soil. Rebels like Napper Tandy and Wolfe Tone planned for the moment of their return to the Emerald Isle, while other Irishmen were, for example, in the forefront of the opponents of Jay's treaty, the Washington administration's major diplomatic initiative to achieve rapprochement with England.

The partisan activities of the French and Irish exiles coincided with the crystallization of the first American political parties and were a matter of concern to the leaders of the opposing organizations. The Democratic Republicans, forming around Thomas Jefferson and James Madison, most often came from areas dominated by agriculture and from rapidly growing states with populations of varied ethnic backgrounds. They accepted the democratization of politics accompanying the Revolution, looked upon events in France as at least a partial replication of their own earlier struggle, and gratefully remembered French support during the War of Independence. The Republicans were aghast at the thought of aristocratic emigrés using the United States as a refuge and a base of operation. The Federalists, aligning behind the administrations of George Washington and John Adams, were strongest in districts heavily involved in commerce and settled largely by people of English origin living in stable communities. This party was uncomfortable with the erosion of the political influence of the social and economic upper class in the wake of the Revolution, looked upon the aims of the French insurgents as much more radical than the goal of national independence they had pursued, and saw the fate of the United States as inextricably interwoven with the success of the English mercantile network. The Federalists were alarmed by those who threatened to thwart Anglo-American rapprochement and to promote political and social leveling. Mutually fearful of foreign agitators, though for almost contradictory reasons, the Republicans and the Federalists by 1795 were willing to accept a new naturalization act that required aliens to reside in the United States for five years before gaining eligibility for citizenship.

After 1795, the Republicans became less worried about outside influences operating in the United States. The inauguration of the First Directory led to the voluntary repatriation of many conservative French exiles. The Federalists, however, found no comfort. France's move to the right did not silence the revolution's supporters in the United States, and the suppression of the uprising of the United Irishmen in 1797–1798 intensified the emigration from Ireland. Indeed, Rufus King, the American minister to Great Britain, had to convince the English not to use the United States as a place of banishment for Irish political prisoners. Federalists, especially those from New England, which had never welcomed Irishmen, found Celtic immigrants obnoxious, democratic, and generally supportive of the well-organized Jeffersonian critics of Adams's administration. The existence of a political party composed of opponents to the elected government was novel and to many Federalists this situation smacked of conspiracy; the adherence of the Irish to the Republican camp only served to make the situation appear more sinister. The Federalists found the opportunity to strike back at their enemies—France, that nation's American friends, alien radicals, and the Democratic Republicans—in the furor caused by the XYZ Affair. The demand by three French diplomats that the United States offer a loan to their nation and a bribe as the price for commencing negotiations on outstanding differences offended all Americans. That incident brought the nation to the verge of war and embarrassed the Republican party.

Striking while the iron was hot, the Federalists in 1798 pushed through four pieces of legislation that limited the political impact that immigrants could have on American politics and at least temporarily deprived their Republican opponents of a potentially important base of supporters. The Naturalization Act included a provision, passed by the narrow vote of forty-one to forty in the House of Representatives, that raised to fourteen years the residence requirement imposed on immigrants who sought American citizenship. The law also demanded that aliens declare their intention to seek naturalization five years before obtaining it and spend five years in the state or territory in which they were to reside as citizens. The law's only concession was to allow foreigners resident in the United States before 1795 to take advantage of the more liberal provisions of the naturalization act passed in that year. The Alien Enemies Act authorized, in time of war, invasion, or attack, the arrest, imprisonment, and deportation of immigrant males from enemy nations who had passed their fourteenth birthday without taking up U.S. citizenship. The Federalists wanted to give the president almost the entire responsibility for implementing the law, but the Republicans managed to put the courts and other agencies in charge of enforcement. A temporary Aliens Act strengthened the president's hand in the immediate crisis by empowering him to order out of the United States any alien suspected of being dangerous to the nation's peace and safety. The Republicans argued in vain that Article I, section 9, of the Constitution expressly forbade congressional action against immigration before 1808 and that in any circumstance the law was so arbitrary as to be invalid. The Federalists proclaimed that the needs of national defense had to be the prime consideration and that aliens were not protected by the Constitution. Finally, the Sedition Act prohibited, among other deeds, the publication of any false, scandalous, or malicious writing against the government. The Federalists used the act, which expired on March 3, 1801, to try to silence several Republican newspaper editors, including immigrants like James Thomas Callender from Scotland, Thomas Cooper from England, and Matthew Lyon from Ireland.

The four Alien and Sedition acts are important in American history less as effective laws than as omens. The two most punitive measures expired within a few years, and the possibility of harassment would not have been enough to discourage potential immigrants had countervailing social and economic forces been at work. But the laws showed how, in a society in which political allegiance is as much a voluntary commitment as an accident of birth, it is easy to doubt the loyalty of the different and the dissident. And they did reveal a tendency common among Americans, but not exclusive to them, to blame domestic turmoil on the intrigues of minority or alien elements in the population rather than to see internal problems as by-products of conflicting values or social inequities. Fortunately, the United States was spared from a recurrence of this phenomenon for the next generation, a period of great importance in the nation's development.

A low level of immigration between 1800 and 1830 allowed the components of the U.S. population to homogenize and this process, in turn, combined with the political maturation of the country to produce a clearer sense of an American nationality. In the years before 1830 the integrity of the non-British cultures present in the United States eroded. The low volume of immigration in the first decades of the nineteenth century deprived the descendants of persons who had come from continental Europe during the eighteenth century, most notably Germans, of the reinforcements that might have allowed them to maintain their ethnic identities in the midst of the dominant Anglo-American society. Technological change, commercial development, and the geographic expansion of the United States also hastened the acculturation of the foreign born. Improvements in transportation and an increasingly broad network of business connections naturally brought people into contact and reduced the isolation that kept ethnic feelings intense. The westward migration that attracted so many Americans of all backgrounds separated people from their national enclaves and recombined them in more mixed communities. The intermarriages that inevitably took place also weakened ethnic ties, though the extent of this amalgamation is in doubt. Marriages between persons of different nationalities seem to have been common among the upper classes. They also occurred frequently enough among ordinary folk, at least on the frontier in the late eighteenth century, to worry ethnic loyalists like the German minister Arnold Roschen of North Carolina. On the other hand, many communities retained a reputation for ethnic homogeneity in the early nineteenth century, and generalizations about the frequency of intermarriage rest more on speculation than on evidence.

Though the new American, whom the French writer J. Hector St. John de Crèvecoeur described as an amalgam of the peoples of Europe, may have been an idealized image, the growing dominance of an Anglo-American culture was real. By the middle of the eighteenth century, colonists of Dutch and Swedish extraction had already begun to succumb to this force. In 1748 Peter Kalm, the Swedish botanist, noted during a visit to New Jersey that Swedish settlers were incorporating English words into their speech. Swedish children were not properly learning their ancestral tongue or hid their knowledge of it for fear of being thought inferior to their English peers. The larger Dutch population in rural New Jersey, and especially in the Hudson Valley of New York, kept their language alive longer but, without enrichment from abroad, the Dutch spoken in America degenerated into a dialect unaffected by the linguistic changes that took place in the Netherlands after 1664. Even German, the most widespread and recently introduced of the non-English languages, withered in most areas. The tongues of the ethnic minorities survived for many decades among older people and in informal conversation, especially in rural areas, but the abandonment of the vernacular by the churches of the various groups was the surest sign of the Anglicization of speech.

America's European sponsored churches were under a dual pressure. As time passed, fewer people understood the languages used in non-English services, and clergymen admitted that they had to make concessions in order to keep the allegiance of their followers. English became the standard language in the services of New York City's Dutch Reformed churches by the 1760s and won even wider acceptance after the Revolution. In 1790 the Dutch Reformed Synod adopted English as the official language of worship in all its churches. Among Lutherans, English replaced German as the language for sermons in Philadelphia in 1806, in New York City in 1807, in Albany in 1808, and in Harrisburg in 1812. German remained alive in the form of Pennsylvania Dutch in some areas of that state, but this language faded in most others and lost out completely to English in North Carolina after 1825. Independence and American national pride also took their toll, and the Protestant churches that had institutional ties to European states cut them: the Dutch Reformed church declared its independence from the Netherlands; the Anglican church became the Episcopal; and by 1800 the

Swedish Lutheran churches of New Jersey affiliated with the latter, at the same time informing Swedish ecclesiastical authorities that missionaries were no longer needed.

The relatively rapid decline of non-British white cultures in the United States during the opening decades of the nineteenth century was of fundamental importance for the future of the nation. This process, for example, helped put the country on a different course of ethnic development from that which eventually emerged in Canada. The British residents of His Majesty's remaining North American colonies expected, like their cousins in the independent United States, to impose a more or less English culture on their corner of the New World. But the British formed such a small minority of the population north of the St. Lawrence that they had to rely on politics, rather than gradual demographic change, to achieve their goal. The Constitution of 1791, which divided old Quebec into Upper and Lower Canada, was seen as the first step on the path to complete British supremacy. That measure not only gave the conquerors control in the former district, in which they were more numerous, but also allotted them majorities in the upper house and executive council of the latter, where the French made up over 90 percent of the population. The British conceded the equality of French for use in legislative debates but made English the language in which laws were officially promulgated. Moreover, they subsequently diverted money generated by the properties of the banned Jesuit religious order—funds that the French had used to underwrite parochial education—to the support of a state sponsored, Anglicized school system.

Despite such measures, French influence refused to fade in Canada, and the British resorted to harsher political pressures. During the Napoleonic era, Governor Sir James Craig, who failed to recognize that the generally conservative French Canadians lacked sympathy for revolutionary France, conducted a repressive campaign against the allegedly subversive French population. Even after the French Canadians proved their loyalty in the War of 1812, proposals to diminish their status continued to surface. The nadir for the French came after French Canadian radicals, known as *patriotes,* joined like-minded English Canadians in an unsuccessful effort in 1837–1838 to extract from the English Parliament more autonomy for the North American settlements. The zeal with which British regular soldiers and English Canadian volunteers put down the uprising left a legacy of bitterness, especially in Quebec, and the report on the crisis made for Parliament in 1839 by the Earl of Durham aggravated in the situation. Durham, who was a liberal in the context of English politics, urged England to give Canada greater self-government, but he saw at the root of the problem a conflict of races rather than of political principles. For the earl the best hope for a complete resolution of Canada's difficulties lay in the creation of a Canadian nationality. He assumed, however, that such a development could be achieved only through the extinction of French Canadian culture, which he deemed inferior to English culture and incompatible with freedom and intelligence.

While the peoples of British North America were struggling in the early nineteenth century to create a Canadian identity, the increasingly homogeneous population of the independent United States was able to discover a set of values and attitudes that would distinguish the American character from the English and all others. It was an era of nationalistic fervor in the republic. Authors like Washington Irving and James Fenimore Cooper created a distinctly American genre and the lexicographer Noah Webster helped distinguish the American variety of the English language from the parent tongue. In politics and diplomacy the public managed to forget the young nation's narrow escape in the War of 1812 by turning General Andrew Jackson's victory over the British at New Orleans into a legend proving the superiority of America's frontier virtue and raw vigor over European wealth and might. Americans also directed their energies to a quest for their so-called Manifest Destiny, in the words of John L. O'Sullivan, editor of *The United States Magazine and Democratic Review*. At face value, the term referred to the apparently inevitable territorial expansion of the United States. Most Americans assumed that the nation would naturally expand to the Pacific coast, and some dreamt of absorbing Canada, Mexico, and even the remainder of the Western Hemisphere. But Manifest Destiny also touched on a long-standing belief that the United States had a providential mission.

From the time of the Puritans, Americans had seen the settlement of the New World as a climactic moment in the history of religion, and by the middle of the eighteenth century they had added an important secular dimension to their understanding. The development of America became, in their minds, the first step toward the establishment of the millennium, a time in which holiness would prevail and Christ would reign on earth. The Revolution, with its strong tones of regeneration, reaffirmed this message, and independence became the political and social complement of the spiritual redemption. In this context, the history of the United States became the unfolding of God's kingdom on earth, and the conquest of the continent loomed as the fundamental assignment in the creation of a new world order.

The goal of American expansion was to create an empire of political liberty, economic opportunity, and, most important, Christian civilization. During the first half of the nineteenth century, the rhetoric of the millennium was common in American churches, especially in the revivalist ones that became the dynamic element of Protestantism. The churches were convinced that they had not only to spread the Gospel to individual souls but also to take part in the salvation of society. Religiously minded Americans were in the forefront of the reform movements of the era. They sought to establish perfect communities and to find the key to rehabilitating the criminal, the mentally ill, and the poor. In the North they led the fight against slavery. Church activists were convinced that an ecclesiastically sanctioned civic morality was necessary to keep the nation true to its mission. Despite the constitutional separation of church and state, they conceived of the United States as a nation whose laws and policies ought to reflect the country's essentially Christian character. Ministers and their supporters deemed it proper that public institutions, including schools, have a specifically Protestant outlook. They also expected that the government would endorse and enforce a broadly shared set of moral standards. These could touch every human endeavor but in the pre–Civil War years the churches focused on the two contemporary abuses whose prevalence symbolized the dangers to America's mission. They stressed the importance of keeping the Sabbath free from profanation, so that the people might turn their minds to God, and they argued forcibly for the prohibition of alcohol, that fundamental threat to spirituality and responsible citizenship.

Cultural homogeneity, national pride, and millennial expectations combined to create the history of ethnic and racial relations in America during the decades before the Civil War. For the most part, these forces set a tone of confrontation. As the diversity of the population lessened before 1830, the majority of white Americans, and especially those of Protestant background, became less tolerant of differences. Paradoxically, at the very time the institution of slavery came under sustained attack, the position of blacks in American society reached new depths of isolation and vulnerability. As the sense of providential concern for the United States and of its special mission in the world became fully articulated, the nation willingly overwhelmed any peoples it encountered on the way west. The Indians, who had symbolized America, were denied a place in the country's future, and the Mexican inhabitants of the West were subjugated in the name of liberty. As the opportunities to achieve an unprecedentedly high level of public and private morality and to establish an almost ideal community seemed to come within reach, even the most generous and optimistic bristled against any threats to reaching these goals. In this regard, the European immigrants, whose arrival signaled their acceptance of the promise of America, felt the sting of those who declared them unworthy of it.

African peoples living in the United States in the early nineteenth century shared an experience superficially similar to that of the descendants of non-English Europeans but in fact profoundly different from it. Congressional action banned the importation of slaves into the United

States after December 31, 1807. Though smugglers thereafter managed to slip an estimated 10,000 slaves into the country during each decade before the Civil War, effective African reinforcement of black culture in the United States became an impossibility. Had race and the stigma of slavery not been more serious distinguishing marks than nationality, persons of African blood, like those of European origins, would have been absorbed at least in part into the dominant society. White Americans, however, thought of blacks as either innately inferior or, in the opinion of the most sympathetic observers, irretrievably damaged by the environment of limited opportunity and apparently insurmountable discrimination in which they lived. Whites also viewed blacks as dangerous, particularly in the wake of various slave rebellions in the late eighteenth and early nineteenth centuries.

Both in the North, where slavery was dying, and in the South, where it held sway, the position of blacks deteriorated. Slave codes became more restrictive, and free blacks had their rights curtailed. By 1840 Rhode Island, Connecticut, New York, Pennsylvania, North Carolina, and Tennessee had eliminated or limited the right of free blacks to vote. Signs of segregation appeared in hospitals, prisons, and other institutions, and America's churches began to cleave along racial lines. Even to foes of slavery, the prospects of Africans in the United States appeared bleak. The common wisdom called for the repatriation of American blacks to Africa, where they would be free and could help civilize the continent. To this purpose, the Reverend Robert Finley; his brother-in-law Elias Boudinot Caldwell, who was clerk of the U.S. Supreme Court; and Francis Scott Key, a lawyer, as well as the composer of the "Star-Spangled Banner," laid the goundwork for the formation late in 1816 of the American Society for Colonizing the Free People of Color in the United States. The colonization movement helped establish the independent republic of Liberia in Africa in 1822 and transported 12,000 blacks there by 1860, but this effort lost its popularity as the financial and practical problems of repatriating millions of former slaves became clear.

Throughout the pre–Civil War era, whites continued to emphasize the differences between themselves and blacks. Leading scientists offered the theory of polygenesis to explain the apparent mental and physical divergences between the races. The thesis, which won the support of Louis Agassiz, the famous French botanist and Harvard professor, proposed the existence of acts of creation in addition to that which made Adam and Eve. According to the theory's adherents, blacks were literally created separate and unequal. Abolitionists, on the other hand, were willing to recognize the equality of the Africans' humanity with their own, but they separated the races in regard to moral characteristics. As can be seen in Harriet Beecher Stowe's novel *Uncle Tom's*

*Cabin,* blacks became for the abolitionists the preeminent possessors of the Christian virtues of childlike simplicity, docility, and unselfishness. Whites, on the other hand, were intellectual, aggressive, and efficient. The contrasting images favored the blacks but suggested that they were at a competitive disadvantage in the whites man's world. Ordinary Americans probably rejected polygenesis as inconsistent with the Bible and dismissed the more benign aspects of the abolitionists' description as sentimentality. For them, the superiority of whites was self-evident, as was the future of the United States as a white man's country once the institution of slavery disappeared. Most people believed that once freed the mass of blacks would have to separate themselves from the white population by concentrating in sections of the South or by migrating to the Caribbean islands or to Latin America or back to Africa. If the blacks insisted on staying among the whites, they would fail in the competitive struggle and their race would gradually die out.

The persistent refusal of white Americans to accept blacks as partners in the New World was less striking than their increasing despair in the early nineteenth century over the possibility of absorbing the Indian population of the continent into Western culture. Africans had been consistently a source of fear and an object of derision in America, but Indians had an ambiguous status in the white imagination. Colonists and frontier dwellers encountered the Indians at their most fearsome and recalcitrant, savagely wielding tomahawks and firebrands to prevent the loss of familiar lands and ways of life. When such incidents became a less frequent part of the white population's experience, however, other components of the Indians' situation gained significance. As the original inhabitants of North America, the Indians were inextricably part of the story of the nation. They could not be seen as an extraneous element, fit, like the blacks, to be returned to their homeland. The worthy foes who managed to escape enslavement and to operate successfully on the periphery of the white man's world seemed superior to the blacks. The standard racial hierarchy placed America's tribal peoples between whites and blacks, and Americans were not particularly disturbed by copper-colored skin. Indeed, intermarriage between Caucasian men and Indian women did not excite strong aversion and sometimes was looked upon favorably by the authorities. White Americans of the early nineteenth century were willing to judge the Indians as having achieved a level of civilization appropriate to the environment in which they lived, and the romantic among them envisioned the natives as noble savages in communion with an idyllic natural world. Reasonable people like Thomas Jefferson assumed that the Indians would soon absorb the benefits of white civilization.

Missionary schools, established with the support of the government by several Protestant denominations, became the primary means of disseminating white culture among the Indian tribes. By concentrating their efforts on the young, on women, and on the offspring of white and native unions, the missionaries were able to make some progress. A number of Indians became nominally Christian, learned English, and abandoned part-time hunting and fishing in favor of full-time agriculture. The expected total absorption of the whole of the whites' ways, however, did not take place. The Indians proved exasperatingly able to adopt bits and pieces of white culture and to use those elements for the ultimate preservation of their own ways. The Cherokee chief Sequoya devised an alphabet that allowed his people's tongue to compete with English as a written language. His tribe also used its knowledge of American laws and institutions to develop a constitution that attempted to make the Cherokee a political entity separate from the federal and state governments. Unfortunately for the Indians, they were not always discriminating in what white cultural elements they chose. Their affection for the wares of Euro-American civilization, including clothes, guns, and sundry implements, made them dependent on that culture without making them fully part of it and went far toward undermining their own skills. Worst of all, the Indians took on the vices, as well as the virtues, of white society; alcohol, in particular, had horribly debilitating effects on the native peoples. By the 1830s the stubborn vitality of some aspects of aboriginal life and the simultaneous deterioration of others, without the substitution of approved new forms of behavior, reflected contrasting aspects of the impact of white culture. But both tendencies pointed to the conclusion that the Indian was not ready to be absorbed into mainstream society.

Once the Indians were judged unready for incorporation in white culture, removing them from their homelands to points beyond the fringe of American settlement seemed the obvious course of action. The policy promised the avaricious quick access to the desirable lands of troublesome neighbors. At the same time, persons sympathetic with the Indians could believe that this policy would allow the tribes more time to achieve civilization. A number of treaties negotiated after 1815 provided for the voluntary surrender of tribal lands east of the Mississippi, and the Removal Act, passed by Congress in 1830, set up a program for sending tribes across that river. The removals were often carried out under dishonorable circumstances. In December 1828, the state of Georgia unilaterally abolished the government of the Cherokee nation, and the tribe's situation became worse in 1829, when gold was discovered on Cherokee land. With President Andrew Jackson supporting Georgia, not even the United States Supreme Court, which denied the state's jurisdiction over the Cherokee, could help the tribe. Some Cherokees agreed by the Treaty of New Echota in 1835 to cede their lands to the federal government, but about three-quarters of the tribe refused to cooperate. The government then removed the recalcitrant in a forced migration that cost over 4,000 lives.

Violence accompanied other removals. The Black Hawk War erupted in 1832, when the Sauk and the Fox refused to honor an agreement made in 1804 to leave the Illinois Territory. The Second Seminole War broke out in 1835, when this tribe would not leave Florida. In 1830 federal troops drove the Creek from Alabama after they attacked whites out of frustration at incursions on the small homesteads left to them as compensation for a major land cession. Soldiers were also used to hurry the Winnebago tribe of the Wisconsin River area across the Mississippi in 1840.

White thoughts of the trans-Mississippi West as a place of protected isolation for the Indians faded in the 1840s and 1850s before dreams of reaching the shores of the Pacific as soon as possible. Explorers and settlers entered the region in large numbers, and the earlier pattern of Indian–white contact was repeated. Epidemic diseases quickly spread among the tribes with disastrous consequences. In the northern Plains smallpox virtually wiped out the Mandan in 1837–1838, and recurring episodes of the disease took a heavy toll among the Blackfoot before the Civil War. Asiatic cholera, which swept the nation in 1849, may have reduced the Comanche population of the southern Plains by more than half and affected other tribes as severely. Treaties negotiated with the U.S. government in the 1850s cost the Indian nations of Kansas more than 90 percent of their land and drove them toward agricultural pursuits, to which they were culturally unsuited. American migrants simply overwhelmed or bypassed the smaller tribes of the arid western regions and drove the Indians of the northern Pacific coast onto reservations. Whenever necessary, force became the ultimate argument against the defiant. In 1849 the army established garrisons at Forts Laramie and Kearney to protect persons traveling the Platte River route to the gold fields of California, and the introduction of expensively maintained cavalry units gave the whites the final edge over the strong tribes of the Great Plains.

The expansion of the United States brought cultural subordination not only to the Indian tribes of the Plains and beyond. As the nation's western frontier touched Mexico's northern, Americans came into contact with a final group to be added to their list of peoples fated for demise. The Spanish-speaking inhabitants of the region from Texas through southern California fell short of American standards in several respects. They bore the political and religious heritage of Spain, a nation excoriated by Americans since the days of English colonization as a bastion of despotism and superstition. Worse, their Spanish blood had been mixed with Indian and black, creating a breed thought by most Americans to be clearly inferior. Visitors to the Southwest in the early nineteenth century forecast that the Mexicans would not be able to hold the area indefinitely, and their prophecy was fulfilled. Migrants from the United States entered Texas in the 1820s and by 1836 were numerous and strong enough to declare their independence from Mexico. Congressional action in 1845 to admit the Republic of Texas to the Union led to a war with Mexico that cost the losers dearly. The Treaty of Guadalupe Hidalgo, signed in 1848, ceded to the United States the lands known today as Arizona, New Mexico, Colorado, Nevada, and Utah, as well as the major prize of California, which had received many American settlers in the 1840s. Time reduced the Mexican proportion of the population to 10 percent in Texas by 1860 and to 25 percent in southern California twenty years later. The Mexicans, moreover, were swiftly relegated to the periphery of the society and the economy, with their Spanish land titles brought into question and their right to participate in America's growth limited by discrimination.

Compared with the blacks, Indians, and Mexicans, the European immigrants of the mid-nineteenth century were in an ambiguous position. As whites they were safe from being categorized as hopelessly inferior and as refugees from the political and economic darkness of the Old World they were evidence that mankind recognized America's mission. But the immigrants were, at the same time, a serious challenge to the establishment of a Christian utopia in the United States. The newcomers became strongly identified with the industrialization and urbanization that was changing the nation in ways disfavored by many socially conscious and concerned people. Foreigners provided the manpower for the growth of the American economy, but their presence also helped make the nation's new factories distressingly similar to those of Europe and their low status belied the magic of the United States as a society of open-ended economic mobility. The arrival of the first wave of European immigrants in an era that saw patterns of familiar communal life waning hastened the decline of these arrangements and stimulated the Americans' fears that the social order was crumbling. Because of the desperate circumstances in which they came, the Europeans were the agents and victims of crime, disease, and disorder with a frequency that far exceeded their proportion of the population. Perhaps worst of all, large numbers of the immigrants flouted Protestant America's version of civic morality and rejected the use of public institutions to propagate this view. Too many immigrants landed on the wrong side of the various reform movements of the era. That the most numerous and troublesome of the early arrivals came from Catholic Ireland, whose people and religion had been hated and distrusted in America since colonial times, only aggravated the multiple problems. Conflict was unavoidable in such an atmosphere, and bitter clashes between natives and immigrants colored American history throughout the pre-Civil War era.

Europeans came to the United States in large part because of America's labor shortage, and their muscles helped propel the nation into the industrial age. But native-stock workers tended to see the immigrants' role in the work force in terms of individual profit and loss rather than of half-understood concepts of societal progress. Those who employed the abundant unskilled labor or rose to advanced positions in new industries dependent on this sector could feel superior to lowly foreign toilers. Those who lost ground had reason for bitterness. The unskilled faced the worst competition from the newcomers, but skilled workers also blamed the immigrants of the 1840s for keeping down wage rates, which had tumbled after the Panic of 1837.

The truth about the newcomers' economic impact is complex. Some jobs taken by them, such as railroad construction labor, had barely existed before their coming. Even in many traditional lines of work the immigrants' effect was mixed. No doubt their presence limited wages, but that curb in turn created employment by coaxing into the marketplace persons who would have been unwilling to hire had higher rates prevailed. The immigrants' coming was most disastrous for native-stock workers in trades that technological and entrepreneurial innovation had already undermined. Mechanization and the division of production tasks reduced the need for skill in endeavors like weaving and vitiated the apprenticeship systems that had controlled the flow of trained crafts workers. Artisans in doomed specialties found it easier to blame their plight on the immigrants who took over their tasks than on the larger revolution that enabled unskilled hands to replace them. The foreigners were a concrete object for the wrath of those who could reason that, had the newcomers been unavailable, labor-replacing technology would have made no headway against their occupations.

The same forces creating the jobs that invited the immigrants to America were simultaneously changing the face of the nation to which they came. This was particularly true in the older cities, where so many of the foreign born were concentrated. The technological revolution of the nineteenth century brought an end to the "walking city," which the absence of public transportation, the rarity of privately owned coaches, and the poor condition of roads had created in the colonial era. Families no longer had to operate their businesses at or near home. The rich no longer had to build their homes at the commercial centers of the cities, as in colonial New York, where the most elegant houses lay adjacent to the docks. The periphery of the town was no longer the preserve of the poorer sort. The introduction of the steam railroad in the 1840s allowed the affluent to commute from as far away as ten miles, and the appearance of streetcars pulled by horses over iron tracks made it possible for middle-class persons to relocate several miles away from downtown. Those willing and financially able to travel daily were the first suburbanites; they enjoyed access to fresher air and more space and escaped the aesthetically displeasing changes associated with the major expansion of wharving and warehousing facilities in the business districts.

America's immigrants inherited the urban void created by the birth of the suburbs. European newcomers were usually trapped near the downtown or in undesirable commercial areas. Several family members usually had to work, and their places of employment changed frequently as they searched for temporary, unskilled jobs. They could afford neither carfare nor travel time added to their long day, and even those with some money could not depend on lines that did not offer crosstown transportation. Immigrants filled the houses left behind in the exodus from the city. The owners subdivided their dwellings and rented them or they leased their buildings to persons who in turn sublet the units. In general, the owners allowed the property to deteriorate with the expectation of selling it at a handsome price as the business district sought space for expansion. The immigrants also crowded into unwholesome areas on the periphery of the downtown; in New York, for example, Irishmen and blacks congregated in the notorious Five Points district. Such changes only hastened the abandonment of the affected districts by the native citizens and transformed them into immigrant slums. In turn, these geographic expressions of the social and economic divisions developing in urban life demonstrated the connection between immigration and the maladies of America at mid-century.

Increases in disease accompanied the deterioration of the old city districts. The expanded commerce of the first half of the nineteenth century made it inevitable that the maladies of Europe would quickly cross the Atlantic to American ports. In the absence of advanced medical knowledge, public health regulations, proper sanitation, and even clean water, virulent epidemics were common. The immigrants, weakened by hardship and unfamiliar with the hygiene demanded by urban life, naturally became prime carriers and victims of such illnesses. Irish residents were the first laid low in the cholera epidemics of 1832 and 1849 in New York City; these outbreaks took a disproportionately large toll among their compatriots and other poor people across the nation.

Crime also flourished in the bowels of the city, where the new wealth and impersonality of life sorely tempted impoverished and marginal people toward wrongdoing. Immigrants received much of the blame for the perceived increase in disorder. Modern experience suggests that the accusations were exaggerated. Discriminatory law enforcement and the glut of young people in the foreign population undoubtedly contributed to the disturbing frequency of immigrants' names on the arrest rolls. Moreover, the vast majority of foreigners in trouble with the law were accused only of minor offenses that a society less concerned with the need for order would have regarded as inconsequential. But crime obviously did play an important role in some immigrants' efforts to adjust to their new surroundings. Theft and prostitution offered desperate people the means to survive, and many young immigrants found acceptance only on the streets among their own kind. Organized in gangs, such as the fancifully named Bowery B'hoys, Dead Rabbits, and Plug Uglies of New York City, Irish males took part in the shenanigans of rival volunteer fire units in the prewar era and provided Election Day muscle for ward politicians. On the slightest pretext, such as the appearance in 1849 of an unpopular English actor at the Astor Place Opera House, they turned the troubles of Ireland into American melees. Most of all, they expressed in battles against each other and equally violent native gangs the anger, frustration, and thirst for adventure endemic among slum dwellers.

The reputed association between immigration, on the one hand, and disease and crime, on the other, hastened the depersonalization of the poor and deviant, a process that had begun in the late eighteenth century with increased rates of internal migration and the rapid growth of cities relative to the countryside. The poor and problem-racked were no longer individual men and women whose problems were handled in the context of small communities or families. They were collectivities of strangers inhabiting social netherworlds. Americans came to see the unfortunate and unpleasant people of the nation less as the victims of luck or societal malfunctions and more as the perpetrators of their own problems. Lawbreakers had never been objects of sympathy, but poverty once had been identified as primarily the lot of the widowed, the orphaned, and the infirm. By the middle decades of the century, however, Americans were inclined to define poverty as a badge of intemperance and shiftlessness rather than as a by-product of the progress that was making so many U.S. citizens prosperous. In the scientific ignorance of the era, even the sick became objects of contempt. During the cholera epidemic of 1832, pastors assured their flocks that the disease was God's scourge against those whose depravity had robbed their bodies of the power of resistance; the virulence of the malady in the darker corners of the cities seemed to confirm this judgment.

Some Protestant ministers, in the millennial flush of the 1820s and 1830s, retained hopes of redeeming the sinners of the slums. Members of the New York City Tract Society, for example, spent much of their time distributing Bibles and religious literature among the poor. They hoped to bring these people an understanding of Christ's work of salvation and assumed that an amelioration in the living conditions of the converts would naturally follow their adoption of high moral standards. Reformers were confident that even those who had already run afoul of the law or proved unproductive might be rehabilitated. They believed that new institutions, like penitentiaries, and revitalized ones, like workhouses, might provide the moral training and exposure to good habits that seemed to have been uniformly absent in the personal histories of their inmates. Such optimism faded in the 1840s and 1850s. The great migration of these decades made the magnitude of the problem seem overwhelming, especially because the newcomers, so many of whom were Roman Catholics, proved as unreceptive as the Indians were to the missionaries' message. In despair, many reformers concluded that the nation's poor were incorrigible. Ministers lost hope in a mass conversion of slum dwellers, and the operators of the society's penal institutions, whose cells were increasingly filled with foreigners, gradually deemphasized rehabilitative aspirations in favor of the custodial responsibility of isolating miscreants from the general population.

The Roman Catholic religious affiliation of many of the residents of the worst districts of the eastern cities was especially galling to American Protestants. Catholicism not only explained the moral recalcitrance of the immigrant poor but also signaled a profound change in the ecclesiastical makeup of the United States. At the time of the first federal census, Roman Catholics constituted less than 1 percent of the American population; 16,000 of the faith's 25,000 adherents lived in one state, Maryland, and the church may have been failing in its efforts to hold the loyalty of Catholic immigrants, particularly Irish servants, settled in strongly Protestant areas. A weak institution, the Roman church hardly seemed a threat; in fact, some Americans found it attractive. Dominated by French clergymen who were refugees from the revolution, the Catholic church had a somewhat aristocratic quality and offered a conservative alternative to Protestants offended by the increasingly evangelical character of their denominations. The influx of immigrants, however, destroyed this equilibrium. By 1850, Roman Catholicism was the largest Christian denomination in the United States, calling 7.5 percent of the population of some 23 million its own. It was a truly national church, with six metropolitan and twenty-seven suffragan bishops in 1852, the year of the First Plenary Council in America. Catholicism was becoming the religion of the great cities, and though many German immigrants also filled the church's ranks, the long despised Irish were quickly taking over its leadership and membership.

For Protestant Americans, particularly those under evangelical influence, the Roman Catholic church remained the fabled Whore of Babylon. Protestant spokesmen used their pulpits and the numerous religious periodicals available to them to rekindle hatreds dating back to the Reformation and the Counter-Reformation. They lashed out at favorite targets, including the primacy of the pope; the doctrine of Transubstantiation; the veneration of the Virgin; vestments; rituals; and miracles. But the central complaints were timely, as well as traditional, and revealed less about Catholicism than about the values and concerns of mid-nineteenth-century America. The supposed subservience of Catholics to the pope caused problems in an age of awakening American nationalism. Commentators frequently expressed doubt that Catholics could be completely loyal to the United States when their spiritual leader was also a temporal prince in the Italian boot. They suggested that the hierarchical structure of the Roman church and its emphasis on obedience, which offended Protestant America's affinity for decentralization, made Catholicism inimical to democracy and liberty. To extremists, the presence of Catholics in the United States was part of the reactionary plot to stymie the fulfillment of America's providential mission. Samuel F. B. Morse—author, artist, and inventor—pointed out the connection between immigration and these machinations. His *Imminent Dangers to the Free Institutions of the United States through Foreign Immigration,* which appeared in 1835, argued that the Jesuits were in control of the transatlantic movement of Catholics and were directing the newcomers to strategic points in the nation in preparation for an attempt to overthrow the government. The next year, Samuel B. Smith, editor of the anti-Catholic newspaper *The Downfall of Babylon,* outlined in a book, *The Flight of Popery from Rome to the West,* the role immigrants would play in a papal military invasion of the United States.

Concerned about Rome's political and ideological threat to the nation, American Protestants also were peculiarly interested in the private morals of Catholic priests and nuns. Criticism of celibacy as unnatural and wasteful was common among Protestants and easy to understand in a youthful, half-empty country. But popular interest went beyond the utilitarian disapproval of abstinence to a lurid fascination with tales of sexual indulgence. Most likely, this obsession was a by-product of the repressive attitude toward sexuality that took hold in the United States in the middle of the nineteenth century. In such an atmosphere, the attribution of immorality to an enemy allowed Protestants to express their misgivings over their own secret desires, and the supposed need to educate the innocent about the danger of Catholicism served as an outlet for their fantasies. As the historian Richard Hofstadter once explained, anti-Catholicism became the pornography of the Puritans. Whatever the underlying cause, literature describing, in almost salacious terms, the depravity practiced by the men and women of the Roman church became enormously popular. The themes were consistent. Priests were seducers who used the confessional to gain control over virtuous young women and to put in their minds suggestions of impurity that would eventually lead to assignations. Convents were brothels, where nuns catered to the pleasures of the priests. When their unions produced offspring, the infants were baptized, murdered, and buried secretly on the covent grounds.

The history of Maria Monk's *Awful Disclosures of the Hotel Dieu Nunnery of Montreal* reveals the pervasive impact of prurient anti-Catholic propaganda on American society before the Civil War. The most notorious of the exposés of convent life, this book purported to recount the experiences of its author before her escape. In fact, Maria Monk had never been a nun, though she had spent time as an inmate of a Catholic asylum in Montreal. Brain damaged as a child, Monk was incapable herself of writing the book, which had been germinated in the minds of several New York City ministers. Harper's, which printed the book through a dummy firm, was the preeminent American publishing house. Responsible critics, including Colonel William L. Stone, the Protestant editor of the *New York Commercial Advertiser,* soon proved the story a sham, and Monk, cut out of the profits by her manipulators, ended her days as a prostitute and pickpocket. The shame surrounding the book, however, failed to hurt its popularity among a good percentage of America's reading public. With 300,000 copies sold between its appearance in 1836 and 1860, *Awful Disclosures* was, next to *Uncle Tom's Cabin,* the best-selling piece of American literature in the pre–Civil War era.

Conflicts emanating from the immigrants' rejection of a package of reforms that were the substance of the program to Christianize America overlapped with and aggravated worries caused by the hold of Roman Catholicism on the mass of arrivals. Protestant efforts to curtail secular activities, including mail delivery, on Sundays and to discourage or prohibit the consumption of alcohol caused much irritation. The Sabbatarian and temperance movements had multiple, related sources of strength. These efforts responded to highly visible and symbolically important affronts to American Protestant morality and, at least in the case of temperance, to a real social problem. Popular neglect of the Sabbath underlined the decline both of religious enthusiasm and of the churches' coercive abilities following the loss of governmental support after the Revolution. Drinking suggested not only worldly pleasures but also alcoholism. The latter equation was not beyond reason: native-stock American drinkers favored hard liquor almost to the exclusion of beer and wine, and such a pattern of consumption is often associated with alcohol abuse. Sabbatarianism and temperance had their initial appeal among conservatives, who used these movements to attack real problems and to reassert the superiority of their values over the looser democratic mores of the early nineteenth century. Congregational and Presbyterian ministers from older Federalist communities, for example, founded the American Temperance Society, which in 1826 became the first national organization devoted to the issue. But Sabbatarianism and temperance quickly grew into broad-based movements. The revivalist ministers of the Second Great Awakening adopted these reforms and even extended temperance from a call to avoid hard liquor to a demand to abstain from all alcoholic beverages. And the advocates of reform adeptly enhanced the attractiveness of their message by arguing that high morals were more than their own reward; they were also the surest guarantee of worldly success.

With the coming of the immigrants, Sabbatarianism and temperance took on new dimensions. The most numerous foreign groups in the United States did not see these movements as reforms. Germans, whether Catholic or Protestant, looked upon Sunday as a time for social, as well as religious, functions, and they had no reservations about the moderate consumption of spirits. They, of course, brought with them skills that substantially advanced the art of brewing in America. Drinking was also well established in Gaelic culture, and in the desperate conditions of life on both sides of the Atlantic alcoholism had become a serious enough problem to bring forth an Irish temperance crusade led by the renowned Father Theobald Mathew. Thus, native-stock Americans viewed the immigrant cultures as alien to their own values and, most notably, as inimical to the American vision of Christian civilization.

By their adherence to Sabbatarianism and temperance, native-stock Protestants convinced themselves of their superiority to foreigners and they turned these movements into weapons to reinforce their dominant position. The native stock found in the Catholic identity of the Irish, the foreign group most reviled for its drinking habits, confirmation of the subversive role of the Roman church, but they also criticized Protestant immigrants for their behavior. Resorting to legislative action, as well as moral suasion, to convince the entire society to adopt their norms, the native-stock Protestants attempted to assert their political advantage over the newcomers. More important, the native Protestants, especially ones in marginal or economically declining positions, traded on their avowed morality in convincing employers to hire and promote them ahead of their numerous immigrant competitors.

No portion of the program to Christianize America caused more bitterness between the native stock and the immigrant than the public school movement. The common schools, as they were called, were perhaps the most noble and practical reform experiment of the first half of the nineteenth century. Their advocates expected to improve American democracy by bringing to the masses of people unable to afford private schooling the knowledge necessary for economic success and responsible political participation. Public school proponents also hoped to curb some of the disorder of American society by bringing discipline to those at the bottom of the social ladder. The supporters of public education were agreed that moral training should be a fundamental part of schooling, but they recognized that the multiplicity of religious allegiances found in the population doomed any effort to foster the beliefs of a single denomination. Therefore, they ordained that the schools attempt to inculcate only generally accepted moral standards and Christian tenets. Within the context of the basically homogeneous American society that the reformers had known since childhood and wanted to preserve, this arrangement was a liberal and advanced compromise. Within the framework of a nation experiencing rapid immigration, this approach became a weapon against the culture of the newcomers.

Catholic leaders, especially clergy, recognized that the public schools were not nondenominationally Christian but nondenominationally Protestant. All parts of the common school regimen were a point of controversy because they reflected the dominant Protestant milieu of the host community. Textbooks routinely presented history from a perspective that lauded Protestantism and defamed the Roman church. That difficulty might have been overcome. In New York City, the private corporation that administered the publicly supported schools offered to cooperate with Catholics to revise or remove offensive literature. Unfortunately, trust was at a minimum and the offer was minimal. The Catholic hierarchy wondered why the school leaders could not act unilaterally, expected that Protestants would soon reinsert new derogatory material, and feared implicitly endorsing whatever items they did not request deleted. Catholics also knew that removing objectionable books would not silence teachers who shared the disdain of average citizens for immigrants and routinely belittled the ethnic and religious heritages of their foreign pupils. Most important, the Catholics were aware that they had no hope of ending what they believed to be the worst abuse. Protestants considered Bible reading the linchpin of moral training in the schools, but Catholics saw this practice as a double threat. The schools' consistent use of the Protestant, King James Bible, rejected the Roman church's position that the Douai translation was the only authoritative version. And the teachers' practice of reading Bible passages without comment, a tactic adopted as a means of avoiding sectarianism, endorsed Protestant doctrine in favor of private interpretation of Holy Writ and denied the Catholic church's claim to be the sole interpreter of the Scriptures. This latter point, of course, had been a central issue in the Reformation.

The Protestant-Catholic split over the public schools concerned policy more than philosophy. Neither party wanted a truly secular system; their differences revolved around the possibility of separating Christian moral training from sectarian indoctrination. The Protestant leaders of the common school movement believed that they had made the distinction; their critics disagreed. Most Catholic spokesmen, indeed, argued that separating morality and sectarian teaching was impossible without resorting to an unacceptable deistic rationalism. The only solution they saw was public support of schools whose outlook corresponded to the beliefs and values of the specific communities being served.

The lines of contention became clearest in a New York City struggle. In 1840 New York's Catholic bishop, John Hughes, asked the common council to allow parochial schools a share of the education funds, which were then given exclusively to the Public School Society, a private corporation led by Protestant philanthropists. Hughes claimed that the church institutions would be as nonsectarian as the common schools; they would employ Catholic teachers approved by the authorities to teach academic subjects in a manner inoffensive to Catholic sensitivities, but they would avoid religious instruction during regular hours. The Public School Society and Protestant spokesmen disagreed with the bishop, and the common council dismissed his petition. Hughes, however, had the support of Governor William Seward. Though a Whig, Seward did not share his party's aversion for immigrants and was sympathetic with the plight of the Irish. He hoped that the immigrants would fully share in American blessings and recognized that clerical disapproval of the common schools was keeping countless young Catholics from receiving an education. The governor urged the legislature to aid the parochial schools. The bishop, in turn, impressed city Democrats with the importance of the Catholic vote; ten Tammany candidates with his endorsement won election to the assembly in 1841; three without his support lost. In 1842 the assembly passed a bill that divided New York City's political wards into separate school districts with locally elected boards. The measure would have given Catholics control of schools in their neighborhoods, but the senate amended the law to prohibit explicitly sectarian instruction in the schools and to establish a central board of education to supervise the local districts. In the end, Hughes's victory was small. His old foes in the Public School Society lost their monopoly of education, but the newly formed elected board of education fell under control of Protestants who continued the old sectarian practices. The alienation of Catholics from the common schools intensified.

The tragic culmination of the immigrants' confrontation with the American reform movement came over the issue of slavery. Despite their disagreements with native-stock citizens on a host of issues, foreign Americans of the antebellum era shared certain fundamental attitudes with their hosts. The most notable of these involved slavery and race. Like the great majority of Americans resident in the northern states, the newcomers disliked slavery and opposed its expansion into the free western territories. They also were unwilling to risk the future of the Union in order to eradicate the institution in Dixie. Only a leaven of articulate, liberal political refugees, particularly among the small band of

German Forty-eighters, endorsed abolition. Immigrants, like other white Americans, assumed that the Africans were inferior, and as the group most directly in competition with free black labor they grasped this belief all the more tightly. The foreign born shared the fetid urban living quarters of the blacks, vied with them for the unskilled jobs available in the eastern cities, and took advantage of their own light skins to oust Afro-Americans gradually from domestic and personal service occupations. Ironically, in asserting cultural and moral superiority over their competitors, the immigrants did unto the blacks what they were suffering themselves at the hands of the natives. The Irish, the most marginal of the newcomers, were probably the worst offenders. But immigrants of other nationalities who were in frequent contact with blacks also showed bias; indeed, members of the large German population in Texas went so far as to own slaves.

Immigrants fed their hostility to abolition on the awareness that it and nativism overlapped. It was only partly fortuitous that Harriet Beecher Stowe, the author of *Uncle Tom's Cabin,* was the daughter of the Reverend Lyman Beecher, whose sermons had helped incite a mob to burn the convent of the Ursuline nuns in Charlestown, Massachusetts, in August 1834. And, though regrettable, the Reverend Arthur Tappan's involvement with the production of Monk's *Awful Disclosures* was not entirely inconsistent with his role as a founder of the American and Foreign Antislavery Society. Abolition and the anti-Catholic agitation that polluted the natives' reception of the foreign born were integral parts of the general Protestant reform movement that distinguished the second third of the nineteenth century. The sense of civic responsibility and Christian perfectionism and the desire to reestablish social preeminence that combined in the Sabbatarian, temperance, and anti-popery movements also infused abolitionism. Morally conscious Americans reasonably felt guilty for the existence of slavery, and the coming of the immigrants inflamed their sensibilities. The nation's willingness to accept benighted foreigners as voting citizens while denying American blacks, free as well as bound, basic rights highlighted the country's racism, and the newcomers' bestowal of their allegiance on the pro-southern Democratic party limited the prospect of ending slavery. The mutual antipathy of abolitionists and major foreign-born groups had unfortunate longlasting results. This situation shut off the possibility of the newcomers' receiving substantial assistance from the most progressive groups in the United States and helped create an attitudinal gulf that has constantly divided America's ethnic groups, particularly the urban Catholic ones, from the Protestant, middle-class reform tradition.

The antipathy between immigrant and native-stock Americans became one of the most disruptive forces in the United States in the 1840s and 1850s. In May 1844, three days of rioting in Kensington, an Irish, working-class suburb of Philadelphia, culminated in the burning of two churches, St. Michael's and St. Augustine's, and of other Catholic property. A network of cultural, economic, and social antagonisms underlay the clash of Irishmen and natives, but the immediate spark was the mistaken belief that Bishop Francis Kenrick was attempting to banish the Bible from the public schools. In fact, the bishop had simply sought and received permission for Catholic students to read their own version of the Scriptures in the classroom. When the threat of violence spread to New York, Bishop Hughes placed armed men around his churches and warned that the city would become a second Moscow if any of the edifices were attacked. Fortunately, cooler heads prevailed. Though undoubtedly the most dramatic, these were not the only instances of ethnic and religious violence in the era. The troubles reached another peak in the 1850s. An American tour in 1853 by a papal nuncio, Gaetano Bedini, who had been involved in the suppression of republican uprisings in Italy a few years earlier, inflamed the populace, and itinerant preachers like John S. Orr, "the Angel Gabriel," kept the fires of anti-Catholicism going. Of course, the problems associated with the massive influx of immigrants in these years immeasurably aggravated the situation. The result was the burning of a dozen Catholic churches, the desecration of many others, and physical attacks on priests and nuns.

Street battles were the most visible, but not the most important, part of the anti-immigrant struggle in antebellum America. Alone, such incidents were inchoate expressions of grievances. The heart of the movement, however, was political action that resembled older traditions of anti-immigrant maneuvering. Candidates from the nativist American Republican party won the municipal elections in New York City and Philadelphia in 1844; the highpoint of nativist political agitation came a decade later. By 1854 a well-organized American Republican party had emerged nationally from a coalition of local political groups in New York and other states. The Know-Nothings, as they were popularly called because of their refusal to divulge information about their ritualistic secret societies, won stunning victories that year and the next, sending seventy-five of their candidates to Congress and taking control of several state governments in the Northeast. The party also did well in the border states and even made inroads in the South. Know-Nothingism appealed to small businessmen and locally based professionals who considered themselves the cultural guardians of their communities. The movement attracted artisans and workers caught up in economic change and threatened by immigrant competitors. The Know-Nothings, who presented themselves as foes of foreign influence, rather than as anti-Catholics, even won support among the old French settlers of Louisiana, whose position within the Roman church and the general society had been disturbed by the Irish influx. In short, the movement offered something to everyone shaken by the wave of recent immigration, and its appeal to an older, more stable America offered refuge to those dismayed by the other crises of the era.

As political leaders the Know-Nothings were failures. On the federal level they did not have the influence to enact their main programs. Had they been able, the Know-Nothings would have subjected future immigrants to a twenty-one-year waiting period before naturalization and barred them from political office. In state governments, they were an embarrassment. Know-Nothing legislators conducted unsuccessful searches for abominations in the convents of Massachusetts and then billed the public for the costs of their own roistering during the inspection tours. The American Republican party quickly faded, and in 1856 its candidate for the White House, former president Millard Fillmore, earned a paltry total of eight electoral votes. The decline of the Know-Nothings coincided with a steep drop in the volume of European immigration from a peak in 1854. The end of the Irish famine, the economic depression that began in the United States with the Panic of 1857, and the increasing political instability associated with American divisions over the issue of slavery made the Old World less desperate and the New less inviting. In 1861 only 81,000 Europeans reached American shores. The reduction alleviated the social strain in communities that had absorbed the brunt of the earlier influx and allowed the assimilation of the alien population to proceed without additional pressure.

As the fears and frustrations sparked by the preceding decade of mass immigration subsided, the even more serious issues of slavery and secession raced to the forefront of the public's consciousness. Regardless of their origins, the people of the United States were swept up in the Civil War. The available statistics on the composition of the opposing forces are incomplete and hard to evaluate, but they show clearly that the immigrants were overrepresented in the military forces of both the North and the South. The foreign born provided approximately 22 percent of the enlistments in the armies of the North, where they accounted for 18 percent of the population. They formed 5–10 percent of the forces in the South, where they constituted 4 percent of the white inhabitants. Overall, however, the Union, which was home to almost 95 percent of America's foreign born, has to be considered the prime beneficiary of the immigrants' military services.

In their individual decisions to join the military, the foreign born were responding to the same principles, emotions, community pressures, and interests that motivated their native-stock neighbors. The presence of sizable numbers of alien soldiers in the Confederate ranks vitiates specialized explanations that attribute Irish participation to hatred of England, which gave succor to the South, or that credit the

Germans' involvement to a supposed detestation of slavery. For many aliens financial necessity was a powerful incentive to enlistment; the foreign born showed a strong inclination toward the military even before the opening salvos were fired at Fort Sumter. In the prewar era at least 50 percent and perhaps 60 percent of the enlisted men in the regular army were immigrants, usually from Ireland or Germany. For these soldiers, as for many marginal members of today's society, the military offered the guarantee of employment, food, lodging, and other care. The inducements expanded during the Civil War years. Union volunteers received bonuses and immigrants became naturalized immediately upon enlistment. After conscription began in the North in 1863, those who had not yet been called but who were willing to serve for a price could substitute for drafted men.

Perhaps the battlefield made brothers of newcomers and natives and won for the foreign born the respect of some of their erstwhile foes. But this idea can easily be exaggerated. Immigrants were among the most vociferous opponents of the war and some of their protests were so socially convulsive as to obliterate the goodwill generated by their countrymen's service. In New York the conscription into the Union army of several Irish members of the Black Joke Volunteer Fire Company sparked a series of riots that nearly tore the city apart in 1863. After learning that their names had been drawn on Saturday morning, July 11, the draftees plotted with friends to prevent the resumption of the process after the weekend and to destroy the records of their selection. On Monday morning a mob of men and women burned the draft office at Third Avenue and Forty-sixth Street and a half week of terror was under way. Rioters fought police and soldiers, invaded houses and stores, seized an armory, looted, and menaced both City Hall and Horace Greeley's *New York Tribune* building. Striking out at the war they disliked and at their traditional enemies, the participants saved their worst atrocities for the blacks whose slum neighborhoods they shared and whose competition for jobs they feared, especially in the wake of the Emancipation Proclamation. They drove 237 children from the Colored Orphan Asylum and burned the abolitionist sponsored institution to the ground, beat to death or lynched several adult blacks, and pummeled an undetermined number of other blacks. The disturbances subsided by Thursday night, but not until military units freshly returned from the battlefield at Gettysburg directed cannon fire at the crowd. Other places like Boston, Milwaukee, and the Pennsylvania coal mining district also experienced anticonscription insurrections, but New York's Draft Riots gained infamy as the bloodiest episode in American urban history. The official records directly tie 105 deaths to the affair, but this estimate remains conservative even with the addition of another score of related fatalities.

The Irish were flagrantly visible in the Draft Riots. Of the 184 persons of known nativity arrested, 117 were Irish. Their participation was more than enough to make the public forget that Irish policemen and soldiers had helped subdue the mob. For many this incident also outweighed the contributions of countless Irishmen serving in the Union army as members of primarily Irish regiments or of ethnically integrated units. Above all, the Draft Riots helped insure that although Know-Nothingism had died nativism would live on in American hearts.

# CHAPTER IV

# Natives and Newcomers: Accommodation

BETWEEN THE END of the Civil War and the beginning of the twentieth century, Anglo-Saxon society finished spreading across North America. At the same time, however, earlier expectations that a variation of British Protestant culture suitable to the New World would obliterate competing cultures had to be either abandoned or considerably modified. In the British colonies that came together in 1867 and the following years as modern Canada, the French population won recognition of the equality, at least in theory, of their culture with that of the English. In the United States, no such constitutional concessions were made to the Indians, the recently liberated blacks, or the foreign-stock residents. Instead, contradictory currents of thought and sets of goals coexisted and clashed; some pointed to the assimilation of the several elements of the population to a single norm, and others to the voluntary or involuntary social isolation of one or more ethnic or racial groups. By the end of the nineteenth century, the pressures toward the creation and acceptance of seemingly permanent separate social networks for some minority groups had proven irresistible. Indians remained on tribal reservations. Blacks found themselves increasingly under legal restrictions that segregated them but failed to provide compensatory advantages. Meanwhile, immigrants and native-stock whites passed from open and occasionally violent confrontations to mutual, though often unequal, accommodation. The native stock abandoned, in favor of more subtle means of control, efforts to block the participation of foreign-stock persons in public life and to strip away their cultural traditions. The newcomers continued, in the less frenzied atmosphere, to seek a share in America's prosperity and a role in its politics. Most important, they made basic decisions about the place of European ways in their new environment. What was attempted and achieved varied with the ethnic group and the demographic, geographic, and socioeconomic circumstances of its communities. No single immigrant experience took shape, but ethnic, religious, and cultural affiliations exerted an unprecedented impact on American life.

The development of ethnic relations in Canada in the years surrounding the American Civil War offers an instructive alternative against which to compare the situation in the United States. After the Earl of Durham's report in 1839 on the recent troubles in British North America, Parliament unified Upper and Lower Canada. The creation of the Province of Canada gave the less populous English district equal weight with the French in the legislature and made the heavy debt of the former the financial obligation of both, but this measure failed to further Durham's goal of erasing French Canadian influence. In the years after the Act of Union, French intellectuals poured forth ethnically conscious works of history and literature, demonstrating the vitality of their culture. Moreover, the French were too numerous and critically located to be ignored by those persons eager to increase popular government in Canada and to exploit the economic potential of the north country. In the 1840s liberal English politicians like Robert Baldwin cooperated with conservative French leaders like Louis Hippolyte Lafontaine. Together, they defied the Act of Union by abandoning the exclusive use of English in government and forcing the executive to become more responsive to the legislature. In the 1850s George Etienne Cartier and a number of Englishmen, including the youthful John A. Macdonald, shared the dream of a transcontinental railroad. By the 1860s such men were convinced of the need for a new, flexible government to facilitate economically progressive projects and to overcome the lack of Anglo-French cooperation that had characterized Canadian politics since the retirement of Baldwin and Lafontaine in 1850. Fear that Washington would attempt to pluck Canada to punish England for its semi-official sympathy for the rebel states during the Civil War finally brought action. At a series of conferences between 1864 and 1866, Cartier and Macdonald took leading roles in establishing the dominion government, which Parliament approved in 1867 for Nova Scotia and New Brunswick, as well as for Lower and Upper Canada, which became the provinces of Quebec and Ontario, respectively.

The British North America Act, which served as Canada's constitution until 1982, conceded to the faster growing English provinces the principle of proportional representation in the new, elected House of Commons and guaranteed the French the right to use their language in the federal legislature and courts, as well as in those of Quebec. The French also retained the right to their own school system. Such stipulations could neither halt the demographic and social trends that pointed toward overall English domination of Canada nor wipe out ethnic feelings rooted in two centuries of history. Manitoba, British Columbia, and Prince Edward Island joined Canada by 1873, and British immigration to the new confederation gained momentum. The central government displayed strong anti-French feelings in putting down uprisings by French–Indian *métis,* or mixed-bloods, in Manitoba in 1869 and in the Northwest Territories in 1885; the authorities in New Brunswick, Ontario, Manitoba, and the Northwest Territories suppressed French Catholic schools; and the goal of bilingualism faded outside Quebec. Nevertheless, the British North America Act at least effectively protected the French Catholics within Quebec, where a defensive yet determined ethnic and religious movement came to the fore in politics and cultural affairs. Most important, the act—which the French regarded not as enabling legislation for an integrated federal republic but as a treaty between themselves and the English—gave constitutional recognition to the idea of permanent ethnic interests in Canada and created a bipolar cultural framework within which later immigrant groups would have to operate.

While Canada at least temporarily gave up the hope of establishing an ethnically homogeneous society, the United States continued down the path determined by the English domination of the formative years of its colonial and early national experience. No non-British group in the U.S. had the numbers, the extent of geographic concentration, the strength, and the historic claims to autonomy that had forced the English in Canada to make concessions to the Quebecers and other French. In the United States, the vastly inferior position of the Indians and blacks, the two largest and most distinctive groups with reason to be antagonistic toward the British, insured that their cultures would not challenge the dominant one. Moreover, the main era of non-British European immigration long postdated the achievement of a unified nation-state that was believed to embody the perfection of the English tradition of political liberty. The immigrants of the nineteenth century were divided among themselves by national origin, religion, and language, and they lacked a plausible claim to having played an equal role with the English in the discovery and formation of the country. They obviously were not in a position to demand concessions like those eventually made to the French Canadians. Thus, no alternative emerged to the ideal of subjugating peoples deemed incapable of assimilation and absorbing those judged worthy of it. Lacking control over their own destinies, the former could do little to oppose the will of the majority. The latter had options but had to maneuver carefully. Those who resisted complete assimilation had to offer the appearance of conformity whenever possible, while protecting those aspects of their heritage thought to be of fundamental importance. Americans operating within these restrictions laid the groundwork for the later development of the broader concept of a melting pot, but in the process they often paid a high social price.

As Americans completed the settlement of the West, the diminution of the lands available to the aboriginal peoples and the consequent destruction of their way of life continued. Before the Civil War, the government put pressure for land cessions on the tribes resident in the Indian Territory, west of Missouri and Arkansas. In the single year of 1854, the tribes there gave up 18 million of the acres that had supposedly been theirs in perpetuity. During and after the war, even the appearance of voluntary agreement to the cessions faded. Surrounded on three sides by southern sympathizers and frequently led by mixed-bloods who held slaves, a majority of the Chickasaw and the Choctaw and minorities among the Cherokee, Creek, and Seminole of this territory made the mistake of siding with the Confederacy. The innocent and the guilty paid alike in 1866 with a new treaty that cost the Indians half of modern Oklahoma. The Civil War also brought disaster to the tribal peoples who took advantage of the withdrawal of federal troops from the frontier. After some Santee Sioux killed about 500 whites in Minnesota in 1862, the government drove the entire tribe from the state. In Colorado, militiamen under Colonel J. M. Chivington avenged a series of small raids with the massacre of 500 southern Cheyenne and Arapaho men, women, and children at Sand Creek in November 1864. In the Southwest, Kit Carson received a colonelcy to drive marauding Apaches and Navahos onto reservations.

Washington attempted to improve the situation after the war by forming an investigatory Peace Commission in 1867, taking pains to appoint better Indian agents, and establishing the nonpartisan Board of Indian Commissioners in 1871. Unfortunately, these measures did not prevent the continuation of warfare on the Plains and beyond until the 1880s. General Philip Sheridan drove restive Arapahos, Cheyennes, Comanches, and Kiowas back to their reservations in the Red River War of 1874–1875. After the northern Arapaho, the northern Cheyenne, and the Sioux scored an isolated victory over General George Armstrong Custer at the Little Big Horn in 1876, they gradually gave up the fight against army regulars, who had the edge of logistical support from the railroads. Across the Rockies, military defeats forced reservation life on the Modoc in 1873, the Nez Percé in 1877, and the Ute in 1879, while in the Southwest the surrender of Geronimo in 1886 concluded the protracted Apache War. The era finally ended in 1890 at the Battle of Wounded Knee, South Dakota. There, troops of the Seventh Cavalry, which had been Custer's unit, massacred 300 Teton Sioux men, women, and children who had left their reservation under the influence of the Ghost Dance movement, a messianic revival with strong ritual elements that promised the eventual restoration of Indian ways to the western Plains.

The reservations on which the Indians were placed after tribal defeats served a purpose similar to that of the antebellum practice of removing across the Mississippi native nations that had impeded the white advance east of the river. Once American settlement reached from coast to coast, restricting the movement of the nomadic aborigines to designated districts became the preferred means of opening, with a minimum of confrontation, desirable lands to sedentary agriculture and cattle ranching. The immediate purpose of the reservations was to protect the Indians from the most exploitative and violent of the white pioneers, but their main goal was to serve as a controlled environment for the peaceful extermination of tribal ways. Missionaries were able to work safely among the carefully supervised natives, and the government introduced a variety of schools on the reservations and in other isolated settings off them to wean young Indians from their elders. The authorities attempted gradually to create a core of Anglicized leaders on the reservations. After 1878, with congressional approval, certain Indians were commissioned as policemen, and soon they were used, with other cooperative natives, as judges on the Courts of Indian Offenses. These specially chosen tribesmen, who were expected to dress and behave in the fashion of whites, helped to undermine the influence of conservative chiefs and to enforce prohibitions against traditional tribal religious and social practices.

Reservation life naturally became a major topic of concern among the numerous reformers who developed an interest in Indian affairs after the Civil War. Pursuing the general indictment of government policy made popular in writings like Helen Hunt Jackson's *Century of Dishonor*, they exposed the official corruption that poisoned the management of some reservations. By showing the terrible hardships inflicted by forcibly relocating northern tribes like the Ponca, Cheyenne, and Nez Percé to the Indian Territory, they successfully stopped the policy of removing natives from familiar grounds to a handful of presumably more efficient, consolidated reservations. Few reformers, however, attacked the reservations' goal of obliterating Indian culture; instead, the large majority complained of slow progress to this end. They especially objected to the continuation of communal landholding on the reservations and urged the introduction of individual ownership. In their opinion, immersing tribal people in the economic basis of white civilization in North America would lead them to adopt all aspects of the dominant culture. Although experience showed that the many Indians who lacked the skills and equipment to operate private farms soon sold their acres or were defrauded of them, the reformers won their point. The Dawes Severalty Act of 1887 authorized, at the president's discretion, the allocation of reservation lands to individual tribal members, the granting of citizenship to the recipients, and the sale of surplus acreage on the open market. As the reformers hoped, the measure proved a death blow to the unique cultures of many tribes, whose identification as legal entities was dissolved by the act. For the Indians, of course, the act was not a panacea. Over the next half century, from their holdings of 138 million acres, the Indians lost 86 million of the best land, and although their old ways were under attack they were unable to achieve integration into white society.

The reformers, who joined organizations like the Indian Rights Association, founded in 1882, perpetuated the concept of Americanization that had flourished in the antebellum period. Indeed, many of them came from the same Protestant ministerial background that had produced earlier reformers who had envisioned the United States as the site of the Christian millennium. The determination with which these latter-day reformers pursued the problem of the Indian may well have been strengthened by the frustrations that had beset the original campaign. The reformers were able at least to win legislative adoption of their plans for assimilating the Indians. They were successful because they concentrated their efforts on the federal government, which controlled so much of tribal life, and avoided dealing directly with the natives. Moreover, these reformers could influence the government because the declining numbers and defeated status of the Indians were turning them, in the minds of most U.S. citizens and lawmakers, into abstractions. On issues that appeared of immediate importance, the reformers experienced failures. They could neither effectively protect the interests of their major client group, the American blacks, nor break down the cultures of their longtime foes among the immigrant groups.

Emancipation, in a basic sense, cut off the black population from the many people who had opposed slavery but were dubious about the innate abilities of the African. The defunct institution's foes had few plans for its victims. Almost everyone rejected the suggestion by General Jacob D. Cox to turn over Florida and the coasts of Georgia and South Carolina to the former slaves. Relocating so many people was obviously impractical. Unlike the policy that gave Indians reservations as the price for taking even more valuable land from them, Cox's proposal would have penalized whites in order to benefit blacks. At the same time, the measure would have duplicated the reservations' key shortcoming by depriving supposedly backward people of needed contact with white civilization. Most important, giving special assistance violated the assumption that the blacks should immediately begin to compete as free men and women. The age was little concerned with the impact of prior socioeconomic conditions on present opportunity. The American public discounted the cumulative, residual effects of the systematic oppression of blacks under slavery in the same way it deemphasized the impact of European life on the immigrants. In politics the northern majority was willing to give blacks the vote not only to protect them but also to guarantee the victory of the Republican party in the South. Accepting the stereotype of blacks as docile followers, whites did not think that their leadership was in jeopardy. Likewise, even the most sympathetic doubted that the former slaves would change the familiar economic order of the South. Sharing the almost universal belief in black inferiority, they anticipated that erstwhile slaves would gravitate to the base of the social structure. Proceeding from old ideas reinforced with arguments loosely derived from Charles Darwin's new theory of evolution, many predicted the disappearance of the African race in the United States as competition proved blacks unfit for survival, and the most scholarly analyses of late nineteenth-century data gave credence to this speculation.

Reform-minded northerners easily accommodated themselves to the programs of moderate southern businessmen who sought, after Reconstruction, to transform their region into the economic counterpart of the North. Advocates of a New South, such as Senator Wade Hampton of South Carolina and Henry W. Grady of the *Atlanta Constitution*, saw no need to restore either the paternalism or the complete subjugation of the antebellum era. They were satisfied to see white employers and former slaves enter an economic relationship much like that being developed by northern capitalists with European immigrants. The northerners also endorsed southern efforts to train the black population and accepted the educational emphasis in schools like Hampton and Tuskegee institutes on work discipline and practical skills. In keeping with their own recognition of the depth of racial differences and their complete rejection of miscegenation, few northerners objected to the rapid increase in barriers limiting social contacts between blacks and whites. In the civil rights cases of 1883, the northern dominated Supreme Court authorized segregation in public accommodations, and in *Plessy* v. *Ferguson* (1896) the Court proclaimed that "separate but equal" schooling for blacks was acceptable.

Ultimately, northern liberals, whose complicity had undermined the position of freed slaves from the start, could complain only weakly when, toward the end of the century, even the guise of racial harmony disappeared in Dixie. By the 1890s the southern leadership recognized that its efforts to turn the region's blacks into a modern work force had

had two dangerous consequences. On the one hand, this policy had created a potential pool of support for those whites, especially among the early Populists, who were willing to look beyond the color line in an attempt to build a viable reform movement. On the other, it had stirred terrible emotions in the hearts of the even larger number of whites who feared that they would soon fall to the social level of the former slaves. To protect themselves, the mass of ordinary whites increasingly resorted to vicious, racist assertions of their superiority. Both in public debates and in popular literature blacks were stereotyped as sex-mad "beasts"; lynching became an accepted phenomenon. The common charge that the mobs' targets had raped white women missed the fact that only a small minority of the black victims had actually been accused of sexual crimes. But this view did reveal the great depth of the psychological threat perceived by the whites in any program for southern development that failed to guarantee the subordination of the former slaves. Doubtful of the future dependability of black voters and worried by the disaffection for the New South being expressed by the white population, even moderate leaders retreated from the policy of racial "accommodationism." Across the South revisions of state constitutions in the final years of the century stripped blacks of the franchise and completed the reduction of them to second-class citizenship.

Hated in the South and looked upon with indifference, at best, in the North, American blacks had few choices by the mid-1890s. The most notable black spokesman of the era, Booker T. Washington, advised members of his race to accept the lowly status being forced upon them. The principal of Alabama's Tuskegee Institute, Washington made the best-known statement of his views on September 18, 1895, in a speech at the Cotton States and International Exposition in Atlanta. He urged blacks neither to expect to start at the top nor to demand immediate equality; instead, they must learn the virtues of ordinary labor and wait until their contributions in the marketplace inevitably gained them privileges. Washington also assured the delighted whites in his audience that in return for some economic opportunity the black population would accept social segregation. His speech avoided the subject of the disfranchisement of blacks, and he never sanctioned the undoing of the Fifteenth Amendment. But as the course of events became clear over the next few years, Washington counseled his followers that they would be wise to avoid political activity and agitation.

Once lauded, Booker T. Washington is an unpopular figure today. His readiness to put off equality for blacks to some distant day and to salve, rather than prod, white consciences is unappealing. Likewise, it is disturbing that he gathered personal glory, including the first honorary degree granted to a black by Harvard University, by telling men and women of his race to humble themselves. Nevertheless, Washington did have tactical and strategic insights beyond understanding the futility for southern blacks of open resistance to the racism of the 1890s. His request of southern whites that they put their faith in familiar, loyal blacks rather than in foreign immigrants matched the common maneuver by which ethnic groups jostled for preferment by claiming close affinity with the Anglo-American majority. More important, Washington seems to have recognized that what crippled blacks was more the lack of self-determination than the absence of integration. Voluntary or involuntary social isolation was a frequent phenomenon among minority groups in the late nineteenth century. The segregation suffered by blacks not only resembled, in the limitations of opportunity, the reservation life faced by most Indians but also had a parallel in the social separation experienced in much less severe form by some European ethnic groups. Foreign-stock whites, however, proved able to mitigate the effects of the isolation imposed on them. By taking control of their own ghettolike neighborhoods and social institutions while making themselves an essential ingredient in the labor force, unpopular ethnic groups, as will be seen, were able to protect their cultural identities, exert political influence, and pretend to an equal position in the larger community. However weakly he phrased the argument, Washington at least implicitly recognized that the blacks' main hope for a full share in American life rested not on the goodwill of whites but on the blacks' ability to create a strong social and economic base from which to enter the mainstream.

European immigrants and the growing band of second-generation Americans were not as vulnerable as other minority groups in the post–Civil War era. Diehard reformers could not manipulate them as they did reservation Indians and the white majority did not condemn them as unassimilable like blacks. Nevertheless, the complete absorption of the immigrants and their children was still the goal of the United States, and men and women of foreign stock were under considerable pressure to yield. To gain full acceptance, the members of each immigrant nationality were expected to conform to a set of generally defined norms that went beyond the minimum requirement of political allegiance and adoption of the ideology of democratic republicanism. Foreign-stock residents were also supposed to recognize the supremacy of Protestantism, to acquiesce in the programs of moral discipline advocated by the opinion shapers within the native-stock population, and to allow their European traditions to dissolve with the passage of time. Of course, some groups were no more able or ready to conform fully to this regimen after the Civil War than they had been before it. Moreover, several decades of life in the United States had given them enough economic, political, and emotional security to resist abuse and attacks more effectively. In the postwar decades, the foreign groups continued to fight to preserve the religions and languages that formed the most cherished elements of their identities. At the same time, however, individual ethnic groups learned how to use their points of conformity with the majority's beliefs and values in the intense competition against other nationalities.

The pattern of combining cultural accommodation with resistance was common to all non-British European immigrant groups. In the most notable examples of this maneuvering, Protestant newcomers gained protection for themselves by joining nativist attacks on Catholic immigrants, and the Irish, whenever possible, made the most of their knowledge of Anglo-Saxon culture and their affinity for American political forms. But the balance between resistance and accommodation and the level of assimilation that was sought varied considerably. A diversity of experience developed within, as well as among, nationalities because ethnic background did not act as an independent force. Instead, this factor combined with others to create a range of contexts in which the lives of foreign-stock Americans were spent and their attitudes formed. In the end, these immediate, local circumstances determined the tactics by which individual ethnic group members pursued economic success, political influence, cultural vitality, and a favorable niche within the broader society.

Geographic and demographic factors were of primary importance in shaping the world of the immigrant American. After the Civil War New York City retained its preeminence among the ocean ports receiving immigrants. New York's domination of commerce guaranteed that the proportion of the foreign population living on the East Coast would remain high. Likewise, the central states continued to absorb a sizable influx, despite the dramatic decline of New Orleans as a port of entry after 1860. In its place, Huron, Michigan, emerged as the second most important customs district in the immigrant trade. Huron's rise was largely the product of a surge in Canadian emigration: 75,439 of the 94,375 people who entered the United States through this inland port during the year ending June 30, 1880, hailed from British North America. In the same period, New York, which landed 263,726 newcomers, recorded only 117 Canadian entries. Huron was also a focus for immigration from Scandinavia and especially from Norway. Some 9,000 Scandinavians, including 7,375 Norwegians, arrived in Huron between July 1, 1879, and June 30, 1880; the much larger port of New York received only 8,577 passengers from Norway that year. Huron's statistics were just one sign of the large-scale movement of Scandinavians to the Middle West—a distinctive demographic feature of the quarter century following the Union victory. The phenomenon was the product of a fortuitous combination: the expansion of American settlement into the states west of the Mississippi, the aggressive recruitment drives in Europe by the frontier states and the railroad companies laying tracks across them, and the extension of the European population crisis to Norway, Sweden, and Denmark.

In 1890 a map showing the distribution of America's foreign population would have looked much the same as its 1860 predecessor; the main changes would have reflected the extension of settlement in the central states. The continuing flow of well-established immigrant streams to familiar destinations and the fecundity of the earlier arrivals reinforced and extended the patterns that had already been established. Cities continued to hold a far greater percentage of the foreign born and of their children than of those Americans whose parents had been born in the United States. New York, Chicago, Philadelphia, and Brooklyn, each of which was home to more than 500,000 people, had 15.7 percent of the foreign-born and foreign-stock population; seven other communities with populations over 250,000 had another 7.7 percent. Overall, 43.3 percent of immigrants and their offspring lived in the 124 communities with more than 25,000 inhabitants; only 14.2 percent of the white Americans born to native parents were in cities of that size.

In 1890 the band of northeastern and north central states once again held the bulk of the foreign residents. New England had 10.5 percent; the middle Atlantic states, 29.0 percent; and the east north central area, 28.7 percent. The recently settled west north central region—which included Minnesota, Iowa, Missouri, North Dakota, South Dakota, Nebraska, and Kansas—had 17.4 percent. The total of 85.6 percent of the foreign-stock population located in these sections exceeded the 62.4 percent of the native white population found there; as in 1860, the imbalance of the former over the latter was most striking in New York, Massachusetts, Wisconsin, Illinois, Michigan and Minnesota. Finally, the peculiarities in the geographic distribution of the major European national groups persisted. New England sheltered 19.7 percent of the Irish and 1.8 percent of the Germans; the middle Atlantic states held 42.1 percent and 27.9 percent of these two groups, respectively. The east and west north central states were the bases, respectively, for 39.2 percent and 19.3 percent of the Germans and for 17.5 percent and 9.7 percent of the Irish. The newly arrived Scandinavians were tightly clustered in the Middle West: 68.6 percent of them could be found in Michigan, Illinois, Wisconsin, Minnesota, Iowa, the Dakotas, and Nebraska (Table IV-1).

In view of the population distribution in the last decades of the nineteenth century, considerable diversity had to exist in the experiences of the foreign-stock residents of the United States. Within a single ethnic group, some members lived in cities; others, in the countryside. Some lived in communities numerically dominated by immigrants and the children of the foreign-born; others, in places populated principally by

TABLE IV-I
Percentage of America's Total Foreign-Stock White and Total Native-Stock
White Populations Resident in Each of the Major Political Units, 1890

| POLITICAL UNITS | FOREIGN STOCK WHITE (%) | NATIVE STOCK WHITE (%) | INDEX[1] |
|---|---|---|---|
| Alabama | 0.18 | 2.31 | 0.1 |
| Arizona | 0.15 | 0.07 | 2.2 |
| Arkansas | 0.18 | 2.27 | 0.1 |
| California | 2.97 | 1.46 | 2.0 |
| Colorado | 0.79 | 0.71 | 1.1 |
| Connecticut | 1.83 | 1.04 | 1.8 |
| Delaware | 0.15 | 0.32 | 0.5 |
| District of Columbia | 0.23 | 0.31 | 0.7 |
| Florida | 0.16 | 0.55 | 0.3 |
| Georgia | 0.15 | 2.75 | 0.1 |
| Idaho | 0.18 | 0.13 | 1.3 |
| Illinois | 9.14 | 5.49 | 1.7 |
| Indiana | 2.18 | 4.93 | 0.4 |
| Iowa | 4.06 | 3.10 | 1.3 |
| Kansas | 1.86 | 2.89 | 0.6 |
| Kentucky | 0.89 | 4.08 | 0.2 |
| Louisiana | 0.71 | 1.20 | 0.6 |
| Maine | 0.73 | 1.48 | 0.5 |
| Maryland | 1.22 | 1.67 | 0.7 |
| Massachusetts | 6.11 | 2.79 | 2.2 |
| Michigan | 5.57 | 2.70 | 2.1 |
| Minnesota | 4.78 | 0.91 | 5.2 |
| Mississippi | 0.12 | 1.51 | 0.1 |
| Missouri | 3.26 | 5.40 | 0.6 |
| Montana | 0.34 | 0.16 | 2.1 |
| Nebraska | 2.19 | 1.73 | 1.3 |
| Nevada | 0.12 | 0.04 | 2.7 |
| New Hampshire | 0.59 | 0.74 | 0.8 |
| New Jersey | 3.40 | 2.03 | 1.7 |
| New Mexico | 0.11 | 0.35 | 0.3 |
| New York | 16.52 | 7.35 | 2.2 |
| North Carolina | 0.05 | 3.03 | 0.0 |
| North Dakota | 0.70 | 0.11 | 6.3 |
| Ohio | 6.07 | 6.79 | 0.9 |
| Oklahoma | 0.03 | 0.15 | 0.2 |
| Oregon | 0.47 | 0.60 | 0.8 |
| Pennsylvania | 9.28 | 9.41 | 1.0 |
| Rhode Island | 0.97 | 0.40 | 2.4 |
| South Carolina | 0.08 | 1.29 | 0.1 |
| South Dakota | 0.97 | 0.37 | 2.6 |
| Tennessee | 0.26 | 3.73 | 0.1 |
| Texas | 1.63 | 4.10 | 0.4 |
| Utah | 0.67 | 0.20 | 3.3 |
| Vermont | 0.51 | 0.66 | 0.8 |
| Virginia | 0.20 | 2.84 | 0.1 |

TABLE IV–I
(*Continued*)

| POLITICAL UNITS | FOREIGN STOCK WHITE (%) | NATIVE STOCK WHITE (%) | INDEX[1] |
|---|---|---|---|
| Washington | 0.74 | 0.55 | 1.4 |
| West Virginia | 0.29 | 1.95 | 0.1 |
| Wisconsin | 6.05 | 1.27 | 4.8 |
| Wyoming | 0.14 | 0.09 | 1.6 |

SOURCE: Derived by Thomas J. Archdeacon from data in U.S. Senate, *Reports of the Immigration Commission* (1911; reprint ed., New York: Amo, 1970), vol. III: *Statistical Review of Immigration, 1819–1910—Distribution of Immigrants, 1850–1900*, table 15, pp. 522–529.

[1] The index was determined by dividing the percentage of foreign-stock residents by the percentage of native-stock Americans. Foreign-stock persons were over-represented in areas with indexes over 1.0 and under-represented in areas with indexes below 1.0. The index was computed from unrounded numbers.

natives of several generations. Some lived in regions, states, or towns in which their nationality constituted the largest foreign group; others, in locales in which their compatriots were a minority even among the aliens. There were additional complications. Ethnic group members could be first- or second-generation Americans; they might even be third-generation, although the census presumed that the grandchildren of immigrants had lost all traces of their European heritage. Foreign-stock persons could be rich or poor; Catholic or affiliated with one of the many Protestant denominations; in favor of adopting American ways or determined to preserve the old norms. Obviously, attempting to generalize about the foreign born and the children of the immigrants is filled with problems.

Despite the dangers of overgeneralization and the difficulties inherent in the analysis, it seems possible and worthwhile to isolate and discuss four basic ethnic experiences—an Irish one in the East; a German, in its Catholic and Protestant variations, in the Middle West; a Scandinavian in the Middle West; and a British and English Canadian case not bounded by geographical limits. This set embraces a sizable proportion of the foreign elements in the United States. Each experience contributed to the formation of an ethnic stereotype that affected even those members of the nationality living elsewhere. Finally, each can serve as a standard against which the differences in attitude and behavior of members of the group operating in markedly different circumstances can be appreciated.

In the years after the Civil War, the Irish of the northeastern states continued to be objects of contempt and discrimination. The organized political assaults of the Know-Nothings on the Irishmen's rights to citizenship and equal status before the law had receded, to be replaced by a widely shared abusive attitude toward this group. The concentration of the Irish and the Irish-American population between Massachusetts and Pennsylvania meant that they lived in older communities, long past the frontier stage of development. The Irish did not have an opportunity to carve settlements from the wilderness and to play a role in creating the social structures and cultural values of their adopted land. Instead, Irishmen usually had to seek places within existing societies gravely disturbed by this influx. As unskilled newcomers or the children of such, the Irish naturally found themselves on the lowest rung of the ladder. Of the 88,480 gainfully employed Irish immigrants in New York City in 1855, 23,386 were domestic servants and 17,426 were laborers; 4,559 worked at dressmaking, the group's next most frequent calling. Twenty-five years later, half the Irish population in Philadelphia was still engaged in basically unskilled endeavors. Conditions in the smaller cities of the region were similar: the Irish formed the largest bloc in the foreign-stock population of many factory dominated communities until the heavy influx of French Canadians and new immigrant groups from southern and eastern Europe late in the century. In such towns, the Irish, even when they had achieved an educational level equal to that of the natives, suffered occupational discrimination either in hiring or in obtaining jobs with prospects for advancement. As a result, the Irish consistently suffered the disdain that society reserves for its poor and marginal members. But the hostility to the Irish outstripped even the heavy burden that always befalls the disadvantaged because this attitude was, in large measure, also a response to their violent resistance to denigration and to their pugnacious, successful efforts to gain political influence.

In the decade after the Civil War, the old equation of the Irish and public violence was repeatedly reinforced in the popular mind. New York's Catholic Irish clashed with the police during the commemoration of St. Patrick's Day in 1867, and they battled Ulster Protestants in both 1870 and 1871 during parades celebrating William of Orange's victory at the Battle of the Boyne (1690). In 1866 and 1870 the Fenian Brotherhood, an organization of Irishmen and Irish-Americans committed to the liberation of Ireland by force, launched attacks from New York State and Vermont into Canada, the closest English target. These escapades made it clear that bellicose Irishmen would try to involve their adopted homeland in the grand struggle against England, but both sorties were pathetically futile. In the late 1860s and early 1870s the activities of the Molly Maguires in northeastern Pennsylvania were of much more serious import in sustaining the image of Irish violence. The Mollies killed mine foremen, destroyed property, and performed other wanton acts in the anthracite coal fields until the testimony of a Pinkerton detective who had infiltrated their ranks sent ten of their number to the gallows and fourteen more to prison in 1875. An offshoot of the Ancient Order of Hibernians, the Molly Maguires was an American adaptation of the secret societies in Ireland that carried on clandestine warfare against landlords and other representatives of English domination. In Pennsylvania, this group also was part of an incipient labor movement that combined the miners' grievances as workers with their resentment as Irishmen oppressed by English, Welsh, and Scottish owners and supervisors. Though the danger was local and short-lived, tales about the Molly Maguires confirmed the worst fears entertained by respectable citizens about the so-called wild Irish.

However much attention it drew in the postwar era, violence was becoming a minor part of the Irish experience in the United States. As large numbers of them achieved citizenship and familiarity with the ways of the nation, the Irish depended increasingly on the political system for advancement and protection. Nevertheless, they did not introduce ethnic politics to the United States: that phenomenon was the product of a society with a broadly enfranchised, heterogeneous population, a frequently strong correlation between national background and economic status, and a prevailing philosophy that played down the idea of permanent class interests. The Dutch and the English had vied against each other in New York in the seventeenth century, and Scotch-Irish and German blocs had existed in Pennsylvania in the eighteenth. The age of mass migration simply reinforced earlier developments. The Democratic party, with its egalitarian outlook and strength among the urban lower classes, appealed to more immigrants, but the Whigs were strong among certain groups. During the Jacksonian era, for example, the Catholic Irish and the Germans of New York favored the Democrats, while the Protestant Irish, the English, the Scots, and the Welsh supported the Whigs. The novelty of Irish and Irish-American politics lay in its success in taking over critically situated American cities and in openly using the powers of elective government as a vehicle for ethnic assimilation.

After several decades of service as the foot soldiers of the Democratic party, the Irish were filling places of leadership in it by the 1870s. In New York City, "Honest John" Kelly, a former congressman and the brother-in-law of John Cardinal McCloskey, became the first Irish Catholic chief of Tammany Hall after the fall of the notorious William Marcy "Boss" Tweed, an Anglo-American Protestant. In 1880, William R. Grace, the founder of the famous shipping line, won election as the first Irish Catholic mayor of the city. Two years later in Boston, Hugh O'Brien duplicated Grace's feat. Elective successes also came in smaller cities with immigrant districts. The Irish had turned the social liability of their cramped urban existence into a political advantage;

they had appropriated the democratic institutions of the society to seize the recognition the nation had been unwilling to give. Irish politicians won the allegiance of the masses not only by capitalizing on ethnic identity but also by shrewdly employing the party apparatus to fill a void in urban America's ability to deliver social services. In a nonbureaucratic manner that placed a premium on personal loyalty and left much room for corruption, the party served its constituents by facilitating naturalization, finding jobs, offering relief in times of distress, and acting as an intermediary with higher authorities. Through the machine's control of patronage, foreign-stock Americans, and especially the Irish, gained a toehold in public service employment. By 1886 one-third of the police force of Chicago, a middle western city with eastern characteristics, was foreign born, and the remaining two-thirds contained many second-generation Americans. Of course, the Irish predominated.

Whether mayors or lesser officials, the Irishmen elected in the post–Civil War era were usually from economic and occupational backgrounds similar to those of their native-stock predecessors. Likewise, they were willing to make the concessions necessary to conciliate the business interests of their communities. Nevertheless, Irish political victories disconcerted many citizens. The emergence of party machines that openly fostered group reaction rather than individual reflection in the making of political decisions offended middle-class Protestant sensibilities, as did the clear exchange by the lower classes of ballots for benefits. Worse, from the natives' point of view, the effectiveness of the new politics threatened to put control of urban America in alien hands at the very time that the cities were becoming the center of life in the United States. In order to push back this incursion on their control, native-stock leaders changed the rules of the political game. After a group of first- and second-generation Irish small businessmen and skilled workers won control of the board of aldermen in Jersey City, the New Jersey legislature in 1871 devised a new municipal charter to strip the board of real power. The altered frame of government not only gerrymandered aldermanic districts to minimize Irish influence but also vested responsibility for the critical areas of fire, police, and public works in commissions appointed by the legislature. Similar manipulation took place in the much larger states of New York and Massachusetts. But even with their powers diminished, city governments remained plums that the native stock, gathered behind the banner of governmental reform parties, would continue to try to wrest back from the ethnic machines.

Calling attention to the social and political threat posed by the Irish became an obsession of the higher toned newspapers and periodicals of the late nineteenth century. Reform-minded journalists were largely responsible for perfecting the stereotype of the corrupt, drunken, ignorant, and priest-ridden Irishman. Thomas Nast, immortalized for his attack on the Tweed Ring, savagely caricatured the Irish in his cartoons. He decried their violence, mocked their assocation with the Democratic party, and repeatedly denounced their religion as a danger to the smooth functioning and survival of the public school system. Even more important, Nast's art inculcated in its viewers the message that the Irish constituted a subhuman species. He invariably endowed the Irish in his cartoons with grossly protruding lower jaws and severely sloping foreheads. Then fashionable theories of physiognomy associated orthognathism, in which the axes of the face and skull intersect to form a high facial angle, with intelligence and virtue. By contrast, the acute prognathism of cartoon Irishmen, which resulted in low facial angles, suggested that they were more apes than men. Nast had borrowed the image of the Irish simian from John Tenniel, a contemporary English cartoonist, and other American press artists, like Joseph Keppler of *Puck*, followed his example. The Americans, however, gave their Irishmen somewhat higher facial angles than the English allowed. Although they usually had more sympathy for the blacks than for the Irish, American political caricaturists, for reasons locked in the history of racism, gave the former more simian features than the latter. Such niceties, unfortunately, did little to mitigate the essential lesson of Celtic inferiority.

While Irish men and women were striving for economic security and advancement and Irish politicians were changing government from a foe to a friend, it fell to the Catholic clergy to combat the potentially debilitating effects of continuous attacks on a group whose most distinctive cultural characteristic was its religion. Their strategy lay in creating for the Irish, and any other Catholics, an insulated niche within the society, served by a series of church sponsored institutions that duplicated those of the larger community. Within these alternative structures, all Catholics would be able to prepare themselves to compete for the nation's material goods, to avoid discrimination, to mature and live without danger to their faith, and to demonstrate in time moral and intellectual superiority. The church sponsored colleges, hospitals, newspapers, and orphanages, but parochial elementary schools were the linchpin of the program. The movement for a separate, self-supporting school system gathered momentum as the political impossibility of gaining public funds for church operated education became clear. As early as 1852 the First Plenary Council of Baltimore, a national meeting of archbishops and bishops, directed pastors to erect schools and support their teachers with church revenues. After the Civil War advocates persuaded the Sacred Congregation for the Propagation of the Faith, located in Rome, to instruct the American hierarchy in the spiritual dangers of allowing children to attend public schools. Finally, in 1884, the Third Plenary Council of Baltimore ordered each parish to erect, within two years, an elementary school for the children of its communicants. The council also commanded Catholic parents to enroll their sons and daughters in these schools unless they could provide religious instruction at home or at other facilities.

The Irish leadership of the church was not entirely united in the drive to isolate Catholics from the mainstream of American society. A handful of clerics, led by John Ireland, offered stiff opposition to this strategy. As archbishop of St. Paul, Minnesota, Ireland appreciated the difficulties of maintaining a separate educational establishment in areas with few Catholics; he believed that all public schools should offer religious instruction appropriate to the sectarian backgrounds of their student bodies. The archbishop grievously offended conservatives by lavishly praising the ideal of the public school in a speech before the National Education Association convention in 1890 and by expressly conceding to the state a coordinate role with parents and the church in the training of youths. Ireland thought that the answer to Catholic concerns lay in negotiations with the secular authorities. In 1891 he permitted the pastor at Faribault in his own diocese to rent the parish school building to the local board of education. The board, in return, certified and paid the Catholic staff to teach regular academic subjects during the normal hours for school instruction. In addition, the teachers were allowed to offer religious training before and after the school day. Ireland's ideas resembled the proposals of John Hughes a half century earlier and, like them, were fought by uncompromising Protestants, who forced the termination of the Faribault arrangement. But the midwesterner was also accused by Catholic critics of having yielded too much to the Protestant majority. Inasmuch as the leading objectors, Archbishop Michael J. Corrigan of New York City and Bishop Bernard McQuaid of Rochester, New York, had allowed arrangements similar to the Faribault experiment in Poughkeepsie and other communities under their jurisdictions, the real source of their dismay must have been Ireland's integrationist attitude, rather than his policies.

Ireland's outlook was both pragmatic and idealistic. As the archbishop of St. Paul, he presided over a diocese in which Catholics, especially Irish ones, were a small minority. At the heart of his diocese, in Minneapolis and St. Paul, persons of Irish stock accounted for only 10 percent of the population, while Germans and Scandinavians, respectively, constituted 17 percent and 23 percent of the population. Ireland's situation recalled that of the Anglo-Catholic prelates of the early nineteenth century, who had had to keep the church out of uneven conflicts with the overwhelming Protestant majorities in their districts. At the same time, as will be seen, Ireland's position enabled him to maximize the Irish Catholics' leverage by uniting them with the Anglo-American population against non-English-speaking foreigners, including their co-religionists who happened to be German. Such political considerations, however, touched only part of his motivation. Brought to the United States as a small boy by his Irish-born parents and educated by liberals in France, Ireland was sincerely optimistic about the future of both his ethnic group and his religion in America. The archbishop was impressed by the success of those Irish who had managed to establish themselves in the rural expanses of the Middle West. With a naive underestimation of the difficulties of moving and an exaggerated sense of the potential of the central states, Ireland repeatedly but fruitlessly called on his people to abandon the slums of the East. Moreover, unlike many conservative clergymen, Ireland and his supporters, including James Cardinal Gibbons of Baltimore and Bishop John J. Keane of the Catholic University, saw no inherent conflict between Catholicism and the central ideas of nineteenth-century liberalism as they were embodied in American democracy.

The battle over the parochial schools was the symbol of a greater division within the ranks of the Irish over the appropriate limits of assimilation into American society. The constant battering by hostile nativist forces and the hardships of life in the ghettoes had hardened in many the perception of themselves as outsiders and heightened their desire for protected isolation. Others, particularly those in happier circumstances, maintained greater hopes. For Ireland and his allies their position on the school question was only one part of their struggle to create an Americanized Catholicism that might eventually win the United States to the church. In 1890 the balance of power between the conservatives and the liberals was not yet clear, and a statement in 1892 by Pope Leo XIII, whose Latin text said that he would "tolerate" or "allow" the Faribault approach, was open to a variety of interpretations. By the end of the century, however, after the debate had extended beyond the Irish community to matters deeply affecting the German component of the American church, the victory would be determined.

Compared with the Irish, persons of German stock faced a favorable situation in the late nineteenth century. Their concentration in the Middle West shielded them from some of the criticism that would have inevitably arisen had they congregated in the opinion-shaping centers of the crowded East. Instead, their small numbers along the Atlantic coast allowed them to be seen as a pleasant contrast to the Irish hordes. The Germans' early arrival and continuing movement to the north central states also enabled them to play an important part in the formation and cultural development of communities there. The Germans constituted at least 60 percent of the foreign-stock residents of Baltimore, St. Louis,

Cincinnati, and Milwaukee, four of the sixteen American cities with populations exceeding 200,000. The last three were the vertices of the so-called German triangle of the West. In those cities, Germans accounted for 60 percent, 70 percent, and 69 percent, respectively, of the first-and second-generation Americans, who, in turn, made up 67 percent, 69 percent, and 86 percent of the total populations. By contrast, among the top sixteen cities, Boston was the only one in which the Irish represented more than half the foreign-stock population. Likewise, the Germans tended to cluster in the nation's smallest communities: 52 percent of those born in Europe lived in settlements with fewer than 25,000 people. Again by contrast, only 44 percent of the Irish could be found in units of such size. Inasmuch as the Germans, according to the 1890 census, were employed more in agriculture and less in factory work than were the Irish, it seems likely that they were concentrated to a greater extent in the countryside and the very small towns of the nation. Often, they dominated those communities. In Dodge, Jefferson, and Outagamie counties in rural Wisconsin, for example, Germans constituted 82 percent of the foreign born in 1895, and Teutonic blood probably flowed in the veins of many of the native-born majority.

Geographic concentration and isolation were only two of the Germans' advantages. The general prosperity and broad distribution of the Germans among the nation's economic classes prevented the equation of their coming with the spread of poverty and social disorder. Their single largest area of occupational specialization linked them with a variety of skilled activities, including brewing, several facets of the food processing industry, and the handicraft trades. Similarly, the presence in their ranks of a sizable, though undeterminable, percentage of Protestants, which probably increased as the center of emigration shifted from the southwestern to the northeastern provinces of the homeland, made impossible the automatic association of the adjectives "German" and "Catholic." History had made Germany's Protestants as intolerant as any Anglo-Americans, and they quickly discovered the advantage of aligning with their hosts. That the two foremost anti-Irish and anti-Catholic cartoonists of the era, Thomas Nast and Joseph Keppler, were German Protestants, was a natural product of immigrant infighting.

In the political arena, the Germans had the benefit, since the pre–Civil War decade, of a coterie of articulate activists sympathetic with the sundry reform movements of the era. These men, many of whom were refugees from the abortive Revolutions of 1848, probably spoke more for themselves than for their countrymen; contrary to their wishes, their fellow Germans, at least through the Civil War, voted strongly in support of the antinativist Democratic party. Nevertheless, among both contemporaries and historians, the Forty-eighters and like-minded leaders gave German immigrants a reputation for progressive thinking. The Germans added luster to their image in the Civil War. Lincoln rewarded the political contribution of the Forty-eighters to the Republican party cause by naming three of their number, Carl Schurz, Franz Sigel, and Peter Osterhaus, to the rank of major general. The German people also gave their share of men and blood. New York alone raised ten infantry regiments made up almost exclusively of Germans, and one of these, the Fifty-second, endured so many casualties that only 200 of its 2,800-man complement returned from the field. Moreover, though some German immigrants forcibly resisted conscription, particularly in Wisconsin, their activities were not on a scale to besmirch the reputation of the whole group. Finally, German prestige continued to rise after the war. Germany's unification in 1870, which, in terms of the developing nationalism of the Western world was reminiscent of the Union victory, and that nation's emergence in the next decades as a world power also created respect for German immigrants.

The advantageous aspects of the German position in America, however, can easily be exaggerated. For example, the handicraft skills and economic resources that brought early success also bred occupational conservatism. Many Germans found themselves locked into declining areas of employment as mechanization rendered the individual artisan relatively less efficient and competitive. Sons who learned treasured techniques from their fathers and attempted to follow in paternal footsteps were often no better off than Irish-Americans engaged in unprestigious but fairly well paid factory jobs. By the end of the century, later generations of Germans and Irishmen were moving toward economic parity as they took their places in the industrial work force. The pattern of geographic distribution and the availability of reform oriented politicians also had negative effects. Besides shielding the Germans from severe criticism and making them acceptable to leading natives, these attributes encouraged the delusion that Germans were an equal contributor to American culture rather than a minority group expected to conform to an Anglicized norm. The success of Germany in international affairs reinforced this feeling, especially among later immigrants, who did not share the political disaffection of their predecessors from the fatherland. In a similar manner, the vitality of German and its high standing among the world's languages intensified national pride and obscured the necessity of adopting English as the main tongue. By keeping the culture of the old country while absorbing the political values of the new, German-Americans thought they could be both German and American. They were wrong; they could not, as some wished, think of Germany and the United States as mother and bride, respectively. Finally, the denominational diversity within the German population, which protected it to some extent from attacks based on religious prejudice, promoted disunity within the ethnic group and reduced the influence that its large numbers might otherwise have generated.

The Catholics within the German population were in the most difficult position. Despite fears provoked by Chancellor Otto von Bismarck's *Kulturkampf* against the church in the newly unified German nation, they fully shared their ethnic group's pride and its aspirations for an influential and somewhat distinct position in the United States. German-language parishes had existed to serve newcomers since the early days of large-scale immigration. Most German priests originally expected these foreign-language units to fade away, but with the mounting immigration of the post–Civil War era, the clergy pushed for their expansion. The Germans were also desirous of having a share of the positions in the American church hierarchy and, within areas they dominated, consistently blocked the advancement of priests of other nationalities. To advance their goals and interests, German-Americans became the first Catholics to organize themselves along explicitly national lines. Their major union, the German American Priests' Society, first met in 1887 in Chicago. What the Germans did was not remarkably different from Irish practices, but the Irish, by virtue of their sharing in the English language and culture, were able to advance themselves as Americans rather than as foreigners. The Irish had overwhelmed the real Anglo-American Catholics in numbers, and they had taken over the main parishes, which were established along territorial rather than national lines. The Irish had no need of separate ethnic organizations within the church; they were on the way to making the institution itself Hibernian in an Americanized style. Thus, German Catholic behavior was in part a defensive response to the Irish-Americans' almost fortuitous claim to leadership of the Catholic religion in the United States. But the Germans' stance was more than a reaction to Irish precedence within the church. For many Germans, language and religion were symbiotic; forgetting the former would lead inevitably to loss of the latter. German leaders feared that parents and teachers would not be able to hold the respect and attention of children who spoke English only. In addition, though their theologians were too prudent to force the thesis, many Germans sensed an almost mystical connection between their mother tongue and their mother church.

German Catholic maneuvering during the 1880s, including the annual conventions of the priests' society, Father Peter Abbelen's plea to Rome for greater autonomy for foreign-language parishes, and the advancement to the archbishopric of Milwaukee of a strong nationalist, Frederick Katzer, irritated the Irish and the Anglo-American members of the Roman church hierarchy. A crisis did not occur, however, until the activities of the St. Raphael Society, an emigrant aid agency begun in Germany in 1871 under the inspiration of Peter Paul Cahensly, raised the specter of direct foreign interference in the American church. In December 1890 representatives of several European branches of the society met in Lucerne, Switzerland. There they devised a memorandum that was signed by fifty-one delegates from seven nations and presented by Cahensly to Pope Leo XIII in April 1891. Some of their proposals, such as a call for priests able to deal with new immigrants in their native tongues, were inocuous. Others, including the establishment of parochial schools along national lines, had problematic implications. But one suggestion, the appointment of foreign bishops to serve immigrant populations, was inflammatory and out of touch with reality. A foe of his own government, Cahensly was not promoting German nationalism and probably was most concerned with the spiritual well-being of recent Slavic and Italian arrivals throughout the Western Hemisphere. He and his associates, however, had made the typical error of tying the survival of Catholicism to the preservation of ethnic culture, and they had grossly underestimated America's nationalistic fervor and that nation's demand for unity.

Cahenslyism, as the philosophy of the Lucerne Memorial was quickly and somewhat inaccurately dubbed, became the albatross of German-American Catholics, who either disavowed the St. Raphael program or claimed that it had been misinterpreted. Conservative Irish-American prelates like Corrigan of New York, who had found the Germans natural allies in pursuing the parochial school question and in fighting the efforts of Ireland to accommodate the church to American social mores, abandoned the Germans on the issue of foreign bishops. All English-speaking clergymen recognized that dividing the Catholic church along national lines would emphasize its alien image and dissipate the power that would accrue to a sizable, united Catholic population. Furthermore, both conservative and liberal Irish-American bishops, whatever their differences on the limits of assimilation, assumed that their ethnic group would lead the American church. The liberals rushed forward to cripple the German cause. From his station in Rome, Monsignor Denis O'Connell warned Ireland that the papal court, which was sensitive to the winds of continental politics, might bow to German pressure unless the possibility of an American *Kulturkampf* seemed real. Leo XIII's quick decision to dismiss the Lucerne Memorial as impractical and unnecessary indicates that O'Connell's fears were overblown, but his episcopal superiors back home pursued the attack. Cardinal Gibbons met informally with President Benjamin Harrison and extracted from him an endorsement of the English-speaking position, a denunciation of European interference with the American church, and permission to release the chief executive's comments to the press. The denouement came when Gibbons, the ranking member of the nation's hierarchy, accepted a conciliatory invitation to preside at the installation of Katzer in Milwaukee. Gibbons took the occasion of the ceremony in August 1891 to deliver a stern sermon that proclaimed "we owe allegiance to one country, and that country is America." The message did not resolve the broader liberal-conservative split within the hierarchy, but it stunned the German-American heartland and made clear the ethnic balance of power in the church.

Lutherans, Protestants of other denominations, and Freethinkers among the Germans were in a position better than that of the Catholics. There was, however, a considerable range of experience among the Protestants. The Lutherans, who formed the largest contingent, were divided internally. Some were remarkably like Catholics in their theology and social values. Usually of north German origin and affiliated in the United States with the Wisconsin Synod, they preferred traditional liturgical practices, doubted the value of prohibition and other efforts to enforce morality, and maintained a strong system of parochial schools. When they lived in heavily Protestant communities, the German Lutherans gave Democratic political candidates as much as 90 percent of their votes. But the presence nearby of their longtime Catholic foes, who overwhelmingly supported the Democrats, usually drove even conservative Lutherans into the arms of the suspect Republicans. The remaining Lutherans more closely resembled the main branches of native-stock Protestantism in the Middle West. Generally from south German backgrounds and joined in the United States with the Missouri Synod, they emphasized individual, rather than institutional, religious commitments and stressed the importance of high standards of personal and public morality. Their views meshed well with those of Germans belonging to pietistic sects and both groups supported a variety of movements to enforce moral behavior, including prohibition. In politics, these Lutherans, as well as Germans of other Protestant denominations, strongly gravitated to the Republicans.

From the perspective of later decades, German Protestants seem to have been well integrated into the American mainstream by the end of the nineteenth century. They certainly partook of the dominant religious and social values and were in tune politically with their native-stock neighbors. But the impression of overall assimilation is misleading. Safe from the most vitriolic nativist criticism, free of the need to accommodate other ethnic groups in a major supranational institution like the Catholic church, and often ensconced in small, relatively homogeneous communities, the German Protestants could preserve as much of their heritage as they wanted. Their response to two controversial pieces of educational legislation passed in Illinois and Wisconsin suggests that they were as imbued as the Catholics with pride in German culture. Both Illinois's Edwards Law and Wisconsin's Bennett Act mandated compulsory education and made ineligible for accreditation elementary schools that did not use English as the language of instruction for reading, writing, arithmetic, and American history. Aimed at the minority of parochial schools that used German exclusively, the measure drew support from a number of English-speaking, Americanizing Catholics, like Bennett himself, as well as from persons suspicious of church sponsored education. But the Edwards and Bennett laws generated a strong backlash, as people fearful of the state's usurpation of traditional parental responsibility for education united in resistance with a cross-section of the German population. German Catholics naturally opposed the laws. This time, however, Pietists, nonbelieving Germans who resented the attack on their culture, and Lutherans, whose children accounted for 30,000 of the 70,000 parochial school pupils in Wisconsin, joined the protest. The defection of the Protestants brought complete defeat to the Republican party, which had endorsed the offending laws, in the 1890 elections in Illinois and Wisconsin. The temporary reunification of the Germans soon ended, and the non-Catholic ones were back in the Republican ranks by the middle of the decade. But the pride that underlay the response to the Edwards and Bennett laws lingered, unobstrusively informing the values of many Germans, particularly in their midwestern enclaves. This pride would persist until the tragedy of World War I brought a death blow to the hopes for maintaining German ethnic identity in the United States.

Less can be said of the process by which the two remaining sizable white ethnic groups adjusted to American society. Both the British and the Scandinavians have by and large escaped historical notice. Relative to the Irish and the Germans, the two groups were small, particularly when the diversity within each is recalled. Indeed, the terms "British" and "Scandinavian" are scholarly conveniences stressing the similarities among men and women who considered themselves English, Scottish, Welsh, or Anglo-Canadian, on the one hand, and Norwegian, Swedish, or Danish, on the other. More important, the British and the Scandinavians are barely discernible in American ethnic history because neither posed a serious economic, religious, political, or cultural problem. The British, though many of them were poor, could hardly be classed as riffraff. If anything, the presence of highly skilled workers in mining, textiles, toolmaking, and business was the striking feature of this group's occupational makeup. In religion, like native-stock Americans they tended to belong to the Protestant denominations that emphasized conversion, personal piety, and informality in worship. Most were Baptists, Congregationalists, Methodists, or Presbyterians. In politics they favored the Republican party, as an expression of their anti-Catholic heritage and their sympathy for publicly enforced morality. The Scandinavians were probably less well off than the British, but they were not among the most visibly exploited of America's workers. No group was more involved in agriculture and, like the Anglo-Canadians, the Scandinavians were heavily engaged in lumbering and fishing. In religion most Scandinavians belonged to the pietistic tradition of Lutheranism and in politics they voted Republican. The Edwards-Bennett controversy created some furor among the Scandinavians and temporary defections to the Democrats, but generally they displayed much less conscious nationalism than the Germans did and made only minor efforts in the direction of parochial schooling and language preservation.

If the assimilation of a minority is taken to mean the absence of social pathology and of conflict with the majority, then the British and the Scandinavians quickly achieved this state. If, however, positive evidence of the loss of a separate identity is required, different conclusions are in order. Indeed, in some ways, the British and the Scandinavians represented opposite poles. British immigrants kept alive traditional celebrations, published a handful of ethnic newspapers, and organized a few ethnic societies, but the pressures toward consolidation with the majority were overwhelming. The British were well interspersed geographically with the rest of the American population and lacked the demographic concentration necessary to sustain an ethnic subculture. In any case, they had so much in common genetically and culturally with the Anglo-American base of the society that distinguishing them past the first generation would have proved difficult. The children of parents raised on cricket and rugby made the easy transition to baseball and football. As adults, the British, far more than any other ethnic group, intermarried with native-stock Americans.

Superficially similar to the British experience, the Scandinavian case perhaps had more in common with the patterns of ethnic group separation seen among other nationalities. With 57.9 percent of their numbers concentrated in Minnesota, Illinois, Iowa, and Wisconsin in 1890, the Scandinavians had a strong geographic base in four relatively young states. Within these bastions, they often lived in undisturbed ethnic enclaves, a phenomenon that may help to explain the apparent lack of concern among Scandinavians about parochial education and linguistic preservation. The Scandinavians were the least urban of all foreign-stock groups: in 1900 only 28 percent of them lived in cities with more than 25,000 people. The Scandinavians, in conforming to the American value system, did not have to dissolve their ethnic group connections, and the evidence suggests that the ties remained firm. In Chicago, the city with the largest number of Scandinavian residents, they showed little inclination to move outside their group. By 1880, 91 percent of the city's married Swedes had spouses of the same nationality, and 51 percent of the remainder were wed to either Norwegians or Danes. Indeed, even the 30,000 Scandinavian Mormons who settled in Utah in the last half of the nineteenth century tended to form a subcommunity within the religion to which they had converted, and, in this regard, they sharply differed from the over 40,000 British Mormon immigrants who quickly integrated with their American-born co-religionists.

During the final decades of the nineteenth century, then, four different approaches to assimilation had taken shape among the main white ethnic groups. In two cases, the balance between accommodation and resistance was obviously tilted toward the former, but with interestingly different outcomes. The British experience most resembled the ideal of assimilation espoused in the United States since pre–Civil War days. The Scandinavians, however, both shared in Anglo-American values and retained much group cohesiveness. Scandinavians either could remain without recrimination among themselves or mingle without discrimination among the general population. In the case of the Germans, the balance between accommodation and resistance was less clear. Their large numbers and growing sense of nationalism initially encouraged cultural pride, symbolized by the determination to keep the mother tongue alive in the United States. Although that effort was doomed, as the first generation passed away and emigration from Germany declined, this failure may actually have strengthened the group's position. With the victory of English, Protestant Germans at least became more like the Scandinavians—able to conform to Anglo-American norms without undergoing immediate amalgamation with the other components of the population or losing the nonlinguistic aspect of their culture.

The fourth case of ethnic adjustment, the effort of the Irish to preserve their Catholic religion, was the only instance in which resistance patently limited accommodation. This case also involved the only long-range challenge to the goal of cultural homogenization. By placing themselves at the head of the American branch of a supranational organization, which was to grow rapidly at the end of the century, the Irish were able to maintain their separate identity longer than any other English-speaking immigrants of the era. But both the Irish and the non-Irish faithful had to pay high social costs for this remarkable loyalty in the face of massive and overt hostility. Subsuming their ethnicity in Catholicism was both a response to, and an encouragement of, the already advanced obliteration of the other distinctive and perceptible features of Irish culture. Likewise, Irish efforts to create an Anglicized, unified church in the United States forced other Catholic immigrant groups to undergo a double process of acculturation; the German Catholics were only the first to have to accommodate the Irish-Americans, as well as the Anglo-Americans.

# CHAPTER V

# The New Immigration, 1890–1930

STUDIES OF THE HISTORY of immigration to the United States often sharply divide an old phase preceding 1890 from a new one following that year. When carelessly used, this distinction can encourage the perpetuation of unfavorable stereotypes formed at the dawn of the twentieth century about the immigrants then arriving, and it can obscure important conditions and trends that bridged the first and second waves of American immigration. Nevertheless, like many other truisms, the idea of a new immigration contains, beneath the layers of inaccurate connotations, a core of valuable insight. In many ways both the immigrants who reached the United States at the turn of the century and the nation to which they came were new phenomena. Foreigners came to the United States in unprecedented numbers between 1890 and 1930, and the majority of these latecomers belonged to ethnic and national groups not commonly found in America during the old immigration. A larger proportion of the immigrants was single, young adults than previously; a greater percentage were males; and more of them saw the trip across the ocean as a sojourn rather than a permanent relocation. In an America whose frontier the superintendent of the census declared closed in 1890, the later immigrants became the mainstay of the industrial force concentrated in the cities of the nation's northeastern quadrant. There they helped create the quilt of ethnic neighborhoods that characterized urban America until the middle of the twentieth century.

There, too, they encountered a task of adjustment perhaps even more complicated than that faced by their predecessors.

More than 18.2 million newcomers, many of them belonging to southern and eastern European ethnic groups, entered the United States between 1890 and 1920. Earlier arrivals had been fewer and familiar: only 10 million immigrants came between 1860 and 1890; just 4.7 million landed between 1830 and 1860; and in both periods the bulk of the arrivals were from western European backgrounds similar to those of their hosts or at least well known to them. But concentrating on the amazingly large numbers of people involved in the new immigration and on the southern and eastern Europeans in their midst can create a distorted impression. Establishing a broader perspective is, therefore, a prerequisite to proper evaluation of the distinctiveness and impact of this second phase of modern American immigration history.

Contrary to first impressions, the new immigration was not a phenomenon exclusive to the United States. The dramatic influx that occurred there formed part of a worldwide movement of people in the late decades of the nineteenth century and the early ones of the twentieth. This process brought the earth's younger nations their largest volumes of overseas immigrants. While the United States was taking in 9.4 million persons between 1906 and 1915, Canada accepted roughly 2.6 million and Argentina, over 2.2 million. Brazil admitted some 1 million persons, just slightly fewer than the number accepted from 1891 to 1900. The Australian commonwealth and New Zealand allowed over 900,000 newcomers to enter between 1901 and 1910. Moreover, at various points after 1890, nearly all the earth's other receiving nations achieved their zeniths, relative to the U.S. experience, as magnets for immigrants (Table V-1).

The new immigration did not have, in relative terms, as much of an immediate demographic impact in the United States as that of the old immigration. Likewise, this era generated a lower rate of population growth in the United States than in other receiving nations. The decades between 1890 and 1929 were not especially noteworthy in regard to the ratio between arrivals and the total American population. Indeed, the most important decade in this respect seems to have been the 1850s: the 2.8 million newcomers landing between 1850 and 1859 amounted to 12.1 percent of the overall population of the United States in the former year. The decade between 1900 and 1909 ranks second, with its 8.2 million immigrants constituting 10.8 percent of the 76 million people counted in the 1900 census. But the 1880s, for which the comparable percentage was 10.4, was about as significant a period as the 1900s. Among the remaining decades, the 1840s stands fourth; the 1870s and 1910s are tied for fifth; the 1860s ranks sixth; and the 1890s, seventh. By contrast, the new immigration seems to have had a greater

## Table V-1
### Immigration to Selected Countries Expressed over Five-Year Intervals in Absolute Numbers and as Percentages of the U.S. Totals, 1821–1924

| Five-Year Interval | United States N | Canada N | Canada % | Brazil N | Brazil % | Australia–New Zealand[1] N | Australia–New Zealand[1] % | Argentina N | Argentina % |
|---|---|---|---|---|---|---|---|---|---|
| 1821–25 | 40,503 | | | 1,035 | 2.5 | | | | |
| 1826–30 | 102,936 | | | 6,388 | 6.2 | | | | |
| 1831–35 | 252,494 | 167,214 | 66.2 | — | — | | | | |
| 1836–40 | 346,631 | 82,562 | 23.9 | 2,838 | 0.8 | | | | |
| 1841–45 | 430,335 | 139,704 | 32.5 | 1,870 | 0.4 | | | | |
| 1846–50 | 1,282,915 | 205,886 | 16.0 | 4,925 | 0.4 | | | | |
| 1851–55 | 1,748,424 | 191,405 | 10.9 | 39,078 | 2.2 | 14,029 | 0.8 | | |
| 1856–60 | 849,790 | 86,274 | 10.1 | 82,669 | 9.7 | 36,705 | 4.3 | 20,000 | 2.3 |
| 1861–65 | 801,723 | 102,020 | 12.7 | 50,970 | 6.3 | 142,206 | 17.7 | 46,874 | 5.8 |
| 1866–70 | 1,513,101 | 181,294 | 12.0 | 46,601 | 3.0 | 52,769 | 3.5 | 112,696 | 7.4 |
| 1871–75 | 1,726,796 | 148,596 | 8.6 | 81,314 | 4.7 | 190,556 | 11.0 | 148,694 | 8.6 |
| 1876–80 | 1,085,395 | 71,187 | 6.5 | 137,814 | 12.7 | 174,565 | 16.1 | 112,191 | 10.3 |
| 1881–85 | 2,975,683 | 477,066 | 16.0 | 135,482 | 4.5 | 236,838 | 7.9 | 255,185 | 8.6 |
| 1886–90 | 2,270,930 | 409,111 | 18.0 | 395,424 | 17.4 | 243,785 | 10.7 | 585,937 | 25.8 |
| 1891–95 | 2,123,879 | 182,413 | 8.6 | 666,370 | 31.4 | 234,800 | 11.0 | 236,252 | 11.1 |
| 1896–1900 | 1,563,685 | 138,889 | 8.9 | 477,532 | 30.5 | 258,603 | 16.5 | 412,074 | 26.3 |
| 1901–05 | 3,833,076 | 521,489 | 13.6 | 288,031 | 7.5 | 337,490 | 8.8 | 526,030 | 13.7 |
| 1906–10 | 4,962,310 | 1,242,986 | 25.0 | 402,836 | 8.1 | 577,891 | 11.6 | 1,238,073 | 24.9 |
| 1911–15 | 4,459,831 | 1,334,873 | 29.9 | 611,360 | 13.7 | 240,624 | 5.4 | 1,011,853 | 22.7 |
| 1916–20 | 1,275,980 | 477,953 | 37.4 | 186,384 | 14.6 | 368,264 | 28.9 | 193,086 | 15.1 |
| 1921–24 | 2,344,599 | 422,808 | 18.0 | 304,084 | 13.0 | 381,858 | 16.3 | 582,351 | 24.8 |

Source: Imre Ferenczi, comp., *International Migrations*, vol. I: *Statistics* (New York: National Bureau of Economic Research, 1929), table 13 of the international tables; percentages derived by Thomas J. Archdeacon.

[1] Data for the period 1851–1870 pertain only to New Zealand; for 1871–1900, to Queensland and New Zealand; for 1901–1920, to Australia and New Zealand; for 1921–1924, only to Australia.

demographic impact outside the United States: in Argentina, Canada, and Australia–New Zealand, for example, arrivals landing between 1901 and 1910 totaled 37 percent, 34 percent, and 20 percent, respectively, of the existing populations (Table V–2).

Putting the later immigration to America into focus also requires lowering the estimate of the total size of this influx to take into account the frequency with which the newcomers returned to their overseas homelands. Remigration was probably a rare occurrence before 1890, but thereafter, for reasons that will be discussed later, it became common. The phenomenon of remigration undoubtedly reduced the new immigration's demographic impact and perhaps weakened its cultural influence, too. Unfortunately, a full discussion of the problem is impossible because the American government did not keep continuous records on the departures of aliens. The best data show that 3,574,974 foreigners left the United States between 1908 and 1924; this figure translates into an annual average of 210,293 persons. The yearly mean number of immigrants was 608,135 from 1890 to 1920; the annual mean reached 678,288 between 1899 and 1924, a particularly important period for which good statistical information is available. A comparison of the tallies of average annual emigration and immigration suggests that if the rate of remigration was fairly constant at the turn of the century, at least 30 percent of the people then arriving in the United States stayed only temporarily. The rate of return derived from the 1890–1920 immigration data is 34.6 percent; from the 1899–1924 figures it is 30 percent. The procedure of using the emigration statistics for 1908–1924 in calculations with data drawn from longer periods is undoubtedly

TABLE V–2

Decennial Immigration to the United States as a Percentage of the Census Population at the Beginning of each Decade, 1820–1929

| DECADE | IMMIGRATION | CENSUS | POPULATION | PERCENTAGE |
|--------|-------------|--------|------------|------------|
| 1820–29 | 128,502 | 1820 | 9,618,000 | 1.3 |
| 1830–39 | 538,831 | 1830 | 12,901,000 | 4.2 |
| 1840–49 | 1,427,337 | 1840 | 17,120,000 | 8.3 |
| 1850–59 | 2,814,554 | 1850 | 23,261,000 | 12.1 |
| 1860–69 | 2,081,261 | 1860 | 31,513,000 | 6.6 |
| 1870–79 | 2,742,137 | 1870 | 39,905,000 | 6.9 |
| 1880–89 | 5,248,568 | 1880 | 50,262,000 | 10.4 |
| 1890–99 | 3,694,294 | 1890 | 63,056,000 | 5.8 |
| 1900–09 | 8,202,388 | 1900 | 76,094,000 | 10.8 |
| 1910–19 | 6,347,380 | 1910 | 92,407,000 | 6.9 |
| 1920–29 | 4,295,510 | 1920 | 106,461,000 | 4.0 |

SOURCE: Derived by Thomas J. Archdeacon from data in U.S. Bureau of the Census, *Historical Statistics of the United States: Colonial Times to 1970* (Washington, D.C.: Government Printing Office, 1975), series A7, C89–119.

risky and rough, but the estimate of remigration generated is consistent with recent findings by students of several key European immigrant groups. The projected rate of remigration appears even conservative when compared with the most complete information available for another nation; Argentinian statistics show that between 1899 and 1924 emigration amounted to 49 percent of immigration. If the projection of remigration from the United States is accurate, then the total number of permanent immigrants coming to America between 1890 and 1920 should be set no higher than 12.5 million.

The final step in placing the new immigration in context involves a modest reassessment of its ethnic composition. Contemporaries were naturally impressed by the prevalence of unfamiliar national groups among the later arrivals, and their observations have led historians to underestimate the ethnic diversity within the new immigration. Scholars have subsumed a variety of peoples under the broad category of southern and eastern European and have slighted the continuing contributions of countries from the northern and western sectors of the continent to the growth of the American population. Of all the leading recipients of transoceanic immigrants, the United States took in the widest and most evenly balanced assortment of ethnic groups. The other major immigrant nations obtained the bulk of their newcomers from less than a handful of sources, and in each case the key contributors had close cultural links with the host society. Between 1901 and 1924 Brazil gathered 77 percent of its immigrants from Portugal, Italy, and Spain; Argentina gained 80 percent from Spain and Italy; Canada got 74 percent from the British Isles and the United States; and Australia took 71 percent from the British Isles. According to the projections of permanent immigration made in this chapter, the United States required additions from at least eight national or ethnic groups to account for 75 percent of the arrivals from 1899 to 1924. The importance of southern and eastern Europe in the American traffic was obvious; the Italians and the Jews contributed about 17 percent and 14 percent, respectively, of the immigrants to the United States. The Germans, however, ranked third and their fellows among the old immigration—the Scandinavians, the British, the Irish, and the Anglo-Canadians—followed in order after the Poles. No other group provided more than 5 percent, although non-Polish Slavic peoples combined to contribute 9 percent (Table V-3).

Even in this modified perspective, the new immigration remains a major chapter in American history. The roots of this massive increase in international human traffic were interacting push and pull forces reminiscent of, but more widespread than, those that underlay the earlier burst of population relocation in the middle of the nineteenth century. On the pull side, the United States was in a period of industrial development, which was a powerful magnet for the unskilled laborers of the world. In addition, the other recipient nations of the world were in phases of frontier settlement and agricultural expansion that called for smaller increments to their work forces, and they were willing to recruit immigrants by incentives judged either unnecessary or undesirable by Washington. In the hope of enticing independent and tenant farmers and agricultural laborers to its western provinces, Canada continued to advertise for settlers in western Europe and the United States and to pay bonuses to agents abroad who arranged the migration of their countrymen to the dominion. The various colonies that made up Australia frequently paid part or all of the transportation costs of immigrants in needed occupations, and they established liberal criteria for financing the purchase of unoccupied lands. Likewise, Brazil and Argentina sought immigrants for their underpopulated and underdeveloped countrysides by offering a host of incentives, including free transportation across the ocean to points of settlement, exemption from military service, and some grants of land and equipment.

The main explanation for the large volume of the later influx of newcomers to the United States and the other recipient nations was, however, the extension of emigration fever beyond northern and western Europe. In the final decades of the nineteenth century and the first quarter of the twentieth, the countries of Asia and of southern and eastern Europe experienced the population explosions and dislocations that western Europe had earlier undergone. For the first time these countries surrendered hundreds of thousands of their subjects to the United States, and recent technological improvements made the number even greater than it might have been under earlier conditions. By the late nineteenth century, railroads made German ports accessible to the towns of central and eastern Europe, and steamships had penetrated to ports deep in the Mediterranean basin. Transoceanic vessels were more numerous, and the newer ones were bigger, faster, and safer than their predecessors had been. With the turn of the twentieth century, turbine-powered ships boasting four funnels and propellers and cruising at speeds of twenty-five knots entered service. Even ordinary vessels surpassed 15,000 tons. Greater speed meant that each ship could make more crossings annually, and increased size meant that on each westbound trip as many as 2,000 or 3,000 souls could be crammed into the steerage sections, where most immigrants rode out their voyages to America. The conditions of travel were also improving. The fortunate poor benefited from the introduction of third-class accommodations by the better lines. Even the hordes in steerage fared better as the time required for a transatlantic crossing from Europe's northwestern ports dropped below twelve days and as the oceanic mortality rate fell almost to zero.

At the end of the nineteenth century, the pressures of overpopula-

Table V-3

Statistical Overview of the New Immigration, 1899–1924

| Ethnic Group | Immigration | Emigration[1] | Projected Emigration Rate[2] (%) | Projected Permanent Immigration[3] | Cumulative Proportion of Permanent Immigration (%) |
|---|---|---|---|---|---|
| Italian | 3,820,986 | 1,137,100 | 45.6 | 2,078,616 | 16.9 |
| Hebrew | 1,837,855 | 52,048 | 4.3 | 1,758,827 | 31.2 |
| German | 1,316,614 | 117,961 | 13.7 | 1,136,238 | 40.4 |
| Polish | 1,483,374 | 320,429 | 33.0 | 933,860 | 48.0 |
| Scandinavian | 956,308 | 96,431 | 15.4 | 809,036 | 54.6 |
| British | 983,982 | 130,054 | 20.2 | 785,217 | 61.0 |
| Irish | 808,762 | 47,311 | 8.9 | 736,782 | 67.0 |
| Anglo-Canadian | 567,941 | 66,249 | 17.8 | 466,847 | 70.8 |
| Slovak | 536,911 | 128,032 | 36.5 | 340,938 | 73.6 |
| Mexican | 447,065 | 70,591 | 24.1 | 339,322 | 76.3 |
| Croatian/Slovenian | 485,379 | 115,114 | 36.3 | 309,186 | 78.8 |
| Magyar | 492,031 | 149,508 | 46.5 | 263,236 | 80.9 |
| French-Canadian | 257,219 | 14,014 | 8.3 | 235,870 | 82.8 |
| Greek | 500,463 | 175,830 | 53.7 | 231,714 | 84.6 |
| Ruthenian | 265,478 | 29,032 | 16.7 | 221,143 | 86.3 |
| Lithuanian | 263,277 | 34,986 | 20.3 | 209,832 | 88.0 |
| Japanese | 260,492 | 44,392 | 26.1 | 192,503 | 89.5 |
| Finnish | 226,922 | 30,931 | 22.0 | 176,999 | 90.9 |
| Dutch/Flemish | 205,910 | 25,720 | 19.1 | 166,518 | 92.2 |
| Bohemian/Moravian | 159,319 | 16,191 | 15.5 | 134,625 | 93.3 |

| Group | | | | | |
|---|---|---|---|---|---|
| Portuguese | 186,244 | 42,991 | 35.3 | 120,500 | 94.3 |
| African | 135,029 | 23,850 | 27.0 | 98,564 | 95.1 |
| Spanish | 190,521 | 64,720 | 51.9 | 91,641 | 95.8 |
| Russian | 258,985 | 110,003 | 65.0 | 90,645 | 96.5 |
| French | 158,025 | 49,829 | 48.2 | 81,857 | 97.1 |
| Syrian | 97,716 | 14,752 | 23.1 | 75,143 | 97.7 |
| Armenian | 76,129 | 8,995 | 18.1 | 62,350 | 98.2 |
| Rumanian | 148,251 | 64,106 | 66.1 | 50,257 | 98.6 |
| Cuban | 77,028 | 24,998 | 49.6 | 38,822 | 98.9 |
| Dalmatian/ Bosnian/ Herzegovinian[4] | 52,130 | 8,987 | 26.3 | 38,420 | 99.2 |
| Bulgarian/ Serbian/ Montenegrin | 165,091 | 94,330 | 87.4 | 20,801 | 99.4 |
| West Indian | 29,257 | 9,056 | 47.3 | 15,418 | 99.5 |
| Korean | 9,214 | 1,022 | 16.9 | 7,657 | 99.6 |
| East Indian | 8,234 | 2,268 | 41.9 | 4,784 | — |
| Turkish | 22,021 | 11,600 | 80.5 | 4,295 | — |
| Pacific Islander | 491 | 59 | 15.8 | 413 | — |
| Chinese | 59,079 | 51,343 | 132.9 | −19,437 | — |

SOURCE: Derived by Thomas J. Archdeacon from data in Imre Ferenczi, comp., *International Migrations*, vol. I: *Statistics* (New York: National Bureau of Economic Research, 1929), tables 13 and 19 in the section on the United States.

[1] Data on emigration pertain to 1908–1924 only.

[2] This figure represents the average annual emigration (1908–1924) divided by the average annual immigration (1899–1924).

[3] This figure represents 1.00 minus the projected emigration rate, with the difference multiplied by the immigration total for 1899–1924.

[4] These groups are geographical, rather than ethnic. Croats and other south Slavs lived in the region.

119

tion, the prospects of economic mobility, and the availability of rapid transportation set persons all over the world on the road. From Asia, the Chinese and the Japanese led the way to the United States; Italians, Jews, and Slavs set the pace from Europe. But the same forces were also at work within the Western Hemisphere: Mexico's population began to filter north across the U.S. border, and Canada's peoples headed south more frequently. Indeed, an intranational manifestation of this global pattern of migration occurred within the boundaries of the United States as large numbers of blacks moved from the southern to the northern states.

Most Chinese immigration to the United States occurred well before 1890, but the features of this influx so resembled those of the new immigration that it deserves to be considered at least a precursor of the movement. The causes that propelled the Chinese across the Pacific to the West Coast of the United States paralleled those that drove various peoples across the Atlantic to America's eastern shores. Like the nations of Europe, China experienced a demographic boom between 1750 and 1850: the population doubled, from 215 to 430 million. The resulting pressure on the limited available arable land probably helps explain China's extensive domestic turmoil, which reached a crescendo with the outbreak of the Taiping Rebellion in 1851. Led by Hung Hsiu-ch'uan, who considered himself literally the brother of Jesus Christ, the Taiping rebels were peasants in search of a new social order based on a zealous pseudo-Christian religion and a communal economy. The uprising, which finally went down to defeat in 1864, aggravated the problems caused by contemporary Anglo-French diplomatic maneuvers and military actions designed to keep China open to Western commercial penetration. Together, the internal unrest and the external attack enervated the inefficient Chi'ing government and unbearably disrupted the daily lives of the populace. In these circumstances, many Chinese, especially those residing near the Pearl River Delta and the southern port of Canton, chose to abandon their homeland. Past emigrations had taken Chinese men and women to Indochina, the Malay Peninsula, and the Philippines; the new outpouring would take them also to Australia, the West Indies, and the recently opened Golden Hills of California.

American records indicate that Chinese immigration was negligible before 1854. In that year 13,100 arrived and an average of 4,567 persons entered the country annually through 1868. A total of 28,614 Chinese reached America in 1869 and 1870 and then, after falling off to 15,923 in the next two years, the influx reached its peak. Between 1873 and 1877, 69,090 Chinese landed in the United States. Soon, however, the prospects for Chinese newcomers deteriorated badly. As nonwhites, the Chinese had been in a tenuous position in California since the beginning, and a combination of conditions in the mid-1870s, including the onset of a serious depression, aggravated their situation. As will be seen, by the early 1880s the white majority, in the hope of improving its competitive advantage in the labor market, had obtained federal legislation that virtually cut off the flow of the Chinese to America.

The exclusion of the Chinese ended the first phase of Asian immigration to the American West Coast; the coming of the Japanese opened the second. Emigration from Japan began after Commodore Matthew C. Perry of the United States Navy forced the imperial government in 1854 to open the country to contact with the outside world. The growth of Western influence contributed to a period of economic expansion. Coincidentally, the Japanese population, which had been held in check for some 125 years by late marriage and infanticide, rose quickly, from a mere 32 million in 1850 to 45 million by 1900. The resulting pressure of population against agricultural resources had its familiar consequence, as young Japanese took advantage of their government's gradual relaxation of the traditional prohibition against emigration. Initially most of the departees went to China, Korea, or Asiatic Russia, but some headed across the Pacific to points as far away as Peru and Brazil. After the Meiji authorities agreed in 1884 to permit agricultural workers to serve as contract laborers in Hawaii's sugar fields, the islands became a favorite destination of the outward bound. The Japanese came to form an important proportion of the Hawaiian population, but the American mainland eventually attracted the largest numbers of them.

Annual Japanese immigration to the United States first exceeded 1,000 in 1891; the movement achieved its greatest intensity between 1900 and 1908. American records show that 136,601 landed by sea in those years, and others came in across the Canadian and Mexican borders. The immigrants to the United States tended to come from the more prosperous points of emigration in Japan and they were often of higher social status than those who went to Hawaii; 39.3 percent of those arriving on the mainland between 1886 and 1908 were farmers, fishermen, laborers, or artisans; 21.5 percent were merchants; and 21.1 percent were students. The large majority of Japanese, however, began their American careers as farm laborers, railroad workers, or servants. Japanese immigration continued after 1908, with a total of 118,872 newcomers arriving before 1925, but, as will be seen, these people represented the tail end of a movement effectively curbed by racial bias and governmental pressure.

The vast majority of the new immigrants did not come from Asia but from Europe; among the nations of the latter continent, Italy surrendered by far the greatest number. The story of Italy in the late nineteenth century is one of hope spawned by the creation of a politically unified nation counterbalanced by despair rooted in continuing economic and social malaise. Life there was not easy under the best of

circumstances. Mountains and hills covered 75 percent of the land-
scape; there were only 19 million acres of plains. Rain was terribly
scarce in the hard-pressed south, and what came fell in the autumn and
winter on impermeable soils. The extensive deforestation of the land
during the nineteenth century aggravated the problem of soil erosion
and contributed to drainage difficulties, which made malaria a plague.
The disease struck a double blow at the rural population, both weakening the peasants physically and forcing them to live in the hills, away
from their fertile but unhealthy low-lying fields.

Italy's social arrangements matched the meanness of that country's
geophysical conditions. The economy displayed some regional variation, and industrialization had begun in the north, but nine out of ten
Italian men were agricultural workers. Not more than 10 percent of
them owned even five acres of land; the remainder, in more or less equal
proportions, either rented land or served as day laborers. Agriculture
was most advanced in the central provinces of Emilia-Romagna, the
Marches, Tuscany, and Umbria and in the southern province of
Apulia; in these districts landownership was concentrated in a few
hands, capital investments were high, and management was efficient.
In the interior of Sicily, landowners leased their estates through *gabbeloti,*
or middlemen, who often violently exploited the sharecroppers and
short-term tenants under them. The peasantry was just as illiterate and
starved in the southern provinces of Abruzzi and Molise, Basilicata, and
Calabria and in most of Sicily's coastal region, but there the land was
divided into such small holdings that almost nobody prospered.

Italy was ripe for a wave of emigration at the end of the nineteenth
century, and a series of crises—including high taxation, the ravages of
the olive fly, and the spread of phylloxera in the vineyards—intensified
the exodus. The southern provinces accounted for approximately 80
percent of the population loss, with Sicily contributing almost 30 percent of it and the region around Naples yielding over 27 percent. The
emigration rates, however, reflected only imperfectly the areas of
greatest economic distress; the exodus was greatest from those impoverished areas in which the nuclear family was the sole unit of social
cohesion and other unifying forces, such as hierarchic employment
systems and trade unions, were absent. Initially, the majority of the
emigrants headed for Argentina and Brazil, but by the last decade of the
century a small plurality was going to the United States. The highpoint
of Italian immigration to the American republic came between 1900 and
1914, when some 3 million arrivals accounted for just less than two-
thirds of the total transoceanic exodus from Italy. After that, except for a
sudden influx of 317,405 persons in 1920 and 1921, the volume of
Italian immigration to the United States tumbled, as World War I and
new American restrictions on admission disrupted the traffic.

Jews from central and eastern Europe ranked second in number to the Italians among the new immigrants. Their coming marked an important, early step in the disintegration of the ancient arrangements that had established the Jews as the links connecting the various components of Europe's premodern social structure. The presence of the Jews in central and eastern Europe dated from the thirteenth century, when King Boleslav the Pious of Poland invited them to settle in his realm. The monarch was aware of the reputation as skillful economic middlemen that these distrusted infidels had developed after having been legally blocked from participating in most of the basic agricultural and mechanical occupations pursued in Christian Europe. As Boleslav had hoped, the Jews fostered Poland's commercial growth. The nation prospered until the middle of the seventeenth century, when it entered a long period of decline. Finally, in 1772, 1793, and 1795, Poland suffered a three-stage dismemberment of its territories at the hands of Russia, Austria-Hungary, and Prussia. The consequences were not happy, especially for the three-quarters of the Jewish population that fell under the jurisdiction of the czars.

Throughout the nineteenth century, Russian policy toward the Jews revolved around a persistent effort to isolate and subjugate them. Russia restricted Jewish settlement to a congested area of 386,000 square miles that stretched along the nation's western border between the Baltic and the Black seas and included Congress Poland, Lithuania, Byelorussia, and most of the Ukraine. The almost 4.9 million Jews living within this so-called Pale of Settlement constituted 97 percent of Russia's Hebrew population; only top-ranking merchants and master craftsmen were allowed to dwell elsewhere. Within the Pale the Jews experienced additional physical and social isolation. Most of them were barred from the countryside and required to reside in cities or towns. As a result, although the Jews formed only 4 percent of the population in all of Russia, they accounted for 12 percent of the inhabitants of the Pale and for 40 percent of the urbanites there. The Jews also formed an almost separate occupational caste. Compared with their Christian neighbors, they had more people involved in commerce and industry, fewer in personal service, and virtually none in agriculture.

With the Jews quarantined, the czars were able to experiment with a variety of ploys to destroy the cohesion of their community. Nicholas I, who ruled from 1825 to 1855, instituted more than 600 anti-Jewish laws, censored Hebrew and Yiddish books, interfered with Jewish schooling, and tore some young Jewish boys away from their families for twenty-five years' service in the army. His successor, the benevolent Alexander II, chose the more liberal and more insidiously effective route of encouraging the spread of Western culture among the Jews; by the end of his reign, Jews accounted for 9 percent of Russia's university students.

Repressive tactics returned to favor after Alexander's assassination in 1881. Under Alexander III and his heir, Nicholas II, who came to power in 1894, the Jews fell under quota laws that restricted their attendance at schools; they suffered expulsion from Moscow, St. Petersburg, and Kiev; and they found their access to traditional employments as innkeepers and restauranteurs impeded. Jews also became the victims of frequent *pogroms,* or organized massacres.

Persecution was only part of the nineteenth-century trauma of European Jewry. Their isolation did not immunize them against broader social and economic changes that ultimately proved as disruptive as anti-Semitism to their world. Like so many other peoples, the Jews experienced rapid demographic growth. Judaism encouraged early and fruitful marriages, and a culturally succored low death rate pushed the pace of population increase even past that of the Jews' equally fecund neighbors across eastern Europe. The commercial sector of the economy could not absorb these rising numbers, and after the emancipation of the serfs in 1863 let loose potential competitors for the role of Russia's middlemen, the pressure on the Jews to find alternative occupational outlets intensified. Necessity uprooted many Jews from their homes in ghetto villages, or *shtetls,* and deposited them in large cities like Warsaw and Vilna, where they could find industrial employment, especially as handicraft workers in garment production. The change inevitably undermined the traditional centers of Jewish authority, including the rabbinate, and left the deracinated masses open to fresh cultural and intellectual currents. Western learning penetrated the consciousness of youngsters whose education had previously revolved around the Talmud; the *Haskala,* or enlightenment, which called for a modernization of Jewish life, spread more rapidly; ideologies like socialism, which made an appeal based theoretically on economic rather than ethnic realities, gained a hearing; and thoughts of escape, including the Zionist dream of a Jewish state, became plausible.

In the last decades of the nineteenth century and the first ones of the twentieth, central and eastern Europe lost more than one-third of its Jewish population. Identifying those emigrants is a difficult task. Over 90 percent of them came to the United States, but the American government listed them only by their country of origin until 1899, when it assigned the designation "Hebrew" to Jewish newcomers. The best estimate is that some 2.4 million Jews landed in the United States between 1881 and 1924. More than 100,000 arrived annually in the years of the heaviest immigration, 1904–1908, when a total of 642,463 Jews entered. In the period 1899–1924, which offers the best comparable data, the roughly 1.8 million Jewish newcomers to America constituted 10.5 percent of the total foreign influx.

Approximately three out of every four Jewish immigrants to the

United States came from Russian territory. Initially, a disproportionately large number came from Lithuania and Byelorussia in the
northwest sector of the Pale. The levels of industrialization, religious rationalism, and gentile learning were highest in these districts. But the
rate of emigration seems to have quickened in the south after the outbreak of *pogroms* there in the first years of the new century. About 19 percent of the Jewish immigrants to America came from the Austro-
Hungarian empire, and another 4 percent left Rumania. The rate of
Jewish emigration from Austria-Hungary, where Jews enjoyed civil
rights and experienced relatively mild treatment, was approximately 60
percent as high as the pace of their flight from the harsh regimes of
Russia and Rumania. The statistics suggest that although persecution
surely swelled the total number of departures from central and eastern
Europe, there would have been a sizable demographically and
economically sparked exodus in any case.

The general themes of ethnic conflict and economic woe that give
form to the saga of Jewish migration reappear in the story of the departure of their Slavic neighbors from central and eastern Europe at the
turn of the twentieth century. But the particulars of the tale of the Slavic
movement are unique and fascinatingly complex. Viewed as a unit, the
Slavs formed the second largest element in the new immigration: 3.4
million of them entered the United States between 1899 and 1924. The
concept of a single Slavic people, however, is misleading. Melding the
several Slavic nationalities into an entity makes less sense than classifying Norwegians, Swedes, and Danes as Scandinavians or grouping
English, Scots, and Welsh as British. The Slavs share a common
linguistic heritage, and some visionaries have dreamt of pan-Slavic
unity, but geography, history, and politics have divided this people into
three separate cultural branches.

The eastern Slavs, centered in what is today the Soviet Union, constituted the largest Slavic bloc at the time of the great migration. Their
ranks included the Russians, the Byelorussians, the Ruthenians, and
the Ukrainians, peoples who used the Cyrillic alphabet and were affiliated with the Eastern Orthodox church or the Eastern Rite of the
Roman Catholic. The western Slavs included the Poles, the Bohemians
(or Czechs), the Slovaks, and the Sorbs of eastern Germany. Nine out of
ten Poles and four out of five Bohemians and Slovaks were Roman
Catholic, and none of these peoples had an independent homeland
before World War I. Poland, as has been noted, was divided among
Prussia, Russia, and Austria-Hungary, and the future territory of
Czechoslovakia lay entirely within Austro-Hungarian jurisdiction. The
southern Slavs included Slovenians, Croatians, Serbs, Montenegrins,
Bulgarians, and Macedonians. The Slovenians, who lived uneasily
under Austro-Hungarian control, were predominantly Roman Cath-

olic, but among the Croatians, Moslems formed the largest element of the non-Catholic quarter of the population. The situation in Bosnia-Herzogovina, which was tied to the Austrian provinces of Dalmatia and Croatia, was even more complicated: there, 40 percent of the inhabitants were Orthodox Serbians; 40 percent, Moslems; and 20 percent, Catholic Croatians. The residents of Serbia, Montenegro, Bulgaria, and Macedonia followed the Orthodox religion; the first three of these Balkan states had gained independence from Turkey during the last quarter of the nineteenth century and they wrested Macedonia from their common enemy by 1913. Today, the southern Slavic peoples, except the Bulgarians, are combined, sometimes uneasily, in the single nation of Yugoslavia.

Political conditions were undoubtedly a spur to the increased Slavic emigration of the late nineteenth century. The era of large-scale Polish departures from Prussia coincided with Chancellor Otto von Bismarck's most strenuous efforts to eradicate Polish culture in Germany's domain. During the 1870s and 1880s he demanded the use of the German language in legal, administrative, and educational communications, put parochial schools under state control, instituted a four-year term of compulsory military service for Polish males, and displaced Polish peasants by buying or forcing out their landlords, whom he replaced with independent German farmers. Emigration from Prussian Poland ebbed after the temperate Leo von Caprivi replaced Bismarck in 1890, but the harsh policies of Czars Alexander III and Nicholas II soon helped to push departures from Russian Poland to unprecedented heights. There, too, much of the attack centered on removing the Polish language as an acceptable medium for official business or education. In Austria-Hungary, the Poles received relatively good treatment, but the nationalist aspirations of the south Slavs caused strain within the empire. Likewise, nationalist movements directed against the Turks and the Austro-Hungarians kept the Balkan states in turmoil during the decade and a half of heavy emigration before World War I.

Despite its importance, politics was probably a supplemental, rather than a primary, cause of the Slavic exodus from Europe. The case of the Poles is illustrative. In Germany, the decision made in 1891 to allow Poles to work in the rapidly growing industrial sector of the economy probably did as much as Bismarck's forced retirement to reduce the number of departures among this group. In Russia, at least a half century of occasionally brutal anti-Polish actions had failed to set off a wave of emigration until economic conditions were right for such a movement. Finally, in Austria-Hungary, a large-scale outpouring of Poles existed independent of a political impetus. Political harassment, it seems, added a leavening of patriotic exiles to the mass of emigrants and, more important, weakened the affective ties that might have convinced an undeterminable number of the eventual migrants to stay at home even in the face of economic adversity.

The economic roots of the Slavic emigration lay in the agricultural crisis occurring in central and eastern Europe in the late nineteenth century. The forces at work in Russia and Russian Poland have already been mentioned in the story of the flight of the Jews. In Austria-Hungary, where the exodus of the Slavs accounted for fully two-thirds of the outward bound traffic between 1901 and 1912, the province most affected by Polish emigration was Galicia, on the Russian border. There 81 percent of the agricultural holdings were under the minimum of five hectares needed for successful operation, and the level of industrialization was insufficient to offer adequate alternative employments. Similar conditions existed in Bukovina, the district of heaviest Ruthenian emigration; in Dalmatia and Croatia, the centers of south Slavic departures from the empire; and in the independent Balkan states.

Most of the Slavs who left Europe went to the United States. The American republic absorbed approximately 83 percent of the total emigration between 1876 and 1910; Canada, the next most frequent destination, took in only 8 percent. Determining exactly the ethnic affiliations of the departees is an impossibility, given the demographic and national complexities of the region. But American statistics show that among the eastern Slavs 258,985 Russians and 265,478 Ruthenians and Ukrainians entered the United States between 1899 and 1924. The same sources record the arrival of 702,600 southern Slavs, with Croatians and Slovenians accounting for at least 69 percent of that total. The western Slavs were by far the most numerous: as many as 1,483,374 Poles and 696,230 persons from Bohemia, Moravia, and Slovakia reached the United States between 1899 and 1924.

Although Italians, Jews, and Slavs formed the bulk of the new immigration, other groups also made their major contributions to America's immigration history in the same period. Several of the latter, including the Greeks, the Magyars, and the Finns, have become important and visible elements of the population. Half a million Greeks arrived in the United States between 1899 and 1924. The stimuli to emigration included hardships stemming from the overproduction of currants, which were Greece's main export, high taxation, tight credit, inadequate facilities for crop transportation, and the difficulties of providing young females with dowries. Moreover, the fact that 29 percent of the 287,600 Greeks who came to the United States between 1907 and 1914 left from the Balkan states, Crete, Cyprus, Egypt, and Turkey suggests that the deteriorating political conditions in the region and the desire of young men to avoid military service were also factors in the exodus. Just under 500,000 Magyars, or ethnic Hungarians, joined their Slavic neighbors in leaving Austria-Hungary between 1899 and 1924, and over a 250,000 Christian Lithuanians departed with the Jewish emigrants from the Baltic borderlands of Russia. Finally, almost 300,000 Finns reached America between 1890 and 1920. Approximately 86 percent of them came originally from rural districts, and over 60 percent were natives of the northern provinces of Oulu and Vasa, where no industry existed to absorb the surplus population and where tales of Scandinavian successes in the New World were in wide circulation. For those who needed more than economic motives to uproot, prospects of political harassment by Finland's Russian masters and of mandatory service in the czar's army offered additional incentives.

Part of the new immigration, like part of the old, was hemispheric rather than transoceanic in origin. The years between 1890 and the Great Depression marked the beginning of the large-scale movement of Mexicans north across the American border, a phenomenon that continues to this day. Emigration from Mexico was rooted in the same general demographic and economic causes that were operating around the world, but the story's unique features deserve recounting. Mexico's population grew very rapidly in the last decades of the nineteenth century, from 9.4 million in 1877 to 15.2 million in 1910. The era of increase coincided almost exactly with the tenure in power of Porfirio Díaz, a general who seized the reins of government in 1876 and managed to hold them until rebels toppled his regime in 1911. Díaz pursued a vigorous policy of modernizing Mexico and of opening the country to foreign capital. Under his rule, foreign investments soared, railroads penetrated the countryside, mining emerged from its slumber, and the oil industry was born. But his policies aggravated as much as alleviated the dislocations that naturally followed the population boom. The dictator reversed earlier reforms aimed at giving land to Mexico's peons and encouraged wealthy landholders to accumulate large estates. By the end of Díaz's administration, there were 900 great landlords and 9 million propertyless peasants in Mexico.

Díaz's policies laid all of Mexico's poor open to exploitation. The dictator's advisors, who were known as *científicos,* or scientists, were imbued with the values of European positivist philosophy and accepted the trials of the less fortunate as the inevitable price of progress. The Indians suffered the most grievously of all the elements of the population. Although Díaz was himself a *mestizo,* he and his associates believed that the country's future depended on a massive infusion of European genius, and they awaited, without remorse, the eventual disappearance of the natives and of their culture. The indigenous Mexicans not only endured discrimination but also fell under the effects of the Ley Lerdo of 1856. The measure, which provided for the forced sale of corporately owned land, had been used originally to strip property from the church for the benefit of the poor. The Díaz regime, however, found the law an equally versatile means to alienate the communally held acres of the native tribes for the benefit of the rich and virtually turned the Ley Lerdo into a Mexican version of the Dawes Act, passed by the American Congress in 1887.

On the eve of the twentieth century, Mexico was filled with people ready to move. The unabsorbable children of the population boom and the Indians displaced by Díaz's policies formed only part of the army of potential migrants. The countryside held large numbers of *rancherías* or villages that served as bases for semitribal groups that frequently relocated in search of seasonal work. In addition, many peasant proprietors found attractive the idea of migrating temporarily to earn extra income that would enable them to return and purchase more land. Deciding to go was in some ways easier for Mexico's would-be emigrants than for their European counterparts. Between 1880 and 1910 railroad lines bound together the United States and Mexico. Railways connected California and Sonora, El Paso and Mexico City, San Antonio and Monterey, and sundry other pairs of points in a way that mocked the idea of an enforceable border between the two nations. Moreover, the call for Mexican labor in the American Southwest was amazingly loud, clear, and specific. The Southern Pacific nonchalantly moved crews of Mexican railroad workers to various points north and south of the border, and the Anaconda Company did likewise in its mining enterprises. *Enganchadores,* or labor contractors, collected Mexican immigrants as they entered the United States, and many southwestern employers never took seriously the provisions of the Foran Act of 1885 against the recruitment of foreign contract laborers.

Statistical data about Mexican entries into the United States are immediately suspect. Undocumented crossings have always been legion, and American inspectors did not keep a full count of legal Mexican immigrants until 1908. If Mexico's overall share of the total foreign immigration to the United States approximated the percentage reached between 1908 and 1914, then over 280,000 persons may have come north between 1899 and 1914. Mexico's proportional contribution to American immigration actually increased with the outbreak of World War I. The interruption of transatlantic traffic increased America's demand for Mexican labor to the point that Congress exempted Mexicans from the literacy test and $8 head tax that the United States had recently imposed on other immigrants. Similarly, the legal limitations imposed by Congress on European immigration in the 1920s helped make that decade the apex of the Mexican influx. According to American tallies, 498,945 Mexicans came north across the border between 1920 and 1929.

During the new immigration, Canada, America's other next-door neighbor, continued its familiar role as a major contributor to the republic's population. The standard statistical record shows 1,385,635 people entering the United States from Canada between 1899 and 1924, but this number requires interpretation. The estimate includes many non-Canadians in transit to the U.S. A tally of 825,150 better approximates the immigration of native Canadians. Close inspection of the data also reveals a shifting in the center of Canadian emigration between the English and the French provinces of the dominion. Between 1890, the first census year for which such information is available, and 1900, the percentage of Quebecers among the Canadian-born residents of the United States rose from 31 to 33 percent; the increase reflected the continuing importance of the post–Civil War movement of French Canadians into the industrial towns of New England. By 1920, however, the percentage of Quebecers fell to 27 percent; the decline was the result, in part, of the end of a period of rapid expansion in the western provinces and the subsequent rise in southward migration by British Canadians.

The statistics on Canadian immigration to the United States, of course, tell only half the story of the population movement across the boundaries of these two neighbors during the early years of the twentieth century. Canada regained about as many migrants from the United States as it lost to America; in the period between 1900 and 1924, approximately 1.5 million Americans headed north. During the pre–World War I boom years in the Canadian West, many farmers moved their families from the Middle West to the cheaper, abundant lands of the prairie provinces of Manitoba, Saskatchewan, and Alberta, and other Americans abandoned West Coast states for the mines, mills, and orchards of British Columbia. For some of the migrants, crossing the Canadian-American border, in either direction, amounted to a form of repatriation. Perhaps half of the American emigrants were from families that had at some time lived in Canadian territory. Overall, it seems that the Canadian-American exchange migration of the early twentieth century continued a longtime pattern of movement in which people on both sides of the border sought their fortunes with little concern for the implications of international boundaries.

The internal shift of some 2 million black men and women from the rural districts of the American South to the states and cities of the North between 1890 and 1930 cannot technically be considered an immigration movement. Nevertheless, discussing this phenomenon in the context of international population changes seems appropriate. The black exodus from Dixie was at least as intimately associated with the new immigration as the push of native white Americans across the continent was intertwined with the old. Indeed, the ex-slaves' children who abandoned the South probably had more social characteristics in common with the southern and eastern Europeans crossing the Atlantic at the end of the century than the pioneers had shared with the Irish immigrants of fifty years earlier. Moreover, the black migration and the new immigration were complementary parts of a larger pattern of peopling the industrial centers of the North; the former waxed as the latter waned with the outbreak of World War I. Finally, the arrival of the blacks in the urban centers of the North, where the old immigrants had carved a niche and the new ones were attempting to establish themselves, completed the setting in which the urban history of the nation would be played out during the twentieth century. For better or worse, the experiences of these three main subgroups of American society would henceforth directly affect one another.

After the Civil War the former slaves began to drift away from the rural South, where more than 90 percent of the black population of the United States had lived in the antebellum era. The volume of emigration was low initially, and most of the movers went west in pursuit of lands being offered along the paths of the expanding railroad network. By 1880, approximately 60,000 blacks had made their way to Kansas, Nebraska, Arkansas, Oklahoma, and Texas. The pace of departure doubled and the predominant destination changed in the following decades. The maturation of the first generation of freeborn blacks, who were unburdened by the limited vistas and affective ties that bound many of their parents to the South, created a large pool of potential migrants. Their independence and ambitions aggravated the resentment and fear felt by southern whites toward blacks, and the explosive racism of the 1890s, in turn, attuned them to calls of opportunity from northern cities. Approximately 200,000 first-generation freeborn blacks abandoned the South between 1890 and 1910 and, as a result, the black population tripled in New York and increased only slightly less dramatically in New Jersey, Pennsylvania, and Illinois.

Black migration continued to increase after 1910. Bad weather and the boll wevil destroyed the cotton crops of 1915 and 1916 and added to the list of woes already pushing blacks from the South. At the same time, the demands of World War I made soldiers and workers out of many young Europeans who otherwise would have ventured across the Atlantic. Suddenly, black Americans, who previously had been relegated to service occupations and menial jobs on the periphery of the industrial economy, became eligible for more desirable employment. Labor agents turned to them to fill the manpower void created by the plummeting number of immigrants. Despite white southerners' efforts to impede the recruiters, their blandishments helped bring 75,000 blacks north in 1917 to the railroad yards, mines, munitions factories, and other heavy industries of Pennsylvania. Once the migration was under way, reports and letters sent home describing the opportunities waiting in the North sustained its momentum. In addition, black leaders encouraged the exodus with more vigor and determination than immigrant spokesmen had ever shown in calling their countrymen from Europe. Robert S. Abbott's *Chicago Defender,* the first black owned, mass circulation newspaper, spread stories about the migration to every corner of the South. The *Defender* promised economic advancement and a chance for racial dignity to all who were brave enough to join the hegira. Approximately 577,000 blacks left the South between 1910 and 1920. The postwar prosperity of the northern states combined with the imposition by Congress of sharp limits on further immigration from abroad to drive the total even higher in the 1920s. During that decade, an additional 926,000 blacks came north, and by 1930 about 20 percent of the nation's black population lived outside the South.

Whether they were natives of Europe, Asia, the Western Hemisphere, or backwater areas of the United States, the men and women who participated in the great migration of the early twentieth century were responding to the age-old goal of emigrants: escape from want and persecution. The story of their coming naturally repeats themes from the old immigration, but it also contains fresh elements. The continuation of economic trends and technological developments dating from the Civil War era combined with the introduction of new sources of emigration to change the immigrant population in demographic features beyond its ethnic balance, to affect the range of opportunities available to the foreign born in the United States, and to alter the newcomers' aspirations and expectations. At the same time, the system of ethnic and racial socioeconomic stratification that had grown out of the earlier waves of immigration to America complicated the situation. The new arrivals had not only to deal with the original native white population but also to establish a place for themselves in the foreign-stock subculture created by their immigrant predecessors.

The changing occupational composition of the immigrant population after the Civil War reflected the changing nature of agriculture on both sides of the Atlantic. The consolidation of small plots into larger holdings worked toward lowering the number of farms, and the beginnings of mechanization further reduced the need for labor in that sector. In the United States, the official closing of the frontier in 1890 marked the end of agriculture's most expansive era, and the rising costs of land and mechanized equipment drove up the amount of capital indispensable to an aspiring farmer. As a result, fewer Europeans could classify themselves as independent farm operators and America was less dependent on immigrants to fill its western expanses. This trend actually predated the Civil War, and among newcomers to the United States who reported an occupational history upon arrival, the proportion claiming to have been owners or managers of farms never exceeded 30 percent after 1855. Between 1865 and 1898 the percentage of farmers in each year's influx of people hovered in the teens, reaching 20 percent only four times and falling below 10 percent twice. In the main years of the new immigration, 1890–1914, the farmers' share of the total ranged from .7 percent to 2.3 percent. The sharp drop in that era, however, probably reflects greater vigilance by the authorities in distinguishing farm owners from tenants and laborers, as well as the continuation in the decline f agriculture's contribution.

As the farmers' share of the immigrant population slipped and as the spread of factories created a large block of new jobs in manufacturing, the proportions of arrivals in a host of occupations inevitably shifted. The percentage of skilled workers in the influx was fairly stable as the old immigration shaded into the new, but a slight decrease was noticeable. In twenty-five of the forty years between 1860 and 1899, skilled workers constituted at least 20 percent of the arrivals; in the following twenty-five years, they reached that level only nine times. By contrast, the percentage of servants or domestics surpassed 10 percent for the first time in 1884 and thereafter fell below that mark on only three occasions before 1924. And the proportion of unskilled persons categorized as laborers showed the most dramatic rise. After the mid-1840s, laborers were consistently the most numerous group among each year's immigrants, and their presence was most obvious when bust in Europe coincided with boom in America. Changes in the definition and organization of occupational categories make precise measurement difficult, but the laborers' share of the incoming total definitely increased as time passed. For fourteen of the years between 1840 and 1859, this proportion hovered between 30 to 49 percent, never achieving a majority. In the next three decades, readings in the 40 percent range became more frequent than lower ones and the 50 percent mark was passed four times. Finally, in the twenty-five years between 1890 and 1914, laborers and farm laborers accounted for between 50 and 70 percent of the immigrant arrivals on seventeen of the annual tallies (Figure V-1, p. 134).

By the first decade of the twentieth century, the menial callings of laborer, farm laborer, and servant were the ones most frequently reported by new arrivals in the United States. According to statistics gathered between 1899 and 1910, laborer ranked first among the occupations claimed by Italian, German, Polish, Scandinavian, Slovak, Croatian-Slovenian, Greek, Lithuanian, Finnish, Portuguese, and Spanish immigrants; farm laborer led the way among Magyars and Ruthenians; and servant or domestic headed the list of Irish, Bohemian, and African employments. Indeed, these unskilled and poorly remunerated callings represented the three main occupations for almost every sizable immigrant group. The Jews were an exception to the rule among the new immigrants: among them the trade of tailor, which was

FIGURE V–1
Immigration of Farmers, Skilled Workers, and Laborers,[1] 1840–1924

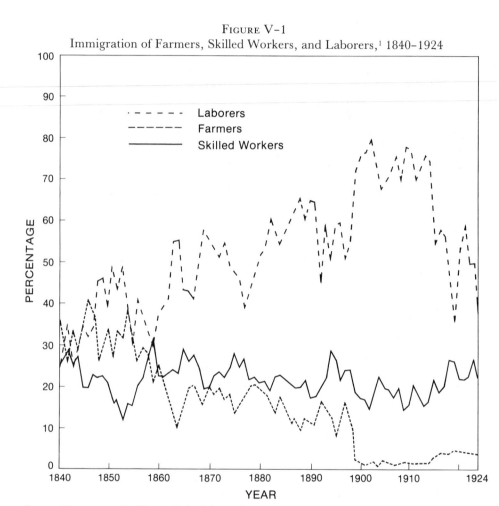

SOURCE: Figure created by Thomas J. Archdeacon from data in U.S. Bureau of the Census, *Historical Statistics of the United States: Colonial Times to 1970* (Washington, D.C.: Government Printing Office, 1975), series C120–137.

[1] Laborers include unskilled workers, domestics, and farm hands.

reported by 25 percent of the employed, was the most frequently mentioned occupation. This calling combined with laborer and servant to make up 47.5 percent of the total. The remaining Jews were scattered in various other occupations; 6 percent were carpenters and 5 percent were merchants, but only 2 percent were farm laborers. The distribution is not surprising considering the town based pattern of Jewish settlement in Russia. And, given the discriminatory limits on their work activities and lifestyles in Russia, the Jews still conformed to the general fact of immigrant poverty. Their skills and experience, however, would prove an asset in America.

As opportunities for family farmers dissipated and as the demand for skilled and especially for unskilled urban workers grew, young unattached adults entrenched themselves as the mainstay of the international migrant population. The existence of a downward trend in the immigration of married couples relative to that of single people appears implicitly in the decline in the proportion of children among the newcomers. Minors usually traveled with their parents, and their presence is thus indirect evidence of the number of family units in the influx. In the five decades between 1840 and 1889, boys and girls under fifteen years of age represented 19–23 percent of the immigrant traffic. Comparing these data with later ones is difficult because the American government's aggregate statistics adopted the fourteenth birthday as the cutoff for classifying youthful arrivals between 1899 and 1917. But the drop of the pertinent comparable figures to 15 percent between 1890 and 1899 and to 12 percent between 1900 and 1914 seems too great simply to be an artifact of the counting procedure. A contemporaneous rise in the ratio of male to female immigrants provides additional evidence of the importance of single adults, and especially young males, in the later phase of American immigration history. In the decades between 1840 and 1899, males constituted 58–61 percent of the arrivals. By contrast, males accounted for 70 percent of the newcomers between 1900 and 1909 and for two out of every three between 1910 and 1914.

The change in the proportion of males to females did not take place evenly across the immigrant nationalities. The Irish were the most striking exception to the trend: women formed a majority of the newcomers only in this group. The other ethnic elements of the old immigration—the Germans, the Scandinavians, and the British—also managed to keep their percentages of males below the average for the later years. Of the groups whose peak years of immigration came early in the twentieth century, the Jews displayed the best balance. With a ratio of fifty-four males to forty-six women, the Jews ranked second to the Irish in having the most even distribution of the sexes. The immigrants classified as Bohemians-Moravians also showed a relatively equal division, as did the Poles and the Slovaks. The greatest discrepancies were limited to other nationalities associated with the new immigration. Males outnumbered females by a margin of three to one among the Italians, who counted in their ranks more than one out of every five foreign arrivals in the United States between 1899 and 1924. The percentages of males were even higher among the immigrants identified as Croatians, Slovenians, Spaniards, Rumanians, and Russians. The Greeks and the Bulgarian-Montenegrin-Serbian group topped the scale, with males constituting 87.8 percent and 90.2 percent of the respective totals.

The proportion of women to be found among the immigrants of a particular nationality reflected, in part, the ability of females from that ethnic background to find employment. Immigrant women were not ornaments. As factory workers, servants, and farm wives, and as city wives and widows who lodged boarders and took in industrial homework, immigrant women either supported themselves or augmented their husbands' wages. The predominance of women among the Irish arrivals probably is a measure of Irish women's success in securing employment as domestics. Indeed, the doings of "Bridget," the ubiquitous Irish servant, were a stock component of late nineteenth-century stories and cartoons. Interestingly, domestic work was also prevalent among blacks, the only other migrant group with a female majority. Singly or in combination, the advantages of belonging to an ethnic group well established in the United States, of speaking English, and of having experience or skills suitable to light industrial employment gave women from old immigrant, French Canadian, Jewish, and black backgrounds a job-seeking edge over their counterparts from most of the new immigrant nationalities.

America's insatiable appetite for male laborers and its greater selectivity in utilizing females goes far toward explaining the imbalance of the sexes in the immigrant traffic, but these reasons are not adequate by themselves to account for all the variation among the ethnic groups arriving in the United States in the decade and a half before the outbreak of World War I. Other factors also had effects. The balanced sex ratio among the Jews probably emphasizes the extent to which persecution directed against the whole people contributed to the volume of their emigration; it possibly also reflects the importance of family unity in Jewish culture and the associated acceptance of marriage as an almost moral obligation. Perhaps too, the proportion of women varied directly with each ethnic group's willingness to allow single females to travel and work outside the protection of their families. Finally, circumstantial evidence indicates that this persistent presence or absence of a balance of the sexes in an ethnic group's migration, in addition to being the product of contemporary push and pull forces, reflected the nationality's attitude toward permanent settlement in a foreign land.

An immigrant group's ultimate success in the United States depended on its ability to reestablish a normal pattern of family life in the new country, and without a doubt the popular image of European men coming to America, establishing themselves, and sending back for their wives and sweethearts has a base in fact. But this view is also exaggerated. For individual ethnic groups, the ratio of males to females, whether low, medium, or high, was fairly consistent until the outbreak of World War I. In the war years, the percentage of males dropped dramatically among some immigrant nationalities. The change, however, was primarily the product of Europe's struggle and of the Russian Revolution, rather than of an acceleration of earlier immigrants' efforts to reunite or to form families. After peace and order were restored, the old pattern reemerged until the introduction of new, restrictive American immigration policies again disrupted it. Rates of remigration from the United States to Europe were consistently low among peoples with reasonably even numbers of men and women; they were persistently high among those for whom the division of the sexes was grossly imbalanced. Perhaps men returned home when they could not find countrywomen to marry in America, but, on the whole, the lack of potential spouses provides a poor explanation for the phenomenon of remigration. Indeed, females from groups with large male majorities also showed a propensity to leave America: Italian and Slavic women, for example, had remigration rates of approximately 20 percent. The continuing absence of female immigrants among some ethnic groups suggests that many people from those nationalities never conceived of the United States as a place of permanent settlement.

Large-scale remigration became a distinguishing feature of the later phase of immigration to the United States, especially among some of the groups new to the traffic. These peoples lacked the cultural toeholds in America that were available to contemporary arrivals from longtime immigrant sources. Likewise, these newcomers bore the brunt of nativism's most virulent outbursts in the twentieth century. Moreover, the new groups came from areas that had no traditions or lore of losing sizable portions of their populations to foreign lands. Such heritages of permanent resettlement were the product of an earlier era when, for the great majority of emigrants, returning home was not a practical alternative. For later immigrants, the improved transportation that made going to America fast, safe, and cheap made remigration equally feasible. In addition, the technology that moved men and women from farms to factories and cities put them in an economy in which fewer ties prevailed and in which property took liquid forms like cash and portable possessions rather than immobile forms like land, livestock, and equipment. The grand volume of remittances sent to Ireland from 1850 onward suggests that even in an earlier age emigrants looked back as well as forward. The changed conditions of the late nineteenth century, however, enabled those emigrants for whom permanent removal was unattractive to contemplate repatriating themselves, as well as their donations. The Chinese thought of themselves as sojourners who would return with honor after spending their working years in America. Among members of European groups with better prospects, the hope became to earn enough money in a brief period to secure the family's homestead, to provide dowries for female relatives, or to reestablish themselves solidly in the mother country. For these people, migration to the United States became an extension of the international seasonal migrations that were becoming common in Europe at the dawn of the twentieth century.

The lack of adequate data complicates the task of defining remigration precisely and of estimating its volume and overall effect on the composition of the American population. The records neither tabulate how often any one person arrived in, or departed from, the United States nor distinguish newcomers contemplating permanent settlement from those better described as migrant workers. Consequently, it is impossible both to tell how many different people were actually counted as immigrants and to judge how many emigrants from America were fulfilling original hopes or escaping unexpected disappointments. Moreover, as has been noted, American statistics on the emigration of aliens in this era cover only the years 1908–1924. Accordingly, in order to estimate the full impact of remigration on the absolute and proportional contributions of each ethnic group to the composition of the American population, it is necessary to reemploy a procedure used previously in this chapter. Taking the ratio of each group's average annual emigration to its average annual immigration and reducing its total immigration from 1899 to 1924 by the resulting percentage makes an allowance for the remigrations known to have occurred before 1908. The adjusted tallies are admittedly projections, but they probably do not exaggerate the amount of remigration that took place. As a matter of fact, a comparison of the new figures with rough data on remigration collected by the Italian government indicates that, at least for one very important group, the former are still conservative estimates.

Remigration apparently had less effect on the nationalities identified with the old immigration than on those associated primarily with the new. None of the former returned to Europe at a rate faster than the average among all the groups, but several of the latter far exceeded that mean. The Irish, the Germans, and the Scandinavians had annual average emigration rates of 8.9 percent, 13.7 percent, and 15.4 percent, respectively; the Bulgarian-Montenegrin contingent, the Rumanians, and the Russians, by comparison, had repatriation rates of 87.4 percent, 66.1 percent, and 65.0 percent, respectively. That conclusion, however, should not obscure the existence of low frequencies of return among several latecoming ethnic groups, including the Jews, whose 4.3 percent rate of emigration from the United States was the lowest of all. The Jews' persistence in America was both a measure of the role harassment played in their leaving Europe and a result of their lack of a real homeland (Table V-4).

The phenomenon of remigration drastically reduced the impact of the Italian influx on the American population. More than 3.8 million Italians landed in the United States, but their high annual emigration rate of 45.6 percent indicates that fewer than 2.1 million of them remained indefinitely. Thus, although they constituted 21.8 percent of the foreign arrivals in the country, the Italians eventually accounted for only 16.9 percent of those who stayed. They remained the largest immigrant nationality, but the gap separating them from the second-ranking group, the Jews, fell from 1,983,131 persons among the arrivals

TABLE V-4
Percentage of Males and Remigration Rates of Major Ethnic Groups[1]

| ETHNIC GROUP | MALE (%) | REMIGRATION RATE (%) |
|---|---|---|
| Hebrew | 54.3 | 4.3 |
| Irish | 46.4 | 8.9 |
| German | 57.5 | 13.7 |
| Scandinavian | 61.3 | 15.4 |
| Bohemian/Moravian | 55.7 | 15.5 |
| Ruthenian | 69.2 | 16.7 |
| Armenian | 71.3 | 18.1 |
| Dutch/Flemish | 62.7 | 19.1 |
| British (including Canadian) | 57.6 | 19.3 |
| Lithuanian | 66.6 | 20.3 |
| Finnish | 63.2 | 22.0 |
| Syrian | 69.5 | 23.1 |
| French (including Canadian) | 55.9 | 23.5 |
| African | 54.2 | 27.0 |
| Polish | 65.9 | 33.0 |
| Portuguese | 63.4 | 35.3 |
| Croatian/Slovenian | 79.7 | 36.3 |
| Slovak | 64.8 | 36.5 |
| Italian | 74.5 | 45.6 |
| Magyar | 67.0 | 46.5 |
| Spanish | 83.2 | 51.9 |
| Greek | 87.8 | 53.7 |
| Russian | 83.3 | 65.0 |
| Rumanian | 83.8 | 66.1 |
| Bulgarian/Montenegrin/Serbian | 90.2 | 87.4 |

SOURCE: Derived by Thomas J. Archdeacon from data in Imre Ferenczi, *International Migrations,* vol. I: *Statistics* (New York: National Bureau of Economic Research, 1929), tables 10, 15, and 19 in the section on the United States.

[1] These data yield a high Pearson product-moment correlation of .689. This statistic is a standard measure of the strength of association between two phenomena.

to 319,789 among the permanent settlers. Among the other numerically important groups, the Poles' slightly above average remigration rate dropped their total long-term contribution to the American population behind that of the Germans, whose proportion of return was relatively low. Similarly, the Greeks' remarkably high annual emigration rate of 53.7 percent lost them five places in the rankings, and differing remigration patterns produced additional alterations in the standings of other numerically small immigrant nationalities.

Skilled or unskilled, married or single, male or female, intent on staying or planning to remigrate, the people of the new era of immigration helped change the face of America between 1890 and 1920. Geographically, the foreign born were still concentrated in the northern states located east of the Mississippi and along the West Coast. According to the census reports for 1890 and 1920, these regions held approximately 66 percent of the total U.S. population and 91 percent of the foreign-born share in both years. In the interim, however, substantial changes had occurred within these regions. In 1890 the east north central and the west north central states had more foreign-born residents than did the New England and the middle Atlantic states. By 1920 the tide had shifted back to the East Coast. Moreover, from 1890 to 1920, the east north central states' share of the total foreign-born population fell from 27.1 to 23.9 percent, and the west north central states' portion dropped from 16.7 to 9.9 percent. Coincidentally, the ratio of foreign-born to native residents declined fom 1.27:1.00 to 1.18:1.00 in the east north central region and from 1.18:1.00 to .83:1.00 in the west north central area. In the same period, the Pacific states of Washington, Oregon, and California raised their share of the foreign-born population from 5.5 to 8.1 percent, but there, too, the ratio of foreign to native decreased, from 1.86:1.00 to 1.53:1.00.

Only the states of the northeastern seaboard experienced increases between 1890 and 1920 both in their share of the total immigrant population and in the ratio of foreign born to natives among their residents. Among the New England states, gains in Massachusetts, Rhode Island, and Connecticut more than offset losses in Vermont and New Hampshire and a static situation in Maine. As a result, the proportion of foreigners in the region rose from 12.3 to 13.5 percent of the U.S. total and the ratio of newcomers to natives climbed form 1.65:1.00 to 1.93:1.00. For the middle Atlantic states, the comparable sets of figures were 29.7 percent versus 35.6 percent and 1.47:1.00 versus 1.69:1.00.

As might be expected, considerable ethnic variations existed within this general geographic framework. Members of the well-established groups were distributed along familiar lines in 1920. The Irish remained centered in the middle Atlantic and the New England areas; 71 percent of them lived in these regions, compared with 49 percent of the total foreign-born population. The Germans were most strongly represented in the east north central states; 35 percent of them lived there, compared with 23 percent of the whole immigrant population. The Scandinavians still favored the west north central region; for example, 45 percent of the Norwegians lived there, compared with 10 percent of the general foreign population. People from the newer national and ethnic groups were heavily concentrated in the band of states between New York and Illinois. More than 57 percent of the immigrants from Italy and over 54 percent of those from Russia, including the vast majority of the Jews, lived in the middle Atlantic region. Indeed, 34 percent of the Italians and 38 percent of the Russians resided in a single state, New York, which by itself was home to 20 percent of the entire foreign-born population. The Poles had 21 percent of their contingent in New York, but they were probably more visible in Pennsylvania and Illinois, where approximately 16 percent and 18 percent of them, respectively, lived. The people classified as Czechoslovaks in the 1920 census had 49 percent of their group in Pennsylvania, Illinois, and Ohio, and those called Yugoslavs had more than 50 percent in the same three states. The Asians and the Mexicans, who entered the country from the west and the south, rather than from the east, naturally differed from the other new immigrant groups. Approximately 45 percent of the Chinese and 83 percent of the Japanese lived in California, while 88 percent of the Mexicans lived in Texas, California, and Arizona.

The concentration of immigrants in the Northeast was a by-product of the decline of agriculture and the rise of industry as America's magnet for the foreign born. By 1920, 51 percent of the total population of the United States lived in urban centers of more than 2,500 people. Among the foreign born the urban proportion was an even higher 75 percent. The trend toward city life was most evident among the newer ethnic groups in the population. Over 84 percent of foreign-born Italians and Poles resided in cities, as did about 89 percent of the immigrants from Russia. The Czechoslovaks and the Yugoslavs were the least urbanized of Europe's latest contributions, but their respective tallies of 66 percent and 69 percent still far surpassed the national average. The Mexicans, 47 percent of whom lived in cities, were the only latecomers with a rural majority. Of the long established ethnic groups, the Irish, who continued to immigrate at a high rate after 1890, were the most urbanized: almost 87 percent of them lived in cities or towns. The percentages of urban residents among the other old immigrant nationalities either approximated the overall average for the foreign born, as in the case of the British, or fell somewhere below it. Only the Norwegians, however, failed to exceed the national norm: according to the 1920 census, a mere 47 percent of them were city folk.

By 1920 the era of the new immigration had altered the meaning of the word "foreign." Although the groups associated with the old immigration continued to arrive, their share of the foreign-born population was falling. The passing of time had shrunk the ranks of the earlier arrivals. In the decade between 1910 and 1920, the numbers of Americans born in Germany, Ireland, Norway, and England dropped by 27.0 percent, 23.7 percent, 9.9 percent, and 7.3 percent, respectively. These people had formed the core of the foreign-born urban population in 1890, but by 1920 the Jews and the Italians were the largest immigrant groups in New York, and the Poles led the way in Chicago, Cleveland, and Buffalo. These changes, however, must be seen in perspective. They were occurring at a time when foreign-born residents were becoming less important than children of immigrants in the makeup of the American population. The percentage of Americans who were foreign born had fallen from 14.3 in 1890 and 14.5 in 1910 to 13.0 in 1920. Meanwhile, the percentage of second-generation Americans in the population had risen from 18.3 in 1890 to 20.5 in 1910 to 21.5 in 1920. And persons belonging to old immigrant nationalities naturally formed an important part of this growing contingent. As a result, although people classified as Russians and Italians constituted, respectively, 10.6 percent and 9.2 percent of America's first- and second-generation inhabitants in 1920, German-born and Irish-born inhabitants and their children still out numbered the former. In 1920, persons of German or Irish backgrounds, accounted for 19.9 percent and 11.4 percent, respectively, of the foreign-stock residents of the United States. Moreover, untold numbers of partly assimilated third- and later generation Americans, all of whom appeared in the census as native rather than foreign stock, still had strong emotional and social ties to the old immigrant groups.

The basic effect of the new immigration was to increase dramatically the heterogeneity of the American population and to make the relationship among its elements enormously complex. A pair of relatively simple divisions had existed within the non–Indian population during the middle of the nineteenth century. In the North the native white stock faced newcomers from northern and western Europe, and in the South they held sway over several million Africans. But by the first years of the twentieth century, the non–Indian population was divided among the native stock, the descendants of the original old immigrants, latecomers from the old immigrant countries, Asians, Mexicans, blacks, and the new immigrants from central, eastern, and southern Europe. Many Americans, especially among the native stock but even within the old immigrant groups, were troubled by this developing situation. They did not see it as the fulfillment of the nation's destiny but as a threatening departure from the social and cultural homogeneity necessary for unity and stability. In their opinion, something had to be done to control the influx of newcomers and to prevent what they feared was the mongrelization of the American identity.

# CHAPTER VI

# The Movement toward Restriction, 1865–1924

As the decades passed between the end of the Civil War and the plunge into the Great Depression, the United States moved with faltering steps from encouraging virtually unrestricted immigration to barring the gates against all but a select few. In the antebellum era the nation's obvious need for settlers and its confidence in a coming American millennium kept the popular animus against the foreign born from becoming a crusade against immigration. Optimists channeled their efforts into Americanizing the newcomers as quickly as possible, while pessimists tried to insure by law that the immigrants could aspire to citizenship and political office only after many years of exposure to U.S. manners and mores. After the Civil War, however, the end of westward expansion, the first signs of a surfeit of labor, and a growing perception of limits to America's assimilative capacity led to efforts to prevent the entry of people whose presence threatened to be economically, politically, or socially disruptive. Most of the early restrictive programs aimed at turning back individually unfit arrivals, but a willingness to exclude whole ethnic or racial minorities existed from the beginning. The Chinese were the first to be judged unacceptable, but some observers became convinced that a number of groups associated with the post–1890 influx also deserved condemnation. The restrictionists based their conclusion on a supposed connection between the onset of the new immigration and an increase in various social problems. They found intellectual support for their negative judgments about the most recently arrived peoples in the scientific and pseudoscientific systems of racial categorization that flourished in the whole Anglo-Saxon world at the turn of the twentieth century. The restrictionists' long campaign for the limitation of immigration culminated during and immediately after World War I. The involvement of the United States on the English side in the war made patriots dubious of the loyalty of anyone who did not fully identify with the nation's basically Anglo-American heritage. And the changing society of the postwar years made many citizens who were not ready to cope with the new realities fear the erosion of older American values and virtues under foreign influences. The result was an irresistible drive to return America to a mythical, pristine state in which immigration and immigrants would never again play an important role.

Early legislative attempts to bar undesirable immigrants originated at the state level and therefore ran the risk of violating Article I, section 8, of the U.S. Constitution, which gave the Congress control over foreign commerce. In the 1837 case of *New York* v. *Miln*, the U.S. Supreme Court upheld a state law requiring masters of vessels to identify and to provide basic information about the passengers they brought into port. Twelve years later, however, in the so-called passenger cases, the Court nullified laws by which New York and Massachusetts had imposed a head tax on each alien who landed in those states. The levy had been intended for the relief of communities burdened with the support of indigent foreigners. New York eventually attempted a different approach to the same goal; the legislature ordered shipmasters either to pay a $1.50 head tax on each of their alien passengers or to post bond that the newcomers would not become public charges for at least four years. In 1876 the Court, in *Henderson,* rejected this subterfuge, but the justices used the occasion to urge Congress to adopt a uniform code of immigration regulations.

Congress reacted piecemeal to the Supreme Court's call. The legislature concentrated much of its effort on prohibiting the admission of aliens deemed to have serious individual shortcomings or to constitute collectively a threat to American workers. Even before the Court spoke, the Congress in 1875 had outlawed the entry of both prostitutes and felons under sentence for nonpolitical crimes. In 1882 the Congress ordered the exclusion of lunatics, idiots, and persons likely to become public charges. Three years later, by the Foran Act, the lawmakers forbade employers or their agents to encourage or assist the immigration of foreigners under contract to perform labor on arrival. The measure, which aimed at undermining the use of southern and eastern Europeans as strikebreakers, was actually misdirected: embattled employers had no need to resort to the importation of contract labor when hordes of voluntary immigrants were already available. In 1891 Congress resumed its effort to identify individually undesirable immigrants by barring victims of loathsome or dangerous diseases, polygamists, and persons convicted of misdemeanors involving moral turpitude. In 1903 the legislature added epileptics, professional beggars, procurers, anarchists, and advocates of political violence to the list of unfit. Four years later, as a means of preventing the exploitation of alien child laborers, the lawmakers denied entry to boys and girls under sixteen who were not accompanied by a parent.

Washington naturally sought to involve the transatlantic shipping companies in the control of the immigrant traffic, which the United States to some extent blamed on their advertising. In 1891 Congress once again displayed its lack of understanding of the causes of immigration by ordering the steamship lines not to encourage people to leave Europe. But the lawmakers also took more constructive steps. The comprehensive legislation of 1891 directed the commanders of incoming vessels to report to federal officers the names of aliens traveling on board, as well as their nationalities, last residences, and destinations. Another provision made the shipping lines liable for the repatriation of inadmissible aliens and for the deportation of immigrants found within a year of their arrival to have entered unlawfully or to have become public charges for reasons that predated their coming. Subsequently the law was made broader. After the turn of the century, the Congress required ship commanders to provide more extensive data about passengers' literacy and finances. In addition, the Congress imposed a head tax on passengers from outside the Western Hemisphere and directed that the proceeds be used to defray the costs of regulating the immigrant traffic.

As time passed, the federal government assumed full control over the reception of arriving aliens. Congress took an important step in this direction in 1882, when it put the secretary of the Treasury in charge of immigration and authorized him to enforce the pertinent regulations through local authorities at the ports of entry. But the Immigration Act of 1891 must be considered the linchpin of the federal program. This law not only created, in the Treasury Department, the Office of Superintendent of Immigration, but also established direct federal responsibility for the screening of new arrivals. The law required all alien passengers landing in steerage class to report immediately to federal immigration officers for questions about background and current status and for physical examinations by doctors from the Marine Hospital Service. Most of the inquiries and inspections mandated by this law eventually took place on Ellis Island, in the harbor of New York City, which continued to be the port of entry for about 80 percent of the foreign influx, and on Angel Island, in San Francisco Bay. Indeed, the immigrant station opened on Ellis in 1892 became the symbol of the new immigration.

From a bureaucratic point of view, the federal admission procedure was not harsh. The physical examination and the process of registration at Ellis Island took about forty-five minutes in most cases. The doctors were skilled at detecting deformities and serious maladies like leprosy, ringworm, trachoma, tuberculosis, and venereal disease. Instructional information was posted in at least nine common languages, and interpreters were available for almost every tongue. Most important, the tests kept out relatively few people: the number turned away from American ports between 1892 and 1910 amounted to only 1 percent of the total admitted.

The Ellis Island story also had a darker side, however. Some officials were gruff with the newcomers; some consciously Anglicized the names of fresh arrivals and thus gave them a taste of America's lack of respect for alien cultures. Some officials extracted bribes from the immigrants or shortchanged those who turned in foreign currency for American dollars. At busy times the press of 5,000 daily arrivals at Ellis exhausted the patience of both staff and immigrants, and perhaps for the same reason sanitary conditions occasionally fell below acceptable standards in the dining halls and elsewhere. Moreover, the experience was traumatic for immigrants who had fed their fears with rumors of the awaiting ordeal. Worries only increased when a doctor chalkmarked an immigrant's coat with a coded reference to a suspected ailment or when a newcomer stumblingly tried to explain how he was neither a contract laborer nor an unemployable person likely to become a public charge. For some of the small minority with problems, detention was only momentary. But for others it meant separation from family members and friends who passed inspection and, finally, deportation. As many as 3,000 persons committed suicide at Ellis Island rather than face the future. Some sensitive officials, like New York's future mayor Fiorello La Guardia, who worked as an interpreter on the island while he attended law school, never forgot the sorrows they saw.

All things considered, the legislation and regulations thus far discussed adequately protected America from undesirable foreigners without being Draconian. But controls designed to keep out individual immigrants who were judged mentally, morally, or physically unfit were not enough to satisfy many citizens. These Americans feared that whole racial and ethnic groups among the current crowd of immigrants constituted a danger to the economic welfare, moral fiber, and cultural purity of the United States. Consequently, they were convinced of the necessity for broad restrictive laws to turn these peoples away at the gates. The call for ethnically and racially based exclusion laws reached its crescendo in the first quarter of the twentieth century. As early as the

1870s, however, when Congress was taking its first steps toward weeding out—without regard to national, racial, or religious background—undesirable candidates for entry, many Americans had loudly demanded the termination of Chinese immigration. Indeed, the story of the modern nativist movement begins in that decade.

Americans had misgivings about the Chinese from the time of their arrival in the United States during the California gold rush. The Chinese came voluntarily but usually in debt to merchants of their own nationality for the costs of ocean passage. Once in America, Chinese workers continued to deal for their daily needs with the same merchant community, which through its Six Companies organized them into gang labor for Caucasian employers. Thus, the Chinese immigrants bore resemblances to the European redemptioners of colonial times, to the then admissible contract laborers, and to the inexperienced newcomers of all nationalities, who were often at the mercy of their more seasoned countrymen. But many Americans drew a harsher analogy; Anglicizing the Chinese term for unskilled laborer, they called the arrivals ''coolies'' and infused the word with strong connotations of slavery. The association ruined the image of the Chinese among the white people of California, who, like other northern whites, knew that bound labor was a plague not only for its victims but also for nearby free workers. Moreover, the dark impression of the Chinese immigrants meshed with the generally negative stereotypes that dominated American ideas about China itself. Western merchants and diplomats repeatedly commented on the inefficiency, corruption, and weakness of imperial China. American Protestant missionaries explained Chinese indifference to Christianity in terms of morality, rather than culture, and charged their unreceptive hosts with maltreatment of women, sexual license, infanticide, opium addiction, and other vices. And most American journalists kept up an anti-Chinese diatribe—from their reporting on the Opium Wars of the 1840s to their accounts of the massacre of Christian missionaries and converts at Tientsin in 1870.

White settlers and Chinese immigrants established an uneasy modus vivendi during the quarter century after their initial encounter in the gold-mad and heavily male society of California. In the 1850s white prospectors used both legal devices, such as license taxes on foreign miners, and force to restrict the Chinese primarily to working old diggings that no longer attracted Americans. When the advent of hydraulic mining, with large capital requirements, reduced formerly independent prospectors to the rank of hired help, the Chinese were relegated to performing menial tasks around the camps. Many Chinese then moved into railroad construction, but the situation there was similar. The Asians could obtain only peripheral jobs, except in those instances in which the danger of the undertaking repelled white workers. In the most notable case, the Central Pacific used 10,000 Chinese laborers to lay railroad track across the Sierras in the killing winters of 1866 and 1867. Other Chinese workers helped in the massive and arduous tasks of clearing, irrigating, and harvesting that accompanied the birth of California agriculture.

The unsubtle division of labor between California's white and Chinese populations broke down in the 1870s. The completion of the transcontinental railroad lessened the demand for unskilled labor and integrated California into a national market network, which subjected local producers to severe outside competition. When the owners of California's shoe and cigar factories and woolens mills turned to cheap Asian labor, the prospect of vying for jobs with people normally forced to accept the humblest standards of living proved more than most whites would bear. Led by a naturalized, Irish immigrant drayman named Denis Kearney, the whites organized in anticoolie clubs and then in the Workingmen's party of California, whose anti-Chinese platform transformed the state's politics.

California's independent efforts to curtail Chinese immigration, which began with an 1858 law forbidding Chinese nationals to set foot on shore except in maritime emergencies, ran afoul of constitutionally defined congressional prerogatives in court tests at the state and federal levels. But by the 1870s opposition to Chinese immigration had become national in scope. Eastern employers, most notably the owners of a shoe factory in North Adams, Massachusetts, and of a laundry in Belleville, New Jersey, had outraged white workers by importing Chinese strikebreakers; in the same years unwanted Asian communities were appearing in several of the nation's older cities. In 1876 Congress dispatched a joint investigative committee to California. Despite voluminous testimony to the contrary, the legislators issued a report that confirmed the familiar and popular suspicions about Chinese morality and the unwillingness of these newcomers to become assimilated. In the same year, the presidential nominating conventions of both parties endorsed restriction, and by 1880 the Congress passed a bill limiting to fifteen the number of Chinese immigrants allowed on board any vessel bound for the United States. President Rutherford B. Hayes vetoed the measure as a violation of the Sino-American treaty negotiated by Anson Burlingame in 1868. That agreement had authorized the free movement of people between both countries, although it did not provide for the naturalization of such migrants. In the hope of extricating himself from a political impasse without creating an international incident, Hayes dispatched several diplomats to China to renegotiate the Burlingame Treaty. The Peking government was reluctant to deal but, after much haggling, accepted the right of Washington, at times when the interests of the United States required protection, to halt temporarily the immigration of Chinese laborers. Congress almost immediately took advantage of this revision. In 1882 the legislature suspended the entry of Chinese laborers for ten years. The lawmakers renewed the act for an equal term in both 1892 and 1902 and in 1904 extended the ban indefinitely.

The movement toward Chinese exclusion is best understood both as a continuation of traditional American prejudices against nonwhites and as an early example of the xenophobia that would eventually lead to the imposition of ethnically based barriers to white immigration. The economic and political development of the United States in the post–Civil War era weakened American confidence in the nation's ability to absorb newcomers. The completion of industrialization in the late nineteenth century eroded the limits on national prosperity and depression and on individual wealth and poverty that were inherent in the simpler agricultural economy of earlier decades. Concomitantly, the congregation of workers in factories and at urban industrial sites increased their ability to join in protests when employers attempted to shift to labor the burden of the recurring economic recessions. But a government that had recently faced armed rebellion and the fortunate citizens who were prospering in the postwar years were not receptive to the spectacle of major and sometimes violent blows against the new economic order. As industrial growth created an unprecedentedly sharp division between the nation's haves and have-nots, America lost the revolutionary quality that had distinguished its early history. Europe not only caught up with the fundamental democratic reforms originated by the United States but also gave birth to various Socialist ideologies whose collectivist prescriptions for the pursuit of happiness assumed that the American cult of individual enterprise was outdated.

Americans of the late nineteenth century were quick to interpret labor unrest, particularly in sectors of the economy manned mainly by foreign workers, as an importation of the new European radicalism. Their association of aliens with disruption was symptomatic of the national habit of blaming real domestic dissent on imaginary foreign machinations. Many conservatives put the general railroad strike of 1877, which led to rioting in Baltimore, Pittsburgh, Chicago, and St. Louis, in the same category as the rising in 1871 of the Paris Commune. Outraged citizens made even more explicit denunciations of foreign radical influence following a tragic incident almost a decade later in Chicago's Haymarket Square. There, on May 4, 1886, a bomb exploded in the midst of policemen who were breaking up an anarcho-communist demonstration in support of the strikes then occurring across the nation in favor of the eight-hour workday. The blast killed seven officers, and editorialists immediately blamed "Europe's human and inhuman rubbish" for the deed. The actual bomb thrower was never identified, but the courts eventually convicted and condemned to death one American and six immigrants, five of whom were Germans.

The identification of immigration with left-wing radicalism added a fresh dimension to American xenophobia; except for a brief period during the French Revolution, American nativists had usually stereotyped aliens as the agents of reactionary regimes. But the new fear of social revolution did not force the abandonment of the old concern that Catholic immigrants were the tools of political despots. Indeed, the most notorious nativist organization of the era managed to appeal, somewhat contradictorily, to both worries. The American Protective Association (APA) originated in Clinton, Iowa, in 1887; its founder, Harry F. Bowers, was a garden-variety anti-Catholic who blamed the church for undermining the public school system. Bowers formed the APA after Irish mill hands, who were members of the Knights of Labor, helped defeat a bid by his associate, Arnold Walliker, for reelection as mayor of Clinton. Those who joined the APA pledged not to hire Catholics, not to strike with them, and, of course, not to vote for them. The organization spread to several other midwestern states by 1890 and reached its zenith after the Panic of 1893. The APA explained that economic downturn with a facile thesis that blended elements of papal subversion, alien labor competition, and foreign radicalism. According to the APA, Rome was attempting to undermine the American economy by flooding the country with immigrants, and American Catholics were doing their part by stirring up labor unrest and making runs on banks.

In 1894, at the height of the economic crisis, the membership of the American Protective Association may have reached 2.5 million. Insofar as it was able to mask the general anti-alien bias lurking behind its anti-Catholicism, the organization was able to build a heterogeneous coalition that included even foreign-stock British, Canadian, German, and Scandinavian Protestants. The movement's long-term importance, however, was minimal. The APA took credit for Republican victories in 1894 and 1895 and for the termination of government contracts with religious groups, including many Catholic ones, for the education of Indian children on reservations. But the Republicans would have naturally made gains against Democratic incumbents in a depression, and the Indian legislation had broad support. At most, the APA seems to have reinforced the familiar ethnocultural component in American politics. On the one hand, this organization strengthened the Republican inclinations of persons who would have voted that way in any case; on the other, it solidified the Catholic immigrant vote in the Democratic corner. As a result, the Republican party was willing to accept the APA's support but saw no reason to adopt its divisive plans to curb all immigration, to tighten naturalization requirements, and to tax church property.

The APA and the other antiradical and anti-Catholic outbursts of the 1880s and 1890s marked a transitional phase in American nativism. These phenomena signaled the revitalization of immigration as a political and social issue in the United States, but they were too broad and, in some respects, too old-fashioned to do more than express momentary frustrations. By the 1890s the educated men and women of America's upper middle and upper classes no longer harbored the most irrational prejudices felt toward immigrants at mid-century. Familiarity had not made them ready to accept members of the old immigrant nationalities as equals, but intimacy had bred tolerance. Editorial writers described the doings of Irishmen and Germans with condescending humor rather than with bitterness, and cartoonists were more likely to sketch St. Patrick as a friendly leprechaun than as a drunken ape. Leading liberal Protestant academics and churchmen occasionally even expressed appreciation of the Catholic church's efforts to inject spiritual values into the lives of the newcomers and to curb urban immorality and disorder. The softened attitude reflected the recognition among more sophisticated  natives that the descendants of the mid-nineteenth-century immigrants had become acculturated and could no longer be imagined a threat to the republic. This change also revealed an uneasy perception, which was magnified by hindsight, that the Irish and the Germans at their worst moments had given more promise than the current hordes of Italian, Jewish, and Slavic arrivals of finding a place in American society.

Any realistic late nineteenth-century discussion of the problems caused by immigration and the presence of foreigners in the United States has to take into consideration the differences between the old European nationalities and the new. By the 1890s the descendants of the Irish, German, and Scandinavian immigrants of mid-century had gained an occupational, organizational, and political toehold in the United States, and their latecoming compatriots from northern and western Europe shared in their half-accepted status. The position of the recent southern and eastern European arrivals, however, was much more vulnerable. They were, of course, sharply distinguished from the Anglo-Saxon native core of the American population and, to some extent, from the early Protestant immigrants who had ensconced themselves in rural niches. But they were also semiseparated from the survivors and descendants of that group within the first wave of immigration with whom they shared a humble background, an alien religion, and adulthoods spent toiling in America's cities. No one had ever proposed that heraldic symbols of these newcomers be made part of the national seal. They were relatively poorer, less culturally familiar, more physically isolated, and less politically strong than their predecessors had been. Most important, to many Americans, either of old native stock or of old immigrant stock, they appeared to have flaws of character that could only lead to insurmountable problems.

The new immigrants' exact position in the American economy is a subject of considerable disagreement among the few scholars who have closely examined the question. Incomplete data, the difficulty of distinguishing causes from effects in economic relationships, and the wide variations among the ethnic and occupational structures of American communities inevitably lead researchers, depending on their assumptions and foci, to differing conclusions. Nevertheless, some generalizations seem safe. Between 1899 and World War I technological developments decreased sharply the capacity of the American economy to absorb unskilled labor. The real wages of the untrained fell, and the influx of laborers from Europe aggravated the decline. Moreover, the developmental gap separating the United States from the major countries supplying America with their peoples had widened with the passing decades. Unlike the first wave of northern and western European immigrants, the masses of southerners and easterners who dominated the ranks of the post–1890 influx did not possess skills on a par with those common in the economy they entered. The Irish, the most unfortunate contingent among the old immigrants, had at least enjoyed the advantage of familiarity with English. Even late arrivals from northern and western Europe had better prospects than did their contemporaries from southern and eastern points of origin. The former, for example, were much more likely than the latter to be literate. Among immigrants who were at least fourteen years of age and who arrived between 1899 and 1909, the Germans, the Scandinavians, the English, and the Irish had illiteracy rates of 5.1 percent, .4 percent, 1.1 percent, and 2.7 percent, respectively. By contrast, the Italians, the Jews, the Poles, and the Slovaks had rates of 46.9 percent, 25.7 percent, 35.4 percent, and 24.3 percent, respectively.

Common sense suggests, and research has confirmed, that the inability to speak English and the lack of even modest amounts of education or relevant job experience condemned newcomers to the lowest rungs of the economic ladder. In addition, most scholars agree that discrimination added to the burdens of the new immigrant nationalities. The slight favoritism felt by employers toward northern and western European immigrants on the basis on long-standing cultural contact reinforced the effects of the advantages in skills that they enjoyed over their southern and eastern European competitors. The new immigrants were the last hired and the first fired, and they suffered frequent layoffs in the interim. Moreover, they had little success in advancing within the industries in which they were employed; even those who learned English and gained job experience remained handicapped. According to a government study of thirty-six occupations in manufacturing and mining, English, Irish, and German adult male immigrant workers at the turn of the century earned average annual incomes of $673, $636, and $579, respectively. Their Polish, Jewish, and south Italian counterparts made $537, $492, and $408, respectively. Similar differentials existed in the wages offered females from the old and new immigrant groups.

Religion, as well as economics, helped define the position of southern and eastern European immigrants in American society. The great majority of them were non-Protestants and, as such, distinguishable from the dominant element of the population. Beyond that, their experiences varied. As non-Christians, the Jews were the most isolated. Moreover, the coming of the eastern European Jews had much the same deleterious effect on the small Sephardic and German Jewish communities already established in the United States that the Irish invasion of the 1840s had had on the Anglo-Catholic minority of that earlier era: the arrival of the newcomers altered the ethnocultural composition of the group, lowered its socioeconomic status, and swelled its numbers to a point that members of the host population considered threatening. Orthodox Christians fared better than the Jews. Theologically, their churches bore kinship with the Catholic, which by the end of the nineteenth century had achieved a secure, albeit second-class, ecclesiastical standing. But the Orthodox immigrants' rejection of the spiritual primacy of the pope was a wedge between them and the Roman Catholics, and their identification with European languages, cultural values, and politicoreligious hierarchies placed them further from the American mainstream than their acculturated cousins found themselves. But even the Catholics, who constituted a majority among the new immigrant peoples, were cut off by contemporary developments in church politics from sharing fully in an Americanized religion.

By the end of the nineteenth century, the band of liberal bishops and priests fighting to create a truly Americanized Catholic church was in trouble. With the cooperation of otherwise conservative English-speaking clerics, they had vigorously reaffirmed the English-language, acculturated character of Catholicism in the United States and had defeated the effort to divide the church along European national lines. But Ireland, Gibbons, Keane, and their cohorts had by their stands on the public schools, the German question, and the possibility of Catholic-Protestant rapprochement generated two phalanxes of English-speaking and non-English-speaking foes. And their optimistic predictions of the church's ultimate acceptance by the native majority had far exceeded the reality of slowly growing and uneven toleration experienced by most Catholic citizens and clergymen. The American church in the 1890s was coming under the control of bishops like Michael Corrigan of New York City and Bernard McQuaid of Rochester, New York who had matured in an atmosphere of rejection. Proud both of personal accomplishments achieved against great odds and of the church's vitality, these leaders had a combative and competitive attitude toward American Protestantism. Socially insecure, they hoped to prove themselves better than those who snubbed them. Finally, trained in Rome, they identified with European aristocratic traditions, advocated the papal prerogative, and had the attention of sympathetic ears in the Curia.

American Catholic conservatives scored their most important coup when, in 1897, they convinced Pope Leo XIII to condemn certain positions ascribed to their church in Abbé Felix Kline's laudatory introduction to the French edition of Isaac Hecker's biography. Leo's encyclical, *Testem benevolentiae*, did not charge the deceased Father Hecker, a convert who had founded the Paulist Fathers, or any other liberal with teaching that the church should dilute its principles to succeed in the United States or with spreading any of the other errors mentioned by the French abbé. The pope simply pronounced heretical the ideas that had become popularly known as Americanism. Nevertheless, *Testem benevolentiae* placed under a cloud all those who had argued that Catholicism could be reconciled with the nineteenth century's secular ideals of progress, liberalism, and democracy, especially as they were practiced in the United States. The so-called Americanists continued their work for many years, but they never regained their dominant position within the church in the United States.

In the wake of the Americanist controversy, Catholics among the new immigrants encountered a church that accepted an American identity but was defensive about its role in the larger society and was unconvinced of the wisdom of complete assimilation. The Irish-American model of an English-speaking church providing a full range of parochial institutional services for the faithful became the norm, especially in the old immigrant settlements of the larger cities. Even the Germans adopted English to meet the needs of their later generations, and the number of parishes using the German language exclusively dropped from about 500 to about 200 between 1906 and 1916. Acculturated Catholics expected that the new immigrants would adjust to the standards of the American church and that they would accept an implicitly subordinate position in it in the meantime. But the hierarchy was willing to allow the southern and eastern Europeans to achieve the semi-assimilation of American Catholics at their own pace. The newcomers were permitted to have services in their own languages, preferably in the basement chapels of existing churches. And when ethnic groups were able to raise money and put enough pressure on the hierarchy, bishops authorized them to erect so-called national parishes, whose boundaries often overlapped those of already established territorial ones. By 1916 over 2,200 foreign-language Catholic churches, including 466 Polish parishes, were in operation.

Catholic policy toward the new immigrant groups mixed political convenience with an understanding of the psychological and spiritual needs of recent arrivals. Allowing the prolongation of ethnic identities enabled Americanized Catholics to remain undisturbed in their control of the church while it reaped the benefits of growing membership. The device of the national parish made it possible to defuse dangerous demands like that of the Poles, who in their ignorance of the implications of the Cahensly affair called for a papally appointed bishop from their homeland. Meanwhile, Irishmen and Gemans, from their superior positions, could promulgate the standards of an American church by railing at the shortcomings of the newcomers. They were especially harsh toward the Italians, for many of whom membership in the unendangered, state supported church of Italy had been a nominal affair. American clergymen denounced nonpracticing Italians for falling away from the faith, charged those who avoided the parochial schools with negligence of their children, and condemned those who did not support the church financially. Moreover, they looked condescendingly on the traditional religious pageants imported from the European countryside and scorned the anticlericalism common among class-conscious Italians used to a church dominated by the aristocracy.

The strategy of creating an Anglicized church with room for ethnic diversity worked reasonably well. Leakages—such as the conversion of some Italians to Protestantism and the defection of some Poles to the schismatic Polish National Catholic church—were minor. But Catholics also paid a price for their church's compromise. The old immigrants suffered from the slowdown of the church's assimilation into the American mainstream and from the prolongation of its identification with foreign ways. And the new immigrants were deprived of the advantages that the more risky and less sensitive policy of demanding their rapid adaptation to an Americanized religion might have brought.

Like economics and religion, politics contributed to the vulnerability of the new immigrants by separating them from the native-stock population and putting them in an ambiguous relationship vis-à-vis the descendants of the old immigrants. The political framework in which the newcomers operated was in large part defined by their concentration in the nation's urban centers and by their patterns of residence within those cities. As has been seen, immigrant neighborhoods predated the Civil War. In the last decades of the century, continued improvements in the technology of transportation, including the electrification of streetcars, broadened the areas available for settlement by lower-class families, and the addition of new national and racial groups to the population made immigrant neighborhoods more ethnically varied and complex. In large cities, each immigrant group tended to have several separate centers individually adequate to support a church and other social institutions. Philadelphia's Poles had a dozen neighborhoods by the second decade of the twentieth century, and Chicago's Italians were dispersed enough to need twelve national parishes. An ethnic group, however, was likely to dominate only a sector of a geographically defined district and, even when able to put its cultural stamp on a neighborhood, usually formed no more than a plurality of the population there. In the area served by the parish of St. Anthony of Padua on Chicago's South Side, for example, the Italians constituted only a quarter of the foreign born. Life in an ethnic neighborhood, therefore, did not mean the gathering of a whole immigrant group in a single location and its complete isolation from other nationalities. Accordingly, the political life of the new immigrants had to be based on multi-ethnic coalitions, including bonds with the descendants of the old immigrants.

By virtue of their low economic standing, non-Protestant religious backgrounds, and residence in the ethnic neighborhoods of America's cities, the new arrivals from southern and eastern Europe were drawn into the political networks that in the middle decades of the nineteenth century had sheltered their predecessors from northern and western Europe. To the respectable, middle-class, native-stock population, these political organizations were machines bereft of the spiritual element needed to sustain morality in government. Worse, they were endowed with a seemingly mechanical ability to marshal the votes of the unthinking masses in favor of their venal candidates. The image, however, overestimated the purity of the political process and the rationality of voting behavior outside the cities at the same time that it underestimated the benefits the machines afforded their supporters. The machines consistently displayed a greater willingness than did their opponents to tolerate the immigrants' deviations from American cultural and religious norms. Moreover, they, in at least an informal and irregular fashion, helped the disadvantaged to find jobs, to obtain financial relief in moments of difficulty, and to protect themselves before the police and other agencies of government. The machines may have been acting primarily to advance their own self-interests at the polls; their piecemeal efforts may have demonstrated a willingness to help, rather than a capacity to provide a viable program of comprehensive assistance; and their approach may have been better suited to encouraging loyalty among the recipients of aid than to restoring their autonomy. Nevertheless, the machines were one of the few official sources of succor for the immigrants in an age that was only beginning to consider assigning government a positive role in promoting the welfare of minorities and the less fortunate.

Before World War I southern and eastern European immigrants lacked the numerical strength and feel for American life needed to be anything more than followers in the political organizations that courted their support. They formed not a single voting bloc cognizant of common interests as new immigrants but a series of independent ethnic units, each with its own proud would-be leaders. The ability of these immigrants to exert influence also suffered because relatively few of them were citizens. Five years had to pass before an immigrant met the minimum residency requirement for naturalization and the concomitant right to vote. Even then many southern and eastern Europeans did not seek naturalization, presumably because they either lacked familiarity with Anglo-American political values or because they viewed themselves as transients in the United States. As late as 1920, when more than 70 percent of foreign-born Irish and German male adults were citizens, the rates of naturalization among their counterparts from Russia, Italy, and Poland were 42 percent, 30 percent, and 28 percent, respectively. The new arrivals, therefore, had to rely on the acculturated descendants of the earlier immigrants to mediate between themselves and the host society.

In politics, just as in economics and religion, the addition of a second wave of immigrants to a society in which the offspring of the first had not been fully absorbed created a three-tiered pattern of stratification. The political dependence of the new immigrants on the old gave a broader base of support to the latter group's leaders and officeholders. Being acculturated but only semi-assimilated, the Irish-Americans in particular found themselves well positioned to be mediators, and they filled the role of middleman so adroitly that they became America's stereotypical ethnic politicians. From their bases in the nation's most heterogeneous cities, the Irish extended their influence to state level politics and beyond. From the perspective of the new immigrants, however, the political elevation of their predecessors to a point from which they could occasionally discomfit the native leadership of the country had mixed effects. On the one hand, the newcomers gained a measure of political influence more quickly than they could have done on their own. On the other, the political success of the better established ethnic groups was another aspect of the general process that threatened to separate their interests from those of later arrivals.

In much the same way that the creation of an Anglicized church by Catholics in the first wave of immigration limited the options of their coreligionists in the second, the emergence among the children of the old immigration of politicians adept at exercising power but disinclined to share it inhibited the advancement of leaders from the ranks of the new immigration. Of course, the situation was modified over time. As the new immigrant groups produced their own Americanized spokesmen, they demanded a greater public role. The party leaders, being practical men, gradually made concessions, starting at the lowest levels. In Chicago, Poles were winning aldermanic elections in the 1890s, and

Italian politicians were challenging Irish bosses in a few districts by the end of World War I. In New York, the strong and compact Jewish community of Manhattan's Lower East Side had its own congressman, Meyer London, by 1914. But progress was slow, and the new ethnic and racial groups in the American population lacked independent political influence during the critical years in which the propriety of restricting immigration on the basis of national origin became a topic of debate.

Some Americans of the late nineteenth century did not see the problems of the new immigration as updated versions of those associated with the first wave of the old immigration. They thought the most recent arrivals a breed apart and expressed their perceptions of them in grotesque caricatures of the newcomers' situations. Not surprisingly, they attributed some of the harshest stereotypes to the Italians and the Jews, the two most numerous immigrant groups.

Many Americans considered Italians and all other newcomers from the Mediterranean basin so accustomed to subhuman standards of living that they would forever work for wages lower than any native would tolerate. Workers believed the Italians so committed to the narrowest, most immediate sense of self-interest that they were lost to the cause of unionization. In the opinion of their critics, Italians and Greeks were nothing but pawns in the hands of vicious labor agents of their own nationalities. These *padrones,* immigrants themselves, sometimes tested the limits of the contract labor law in their efforts to convince compatriots in the old country either to immigrate or to send over their children. Often the *padrones* cruelly exploited those who actually came and were dependent on them for jobs and assistance. Native-stock Americans also associated the Italians with violence and readily assumed that their ranks were filled with members of the various criminal brotherhoods, including the Mafia and the Camorra, that flourished in the social disorder of late nineteenth-century Sicily and southern Italy.

American stereotypes of the new Jewish immigrants borrowed heavily from European imagery, in part because the United States lacked an indigenous anti-Semitic tradition. Colonial Americans, with their penchant for biblical allusions, frequently had identified themselves with the Chosen People and the wandering tribes of Israel. In the nineteenth century, the removal of religious tests in politics and the presence of affluent, Westernized Jews in the great German immigration had established the group on an even firmer footing. Unfortunately, the influx of a ragtag, exotic collection of eastern European Jews into a nation confused by the changing world of the late nineteenth century reversed this trend. In the more credulous backwaters of the nation, men and women associated Jews with the faraway cities and half-understood market systems that kept them on the margin of economic ruin. The Jews, whom they rarely met and whom they never saw in the sweatshops and slums, became international financiers, producing nothing themselves but capable of manipulating the world's economy for their own ends. Even sophisticated conservatives of refined social backgrounds were wont to exploit the Jews' supposedly complete involvement in the pursuit of money as an explanation for the apparent victory of crass materialism in late Victorian society. More portentous, the detractors of the Jews spread in the United States poisonous lore of the Hebrews' heathenism and of their supported enmity, even to the point of bloodletting, toward Christians.

The assumptions Americans made about Italian and Jewish degeneracy rationalized the use of violence to keep such dangerous groups under control. On several occasions southern mobs lynched Italians. The most infamous incident took place in 1891 after a jury found the evidence against nine Italians insufficient to convict them of the ambush murder of David Hennessey, New Orleans's popular Irish-American police chief. In that instance a crowd stormed the jail in which the defendants were being held and beat them and two other Italian prisoners to death. In 1915 a band of Georgians negated with a rope their governor's commutation to life imprisonment of the death sentence imposed two years earlier on a young Jew named Leo Frank. The part owner and superintendent of Atlanta's National Pencil Factory, Frank had been convicted on the basis of very incomplete evidence of the rape and murder of Mary Phagan, a thirteen-year-old employee at the plant.

However tragic the episodes in New Orleans and Atlanta were, they must be kept in perspective. They did not prove, in themselves, the existence of special hostility toward Italians, Jews, or other new immigrants. Occasional outrageous acts of violence had marred the early experiences in America of almost every immigrant nationality. But those crimes faded into faint memories as the passage of time weakened both the fears born of unfamiliarity and the hostility inevitable when natives and newcomers jostled for social and economic advantages. What distinguished the situation of the later immigrants was the persistence of the stereotypes that rationalized hatred of them. Even as America made the social and economic adjustments necessary to absorb the southern and eastern Europeans, fresh currents reinforced the intellectual foundations of the belief that they were innately inferior to their predecessors, were unassimilable, and constituted a permanent threat to the well-being of the nation.

Insofar as the new immigrants were concerned, the most important intellectual developments in the United States between the Civil War and World War I were the introduction of the ideas of Charles Darwin and the extension of them from the realm of biology to that of the study of society. Many Americans became convinced not only that Darwin had correctly linked the evolution of organisms to their environmental adaptability but also that his thesis provided a vital insight into the growth of civilization. Social Darwinism, the idea of applying evolutionary theory to human affairs, enjoyed quick success in American universities and among the better educated portion of the general public. The advance of this view was a measure of the country's increasing contact with, and receptiveness to, European thought. Indeed, the most important person in the transfer of the ideology from Europe to the United States was an Englishman, Herbert Spencer, who coined the phrase "survival of the fittest" and produced many of the scholarly works considered seminal by the first generation of American sociologists. But the attraction of Social Darwinism also reflected a need felt by many citizens to find an explanation for the growing disparity of wealth evident in the new industrial order and for the appearance within the population of an underclass seemingly incapable of achieving the economic mobility believed integral to the promise of America.

Social Darwinism's basic tenet, that progress was the product of a sometimes brutal but necessary struggle, was a comfort to the conservative and the prosperous. It could be used to defend cutthroat competition as natural, to condemn governmental interference in the economy as contrary to the more efficient action of natural laws, and to dismiss radical efforts to ameliorate social conditions as inconsistent with the inevitably slow improvement inherent in an evolutionary scheme. At the same time, Social Darwinism could be interpreted to show that the United States was still heading toward its longtime goal of creating a perfect society. Finally, Social Darwinism offered scientific substantiation for the perception that some of America's people—including the bulk of the new immigrants, as well as the blacks and the Indians—were truly inferior.

Despite its apparent foundation in the most rigorous thought of the era, the philosophy of Social Darwinism was vulnerable at too many points to go unchallenged. On the crudest level of observation, the almost indiscriminate slaughter of the young and the able in modern warfare cast doubt on the thesis that the fittest always survived the struggles of humankind. On the level of values, Social Darwinism threatened to equate man and animal and to leave no room for the spiritual and intellectual dimensions of God's highest creatures. Some liberal Protestant religious leaders, including Washington Gladden and Walter Rauschenbusch, offered the Social Gospel, the idea that evolution could work through the application of Christ's teachings to worldly problems, as an alternative to the conflict demanded by Social Darwinism. Liberal academics, most notably Lester Frank Ward, argued that human minds could decipher nature's laws and then direct them in purposeful way that would be more conducive to progress than the wasteful process of unregulated competition.

The proponents of the intellectual countercurrents to Social Darwinism created an atmosphere more favorable to private and public efforts to alleviate the lot of the poor and unfortunate, of whom the foreign born composed a sizable percentage. But many in this camp favored neither immigration in general nor the new immigrants in particular. Moreover, their teachings were compatible with the hypothesis of evolution and with the use of biological findings related to this process to improve society. Not surprisingly therefore, while Social Darwinism, the questionable philosophic spin-off of evolutionary theory, lost its hold on the popular mind toward the end of the nineteenth century, the eugenics movement, a more explicitly scientific descendant, gained strength. Led in the United States by Charles B. Davenport, the eugenicists by the second decade of the twentieth century expanded their concerns from the propagation of better grades of domestic animals to the improvement of the human stock. The eugenicists were convinced that heredity determined almost all of a person's capacities and that genetic inferiority predisposed men and women to crime, poverty, and sickness. Accordingly, they argued that the only realistic means to ease social ills was to encourage the reproduction of the fit and to discourage that of the unfit. The eugenicists hoped especially to make large families a liability, rather than an asset, for the poor by making the education of children compulsory and the employment of them illegal. Of course, even the most prudent domestic programs would be for nought if the government allowed undesirables to enter the country as immigrants.

Eugenics was much in vogue in the United States on the eve of World War I; according to one study by the government, popular magazines devoted more articles to this subject than to a variety of pressing social issues, such as tenement housing reform. The spokespersons for the movement, however, were better at providing a rationale for excluding some immigrants than at identifying specific unfit groups. Their bias against the poor was too general to be an effective criterion for exclusion; this prejudice was obviously incongruent with the fact that many disadvantaged immigrants had to overcome their handicaps and become valuable members of American society. To find the definitive information that would make possible sweeping judgments about the worthiness of individual nationalities, Americans had to turn to anthropology, another of the new social sciences. Like the Darwinist sociologists, American anthropologists were working within a European intellectual framework in which cultural and supposedly scientific theories of race were playing an increasingly important part. The Americans not only accepted the Europeans' assertions of the superiority of whites over the black and yellow peoples but also their inclusion of the Jews in the ranks of the inferior. Moreover, the Americans went beyond the discussion of a vaguely defined Aryan race, which seemed to satisfy most Europeans, to analyses that sought more precise divisions among the Caucasians. Through the works of men like William Z. Ripley, the Americans settled on a tripartite classification of whites and, although scholars had not consistently implied a hierarchy within this system, used it to make qualitative comparisons among groups. According to the popular understanding, at the apex of the white race were the Nordics, or Teutons, who represented the highest grades of intelligence, initiative, and leadership among humans; in the middle were the Alpines, who were described as the prototypical peasants; and at the bottom were the Mediterraneans, along with the Jews, who constituted something of a hybrid race.

Darwinism, eugenics, and scientific racism combined to give Americans apparently strong theoretical grounds for concern about the foreigners in their midst. Taken together, they created substantial arguments for curtailing the volume of immigration and controlling its ethnic composition. Aliens from inferior stocks constituted a twofold threat to the United States. Their presence within the society would drive superior whites unthinkingly to commit race suicide because they would reduce their rate of reproduction as a means of maintaining high standards of living in the face of competition from people willing to accept much less. In addition, interbreeding between whites of better and worse stocks would inevitably, according to the principles of genetics, perpetuate inferior qualities and terminate superior ones. The awareness of such clear and present dangers was more than enough to spur the concerned to action.

The Immigration Restriction League, founded in 1894 by a handful of recent Harvard graduates of distinguished social backgrounds, was the primary forum through which America's patrician elite expressed their fears. The historian John Fiske served as the league's first president; Henry Cabot Lodge, Massachusetts's Republican senator, gave it an influential voice in Congress; and a host of academics, including the reform-minded John R. Commons and Edward A. Ross, provided it with intellectual ammunition and access to educated, receptive audiences. The league was probably the most effective group propagating the new scientific arguments against the free admission of the foreign born. Nevertheless, the league kept the restriction debate on a relatively sophisticated, albeit prejudiced, level in the years before World War I. Though not above political cooperation with know-nothing organizations like the Junior Order of Mechanics, the league nevertheless avoided in public the blatant anti-Catholicism preached by some middle-class, small-town, Protestant foes of immigration. The league's point of view was not mainly a reaction to economic downturns and upturns, and therefore its power to attract members and push its cause showed less of a tendency to wax and wane than did that of other nativist groups. Finally, despite its sophistication and intellectuality, the league offered a simple solution for the crisis facing the United States: a literacy test for would-be immigrants. The literacy test offered a mechanically fair means to a desired discriminatory end. Only those persons unable to read and write their native language would be barred from entry. But because illiteracy was much more common in southern and eastern Europe than in the northern and western quadrants of the continent, the test would have the effect of excluding those nationalities identified as the least fit elements of the white race.

In 1897 President Grover Cleveland vetoed a bill that would have established a literacy requirement for immigrants. Cleveland argued that the test was contrary to American traditions and measured prior opportunity rather than innate ability. The league, however, did not give up its drive. In a twist of fate, congressional opponents of the literacy test unintentionally set the stage for the league's greatest propaganda victory when, in 1906, they asked for a legislative commission to study the issue. Their goal was to delay a bill presented by the restrictionists, but President Theodore Roosevelt saw the opportunity to find a definitive solution to the immigration problem. Under pressure from the White House, the Congress created, instead of an in-house board of inquiry, a full-fledged immigration commission composed of three representatives, three senators, three outside experts, and a large staff. Senator William P. Dillingham chaired the investigation; Dr. Jeremiah W. Jenks, a government economist, established its analytical tone; and the league lobbied effectively to insure that the body would evaluate its findings from the proper perspective. The Dillingham Commission, as this body became known, worked more than three years before publishing its forty-two-volume report. Much of the material presented contained useful, noncontroversial statistics and factual information on subjects such as European social and economic conditions, the demographic characteristics of the foreign-stock population, and the contemporary situation in other receiving nations. The major thesis of the study, however, reaffirmed the charge that the new immigrant nationalities were a less desirable addition than the old and constituted a threat to the welfare of the United States.

According to the Dillingham Commission, the new immigrants were less skilled than the old, were motivated by economic considerations rather than political idealism, and were uncommitted to staying in America. The investigators also repeated the standard charges that the recent arrivals drove old-stock citizens out of some lines of work, undermined unions, resisted assimilation, and were inclined toward violent crime. The bias in the commission's report was obvious. Its favorable portrayal of the earlier era of immigration was fanciful, especially in light of the bitter comments made about the foreign born in the middle of the nineteenth century, but its main failing came in the heavy-handed use of current racial theories in the analysis of data. The hostility expressed toward the new immigrant groups did not fit the commission's own evidence. The socioeconomic differences separating recent immigrants from their predecessors were not easily attributed to racial factors; moreover, as has been seen, the undesirable features associated with the later arrivals were not exhibited uniformly by all the southern and eastern European groups.

Despite the findings of the Dillingham Commission, the proponents of using the new science of race to evaluate the fitness of potential immigrants were not able to have their favorite idea made law before World War I. In 1912 and 1915, respectively, Presidents William H. Taft and Woodrow Wilson repeated the arguments of Grover Cleveland and vetoed bills incorporating a literacy test. The restrictionists, however, could take consolation from other recent developments. In the United States they won the extension of the principle of racial exclusion to the Japanese, and in the other receiving nations of the world their drive for stricter controls on immigration was being duplicated. Advocates of restriction could face the future with confidence that momentum in the struggle was on their side.

Resistance to Japanese immigrants ran high on the West Coast of the United States in the opening years of the twentieth century. As members of a nonwhite race, they were considered ineligible for naturalization under the standard legal interpretation of the Naturalization Act of 1790. Like the Chinese, the Japanese were charged with undercutting American workers and of being sexually immoral; however, unlike their Asian predecessors, the Japanese were also the objects of envy and fear. They enjoyed remarkable success in California agriculture and they were citizens of a nation that many observers believed would soon become a rival of the United States. Within and without, then, the Japanese were deemed a Yellow Peril. The issue of Japanese immigration reached a crisis in 1906, when the San Francisco school board ordered the segregation of Chinese, Korean, and Japanese students. Japan protested that the action violated its status as a "most favored nation." President Theodore Roosevelt denounced the school board but at the same time took diplomatic steps to curb Japanese immigration. Through a series of notes exchanged between Tokyo and Washington in 1907–1908, Japan promised not to issue passports to laborers desiring to emigrate to the United States. Tokyo also recognized the Americans' right to turn back Japanese who attempted to enter on documents issued initially for travel to other places, including Hawaii, Mexico, and Canada. Satisfied by this Gentlemen's Agreement, the San Francisco school board exempted the Japanese from its segregative policy, but the state continued seeking ways to keep these new Asian immigrants in as tenuous a position as possible. Most notably, by laws enacted in 1913 and 1920, California forbade aliens ineligible for citizenship either to own or to lease farmland.

To be understood in its proper perspective, the prewar movement in the United States toward the adoption of racial criteria for denying entry to the country must be seen not as an American oddity but as part of a broader phenomenon occurring in receiving nations around the world in the last decades of the nineteenth century and the first ones of the twentieth. In 1885, the Canadian government responded to pressure from the western provinces by imposing a head tax of $50 on each Chinese immigrant entering the country; by 1904 the levy was $500; and, finally, in 1923, the Canadians declared almost all Chinese ineligible for admission. In addition, by the informal Lemieux Agreement of 1907, Ottawa extracted from Tokyo a promise analogous to that given the United States in the Gentlemen's Agreement. In 1888, the Australian provinces virtually banned Chinese immigration and they then turned their attention to the growing influx of Japanese. In 1901 the first federal parliament authorized immigration officials to single out arrivals they thought to be undesirable and to subject them, regardless of their origins, to reading tests in European languages. In each case, the tester was to choose the language. The wording of the law was later changed to assuage Japanese sensibilities, but the effect of testing in "any prescribed language" was the same. Customs officials protected the goal of a "White Australia" by forcing almost all Asians and, in later years, some southern and eastern Europeans to take the impossible Dictation Test. Even England, which had advised Australia to eschew explicitly racial prohibitions on entry, adopted restrictive legislation in these years: the Aliens Act of 1905 empowered the secretary of state to deny admission to persons recently convicted of crimes, associated with prostitution, lacking visible means of support, or likely to become a public charge. Despite vague wording, the act was widely recognized as a means to regulate and decrease the sizable flow of Jews entering the country.

The most interesting shift in opinion toward immigration took place in South America. In the late nineteenth century, Argentina vigorously recruited European settlers for its sparsely populated agricultural districts and Chile sought foreign laborers to work in the production of nitrate and in other industrial endeavors. Advocates of immigration happily forecast that the newcomers would be able and docile workers. In addition, they predicted that the Europeans would "whiten" Argentina and Chile by reducing the proportionate importance of the supposedly inferior *mestizo* elements of the population. The friends of immigration looked with special fondness on the Germans and Anglo-Saxons in the influx, but they saw even the numerically predominant

Mediterraneans from Italy and Spain as standard-bearers of European modernity.

South American attitudes toward immigration changed drastically after 1900. The newcomers turned out to be a mixed blessing. Immigrant businessmen came to dominate commerce and industry: in Argentina they created an urban middle class that challenged the traditional power of the landowning elite; in Chile they proved to be strong competition for the emerging native middle class. The disaffected in both countries were soon denouncing sharp-dealing Europeans and reviving stereotypes of usurious Jews that lay dormant in their Iberian heritage. Critics cast upon the immigrants, who tended to gather in the cities rather than in the hinterlands, where their presence was most needed, the blame for an assortment of urban problems, including crime, prostitution, alcoholism, mendicancy, and labor unrest. They also complained of the clannishness of the newcomers and of their resistance to assimilation. In both countries, but especially in Argentina, legislators and opinion shapers abandoned their early optimism about immigration. Argentina's Social Defense Law of 1910 pinpointed the newcomers as the cause of the nation's troubles; the act prohibited the entry of criminals and political radicals and authorized the expulsion of alien troublemakers. More important, the country's intellectuals recast the images of the native and the immigrant. The former took on a romantically nationalistic and noble character, which was personified in the *gaucho,* and the latter was ascribed a biologically and morally inferior status similar to that current in the United States.

In the United States, World War I and its outcome created the conditions needed by the restrictionists to overcome the tradition of open immigration from Europe. The bitter debate over foreign policy that took place between the outbreak of hostilities in 1914 and America's entry into the fray in 1917 provided ammunition for those who thought the foreign born a threat to the security of the nation. The controversy called into question the loyalty of the old immigrant groups, which had created the ethnic subculture that mediated between the host society and the newest arrivals. Both Irish-Americans and German-Americans were probably more sympathetic than most other citizens to the Central Powers. Irish-Americans hated Great Britain rather than loved Germany, but they easily found virtues in a nation whose victories weakened England and thereby improved the chances of the rebellion that erupted in 1916 on their ancestral island. German-Americans obviously had direct emotional ties with their fatherland, and many of them had long expressed pride in German accomplishments and culture without realizing the extent to which such an attitude was incompatible with America's own growing nationalism. The Irish and the Germans both took too literally President Woodrow Wilson's declarations of American neutrality in the European conflict. They, and perhaps Wilson himself, failed to recognize that economics tied the United States to the Allies and that America's intellectual and social leaders, although respectful of German culture, were basically Anglophiles.

Americans of Irish or German ancestry risked opprobrium when they, through agitators like Jeremiah O'Leary of the American Truth Society or through organizations like the National German-American Alliance, vehemently protested the pro-British impact of the Wilson administration's posture of neutrality. The president and his openly pro-Ally predecessor, Theodore Roosevelt, won wide support when they condemned Irish-American and German-American complaints as "hyphenism" indicative of unacceptably divided national loyalties. The hint of treason made the so-called hyphenates pariahs whose aid could not be welcomed by either major party. Even though Irish and German voters gave greater than usual support to the Republican presidential candidate in 1916, they could not prevent Wilson's reelection over Charles Evans Hughes.

America's official entry into the war further poisoned the political atmosphere. Finally heeding the restrictionists' warnings about the dangers of outsiders, the Congress passed the long sought literacy test over President Wilson's veto in 1917. Thereafter, candidates for entry who had reached their sixteenth birthdays had to be able to read passages of thirty to eighty words in a language of their choice. In 1918 the Congress barred the admission of anarchists and other advocates of overthrowing the government. Within the nation the emphasis was on conformity and overt displays of loyalty. The National Americanization Committee, an offshoot of the Committee for Immigrants in America, which the Progressive reformer Frances A. Kellor had established in 1914 to educate aliens in the ways of the society, became more aggressive in its tactics. As the war approached, the organization changed its motto from Many Peoples, But One Nation to America First, and it subsequently demanded that all aliens learn English and apply for citizenship within three years of their arrival or face deportation. The appearance across the nation of extralegal bodies whose members were pledged to ferreting out subversive activities was even more ominous. The best known of these groups, the American Protective League, which grew to include more than 1,000 posts and enjoyed semi-official recognition from the government, conducted numerous irresponsible investigations of aliens on behalf of both the Justice Department and the War Department.

For German-Americans the war years were a tragedy. The vast majority of them responded to the call to the colors, but they could not convince many of their neighbors of their loyalty. During the conflict, angered superpatriots engaged in a rampage designed to eradicate all visible vestiges of German influence in American culture. The National Security League, which had argued for "preparedness" before the war, urged banning the German language, and several states, as well as many individual school districts, actually barred instruction in German. Popular pressure forced the German Hospital in New York City to become Lenox Hill Hospital; in St. Paul, Minnesota, the Germania Life Insurance Company became Guardian Life; and elsewhere, other institutions and even whole communities dropped their Teutonic names. At the extreme the "100 percent Americans" resorted to violence; the best-known incident, which took place on April 5, 1918, in Collinsville, Illinois, was the lynching of Robert Prager, a Socialist-leaning and loose-talking German immigrant whose last request was that his body be wrapped in an American flag.

Victory for the Allies only partly relieved the bitterness engendered by the war. The Anglicized Irish, whose ultimate loyalty to America was beyond serious doubt and whose homeland posed no threat to the United States, rebounded to their position of growing strength in domestic politics and noisy impotence in foreign affairs. After the war they were able to win vague congressional resolutions including Ireland in Wilson's pledge of self-determination for peoples aspiring to nationhood; of course, in light of America's unwillingness to offend England, such statements meant nothing. The German-Americans, however, were finished as a culturally vital element in the United States. They could no longer pursue the illusion that success and acceptance in America did not demand complete Anglicization. After the war German-Americans did not dare to speak against the harsh terms imposed on the fatherland at the Versailles peace conference, and the disintegration of their separate identity in the population of the United States accelerated.

The aftermath of World War I was even more baneful for the foreign born than the period of conflict had been. External peace brought internal unrest. Labor sought to recoup compensation deferred during the fighting and to extend the strides taken under the aegis of the National War Labor Board toward the unionization of basic industries. Business, on the other hand, was ready to rescind concessions made out of its wartime labor hunger and under governmental pressure. In the most important industrial crisis of 1919 management was able not only to put down an ill-timed and poorly coordinated strike by a some 250,000 steelworkers but also to attribute the trouble to the southern and eastern European backgrounds of the majority of the participants. The slur against ethnic groups that had recently received some sympathy as victims and opponents of the Central Powers marked the return of prewar patterns of hostility. The attack gained all the more credence in light of the Bolshevik revolution in Russia and the spread of Communist agitation in central Europe. Indeed, the specter of foreign radicalism also colored many Americans' reactions to the Boston police strike, the Seattle general strike, and other disturbances in 1919. Together, these events set the stage for the great Red Scare.

After a series of urban riots on May Day 1919, the simultaneous discovery of thirty-six letter bombs destined for leading politicians and businessmen, and the explosion on June 2 of a powerful device at the door of Attorney General A. Mitchell Palmer's house, the United States was on the verge of hysteria. In August Palmer set up the General Intelligence Division in the Department of Justice under the youthful J. Edgar Hoover. The new agency had the assignment of ferreting out alien anarchists and subversives who, under the wartime revisions of the immigration legislation, were liable to deportation. With little concern for due process and a free application of the principle of guilt by association, Palmer's agents arrested about 1,000 members of the Union of Russian Workers and over 3,000 members of the Communist and Communist Labor parties in raids on November 7, 1919, and January 2, 1920. Very few of those arrested constituted a real threat to the government, but more than 8,000 of them were eventually deported. Congress endorsed the expulsion of enemy aliens and anarchists, the media were solidly behind Palmer, and the number of deportations might have gone much higher had not Acting Secretary of Labor Louis F. Post, whose department took jurisdiction over immigration matters in 1913, courageously protected the detainees whose civil rights had been most grossly violated.

The Red Scare was over by 1921. Palmer's prediction that radicals would start a revolution on May 1, 1920, proved embarrassingly false, and the attorney general's critics gradually showed that his hunt was more dangerous than its prey to America's liberties. The fate of Nicola Sacco and Bartolomeo Vanzetti, however, indicates that an increase in sympathy for foreign radicalism did not follow the decline in fear of it. Sacco, a shoemaker, and Vanzetti, a fish peddler, were Italian anarchosocialists and draft evaders accused of a payroll robbery and murder committed in South Braintree, Massachusetts, during the height of the Red Scare in 1920. To this day, experts are divided on their guilt or innocence but agree that the two Italians were convicted on misleading and prejudicial evidence at a trial presided over by a judge incredibly hostile to them. Intellectuals and social activists across the nation and the world protested the proceedings. Nevertheless, the spirit of the times was such that Sacco and Vanzetti, although they lingered in jail until 1927, could neither win a new trial nor escape execution.

For most foreign-born and foreign-stock Americans, the great majority of whom had no contact with radicalism, the Red Scare and the fate of Sacco and Vanzetti were not traumatic. Indeed, given their conservative social and religious orientations, many immigrants and their offspring undoubtedly shared in the general distaste for the purveyors of unsettling ideologies. For these people, the danger of the 1920s lay in the reassertion, through religious fundamentalism, prohibition, and the Ku Klux Klan, of what the old-stock population understood to be threatened American values. Fundamentalism, especially in the form of biblical literalism, resisted efforts to reconcile Protestantism with modern science and scriptural exegesis. This movement did not pose a theological problem for the immigrants, who were also dubious about such potentially antireligious theses as human evolution; however, fundamentalism did affect them insofar as it represented a revival of narrow, chauvinistic religious feelings and a rejection of the modern, urban milieu in which the foreign-stock population lived. The renewed drive for prohibition, which finally achieved victory in the adoption of the Eighteenth Amendment and the passage of the Volstead Act in 1919, was more of a challenge for the immigrants. The assault was indirect, and prohibition created divisions within, as well as between, ethnic and religious groups. But in the United States, prohibition historically had represented the struggle of native-stock, rural, and Protestant values against immigrant, urban, and Catholic ones, and this movement's success showed that the former could still muster legislative affirmation of their priority. Finally, the resurrection of the Ku Klux Klan—with its commitment to racial purity, Protestantism, and so-called Americanism and its willingness in some cases to resort to extralegal tactics— constituted the clearest attack on the foreign-stock population. Except in a few areas of the rural South, the Klan was not primarily an antiblack organization in the 1920s. On the contrary, the Klan, which recruited approximately 2 million members in that decade, had its greatest strength in the nation's cities, where residents of Catholic or Jewish backgrounds were the special targets of its wrath.

From the perspective of more than half a century, fundamentalism, prohibition, and the Klan seem losing causes, the last gasps of a dying culture. This point of view has merit: adherents of these movements surely felt under attack, and they ultimately failed to impose their vision of the good on the whole society. Unfortunately, concentration on the excesses of fundamentalism, prohibition, and the Klan and on particular defeats they suffered encourages an underestimation both of their influence in the 1920s and of the residual strength of the values they expressed in extreme fashion. Commentators emphasize how the urbane and agnostic defense attorney Clarence Darrow revealed the theological naïveté of the countrified and credulous prosecutor William Jennings Bryan at the *Scopes* trial of 1925. But the trial, a set-up case in which a young man challenged Tennessee's law against teaching evolutionary theory, was decided on narrow, factual grounds. It did not resolve any constitutional principles, and religious conservatives with right-wing political leanings remained as dynamic a force as any in American Protestantism. Likewise, historians pay more attention to violations of prohibition and to its repeal in 1933 than to the continued vitality of stereotypes about the dissipation of urban dwellers. And scholars, in recounting how the Klan fell apart after the arrest of several of its leaders for fraud and sexual offenses, tend to confuse the dismemberment of the organization with the demise of the bigotry it represented.

For persons influenced by fundamentalism, prohibition, and the Klan and for many other citizens simply concerned by America's inability to control the growth and composition of the U.S. population, the various immigration and antisubversive laws passed in the war years were inadequate. The literacy test had not lived up to its promise as a convenient means for keeping out aliens of undesired nationalities; reading skills had spread rapidly into the recesses of Europe during the first decades of the century. Worse, no law existed to protect the United States from the flood of emigrants that, according to writers like Kenneth Roberts and publications like the *Saturday Evening Post*, was ready to burst forth from the ravaged continent. When the average monthly number of immigrants passed 50,000 late in 1920, a time of economic downturn in the United States, Washington quickly reacted. Over the veto of the lame-duck President Wilson, the Congress in 1921 temporarily limited annual immigration from each European country to 3 percent of the number of its natives counted in the 1910 American census.

The Immigration Act of 1921 limited entry to the United States to a yearly maximum of 357,000 persons, but the restrictionists thought that the law still allowed in too many immigrants and too high a proportion of southern and eastern Europeans, especially when the northerners and westerners did not fill the quotas allotted them. Led by Representative Albert Johnson of Washington, the chairman of the Committee on Immigration, and by eminent private citizens like Harry H. Laughlin, the eugenicist, and John B. Trevor, a socialite lawyer from New York, the restrictionists searched for a more efficient tool. They soon asked that Congress limit annual European immigration to 2 percent of the number of foreign born counted among each nationality in the census of 1890, a time in which few southern or eastern Europeans were living in the United States. Ironically, the restrictionists' main argument for this action was best expressed in the writings of Gino Speranza, an American lawyer of Italian descent: he claimed that the United States had been settled and developed by culturally homogeneous Anglo-Saxons, whose race had been fully formed before the dawn of the new immigration in 1890.

To placate those critics who complained of the blatant discrimination evident in the choice of the 1890 census, Senator David A. Reed of Pennsylvania proposed that the quotas for future immigration be based on the national origins of the whole current white population of the United States. The restrictionists were aware that this program, because of the weight it would give to long established components of the population, would produce the desired effect while provoking fewer democratic qualms. Accordingly, the Johnson-Reed Immigration Act of 1924 provided that the 2 percent plan based on the 1890 census would go into effect until 1927. Thereafter the maximum allowed immigration to the United States would be approximately 150,000, to be allocated in proportion to the representation of the various nationalities in the whole white population counted in the 1920 census. In the years from 1924 to 1927 a panel of experts would determine the ethnic origins of the people present in America before 1790, who were to be considered the native stock, and of the immigrants since arrived. From these data, they would make the appropriate demographic projections to establish the final quotas.

# CHAPTER VII

# From Immigrants to Ethnics

CONGRESS'S DECISION in 1924 to limit sharply the annual number of immigrants admitted to America reversed earlier practices and became a permanent feature of the nation's official population policy. Moreover, the legislature's coincidental resolution to control the demographic composition of future immigration according to ethnic and racial criteria remained in force for over forty years. During those four decades the restrictive package of laws was refined and extended. Before the end of the 1920s the non-British components of the old immigration discovered that even they were not exempt from the national origin provisions of the program enacted in 1924, and in the dark days of the Depression the government looked critically for the first time at the issue of immigration from the Western Hemisphere. As the Nazi menace grew, Americans proved unwilling to allow most of the victims of Hitler's atrocities a refuge in the United States. The harsh treatment meted out to Japanese-Americans during World War II more than offset the few indications that popular attitudes were becoming more liberal as the country learned the political and moral lessons of the conflict. Indeed, the passage of the McCarran-Walter Immigration Act and the rise of McCarthyism in the 1950s were strong evidence that most Americans were content with the decisions made thirty years earlier about immigration.

Freed from the pressure of heavy annual immigration, the United

States was able, from the mid-1920s, to make substantial progress toward absorbing the foreign element already in the population. Governmental and private agencies continued their search for effective programs to Americanize alien residents and their offspring, but the main changes that occurred were primarily the result of demographic alterations produced naturally by the passage of time. Acculturation inexorably took place as men and women of the second and later generations became increasingly important in the makeup of the nation's foreign stock. Individual members of ethnic groups adapted their behavior to the manners and mores of the country, and the institutions that served and were led by them experienced analogous alterations of values. Moreover, the religious, economic, and political conditions affecting foreign-stock Americans worked to transcend their particular ethnic identities and to bind them into a common subculture. As a result, the heterogeneity of the population was much less of an issue in the United States during and after World War II than it had been in the decade between 1915 and 1925. The consensus was that the United States had avoided the danger of ethnic Balkanization and had managed to combine peoples of diverse backgrounds in a small, more manageable number of mutually respectful groupings tied to the three great Western religious traditions. The situation, however, obviously fell short of the nation's original goal of producing a homogeneous population and left in doubt the ultimate efficacy of the melting pot.

Support for the restrictive legislation of the 1920s was widespread. Virtually all groups, from the American Federation of Labor, which had consistently demanded curbs on immigration, to the National Association of Manufacturers, which had persistently opposed them, praised or accepted with resignation the imposition of numerical limits. The establishment of ethnic quotas stirred more dissent, but the popular response was still markedly favorable. In the House of Representatives, congressmen from the South and West voted 150 to 0 for the 1924 law; those from the Middle West, a center of the old immigration and of German and Scandinavian strength, were in favor 125 to 15. Only the representatives of the Northeast, by a margin of 53 to 56, rejected the proposal. The Northeast, of course, was the center of new immigrant settlement, of the Irish Democratic political organizations that shielded the recent arrivals, and of the Catholic church, which correctly interpreted the quota system as an attack on itself.

Some of the assimilated descendants of the old immigrants obviously approved the decision to close the door on the new immigrants, but their cheering subsided when they discerned the implications of changing the basis for the allocation of annual immigration quotas from the temporary criterion of the ethnic backgrounds of America's foreign-born residents in 1890 to the permanent one of the composition of the total white population in 1920. The Quota Board, entrusted with making the final determinations, not only scrutinized the available statistical data concerning nineteenth- and twentieth-century immigration but also sought to delve into the ethnic composition of the colonial American population. To acquire this information, the board resorted to an analysis of surname patterns in the federal census of 1790 that the historian Marcus Hansen and the genealogist Howard Baker had skillfully produced for the American Council of Learned Societies. The board concluded that persons of colonial stock comprised 43.5 percent of the 1920 population of 94,820,915 and that later immigrants and their descendants accounted for 56.5 percent of this number. As a result, the board decided that Britain and Northern Ireland, which had played the major role in the formation of the white colonial population, deserved greater recognition than did countries whose contributions, for the most part, postdated the Revolution. Accordingly, the board raised the annual British quota to 65,721 from the 34,007 it would have been under the 1890 rubric. It then lowered the southern Irish allotment from 28,567 to 17,853, the German from 51,227 to 25,957, and the Scandinavian from 18,803 to 6,872. Societies representing the old immigrants—and especially the Germans and the Scandinavians, who believed their Nordic blood and Protestant faith put them beyond reproach—cried foul. Their anger was so great that Albert Johnson and some other Republican restrictionists, who feared the defection of German and Scandinavian voters from their party, contemplated scrapping the national origin quotas in favor of allocations based on the 1890 census. But more politically secure restrictionists held fast, the furor faded, and a reluctant President Herbert Hoover put the new system into effect, two years late, in 1929.

Just under 154,000 men and women could enter the United States each year under the quota system. The visas set aside for British, Irish, German, and Scandinavian immigrants accounted for almost 76 percent of the total. The remaining entry permits were distributed thus: the Poles were allowed 6,524; the Italians received 5,802; the Dutch got 3,153; the French were assigned 3,086; the Czechoslovaks were given 2,874; the Russians got 2,712; the Swiss were assigned 1,707; the Austrians received 1,413; the Belgians were allotted 1,304; the Hungarians got 869; the Yugoslavs were granted 845; the Finns received 569; the Portuguese were permitted 440; the Lithuanians got 386; the Rumanians received 377; and the Greeks were given 307. No other group was permitted more than 300 entrants, and most received only the token minimum of 100. Moreover, the United States established strict guidelines to control the kinds of people who could receive even these limited numbers of visas. The fathers and mothers of adult American citizens and, in the case of countries with quotas in excess of 300, skilled agriculturalists, their wives, and their minor children (under eighteen years of age) had the first claim on up to half of the annual quota for each country. The wives and minor children of legally admitted alien residents of the United States had the right to whatever number of visas remained. Only after persons in these preferred categories had been satisfied could applicants without familial connections or agricultural skills be considered. The system, however, did offer some flexibility in the form of a category of nonquota immigrants, including the spouses and unmarried minor children of American citizens; such people were immune from special requirements and their entry did not count against the legal ceilings on admissions from their countries.

Perhaps the most notable groups of potential nonquota immigrants to the United States were the peoples of the Western Hemisphere, especially the inhabitants of Canada and Mexico. Americans felt a natural affinity with Canadians and had no desire to alter the history of free movement across their mutual border. The American attitude toward Mexicans was less noble and more divided. Some defenders of unrestricted immigration across the Rio Grande saw this policy as a corollary of the government's official policy of Pan-Americanism, but many more viewed it primarily as a means to insure a supply of extremely cheap, docile labor for the agriculturalists and other employers of the southwestern states. Opponents of an open border challenged the claim that Mexicans took only jobs unwanted by natives and charged that the immigrants' acceptance of starvation wages undercut American laborers' efforts to achieve a decent standard of living. The foes of the Mexicans described them as permanently sunk in crime, disease, and poverty and categorized them as a dangerous racial mixture of black, Indian, and inferior Mediterannean stock. The news that the average annual Mexican immigration had fallen to approximately 50,000 persons in the late 1920s did not satisfy advocates of restriction. Indeed, they worried that with the imposition of limits on European immigration the number of Mexican arrivals would represent an increasingly large proportion of the total foreign influx to the United States. Politicians like Representative John Box of Texas were soon seeking the imposition of a quota on Mexico. After four years of debate, the Senate in 1930 passed such a measure, but the administration of President Herbert Hoover was able to dissuade the House from bringing the bill to a vote.

Despite this defeat, the restrictionists achieved the heart of their goal in the 1930s. Reacting to their pressure, the State Department more carefully supervised Mexican immigration and strove to weed out from the applicants for visas legally ineligible contract laborers, illiterates, and potential public charges. The restrictionists' real triumph came with the deepening of the Depression. As a result of the general economic collapse, Mexican immigrants found themselves faced with stiff competition from Americans for even the most menial jobs. In 1931, California prohibited the hiring of aliens for any public works project, and the situation worsened when an army of southern tenant farmers and sharecroppers, as well as Okies and Arkies uprooted from the Dust Bowl, relocated in the western states during the following years. In these circumstances many Mexicans chose voluntarily to repatriate and others came less willingly to the same decision under pressure from American authorities. Between 1929 and 1935 the federal government deported or assisted the voluntary return of approximately 82,000 Mexicans who had entered the United States illegally. Moreover, local governments in several states used offers of free transportation, food, clothing, and medical care to encourage the repatriation of legally resident Mexican aliens who had happened to fall onto the welfare rolls.

Determining how many persons of Mexican background left the United States during the 1930s is virtually impossible. Texas, California, and the Illinois-Indiana region are known to have suffered the sharpest declines, and the census shows that the number of foreign-born Mexicans in the national population fell from 639,000 to 377,000 during the decade. As many as 500,000 persons of Mexican stock left some official record of quitting the United States between 1929 and 1935, and perhaps half of them were American citizens by birth. Many of the Mexicans assumed or were led to believe that they could reenter the United States at a later date, but those who had accepted assistance ran the risk of being barred as potential public charges. Even those born in the United States faced difficulties if they could not prove their place of birth or if they had unwittingly violated their claim to citizenship by voting in Mexico or serving in its army.

While the Depression was reducing the number of men and women able or willing to cross international boundaries in search of economic opportunity, the rise of Adolf Hitler was simultaneously creating a new bloc of people for whom flight offered the only prospect of escaping political, religious, and racial persecution. In the years before World War II the mass of these victims were Jews from Germany and from the other lands that fell under the Reich's control. Before the Nazis turned to their infamous Final Solution, the goal of their increasing harassment of the Jews was not only to make them a scapegoat for Germany's problems but also to force them to abandon their property and accept exile. Under such circumstances, no country rushed to the rescue of the Jews. Each recognized that an offer of asylum might have the unintended effect of encouraging Hitler to persevere in his policy of driving out minorities and opponents. Moreover, the politicians of the economically beleaguered Western nations dared not risk the popular outcry that would have followed any decision to add to the populations of their countries sizable contingents of refugees from a group as ethnically distinct and unpopular as the Jews. In the United States, labor unions predicted that creating a loophole in the quota system would aggravate the already disastrous unemployment problem; isolationists warned that succoring Hitler's victims would draw America into war; and racially minded restrictionists decried the possibility of increasing the Jewish population. Even Franklin D. Roosevelt moved carefully in the face of such opposition. The president sympathized with the Jews, directed American consuls in Europe to do all that was legally possible to aid political refugees, and called for an international conference on the problem to meet at Evian, France, in June 1938. But Roosevelt's unwillingness to challenge the quota laws and his envoy's announcement of the U.S. position that each nation had to respond to the crisis within the terms of its own immigration regulations insured that the Evian conference would do nothing except issue a statement of principle.

The anti-Semitic core of America's resistance to accepting refugees became ever more clear as the situation of European Jewry disintegrated in the final months of peacetime. In the wake of Hitler's annexation of Austria and the intensification of the anti-Jewish terror campaign, beginning with the *Kristallnacht* of November 1938, liberal political leaders, philanthropists, and clergymen from all faiths endorsed a proposal to admit 20,000 German youths as nonquota immigrants. Most of these boys and girls were of the Jewish religion; others were Christians of Jewish ethnic stock. In the Congress, Democratic Senator Robert F. Wagner of New York and Republican Representative Edith Nourse Rogers of Massachusetts introduced a bill embodying this idea. Unlike some refugee programs, this one enjoyed support from labor and the newspapers. Nevertheless, opponents were able to derail the Wagner-Rogers bill with arguments that it was merely a wedge to be used against the quota system and a slight on the deserving poor youth of America. These objections, however, did not come up again when, in 1940, Congress did all in its power to expedite a tentative plan to bring 15,000 ethnically acceptable English children to the safety of the United States for the duration of the war.

World War II and its aftermath created several major problems for American immigration policy, but the country managed to find responses that kept intact its practices of strictly limiting the issuance of entry visas and of discriminating on the basis of national origin among the applicants for admission. The most pressing problem during the war was guaranteeing an adequate labor supply for the nation. The fighting put people back to work, whether in the military, war industries, or other areas stimulated by the economic recovery. With the Depression defeated, the United States once more had room for unskilled men and women, especially in the agricultural sector, which had lost laborers to the services and to more lucrative employments just when wartime needs called for an expansion of production. Inasmuch as parallel developments across the Atlantic and the hardships of travel in wartime had dried up the pool of potential immigrants from Europe, the United States became again willing to welcome an influx of Latin Americans. In 1941 the U.S. government asked Mexico to help it recruit temporary workers among the Mexican citizenry. Although stung by past slights, the Mexicans agreed to cooperate, especially after their country joined the Allied effort against the Nazis. They demanded, however, that the United States act upon their long-standing call for protection of Mexicans working north of the border. Accordingly, in 1942, the two governments agreed that the United States would pay a large share of the costs of the recruiting, which Mexico would actually carry out, and that Americans would furnish round-trip transportation and support for the workers selected. In addition, the governments agreed that the Mexicans, once in the United States, would be draft exempt, would not be used to displace American workers or force down their pay, and would receive guarantees concerning wages and living conditions. More than 200,000 temporary Mexican immigrants actually entered the United States under this program between 1942 and 1947. The vast majority of these *braceros* went to the Southwest, where over half of them were employed in California agriculture. Of the remainder, most worked as farm laborers in other states or in unskilled railroading jobs.

The *bracero* program of World War II appeared to offer the United States a means of recruiting cheap, short-term labor without encouraging large numbers of men and women judged inferior by the general population to become permanent immigrants with rights to make claims on the country's welfare system. The wartime arrangement ended in 1947; however, after fitful negotiations and several brief agreements, the United States and Mexico reached a new understanding during the manpower crisis created by the Korean conflict. Public Law 78, passed in 1951, stipulated that the American secretary of labor would have the authority to declare when *braceros* were needed, to undertake their recruitment and importation, and to enforce contracts that would guarantee them employment at prevailing wages for periods ranging from six weeks to six months. Conservative Republicans and Democrats, most of whom had strong agricultural constituencies, kept the law alive long past the original two-year limit, and approximately 4.3 million *braceros* entered the United States before PL 78 finally expired at the end of 1964. Long before that date, however, the abuse of workers supposedly protected by the act and the massive growth of undocumented immigration across the Rio Grande made it clear that PL

78 had outlived its usefulness as a means of controlling the movement of unskilled laborers across the U.S.-Mexican border.

After the war, the major immigration problem facing the United States became the presence in occupied Europe of about 5 million permanently displaced persons. Approximately 1 million of them were Slavs and Jews dispersed through West Germany, Austria, and Italy. Some of these refugees had been brought to the West by the Nazis and some had survived the concentration camps; others had simply fled combat zones or escaped their countries in the wake of Communist takeovers. The remaining 4 million were ethnic Germans, or *Volksdeutsche,* repatriated by the terms of the Potsdam Agreement from their longtime homes in Czechoslovakia, Hungary, and Poland. In 1946 President Harry S. Truman reserved half of the appropriate European immigration quotas for displaced persons, but he soon realized that this step was not enough to help many or to relieve the burden the refugees were placing on the already ravaged economies of their temporary homes. The following year, the president, with the support of liberal groups like the Citizens Committee on Displaced Persons, proposed that the United States take in a sizable number of these unfortunates as nonquota immigrants. The idea, embodied in a plan by Representative William Stratton of Illinois to admit 400,000 persons over a four-year period, encountered bitter opposition. Organized labor favored the measure, but veterans' organizations claimed that the newcomers would adversely affect American workers. Conservatives argued that the United States had no moral obligation to the refugees and particularly to those who fled west after the fighting had ended. Indeed, they warned that Communist agents had probably infiltrated the ranks of the later arrivals. Finally, in 1948, the Republican dominated Eightieth Congress agreed to allow the entry of as many as 202,000 displaced adults. The lawmakers demanded, however, that only those who had reached refugee camps before the end of 1945 be admitted; that at least 40 percent of the places be reserved for Baltic natives, who would face Russian persecution if they returned home; and that the number of persons of each nationality allowed to enter be charged against future annual national quotas, but not against more than half of the visas to be issued for any single year.

America's refugee policy became somewhat more liberal in the ensuing years. In 1950 the Congress amended and expanded the Displaced Persons Act, but without abandoning the required mortgaging of future annual quotas. The lawmakers deferred the cutoff date for eligibility until January 1, 1949; eliminated the 40 percent perference for persons from annexed countries; raised to approximately 341,000 the total number of refugees to be allowed entrance; doubled from 27,377 to 54,744 the contingent of repatriated *Volksdeutsche* to be admitted; and created places for immigrants in additional categories, including Greek, Italian, and Polish refugees and veterans. Under President Dwight D. Eisenhower, the Congress in 1953 agreed to authorize nonquota visas for 60,000 Italians, 55,000 Germans, 45,000 escapees from Iron Curtain countries, and 45,000 other persons; in addition, all of these were permitted to bring their spouses and unmarried minor children.

The demise of the conservative Eightieth Congress helps explain this modest change of policy, but other, deeper forces were also influential. World War II taught Americans that combating totalitarianism required their cooperation with peoples they had scorned. As early as 1943 the United States, in order to refute Japanese propaganda about American racism, dropped its prohibition against Chinese immigration and allotted America's Asian allies an annual quota of 105 visas. The war also demonstrated the depravity to which unbridled racism could lead and, in the ashes of the Holocaust, the American nation began to redress its own concessions to anti-Semitism. The conditions of the postwar world confirmed the lessons learned in the conflict, and the immigration policy of the United States became increasingly intermeshed with its hope of containing the Soviet Union and communism. The formerly derided peoples of central and southern Europe became valued allies, and restrictionists became as concerned with the political philosophy of would-be immigrants as with their ethnic background. Indeed, in a landmark enactment in 1950, the Congress passed, over President Truman's veto, the sweeping Internal Security Act, which declared present and past members of Communist and Fascist organizations ineligible for admission to the United States and made resident aliens with such ties liable to deportation.

Concessions to the exigencies of the late 1940s and early 1950s did not constitute a disavowal of earlier ideals of sharply limited immigration and of quotas distributed according to ethnically discriminatory criteria. Few persons continued to proclaim boldly that groups allotted low quotas were racially or genetically inferior. But restrictionists were content to argue that such peoples were so culturally different from the American population that they could not successfully blend into it as immigrants. In 1950 the Senate Judiciary Committee, headed by Nevada's Democratic Senator Pat McCarran, himself a second-generation Irish Catholic, confirmed this position in the first major report done on immigration in four decades. The committee's findings became the basis for the Immigration and Nationality Act, passed, over President Truman's veto, in 1952. The McCarran-Walter Act, as this law became known, continued the existing system of quotas and incorporated Asia into the plan by assigning approximately 100 visas to each nation in the region and by setting aside an extra hundred visas for the geographic area defined in the act as the Asia-Pacific triangle. The law abandoned race as a bar to immigration and naturalization but continued to treat European and Asian applicants for visas differently. The former, regardless of their genetic background, fit under the quotas assigned to the countries from which they emigrated; the latter came under those reserved for their countries of ethnic origin or under the special set of 100 reserved for the whole triangle.

Other features of the McCarran-Walter Act made noteworthy changes in the Reed-Johnson Act of 1924 but did not affect the basic goal of limiting the flow of immigrants to America and regulating the composition of this influx. Most important, the new measure revised the preference order for applicants. Would-be immigrants possessing skills needed in the United States could claim up to half the visas assigned to each country, and immediate relatives of American citizens or of aliens legally residing in the United States had first call on the remainder. A person in a lower, or nonpreference, category could obtain a visa only if his or her country's quota was undersubscribed.

The immigration policies developed and amplified in the United States between the 1920s and the 1950s fit in well with those put into effect in the other major receiving countries in the same era. Australia, for example, manipulated its Dictation Test and used incentives, such as subsidized passages offered after World War II to veterans from the United Kingdom and the United States, to guarantee that English-speaking people would continue to be preponderant among immigrants to the continent. Argentina carefully selected among applicants for admission to give preference to those with needed occupational skills or ties to the Spanish, Italian, Portuguese, German, and Swiss communities already well established in that country. Brazil implemented quotas in 1934 for all nationalities except the Portuguese. When the system, which made allotments on the basis of 2 percent of the cumulative total average of each nationality present in the country from 1883 to 1934, proved too generous to the Japanese, the Brazilians counterattacked by severely limiting the admission of unskilled laborers. Canada eschewed numerical limitations and quotas but nevertheless sought to discourage the same groups restricted by the United States. Starting in 1923, Canada allowed open access only to American, British, and Irish citizens. Among other groups only agriculturalists, farm laborers, and female domestic servants were eligible for admission; Asians in these categories also had to have $250. During the Depression the only persons from nonpreferred groups allowed to enter were agriculturalists with enough capital to establish and maintain farms. After World War II, Canada extended open admission to persons born either in France or in certain French possessions; added persons with experience in mining, lumbering, or logging to those eligible from the nonpreferred nationalities; authorized the entry of men and women intending to marry legal residents; and eased some of restrictions against the entry of Chinese and other Asian immigrants. Nevertheless, the general policy remained restrictive and an order-in-council of 1950 defended the propriety of excluding potential immigrants thought to display "probable inability to become readily adapted and integrated into the life of a Canadian community and to assume the duties of Canadian citizenship."

America's decision to reduce the influx of transoceanic immigrants to U.S. shores marked a turning point in the history of the nation's population. Determining the exact impact of the restrictive program and measuring the success of the quota system are difficult tasks. Only 1,873,479 immigrants, including 388,818 persons eligible outside the quota limits, arrived in the United States from quota countries between 1925 and 1948. That number actually fell short of the 1,879,815 landing in America from the same areas between 1920 and 1924, when numerical ceilings were first used, and of the 2,183,877 coming in 1913 and 1914, on the eve of World War I. The Reed-Johnson Act undoubtedly contributed to the reduction, but the Depression and World War II also worked to discourage immigration. Indeed, only 22.5 percent of the 2,306,709 visas available for quota immigrants between 1930 and 1944 were used. In a similar fashion, the national origin provisions of the legislation did change the composition of the immigrant traffic but not to the extent that the restrictionists had hoped. Between 1924 and 1946 northern and western Europe provided 43.1 percent of America's immigrants; southern and eastern Europe, 18.9 percent; Canada and Newfoundland, 21.5 percent; Mexico, 11.5 percent; and an assortment of other countries in Latin America, Asia, Africa, and the Pacific, 5.0 percent. The corresponding figures from 1900 to 1910, the last uninterrupted decade of the new immigration, had been 21.7 percent, 70.8 percent, 2.0 percent .6 percent, and 4.9 percent. Thanks, however, both to the existence of the nonquota preference categories in the Reed-Johnson Act and to the demographic and economic realities of the world, the reversal was not as great as restrictionists might have hoped. Between 1925 and 1948 southern and eastern Europeans outnumbered northern and western Europeans by a margin of 247,918 to 102,359 simply because the former were more likely than the latter to have immediate relatives among America's new immigrant population. Likewise, the decision of northern and western Europeans to use under 40 percent of the quotas available to them in the same years had the effect of raising the less favored peoples' share of the restricted traffic to an actual 23 percent instead of the originally intended 17 percent.

One fact is certain. The decline in immigration after 1920 deprived the foreign-stock people resident in the United States, and especially southern and eastern European immigrants, of the reinforcement previously provided their cultures by the constant influx of newcomers from abroad. Accordingly, these people became much more vulnerable to the society's conscious efforts to absorb them. From the very beginning of the new immigration in the late nineteenth century, most native-stock citizens had been convinced of the need rapidly to Americanize the aliens spilling into the nation's cities. The word, however, had various connotations. For the social activists who moved into immigrant neighborhoods and established settlement houses, the term meant giving the newcomers the wherewithal to survive in a modern industrial society. They tried to teach those who came to their settlement houses English, American social customs, and, when necessary, the rudiments of household management, health care, and sanitation. The best of those reformers, including the renowned Jane Addams of Chicago, performed their work without purposefully assaulting the immigrants' native cultures. On the other hand, more conservative advocates of Americanization increasingly interpreted their primary objective to be neutralizing the newcomers' potentially subversive impact on the nation's political and economic systems. Patriotic organizations, like the Sons and Daughters of the American Revolution, preached to immigrant audiences about responsible voting and obedience to law. With the outbreak of industrial strikes in Lawrence, Massachusetts, in 1912, the North American Civic League for Immigrants, which had been founded in 1908 by a group of New England businessmen, deemphasized the paternalistic aspects of its original program and concentrated on spreading the message of anti-unionism and antiradicalism among the newcomers.

Proponents of 100 percent Americanism often looked to education as the key to eradicating alien cultures. In the years before World War I Henry Ford established a compulsory English school for his foreign workers and the Saxon Motor Company likewise required its non-English-speaking employees to attend language classes at night. For a five-year-period beginning in 1915, wealthy friends of the social activist Frances Kellor subsidized, within the federal Bureau of Education, a Division of Immigrant Education, which encouraged schools across the nation to establish special Americanization programs. Teachers proved willing participants in such endeavors, and state governments, especially during and after the war years, provided new funds for educating immigrants. Numerous school districts instituted or increased night classes in which foreign students could learn English and gain enough knowledge of American government to acquire citizenship. Instructors in daytime classes began to grade children on their level of acculturation, as measured by behavior in school. And state legislatures established more stringent compulsory attendance laws to insure that children receive adequate exposure to the assimilative influences of the schools.

Before the imposition of general restrictions on the volume of immigration, perhaps the only Americanization tactics to have had a visible effect were the blatantly repressive actions taken during World War I against the propagation of German culture in the United States. These measures, which have already been discussed, did not directly inculcate an American culture. They did, however, undermine the only European group that had ever enjoyed the numerical strength, prosperity, high racial status, and ties to a powerful homeland needed to sustain in the United States a culture competitive with the British. It is debatable whether the assortment of ongoing peacetime Americanization programs would have achieved their intended effect had immigration returned after 1920 to prewar levels. Even sympathetic judges of the settlement house movement admit that an enormous cultural gap separated the upper middle-class, well-educated, native-stock Protestants who operated the centers from the immigrant populations served by them. Most academic accounts of the movement's impact take an institutional point of view, stressing the programs offered and the participants involved. But recognizing the unknown number of people who, by circumstance or choice, lived beyond the houses' reach might provide just as informative a perspective. In addition, recent investigations of public school operations at the beginning of the twentieth century have demythologized the role of these authoritative, ubiquitous agencies as positive acculturative forces. Apparently, as late as the mid-1940s, approximately two-thirds of New York City residents over twenty-five years of age had spent only eight or fewer years in school.

Whatever impact programs consciously designed to Americanize may have had, they could not match the acculturative effect that the passage of time exerted on the foreign-stock population of the United States. With the influx of aliens significantly reduced by law, the Depression, and war, each new decade sped along the process that changed the country's immigrant groups into ethnic groups. Demographic changes consequent upon the decline in immigration aged the nation's foreign-stock population. The median age of first- and second-generation Americans rose from 16 years in 1890 to almost 25 years in 1930; that of longer established white groups increased from 21 years to 23 years during the same period. By 1950 the median age of the foreign stock, almost 37 years, exceeded that of the native population by more than a decade. The excess of deaths over arrivals inevitably reduced the number of immigrants in the population. Russian-born residents of the United States reached their numerical peak in 1920, while those born in Italy or Poland achieved theirs a decade later. At mid-century the contingents of Americans born in Ireland and Germany were only 32 percent and 37 percent, respectively, of the size they had been in 1900. The foreign-stock population became increasingly composed of the children of immigrants, plus an untold number of third- and later generation persons who were classified by the census as having native origins. Between 1910 and 1950 the proportion of second-generation members in the Italian population of the United States rose from roughly 37 to 71 percent; in the Polish-American community, from 44 to 71 percent; and in the Russian-American community, from 40 to 65 percent. Thus, as the United States faced the second half of the twentieth century, its foreign-stock population was composed overwhelmingly of people who had spent their entire lives or at least all their adult years in America. Moreover, for these men and women the experiences they shared in the neighborhoods of urban America, in the Great Depression, and in the two world wars combined with the traditions of their homelands to shape their identities and values.

In the repressive cultural environment of the postwar years, the drying up of the immigrant stream and the consequent gradual diminution of the size of the foreign-born population greatly reduced the number of people in the United States who claimed mother tongues other than English. After reaching a highpoint of 10,844,151 with the 1930 census, the count of foreign-born residents whose first language was not English fell to 8,354,700 in 1940 and to 7,176,280 in 1960. A similar pattern emerged among second-generation Americans. Between 1910 and 1920 the number of native-born citizens who had at least one foreign-born parent and who claimed a non-English primary language rose one-third, from 12,027,437 to 15,951,601. Over the next two decades this number fell one-third, to 10,712,480. Benefiting by their late arrival, some southern and eastern European groups, like the Poles and the Italians, managed modest increases in this category between 1920 and 1940, but most other nationalities suffered devastating losses. The number of second-generation claimants of German, for example, skidded almost 60 percent, from 5,896,983 to 2,435,700. The withering of the foreign-language communities became indisputable at the level of the third and later generations. By 1940, out of a total of some 84 million persons described in the census as "native whites of native white parentage," fewer than 3 million reported a non-English mother tongue. Indeed, after World War II, even the simple retention of foreign-language skills seemed possible only among the most recent arrivals and in certain isolated, homogeneous, rural communities composed of old immigrant Germans and Scandinavians.

Across the nation leaders of ethnic communities attributed the declining use of foreign languages not only to the passing of the first generation but also to a lack of interest among the second and later generations in any tongue except English. For younger Americans of foreign stock, non-English languages were tools needed to communicate with their elders and with newcomers from overseas. As demographic changes reduced the need for these instruments, practicality demanded that the children and grandchildren of immigrants give priority to learning and using the language of the host country. Moreover, for foreign-stock Americans non-English tongues were a symbol of their isolation from the mainstream of the society. Disuse of these languages among second-generation Americans also reflected a general rejection of the ways of their parents. This aversion was inevitable and psychologically necessary for the second generation because they could not fulfill the immigrants' hope of re-creating the Old World in the New. No matter how hard they might try, these young men and women could not completely belong to the cultures of their parents; too much of their experience was rooted in America.

Reduction in the number of Americans with primary languages other than English removed or at least minimized the most obvious evidence of the heterogeneous ethnic and cultural origins of the Euro-American population. This trend also had practical consequences that worked against the preservation of Old World cultures and the maintenance of exclusive ethnic communities. One study has shown that between 1920 and 1960 the number of daily newspapers in non-English languages declined by 57 percent: German dailies, which had accounted for over half of the foreign-language papers published in 1910, amounted to only 7 percent of the total in 1960; daily newspapers in Scandinavian languages had disappeared entirely by 1960; and even those publications associated with new immigrant tongues were fading rapidly. Likewise, the use of foreign languages in religious services and in church operated schools became less common. From America's entry into World War I until the outbreak of World War II, the proportion of Lutheran churches in the Norwegian Synod that employed English rose from less than 30 percent to approximately 90 percent. Between the mid-1920s and the mid-1930s the percentage of Lutheran day schools in the Missouri Synod that used only German in religious instruction fell from 17 to 2 and the percentage employing English alone rose from 45 to 83. By 1960 under a quarter of the ethnic parishes of the Catholic and Orthodox churches were relying more on foreign languages than on English in sermons and fewer than a third of them offered mother-tongue instruction in their parochial schools.

As English became the first language of almost all Americans, a major barrier to the intermingling of the key ethnic groups with each other and with the native stock disintegrated. Passing this critical point on the road to acculturation, however, did not constitute a signal that complete assimilation was imminent. In reality, the situation of most second-generation Americans was terribly awkward. Just as their birth and life in the United States prevented them from empathizing entirely with the cultures of their parents, so also their nurture in the homes of immigrants partly cut them off from their longer established fellow citizens. Even those young men and women who, with or without the support of their immigrant parents, claimed to want to achieve thorough Americanization could rarely, if ever, achieve that goal. They neither knew what beliefs and forms of behavior full assimilation entailed nor had adequate personal contact with mainstream Americans, from whose attitudes and actions they might have taken cues. Moreover, very few of them wanted or would have wanted to endure the divorce from family and heritage that total assimilation might have entailed. Most members of the second generation were permanently caught between two cultures. In these circumstances, many of them consciously or unconsciously sought a level of assimilation that allowed them to feel American while remaining in the good graces of their ethnic communities. Some took the path of almost passively accepting the dual identity of the hyphenate while they generally dismissed the importance of their foreign background in forming either their personalities or the society's response to them. Others vigorously identified with the United States and even clashed openly with their peers and parents over relatively minor issues such as the value of languages other than English. But, regardless of their attitudes, almost all tended to remain firmly among their own people in fundamentally important matters such as choosing friends and spouses. To the first group this behavior seemed to signal nothing except accidents of neighborhood life. For the second the lack of outside contacts was more frustrating, but it allowed them to have the fantasy of being Americans without requiring too great a price for this status.

The history of America's Jews between the world wars clearly exemplifies the search for an intermediate path that would facilitate participation in the broader community without complete loss of a separate identity. The most economically mobile people ever to come to the United States, the Jews by the 1930s were quickly becoming a middle-class collection of business people, white-collar workers, and professionals. By that time, more than half of them had abandoned the Lower East Side and other crowded immigrant districts in favor of more comfortable communities, in which they were often surrounded by Christian neighbors. Many of them left behind in the poverty of the ghetto the religious orthodoxy of the first generation. Distinctive modes of dress and grooming faded from use; a variety of ritualistic practices, including the postmenstrual bath, virtually disappeared; and, perhaps most important, observance of the *kashruth,* or dietary laws that served to isolate Jews in their social contacts, also weakened. But in religious matters most of the progeny of the new immigrants did not follow the precedent of the super-Westernized Germans of the old immigration, whose Reform Judaism attempted to obliterate most distinctive rites and festivals, as well as messianic expectations and dreams of a Palestinian homeland. Especially in areas without a Reform temple, the Jews of the new immigration developed an amorphous, pragmatic Conservative Judaism, which reflected the needs of lay men and women desirous of balancing public involvement in a gentile society with their private identities as Jews. Conservative synagogues, like Reform temples, operated in English and transformed rabbis, who did not play the principal role in Orthodox congregations, into liturgical leaders like Protestant ministers and Catholic priests. Moreover, the Conservative synagogues allowed female participation in religious services, which emphasized decorous, well-ordered ceremonies. In contrast with Reform Jews, however, the Conservatives maintained traditional holy days and prayers and encouraged the preservation of convenient elements of Mosaic law. Most important, the Conservatives—as their foremost spokesman, Mordecai Kaplan, urged—made their synagogues centers for social and cultural activities that emphasized the ethnic, as well as the religious, dimensions of Judaism. In this respect, the Conservatives, while avoiding the complete parochial apparatus of the Catholics, took the critical step toward creating a community that would foster the preservation of a distinct Jewish secular and religious civilization within the United States.

After the mid-1920s politics offered foreign-stock Americans an increasingly important opportunity to participate in the broader society. In the political arena each ethnic group became able, without seriously risking cultural contamination or the loss of its identity, to forge ties with other nationalities and to pursue mutually desirable ends. By 1940 most members of the largest new immigrant groups had become citizens. According to that year's census, 59.7 percent of first-generation Poles were naturalized; the comparable figures for Italians and natives of Russia were 62.5 percent and 69.6 percent. Among males in these groups, the percentages were even higher, reaching 68.0, 71.1, and 75.7, respectively. Of course, members of the second and later generations enjoyed citizenship and the vote as their birthright. The growth and changing composition of the foreign-stock electorate called to the fore a new breed of non-Irish ethnic politicians, the first cohort of whom was achieving national prominence by the 1930s. Fiorello La Guardia was perhaps the best known of these men.

Born in New York City in 1882 and raised on army posts in the West, La Guardia was the son of a lapsed Catholic Italian father and a Jewish mother. The couple raised their son as an Episcopalian. La Guardia eventually returned to New York, where he became a reform-minded and politically ambitious attorney. He rejected the Irish dominated Tammany Hall democracy to join the Republican party and in 1916 won election as the first Republican congressman from the Lower East Side since the Civil War. In and out of Congress during the following years, La Guardia established a strong liberal record and in 1933 won election as mayor of New York on a fusion ticket committed to cleaning up the city's government. He won reelection in 1937 and 1941 and during his twelve-year tenure in city hall became a powerful and beloved figure. Concentrating on La Guardia, however, can be misleading. The "Little Flower," who worked hand in glove with Franklin D. Roosevelt's New Deal, was a maverick in his own party. La Guardia's popularity was personal and his career was perhaps not as relevant as that of a contemporary, Anton Cermak of Chicago, to the overall development of ethnic politics in this period.

Fiorello La Guardia may have been the era's best-known ethnic politician, but Anton Cermak was its premier practitioner of ethnic politics. Cermak's career was cut short, he lacked La Guardia's flair, and as Chicago's mayor he missed out on the publicity bestowed automatically on New York's chief executive. But Cermak's legacy was the modern, multi-ethnic Chicago Democratic machine. Born in Bohemia in 1873 to Protestant parents, Cermak arrived in America before his first birthday. He eventually became a self-employed businessman in Chicago and entered the Democratic party under the wing of two Irish leaders, George E. Brennan and Roger Sullivan. In 1922 Cermak won election to the chairmanship of the Cook County Board of Commissioners. During the years that followed he shrewdly used patronage and appeals aimed at a broad spectrum of Chicago's national groups to build a strong political organization. Backed by the Czechs, the Jews, and Irish dissidents allied with Alderman Patrick Nash, Cermak took over the Democratic party after Brennan's death in 1928, even though the deceased leader had wanted his mantle to go to another Irish-American. In the 1930 county election the Czech politician headed a Democratic slate that included a German, an Irishman, an Italian, and a Pole; the balanced ticket signaled the end of the era in which the party had been completely under the control of a single group. Cermak reached the pinnacle of his power in 1931, when he won election as mayor of Chicago. Less than two years later he was dead, the unintended victim of a bullet fired at his political ally, President-elect Franklin Delano Roosevelt.

The association of Cermak and Roosevelt was a fitting symbol of another major change that took place in ethnic politics after the mid-1920s, the alignment of the great nationality groups under the aegis of the national Democratic party. For many decades before the 1920s the Democrats had possessed, at the level of local politics, a stronger reputation than the Republicans had enjoyed as friends of the foreign born and their offspring. The same claim could not be made at the national level without serious qualifications. In the Congress the Republicans pandered to their native, rural, Protestant constituents and castigated their opponents as excessively pro-alien and pro-Catholic. But although northeastern Democrats provided the foreign stock with their only consistent base of support in Washington, their party was not identified on a national scale with the country's immigrant and ethnic groups. During the time of William Jennings Bryan's prominence, at the turn of the twentieth century, the Democrats displayed little interest in the foreign born and even less understanding of the urban milieu in which these strangers and their descendants lived. Given control of the White House, the party, thanks to Woodrow Wilson's foreign policy during his second term, dissipated its major reservoirs of support among the foreign population. And in the bitter days of the early 1920s, the party gave signs of falling under the sway of the racists, bigots, and xenophobes in its powerful southern wing. In 1924, this bloc persuaded the Democratic national convention not to denounce the activities of the Ku Klux Klan.

The Democratic party became the national voice of ethnic Americans only with the rise of Alfred E. Smith. Born on the Lower East Side of Manhattan in 1873, Smith was himself a representative of the special kind of assimilation occurring in America. Smith's paternal grandfather was Italian and his paternal grandmother, German; his maternal grandfather was an Irish Catholic and his maternal grandmother, an Anglo-Irish Protestant who converted to her husband's faith. Nevertheless, Smith's identity always remained that of an Irish Catholic off the streets of New York. Orphaned at the age of twelve, he dropped out of school in the eighth grade and took a series of jobs before finally settling down at a boiler manufacturing plant in Brooklyn. Popular and talented, Smith entered politics as a Tammany Democrat, won election to the assembly in 1903 and became speaker of that body in 1913. Despite his machine connections, Smith earned a reputation for honesty and a sincere interest in alleviating the sufferings of the poor and of the working class. He won election to a two-year term as governor of New York in 1918 and came back after a loss in 1920 to hold that post again between 1923 and 1929. Smith vied with Wilson's son-in-law, William Gibbs McAdoo, for the Democratic presidential nomination in 1924, but the disastrously divided convention, after 103 ballots, finally chose the little-known John W. Davis. Four years later, however, the party was ready for Smith. But the challenge of running against the popular, respected nominee of an incumbent party during prosperous times proved unenviable and Smith lost to Herbert Hoover in the November election. Moreover, opposition to Smith's Catholicism, East Side origins, and stand against prohibition undoubtedly made the defeat worse that it would have been otherwise. Nevertheless, the candidacy of this most ethnic of Americans succeeded in galvanizing politically the foreign-stock population. Italians and Germans, although often at odds with the Irish, could support Smith as a wet, and Jews could identify with him as a victim of religious bigotry. Even blacks, who had formed a solidly Republican group since Reconstruction, showed sympathy for the governor who virtually banned the Klan in New York State.

Smith's candidacy drew a host of foreign-stock Americans to the national Democratic party. He won more popular votes than had any previous Democratic presidential candidate and carried the country's twelve largest cities, which, of course, were centers of immigrant and ethnic strength. Between 1924 and 1928 the Democrats' share of the presidential vote in New York County rose from 40 to 61 percent; it rose from 36 to 67 percent in the Boston metropolitan area; from 10 to 54 percent around Milwaukee; from 10 to 51 percent around St. Paul; and from 7 to 37 percent around Detroit. Chicago's ethnics also shifted their allegiance to the Democratic presidential candidate between the elections of 1924 and 1928. Support for that party's nominee rose from 35 to 71 percent among the Poles, from 31 to 63 percent among the Italians, from 19 to 63 percent among the Jews, and from 14 to 58 percent among the Germans. The Protestant Swedes and the blacks remained Republican, but the Democrats did manage to increase their share of the former's vote from 15 to 34 percent and of the latter's from 10 to 23 percent. The Depression undermined Republican hopes of recouping their losses among the ethnics, and Franklin Delano Roosevelt's campaign in 1932 and his performance thereafter solidified the reputation of foreign-stock Americans as presidential Democrats. In 1932 the white ethnic groups gave Roosevelt a greater share of their votes than they had given Smith, and even the Swedes edged into the Democratic column. Chicago's blacks, who cast just 21 percent of their ballots for FDR in 1932, joined the Democratic fold by the next national election.

As a result of America's patent hostility during the 1920s and 1930s to the preservation of ethnic diversity, the demographic consequences of immigration restriction, and the increasing economic and political integration of the foreign-stock groups into the national mainstream, the United States was able to approach World War II with fewer real worries than had existed on the eve of the first global conflict about the potential impact of European events on the American population. The change was most evident in the case of the German-Americans. Through the interwar period both reputable German scholars and Nazi party leaders continued to think that the German population in the United States remained physically and culturally unassimilated, that this community was ready to take the leading social role appropriate to its large numbers and great talents, and that German-Americans would unite with their racial kin in the fatherland under the aegis of national socialism. Nevertheless, despite organizational and financial support from abroad, pro-Nazi movements were unable to gain a serious foothold among Americans of German descent. The existence of the German-American Bund, which from 1936 was the key Nazi group in the United States, naturally caused concern among American authorities, but this body's membership probably never exceeded 20,000 persons, and most of them had come to the United States after World War I.

Italian-Americans were initially more impressed than German-Americans with the goals and accomplishments of Europe's postwar totalitarian movements. Immigrants or persons in intimate contact with members of the first generation made up a large portion of the Italian population in the United States, and they stood much lower than the long established Germans in the esteem of most Americans. Defined as inferior by their fellow Americans, many Italians took pride in Italy's Fascist regime, which seemed capable of propelling the backward land of their ancestors into the modern world. Italo-Americans were not alone in this view. According to public opinion polls, many people in the United States, especially among the Catholic population and among the prosperous members of other religions, looked upon Mussolini's fascism as a preferable counterweight to the supposedly greater menaces posed by Hitler's nazism and Stalin's communism. Nevertheless, a substantial core of Italian opposition to Mussolini, personified in La Guardia and the labor radical Carlo Tresca, existed from the 1920s in the United States. This movement gained strength in the late 1930s, and Italo-American support for fascism slackened as Mussolini made war in Albania, Ethiopia, and Spain, publicly endorsed the anti-Semitism and racist philosophies of the Nazis, and formally aligned with Germany. By the eve of America's entry into the European war, even formerly stalwart supporters of Mussolini, including Generoso Pope's influential newspaper, *Il Progresso Italo-Americano*, had abandoned the Fascist cause.

As the likelihood of entry into the war against the Axis increased and finally turned into a reality, the country's concerns narrowed from generalized worries about the loyalty of foreign-stock European-Americans to specific fears related to the presence within the existing population of aliens from hostile countries and of apparently unassimilable ethnic and racial groups. According to the 1940 census 1,237,772 German, 1,623,580 Italian, and 126,947 Japanese nationals lived in the United States. In that year the Congress, through the Alien Registration Act, ordered that they and all other resident aliens begin annually to report their addresses to the government. At approximately the same time, President Roosevelt transferred the Immigration and Naturalization Service from the Labor Department to the Justice Department. Within the latter agency, the Federal Bureau of Investigation assumed responsibility for uncovering and thwarting subversion, and in this connection the FBI began gathering information about the leaders of ethnic organizations that maintained close ties with Axis countries or governments. These measures, although potentially dangerous to civil liberties, were inherently neither unreasonable nor intolerable. Indeed, advocates of them could argue that the federal government's moderate preventative steps discouraged radical actions by state and local authorities and by vigilantes. Unfortunately, when the warfare actually began, Washington's program became much more severe and reflected the impact more of past internal tensions than of immediate external dangers.

The attack on Pearl Harbor in December 1941 shocked the United States. Residents of the West Coast, although 3,000 miles from the Hawaiian Islands, fantasized that bombardment or invasion was imminent. The government quickly arrested 16,000 allegedly dangerous aliens, and civic, military, and political authorities gave thought to relocating all nationals of Axis countries then residing near key defense installations and factories. But the popular temper gradually changed. The threat of an immediate attack on California passed; the government released about two-thirds of the aliens initially detained; and the main focus of concern shifted from Axis citizens in general to Japanese residents in particular. Germans and Italians aroused less hostility and were less attractive targets than Japanese. The former were spread across the country; the latter were tightly concentrated in the West, and especially in California. The German and Italian elements of the population were numerically large and politically articulate; witnesses at congressional hearings held early in 1942 in California on the disposition of enemy alien populations strongly opposed any punitive action against these groups. The Japanese, by contrast, were few in number and historically unpopular, as the same hearings confirmed. Most important, the Germans and Italians were Europeans while the Japanese were Asians. Persons of Japanese birth, as nonwhites, were ineligible for naturalization according to the prevailing constitutional interpretation, and Tokyo's recent surprise attack had confirmed all the negative racial stereotypes antecedent and consequent to that viewpoint. Moreover, the white citizenry's fear and distrust of the Japanese extended not only to the immigrant generation but also to their American-born descendants. Despite the Constitution's guarantee of citizenship to all natives of the United States, many people refused to accord to Japanese-Americans the same protections and presumptions of loyalty that they gave Germans and Italians of the second or later generations.

During the first quarter of 1942 a consensus formed around the necessity of removing Japanese residents, regardless of their place of nativity, from strategic areas on the West Coast. John L. DeWitt, the lieutenant general in charge of the Western Defense Command, was antipathetic toward the Japanese and worried that he, like Lieutenant General Walter C. Short in Hawaii, might be caught unprepared by a surprise attack. DeWitt favored a relocation program but vacillated on its scope and finally called for a policy that would have relocated as many Germans and Italians as Japanese. But the army's provost marshall, Major General Allen W. Gullion, and the chief of his aliens division, Major Karl R. Bendetsen, singled out the Japanese as especially dangerous, and western public opinion reinforced their position. California's Democratic governor, Culbert Olsen, and a number of Republicans, including Attorney General Earl Warren, Senator Hiram W. Johnson, and Congressman Leland Ford, spoke out against the Japanese, as did Mayor Fletcher Bowron of Los Angeles and major elements of the media such as the *Los Angeles Times.* In the nation's capital, Secretary of War Henry L. Stimson favored sequestration and his assistant secretary, John J. McCloy, argued that considerations of national security negated any constitutional scruples about forcibly uprooting American-born Japanese. In the Justice Department, Thomas C. Clark, the West Coast coordinator of the Alien Enemy Program and a future member of the Supreme Court, worked to undercut Attorney General Francis Biddle's opposition to relocating Japanese-Americans. President Franklin D. Roosevelt, who shared his countrymen's stereotypes of the Japanese, found it easier to accommodate than to oppose this coalition. On February 19, 1942, FDR signed Executive Order No. 9066, which authorized the secretary of war and military commanders selected by him to designate military areas and to exclude any or all persons from them. This sweeping order could have been used to require the relocation of any citizen or alien, but it actually was used only against the Japanese population in the United States. Acting under that order, the army removed 110,000 Japanese nationals (Issei) and Japanese-Americans (Nisei) from Alaska, the West Coast, and southern Arizona by August 1942.

The Japanese were dispersed first among twelve makeshift assembly centers, where some stayed as long as seven months. They were then divided among ten remote internment camps. Soon after these sites were filled, however, the government began administering loyalty tests to the Japanese. The critical questions called on males to pledge their willingness to accept military service and asked all adults to pledge their support of the United States and its war effort. Between 80 and 90 percent of Japanese adults answered affirmatively. Among those saying no, a large proportion were either Issei, who feared that affirmation would deprive them of their Japanese citizenship and leave them stateless, or Nisei, who resisted the thought of military induction. For those inmates who answered yes, the process of release began. The government allowed several thousand Nisei to go off to college, freed agricultural laborers to work in labor-hungry nonstrategic areas, and, beginning early in 1943, authorized Japanese to enter the military. About 33,000 Japanese eventually served in the war as interpreters, intelligence personnel, or combat soldiers in two segregated units, one of which, the 442nd Regimental Combat Team, won over 18,000 decorations. Finally convinced that the crisis was over, Washington announced on December 17, 1944, that the camps would close within a year; the Western Defense Command reopened the coastal states to the Japanese. The next day, the Supreme Court in the case known as *Ex parte Endo* declared that the War Relocation Authority, the agency in charge of the camps, had no right as a civil body to detain persons whose loyalty was not in doubt. As the war drew to a close, the Japanese began to drift back to their old homes to rebuild their lives. In later years the government offered to compensate the internees for lost real and personal property, but it is estimated that the reimbursement eventually amounted to less than 10 percent of the approximately $400 million claimed.

Although emotional ties of foreign-stock Americans to the Axis countries did not generate a dangerous fifth column during World War II, intergroup tensions of wholly domestic origin at least momentarily posed a threat to the war effort. In the spring and summer of 1943 major riots rooted in ethnic and racial antagonisms disrupted three key American cities. Early in June, soldiers and sailors roamed through Los Angeles beating Mexican-Americans. The ostensible objects of their wrath were second-generation, teenage hoodlums who proclaimed their membership in street gangs by dressing in zoot suits. But in many cases the victims' only offense was a Mexican-American appearance. Prompted by protests from the Mexican ambassador and Washington's worries about the Axis propaganda machine, military commanders around Los Angeles canceled passes and leaves and managed to bring the situation under control by the end of the second week of the month. Hardly a week later, however, rioting between whites and blacks tore apart Detroit. The fighting began on Sunday, June 20, at Belle Isle Park. Black teenagers, who had been previously barred from a white amusement area, initiated the trouble, but the brawling soon became general. About three-quarters of Detroit experienced mob violence before federal troops entered the city on Tuesday and restored order. The riots cost thirty-four lives in all; twenty-five of the victims were black, and of that number seventeen had been killed by the police. Later in the summer, on the evening of August 1, rioting erupted in New York City after a white policeman shot a black soldier who had interfered with his arrest of a woman in a Harlem hotel. The soldier's wound was super-ficial, but rumors of his death circulated, and soon rioters and looters filled the streets of the large Manhattan ghetto. Mayor La Guardia ordered taverns closed, dispatched thousands of policemen into Har-lem, and had the situation calm by morning. Six blacks died, but overall the riot in Harlem was much less serious than its Detroit predecessor had been. New York's leadership responded more quickly and the police showed great restraint. Moreover, the violence was confined to Harlem, was aimed mainly at property, and did not degenerate into direct confrontations between civilians.

Los Angeles, Detroit, and New York were the most notable hot spots of 1943, but smaller crises flared in Beaumont, Texas, and in Mobile, Alabama. Racial tension pervaded the nation. To a large extent the troubles reflected changes caused or accelerated by the war in the rela-tions between whites and minority groups. Perhaps the single most notable development was the resurgence of black migration out of rural areas of the South and into urban zones, especially in the North and West. After slackening during the Depression, the exodus from Dixie recovered its momentum and surpassed the numerical records estab-lished between 1910 and 1930. After 1935 the increased mechanization of southern agriculture combined with the crop-limiting programs in-troduced by the New Deal to lessen the demand for black farm laborers. This push soon joined with the pull of war related industrial expansion in the North to create an ideal environment for an internal migration that brought 750,000 blacks across state lines between 1940 and 1944. Overall, the South experienced a net out-migration of 1.6 million blacks in the 1940s. The demographic impact of this loss was remarkable: dur-ing this decade the South's share of America's black population fell from 77.0 to 68.0 percent, while the Northeast's increased from 10.6 to 13.4 percent; the Midwest's, from 11.0 to 14.8 percent; and the West's, from 1.3 to 3.8 percent.

To black leaders the move out of the South and into the war econ-omy appeared to be an opportunity for Afro-Americans to win one democratic victory for themselves at home while contributing to a sec-ond overseas. In many respects, however, the so-called Double V cam-paign proved a disappointment: blacks encountered in the North the very problems they had hoped to leave behind in the South. When they looked for housing, poverty and prejudice forced them to crowd into the ghettoes that had taken shape during the last great wave of migration. When blacks looked for work, discrimination and their lack of skills con-fined many of them to menial jobs unwanted by whites. Sometimes they found themselves in the midst of old foes; Detroit, for example, received an influx of 500,000 white southerners, as well as 50,000 black ones, during the first years of the war. Official insensitivity stung the black community not only in cities like Detroit, where the rate of in-migration was high and the municipal government's attitude was hostile, but also in New York, where the lack of defense industries kept the influx low and the authorities were progressive. The La Guardia administration offended black sensibilities three times in the months preceding the Harlem riot. The mayor authorized Metropolitan Life Insurance, despite the company's preference for residential segregation, to begin the quasi-public housing project known as Stuyvesant Town; he allowed the police to close Harlem's Savoy Ballroom for being a place of prostitution, although the establishment's defenders claimed that the real cause was its acceptance of interracial dancing; and he permitted the navy, which barred the enlistment of black women, to use Hunter College's publicly owned buildings as a training center for WAVES. Of course, the navy's policy was just a symptom of the broader policy of military segregation that threatened to make a mockery of the Double V campaign.

However much the faltering progress of the Double V campaign contributed to the malaise of 1943, explaining that year's explosions solely in terms of the frustrations of the minority groups involved misses the significance of the outbreaks. It also overlooks the motivations of the whites who were the protagonists in several incidents. From another perspective, the riots seem to show both rising black expectations and increasing white resentment at the erosion of their privileged place in the society. The renewed movement from the rural South was a prerequisite for the integration of blacks into the urban, industrial world of the twentieth century. And the expansion of Mexican and black neighborhoods in northern cities, as well as the employment by labor-hungry businesses of dark-skinned people in jobs formerly closed to them, posed a challenge to the whites. It is not surprising that young servicemen, who were at least temporarily forfeiting their own chances for advancement, were so involved in the disturbances. The immediate fears of the whites were, of course, exaggerated, but their premonition that the times were irrevocably changing ultimately proved true.

The outcome of World War II left Americans of European or Asian ancestry in the best political position they had ever enjoyed in the United States. With the defeat of the Axis, suspicions about the loyalty of the foreign stock dissipated and racial philosophies of the kind that declared whole ethnic groups unfit for absorption into the society fell from favor. The Germans and the Italians had rallied to the flag, and the level of Japanese-American sacrifice, in the face of insult, had been remarkable. In the light of the continuing limits on immigration, even the most nativist Americans could entertain hope for the ultimate absorption of culturally alien peoples already in the population. The most important change for American ethnics, however, was the United

States's postwar confrontation with the Soviet Union and revolutionary communism. Russia's absorption of some small Slavic states, its military and political domination of others, and its cooperation with leftists and insurgents throughout central and southern Europe suddenly created a bridge of common interests across the broad chasm that had separated most American conservatives from the descendants of the new immigrants. Although the most strident critics of the Soviet Union continued to be the strongest foes of liberalizing the immigration law or revising the quota system, they eagerly recruited Americans of eastern or southern European backgrounds for their anti-Communist crusade. Moreover, communism's officially atheistic world view convinced many conservative Christians that the seat of the gravest threat to America's religious heritage was no longer Rome but Moscow. This development made possible rapprochement and political cooperation between fundamentalist Protestant sects and the Roman Catholic church, which had consistently opposed Communist ideology and faced severe repression under Communist governments.

Seeking to capitalize on the anti-Communist leanings of America's ethnic groups, Republican politicians of the postwar years attributed the fate of eastern Europe to the Yalta Agreement, negotiated by President Roosevelt and accepted by his successor, Harry S. Truman. The GOP believed their argument would win Slavic voters away from the Democrats in the 1948 presidential election. But the president's program to contain communism, which took shape in the Marshall Plan, the Truman Doctrine, and the Berlin Airlift, combined with the Democrats' pro-labor tradition to keep not only the Slavs but also other ethnic elements of the party's coalition in line. Four years later, however, the Democrats bore the blame for continuing Communist successes, most notably the fall of China, and for the ongoing Korean War. Popular dissatisfaction was so high that Senator Joseph McCarthy's wild allegations of massive Communist infiltration of the Democratic administration received a serious hearing. Armed with a platform pledged to the liberation of eastern Europe and led by the truly popular Dwight D. Eisenhower, the Republicans finally managed in 1952 to reduce substantially the Democrats' ethnic base. According to a study done by the Survey Research Center of the University of Michigan, Eisenhower took solid majorities among German and Scandinavian voters and won by a narrow margin among Poles. Overall, the Republicans increased their share of the Catholic vote from 25 to 41 percent between 1948 and 1952. The Catholics' drift to the right seemed even more pronounced during the first years of Eisenhower's tenure, as public opinion polls frequently showed Catholics among the strongest supporters of Senator McCarthy's anti-Communist rampage.

To some extent the shift of ethnic Americans toward the Republican party and conservatism in the 1950s reflected a desire for change and a fear of Communist subversion that moved all segments of the population to the right. In the case of Protestant ethnic groups like the Scandinavians, a vote for Eisenhower in 1952 was a reassertion of traditional party loyalties. The significance of the Catholic ethnics' behavior is more difficult both to measure and to interpret. On the one hand, a majority of Catholics remained loyal to the Democratic party and the sympathy felt for Joe McCarthy by those who were not already Republicans did not regularly translate into support for other GOP or conservative candidates. Catholics formed only a minority of McCarthy's supporters and also ranked among his loudest critics. Two leading Catholic magazines, *America* and *Commonweal,* editorially denounced McCarthy, and in an address to the United Auto Workers meeting in Chicago in 1954, Bishop Bernard Shiel of that city delivered one of the sharpest attacks ever made on the senator's brand of anticommunism. On the other hand, their own increasing prosperity and the church's long-standing opposition to communism did draw some Catholics, especially among the better established groups like the Irish, toward political conservatism and, to a lesser degree, to the Republican party. Although their support of McCarthy waxed and waned along with that given by the general population, Catholics, according to opinion polls, were invariably more favorably disposed than other religious groups to the senator. In addition, the Catholic spokesmen who took public stands in defense of McCarthy always seemed to outnumber his prominent Catholic foes. And, as in the cases of men like Francis Cardinal Spellman of New York and organizations like the Knights of Columbus, they were better known to average Americans.

The burst of Catholic conservatism in the mid-1950s is perhaps best understood not as something rooted in religious values but as the culmination of a discrete phase in the church's history in the United States. Between the 1920s and the 1950s the Catholic church became a community of primarily second- and later generation Americans, a substantial number of whom, especially among the descendants of the old immigrants, had gained at least moderate prosperity. As many churchmen were aware, the circumstances appeared right for Catholics to make substantial contributions in all phases of American life. In that turbulent era, the church did produce a number of social activists, including Monsignor John A. Ryan, whose thinking influenced the New Deal, and the convert Dorothy Day, who brought to life Catholicism's inherently radical message. But after the demise of the Americanists, Catholicism failed to develop a core of intellectual leaders committed to finding a common ground between the church and the contemporary world. For the most part, the church's intellectuals operated within the confines of Catholic organizations, most of which were founded between the world wars as parochial parallels to national associations of scholars in various academic disciplines. From these platforms they railed against supposed weaknesses in current secular learning, including, for example, the relativist attitude toward truth embodied in the so-called new history espoused by Charles Beard and others. To their dismay, however, few outside the church heeded their call for a return to a coherent and rational world view based on a revitalized version of the philosophy of St. Thomas Aquinas. For persons raised in this intellectual milieu, the conservative message of the 1950s was a confirmation of the obvious and a form of belated recognition. The conservatives' denunciation of communism implicitly acknowledged Catholic warnings about dangerous modern ideologies. Its accusations of treachery by the nation's political and intellectual leadership constituted payment due for the absolute lack of interest the elite had shown in the Catholic critique and alternatives. And the embodiment of anticommunism in the person of McCarthy reaffirmed the belief of some Catholics that they were ready to pick up the torch in the pursuit of America's providential mission in the world.

By the 1950s, therefore, the ethnic history of the United States had reached a critical moment. Since the government's decision thirty years earlier to close America's gates against the immigrant flood, the nation had survived an earthshaking war that mocked its doubts about the loyalty of the foreign born and internationally disgraced the racist philosophy underlying the restriction movement. When, after the war, Americans persisted in discriminating against some would-be immigrants on account of their ethnic backgrounds, the authorities had to rationalize the immigration program in terms of protecting the nation's cultural unity rather than its biological purity. Of course, in light of the great strides toward acculturation taken by the foreign-stock population of the United States in the interwar years, such arguments could no longer justify uncharitable attitudes toward this sector. Moreover, the political and ideological struggle against the Soviet Union that took shape after 1945 substantially improved the image of southern and eastern Europeans and of Catholics in general. In the aftermath of the Holocaust and with the emergence of the pro-American, democratic state of Israel in the volatile Middle East, even Jews received protection from most criticism despite their predilection for liberal politics and rumors of excessive left-wing influence in their ranks. Nevertheless, it remained clear in the 1950s that ethnicity and religion still counted in American life and that complete absorption of the foreign born and their descendants into the general population had not occurred. It remained unclear, however, whether the notable level of assimilation achieved by the 1950s was merely a benchmark on the road to the old goal of a homogeneous population or a permanent condition that fell short of the ideal. The answer to this question would become a matter of great concern in the latter half of the century.

# CHAPTER VIII

# The Triple Melting Pot and Beyond

BETWEEN 1950 AND 1980 Americans moved from a hopeful expectation that ethnicity was dying as a factor in their national life to a disturbing sense that the impact of this phenomenon could not or should not be eradicated. As demographic changes in the foreign-stock population inexorably pushed forward the process of acculturation, it seemed at mid-century that differences in language and dress and lingering memories of faraway homelands would soon exercise no hold on Americans. Only religious loyalties appeared strong enough to maintain stable divisions within the white population, but even long-standing animosities among Protestants, Catholics, and Jews had faded after the 1920s.

America had successfully absorbed the great waves of a century of immigration and could confidently look forward to an era of relative homogeneity. The favorable situation encouraged the United States, as well as other English-speaking nations in which parallel developments had occurred, to reassert its belief in human equality, to disavow racism, and to repeal or modify ethnically discriminatory legislation affecting immigration. At the same time, however, the new American policies did not amount to a reversal of the past. The country's reformed immigration laws still worked to limit severely the addition of aliens to the population, and the government's administrative practices were designed to discourage, as much as possible, geographic concentration of the foreign born in recognizable and self-conscious subcommunities.

Nobody suggested that racial equality was at hand, and thoughtful observers found deep economic and persistent political divisions even within the triple melting pot formed by the white adherents of the three great religious traditions of the United States.

More than anything else, America's failure to satisfy the aspirations of the mass of its black citizens in the late 1950s and early 1960s undermined the closely related values of racial integration and ethnic assimilation. The extreme resilience of racial and deep-seated cultural barriers gave weight to the demands by blacks and other especially deprived groups for official recognition of their plight and status within American society. In turn, the implicit acceptance of the existence of permanent minorities in the United States popularized, in certain circles, the idea of accepting and encouraging cultural divisions in the nation. This modification of the country's historic goal of adapting all Americans to Anglicized norms left the European ethnic groups in a vulnerable position. It neither recognized the socially and economically marginal ranking of some of these groups within the American population nor legitimated the retention of white ethnic identities, whose erosion the society continued to encourage. Moreover, the emergence of the culturally pluralist outlook coincided with the rapprochement of Catholics and Protestants and the decline of the institutional churches, trends that stripped religion of much of its potential to serve as a surrogate for ethnicity.

The developments of the late 1960s and the 1970s highlighted the points dividing the descendants of the old and especially of the new immigration from other minorities in the U.S. population. On the one hand, blacks and their liberal sympathizers saw the European ethnics as blocking the paths of advancement that offered minorities the most reasonable hope of progress. On the other, the European ethnics resented doing penance for the sin of slavery—in which they arguably had not participated—and they found a coalition of minority and upper middle-class reform interests ready to block their final achievement of economic and social parity with other whites. The conflict inspired a revival of overt ethnicity that was, for the most part, shallow. But, at least in academic circles, this episode also brought an important recognition of the covert, persistent impact of ethnicity and religion in political, economic, social, and cultural behavior.

At mid-century immigrants and their children were clearly on the way to becoming a minute portion of the U.S. population. Between 1950 and 1960 the number of foreign residents fell from 10,161,168 to 9,738,143 and the proportion of the overall population formed by this group declined from 6.6 to 5.3 percent. In 1950, second-generation Americans accounted for 15.3 percent of the general population; ten years later their share was 13.2 percent. Moreover, many of the distinctive ethnic communities that had dotted the nation's cities were disappearing. To some extent these immigrant settlements were simply following the pattern of high population turnover that has been a familiar part of American urban history since colonial days. The hard work of the foreign born made it possible for some of them and their children to take part in the postwar exodus to the suburbs, but, with the restrictive immigration laws in place, not enough countrymen came to take their places and keep alive the ethnic character of the old neighborhoods. In many cases, however, the demise of these neighborhoods was caused or accelerated by evictions of residents from their homes and the destruction of the buildings in which they had lived. Made up of old, low-rent tenements located on prime real estate near the central business districts of American cities and towns, the nation's immigrant quarters were prime targets for the urban renewal movement of the 1950s and early 1960s. The people of these areas were poor and their houses substandard, but their neighborhoods were neither physically dangerous nor socially pathological. Nevertheless, many people saw these communities as unattractive, unprofitable relics of a bygone era, and the inexperience of their residents with cooperative action impeded the few efforts to save them. The West End of Boston, Yorkville and Lincoln Square in New York, and the Valley, southwest of Chicago's Loop, were among the more notable districts to fall as the wrecker's ball worked its way across the country. Urban planners defined the process as slum clearance, but it often did not add measurably to the stock of housing for lower income people. The new structures tended to be either luxury apartments, which generated big rents and high taxes, or civic institutions, like New York's Lincoln Center, whose function was to restore the spirit and the pride of the broader community.

Although the presence of foreigners in the population was becoming much less obvious by mid-century, other divisions related to the immigrant experience were still very evident. Differences in religious affiliation seemed the most noteworthy of these. The focus on religion was partly the result of shortcomings in the amount of information available about the persistence of ethnic identities. Inasmuch as the American government, unlike the Canadian, declines to ask about the remote national origins of citizens whose parents were born in the country, the census statistics of the United States in effect limit ethnicity to a two-generation phenomenon. Scholars therefore accustomed themselves to using religious background as a substitute for summarizing characteristics formerly expressed in terms of ethnic heritage. Church records were abundant, and the Census Bureau indirectly encouraged the trend when, in February 8, 1957, with the release of one of its Current Population Reports, the bureau for the first time published data on the religious preferences of the American people.

The reliance on religion, however, was not simply a case of settling for second best. Strong support was available for the argument that religious affiliation had eclipsed national background as the crucial criterion by which white Americans identified themselves. Marriage patterns offered a particularly good illustration of this development and of its social impact. In New Haven, Connecticut, for example, British German, and Scandinavian Protestants frequently intermarried by 1950, as did Irish, Italian, and Polish Catholics. But while increasing numbers of people were willing to choose mates from other ethnic groups, few were yet ready to cross religious lines in their search for partners. Among the residents of New Haven who wed in 1948, 98.5 percent of the Jews, 93.4 percent of the Catholics, and 76.2 percent of the Protestants married within their faiths. The data from Connecticut and elsewhere indicated that ethnic differences were being melted down in America, but in three pots rather than one.

Recognition of the existence of a triple melting pot occurred at a time in which public expressions of faith and church affiliation were becoming the order of the day in the United States. A Gallup poll taken in 1954 found that almost 80 percent of American adults claimed membership in a church, and over 99 percent of the population was able to express a religious preference in the Census Bureau's survey taken in 1957. Contrary to what might have occurred in an earlier age, however, the growing awareness of persistent divisions and the heightened sense of religiosity in the country did not combine to aggravate tensions among Protestants, Catholics, and Jews. Nine out of ten Americans denied feeling hostility toward persons of different religions, and a majority even of those who described religion as very important in their lives denied that it had an impact on their political behavior. According to astute observers like Will Herberg, the movement to join churches reflected a search for roots in a quickly changing world and a quest for personal spiritual growth in an age of mass consumer culture. For many Americans at mid-century religion was theistic but not theological. Issues such as private versus corporate interpretation of the Bible and the relative importance of God's grace and human effort in the process of salvation continued to divide Protestants from Catholics, but these hardly were matters of public debate. Not even the assertion of Jesus's divinity by Christians or the Jews' self-identification as the Chosen People created confrontation. Americans emphasized instead the bonds among Western religious traditions, especially insofar as they revealed a common spiritual foundation for the nation's political and social values. Herberg described these ideals as the ''American way of life'' and included among them democracy, social equality, economic opportunity, and the aspiration to make the world perfect. In many respects this civic religion was a fresh manifestation of the nation's historic vision of

America as the tool of Providence. But the twentieth-century version of the millennial impulse was not exclusively Protestant: Catholics and Jews were welcomed as allies and the chief obstacle to America's mission became not alien religions but an ideology of atheism, especially as practiced politically in the Communist world.

The best evidence of the newly achieved parity among America's major religions was the election in 1960 of John F. Kennedy, the first Roman Catholic to hold the office of president. His victory invalidated the long-standing assumption that in a political, if not in a constitutional, sense only Protestants were eligible for the White House. This election also marked the culmination of the postwar era, in which Catholics had fully demonstrated their sharing in the values of America's mainstream. The outspoken anticommunism prevalent in the church in the 1950s had dispelled any doubts lingering among informed citizens about the patriotism of the faithful, and Catholic apologists in the era had painstakingly redefined and clarified Rome's teachings on the proper relationship between spiritual and temporal institutions. John Courtney Murray, a leading Jesuit theologian, militantly claimed that his religion and the American system of government were especially well tuned to each other; unlike modern Protestantism, Judaism, and secularism, Catholicism still adhered in the twentieth century to the philosophy of natural law, from which the Founding Fathers had derived their ideas of limited government in the 1700s. Murray denied, moreover, that Catholics, if given the opportunity, would use the power of the government to suppress religious beliefs other than their own. He explained that even the popes accepted the rationale behind the First Amendment and that the toleration of error was the necessary price paid for the greater good of preserving the public peace.

Operating within this cultural framework, Kennedy was able confidently to confront the religious issue from the beginning of his campaign. During the Democratic primary contest against Hubert H. Humphrey in heavily Protestant West Virginia, Kennedy declared on television that anyone who violated the constitutional oath to keep church and state separate would be committing not only an impeachable offense but also a sin. After winning the nomination, Kennedy daringly submitted himself to public questioning by the hostile Greater Houston Ministerial Association; he told this group that his church would not attempt to influence him politically, that he personally would not tolerate ecclesiastical interference, and that he would resign if the responsibilities of the presidency became incompatible with his conscience. In November, the voters proved that Kennedy had been correct when he said, "I refuse to believe that I was denied the right to be President on the day I was baptized."

As the proportion of aliens in the population steadily fell, as the offspring of the foreign born quickly shed the extrinsic elements of their families' Old World cultures, and as the level of mutual understanding rose among America's religions, the inconsistency between ethnically discriminatory immigration laws and the nation's professed ideals became more obvious. Americans had little reason to fear that the annual admission of a modest number of newcomers, regardless of their origins, would seriously challenge the integrity of the country's basically Anglo-Saxon heritage or endanger the economic well-being of the citizenry. If anything, the national interest required the abandonment of racist policies that potential enemies could use in propaganda campaigns in various corners of the world. Efforts to change the McCarran-Walter Act started immediately after its passage. In January 1953 a study commission appointed by President Harry S. Truman harshly criticized the bias existing in America's immigration laws since the 1920s. Later that month the nation's new chief executive, Dwight D. Eisenhower, used a portion of his first State of the Union Message to draw attention to the inequities of the McCarran-Walter Act. Eisenhower subsequently called for reform of the system in messages to Congress delivered in 1956, 1957, and 1960. It seems fitting, however, that John F. Kennedy became the first president of the modern era to submit to Congress a specific body of legislative proposals pertinent to immigration. In letters to the speaker of the House and the president of the Senate, Kennedy in July 1963 called for the elimination, over a five-year period, of all quotas based on national origin, including the special restrictions imposed on persons from the Asia-Pacific triangle. After Kennedy's assassination, President Lyndon B. Johnson, in his State of the Union Message in January 1964, reaffirmed the commitment to reform the immigration laws. Under Johnson's guidance, the Congress overhauled the existing structure of rules and regulations and passed a comprehensive set of amendments to the McCarran-Walker Act. The president signed these revisions into law at a ceremony near the base of the Statue of Liberty on October 3, 1965.

The 1965 amendments to the Immigration Act abandoned the discriminatory features of the national origin quota system. The new provisions restricted annual immigration from the Eastern Hemisphere to 170,000 persons, of whom not more than 20,000 could enter from any single country. In addition, Congress responded to new concerns about a potentially large increase in the volume of immigration from Latin America, where rapid population growth was occurring, by imposing the first ceiling on annual admissions from the Western Hemisphere. The law did not initially include checks on the contributions of individual Latin American countries to the overall limit of 120,000 persons. The complete set of quota revisions did not go into effect until July 1, 1968. Thus, the old national origin rules remained in force for more than two and one-half years after the implementation of the new law on December 1, 1965. For this lengthy transitional period Congress allowed the reallocation of the unused portion of the quotas assigned to countries that produced few immigrants to a pool available for the relief of candidates for admission from nations in which the demand for visas exceeded the authorized allotment of them.

Besides discarding the most inequitable features of the national origin quota system, the Immigration Act amendments of 1965 changed the priorities according to which candidates for admission to the United States established their claims to the entry visas available in their homelands. The new law's relevant provisions, which went into effect on December 1, 1965, and pertained only to immigrants from the Eastern Hemisphere, gave higher preference than had the McCarran-Walter Act to relatives of American citizens and of legally resident aliens. Overall, family members could claim as many as 74 percent of the available visas. The 1965 legislation added the parents of adult U.S. citizens to the category of nonquota entrants and kept spouses and minor children in this group. The unmarried sons and daughters of American citizens had first call on up to 20 percent of the available visas. The spouses and unmarried sons and daughters of aliens legally admitted to permanent residence received second preference, with rights to 20 percent of the visas, plus any not required for first-preference immigrants. The married sons and daughters and the brothers and sisters of American citizens gained the fourth and fifth preferences, respectively. The former won entitlement to 10 percent of the visas, plus any not used by the first three groups; the latter, 24 percent, plus any not used by the first four. The law established a seventh preference category for refugees, who could claim up to 6 percent of the visas. Under the McCarran-Walter Act, skilled laborers, along with their spouses and children, had enjoyed the highest preference and the right to at least 50 percent of the visas. By contrast, the new legislation assigned the third preference to professionals, scientists, and artists; the sixth, to skilled and unskilled workers whose specific occupational talents were needed in the United States. Each group could claim a maximum of 10 percent of the visas, but prospective immigrants in these categories had to obtain certification from the secretary of labor that workers were needed to do their jobs and that their presence would not drive down the wages of Americans similarly employed. All candidates for admission from the Western Hemisphere who were not immediate family members of U.S. citizens also had to obtain this certification.

A marked liberalization of American policies toward refugees accompanied the relaxation of the country's immigration laws. Ironically, the McCarran Walter Act of 1952 sowed the seeds of this change. That otherwise Draconian measure authorized the attorney general, acting either in response to emergencies or in the national interest, to grant temporary sanctuary to any alien applying for admission. In 1965 the amendments to the Immigration Act retained this parole provision and set aside an annual allotment of 17,400 visas for refugees. The new law, however, included the rather limited definition of refugees as persons who "because of persecution on account of race, religion, or political opinion . . . have fled from any Communist-dominated country or area, or from any country in the general area of the Middle East, and are unable or unwilling to return to such country on account of race, religion, or political opinion." Using the mechanism of parole, which was usually followed by a grant of permission to stay permanently, and the new immigration laws, the government offered asylum to over 1 million people between the mid-1950s and 1980. More than 30,000 Hungarians gained admission after the Russians suppressed their revolution in 1956; over 650,000 anti-Castro Cubans arrived between the early 1960s and late 1970s; and about 360,000 Indochinese refugees found their way to America between 1975 and 1980. The attorney general reported that the United States accepted 231,700 refugees in fiscal year 1980, including approximately 130,000 Cubans, whose flight captured worldwide attention. Moreover, this pattern is likely to continue, inasmuch as the Refugee Act of 1980 raised the annual number of refugee visas to 50,000, authorized Congress to admit even greater numbers, and extended the benefits of the law to persons from countries that are neither Communist nor Middle Eastern.

As had been the case in past eras, changes in the immigration laws of the United States coincided with similar developments elsewhere in the world. Close to home, Canada declared in 1961 that "anyone regardless of origin, citizenship, country of residence, or religious beliefs, who is personally qualified by reason of education, training, skills, or other special qualifications" would henceforth be eligible for permanent admission. The Canadian system, like the American, put a premium on attracting skilled workers and reuniting families, but it did not identify a numerical goal or limit for the volume of annual immigration. Canadian legislation passed in 1967 categorized potential immigrants as sponsored dependents, for whom a close relative already in the country was willing to take responsibility, nominated relatives, and independent applicants. To gain entry, persons in the last two classes had to earn at least fifty out of 100 possible assessment points. Nominated relatives could get between 15 and 30 of these points by virtue of short-term living arrangements provided by kinsmen already in Canada, but they had to achieve the remainder of their score on the basis of their education and training, the personal impression they made on immigration officers, the demand for their occupation, the level of their skills, and their age. Independent applicants had to earn all 50 of their points on the basis of these individual attributes and a variety of other ones, including knowledge of French or English. Like Canada and the United States, Australia in these years also rid its immigration policy of blatantly discriminatory features. During and after World War II Australians suffered embarrassment for a series of incidents in which they barred or deported Asian war brides and refugees. The semi-official White Australia policy became an object of scorn in international diplomacy and an obstacle to the country's growing political and economic involvement with the noncolonial nations of its region. Change came gradually, with the most important step taken in 1966, when the minister for immigration announced new criteria for admission that emphasized individual skills and omitted familiar expressions of preference for persons of European origin.

Despite these programmatic similarities, the United States has in several respects come closer than the other major receiving nations of the world to fulfilling the new international commitment to liberal and equitable immigration laws. Canada, which has experienced shifts in the composition of its immigrant population similar to those felt in America, has gradually introduced greater controls on the influx of newcomers. In 1972 Canada ended the five-year-old practice by which visitors could apply for landed immigrant status after arriving in the country; this practice had allowed up to a third of all newcomers to circumvent the normal channels for obtaining entry and the right of permanent residence. Two years later the Canadians in effect raised the number of points required of an applicant for admission from fifty to sixty by ordering immigration officers to deduct ten points from the score of any arrival who was without prearranged employment or skills in a needed occupation. In Australia the disavowal of color-conscious admission procedures has had fewer practical than symbolic consequences. Between March 1966 and March 1968, for example, Australia granted the right to acquire citizenship to approximately 3,000 Asians, many of whom were already temporary legal residents. During the same period the country admitted about 300,000 Europeans as permanent settlers. And, in April 1982 Australia limited immigration to persons with close relatives in the country, needed skills, or the experience and assets necessary to start a business.

The most notable contrast perhaps lies between the immigration policies and practices of the United States and those of European nations, where the presence of foreign workers has become increasingly evident since World War II. By the late 1960s immigrants constituted over 6 percent of the labor force in Britain and France, 7 percent in Germany, and almost 30 percent in Switzerland. Drawn primarily from less developed areas—including Ireland, Italy, Yugoslavia, Turkey, Africa,

Asia, and the West Indies—these newcomers are concentrated at the bottom of the occupational scale. Their presence is Europe's answer to manpower shortages created in part by the demographic effects of wartime deaths and by the unwillingness of better educated, relatively scarce, and socially mobile youths of the postwar era to take menial jobs. The admission of aliens, therefore, is an economic expedient that does not indicate complete acceptance of the idea of their permanent settlement. No European country encourages the immigration of the self-employed, except for small numbers of needed professionals; some governments have deported foreigners for taking up independent pursuits after their arrival; and, during the economic downturn of the 1970s, several nations sought to reduce the numbers of foreigners resident within their borders. Furthermore, the Common Market's endorsement of the free movement of nationals among the member states of the European Economic Community did not constitute a commitment to ethnically nondiscriminatory criteria for entry. Since 1971 the British have curtailed the admission of nonwhites who hold Commonwealth citizenship; free immigration is the right only of persons from the travel area of Ireland, the Isle of Man, and the Channel Island and of *patrials,* at least one of whose parents or, in some cases, grandparents was born in the United Kingdom. The French prefer European over North African immigrants, whom they encourage to return home after short stays. Finally, the Dutch are determined to discourage an influx of colonial West Indians.

Since mid-century, therefore, the United States has made progress toward accepting the demographic and social consequences of earlier eras of immigration and toward reconciling the criteria governing the admission of aliens with the nondiscriminatory ideals professed by the nation. These developments, however, must be seen in perspective. The modification of the quota system has neither constituted a reopening of the gates nor provided a satisfactory mechanism for managing the most pressing contemporary immigration problems, which involve the movement of people from the poorer nations of the Western Hemisphere. Moreover, behind the apparent optimism of this moment of reconciliation and reform lies continuing confusion about the meaning of America's ethnic history. The triple melting pot has proved to be an ambivalent metaphor. The concept is both an admission that the country has not achieved cultural homogeneity and a declaration that it has traveled a notable distance toward that original goal. What remains unclear is whether the United States has reached an interim point on a longer road to full assimilation or the terminus of a shorter route to a limited version of integration. Indeed, the most frequently voiced opinion in recent years has alleged that the appraisal of America embodied in the triple melting pot inadequately describes a society beset by deep racial cleavages and even exaggerates the extent to which differences within the white population have declined.

Under the revised 1965 immigration law and subsequent legislation, the United States remains committed to the retention of relatively strict limits on the number of people allowed to enter the country each year. Of course, the arrival of nonquota immigrants, the vast majority of whom are the parents, spouses, or children of men and women already here, can add substantial numbers beyond the ceiling. Between June 1974 and September 1977, for example, the 556,183 nonquota arrivals amounted to almost 32 percent of the total number of newcomers. But even with increments like these, the annual rate of immigration during the 1970s hovered around 2 percent of the country's population; for the decades between 1830 and 1920 the rate ranged between 4 and 10 percent. Moreover, the favoritism shown by the United States toward educated and skilled applicants for entry indicates that America is not eager to become once more a refuge for the poor of other nations. Persons with professional, technical, or related backgrounds formed the largest employment category among the 189,378 men and women who landed in the year ending September 30, 1977, and who reported an occupation. They accounted for 24 percent of the overall total and for 40 percent and 49 percent of Asian and African immigrants, respectively. Figures like these have prompted charges that the United States is creating a "brain drain" abroad, especially in developing countries, which cannot compensate their most talented people at levels equivalent to those available in the West. Americans can counter that some Third World countries produce more skilled people than their economies can absorb and that the United States is probably not the worst offender in this affair. Estimates by the United Nations indicate that the United States regains, through the acquisition of talent it has not trained, approximately 11 percent of the technical and economic aid Washington sends less developed nations. By comparison, Switzerland takes back 24 percent; Sweden, 31 percent; West Germany, 40 percent; and Austria, 72 percent. The issue is complex, but immigration to the United States now obviously plays a different role from that which inspired Emma Lazarus to have the Statue of Liberty call to the world's tired and hungry.

Popular opposition to the resumption of large-scale immigration is rooted mainly in fears of adverse economic consequences and perhaps also in residual disdain for groups formerly defined as ethnically inferior. But the concerns felt by Americans also reflect an awareness of the cultural fragility of their society and an unwillingness to risk further tests of U.S. society's absorptive capacity. Despite their increasing recognition of the past contributions of the foreign born, neither the government nor the public has abandoned the desire that newcomers adapt quickly to vague but generally understood American norms. This preference to avoid, whenever possible, further cultural diversification was apparent in the official response to the two major groups of political refugees admitted in recent years. The more than 360,000 Indochinese who fled Southeast Asia after the Communist conquest of Saigon in 1975 included an important core of persons from the educated, urbanized elite and of others previously exposed to Western culture. The approximately 125,000 Cubans who sought asylum in the United States during and after the spring of 1980 were less affluent than the anti-Castro exiles of the 1960s but their social standing was above average for the island. Nevertheless, the American government offered only a wary welcome to these newcomers. The authorities even urged Asian arrivals to consider remigration to other nations, and in both cases Washington sought, with only mixed success, to discourage the concentration of these refugees in ethnic enclaves.

The policy of sending refugees to a variety of geographic locales was probably based more on practical than on philosophical considerations. Dispersal minimized the possibility that a handful of communities would have to shoulder an overwhelming proportion of the costs of receiving the refugees; such might have been the case had the arrivals been allowed to stay at ports of entry, seek out locales climatically similar to their homelands, or gravitate to existing centers of their countrymen, like the Cuban districts of Miami. The policy also served to diffuse political protests by the majority of Americans, who, according to Gallup polls taken in 1979 and 1980, opposed the entry of both the Indochinese and the Cubans. Finally, this policy was an inevitable by-product of the nationwide effort to recruit institutional and private sponsors who would take responsibility for helping one or more refugees to find jobs and homes. But if the policy of dispersal did not explicitly seek to facilitate the breakdown of the newcomers' native cultures, it at least implicitly assumed that old customs and manners ought to be abandoned quickly and that the alternative of offering the arrivals the option of settling in ethnic subcommunities, where cultural decompression might proceed less traumatically, was unnecessary, inappropriate, or not worth the consequent social costs.

The continuation of a relatively large-scale influx of immigrants, many of whom came from the grossly underdeveloped countries of the so-called Third World, and the ability of even the most vulnerable newcomers to resist disappearing into the general society gave evidence after 1950 that announcements of the emergence of a culturally homogeneous American population were premature. Nothing, however, did more than developments in the area of race relations to disprove claims that ethnicity was a moribund force in the United States. The experience of

black Americans in the third quarter of the twentieth century made it
clear that true equality remained a distant hope rather than an imminent goal even after the demise of racism as an accepted ideology and the
official rejection of discriminatory practices based on color differences.
More important, the resulting political demand for public recognition of
the special plight of black Americans not only implied the existence of a
perhaps permanent separate status for racial minorities but also led to a
reformulation of attitudes about the present position and prospects of
the country's white ethnic groups.

At first glance the image of the triple melting pot, which offered such
an intriguing insight into the changing patterns of group interaction
among whites at mid-century, does not seem to have been germane to
the contemporary situation of black Americans. The central thesis on
which this notion rested held that religion was replacing national origin
as the prime determinant of ascriptive identity in the United States.
Race did not properly fit the paradigm and, by Herberg's admission,
the isolated position of the main body of black Protestants and their
strong churches constituted an ''anomaly of considerable importance.''
On closer inspection, however, the pertinence of the metaphor for the
aspirations of racial minorities becomes apparent. The broad model of
the process of assimilation that was fundamental to the triple melting pot
theory showed that groups of remarkably different origins could put
aside the most isolating aspects of their pasts, adapt to a common
American way of life, and still maintain their ethnic integrity. This
revelation had somewhat different implications for whites and blacks.
The knowledge that groups of white Americans could come to have so
much in common and yet refrain from marrying across religious lines
was a surprise for some; the prospect that blacks might attain a similar
level of integration without consequent racial amalgamation was probably the sine qua non for popular acceptance of the civil rights movement.

In its initial phase, the black revolution proceeded from the convic-
tion that racism was an intellectually discredited ideology to the conclusion that color could no longer be considered an inherent limit to a person's capacity to take part in American society. In his important study
of American slavery, Stanley Elkins argued that the triple shock of capture, involuntary transfer across the Atlantic in degrading conditions,
and life in an emotionally draining bondage virtually eradicated the
ethnic identities, languages, religions, and other cultural traits of slavery's African victims. From this perspective, the black population of the
United States was, with the possible exception of the Indians, the most
purely indigenous group in the country. Were it not for the policy of
segregation, which artificially distinguished the black population from
the white, racial differences would, like the national origins of the ethnic

groups, disappear as impediments to assimilation. From the mid-1950s through the mid-1960s, therefore, advocates of integration urged that blacks be assured the same legal rights that their white fellow citizens enjoyed. Litigation led to the famous case of *Brown* v. *Board of Education*, in which the Supreme Court guaranteed blacks access to integrated schooling. Boycotts and the nonviolent civil disobedience of sit-ins and Freedom Rides brought the desegregation of the Montgomery, Alabama, bus system in 1956, of numerous lunchcounters in the South in 1960, and of some interstate conveyances in 1961. A decade of peaceful demonstrations culminated in August 1963 with the massive march on Washington led by Dr. Martin Luther King, Jr. This orderly turnout by 250,000 unified blacks and whites helped pave the way for passage of the Civil Rights Act of 1964, which decreed an end to segregation in public accommodations, and of the Voting Rights Act of 1965, which committed the federal government to making enfranchisement a reality for southern blacks.

Court action and nonviolent protest succeeded in destroying the sanctions for racial segregation and discrimination. Long-closed doors opened for blacks who by hard work and good luck had already achieved the skills and savoir faire associated with middle-class life, and the prospects were bright that more would immediately enjoy unprecedented educational and occupational opportunities. Unfortunately, the progress of the few could not satisfy the expectations of the many. Calls to be patient while the next generation equipped itself with the tools needed for the future offered little to men and women beyond adolescence. Blacks whose families had been here for hundreds of years rejected the argument that they had achieved the status of immigrants to the urban world of twentieth-century America. Blacks understood that although laws could end segregation, prejudice was a matter of the heart, and they recognized that they could not shed their skins as Europeans had sloughed off their alien and alienating manners and mores. Blacks also came to see that the masses of their people in both the North and the South confronted daily the special legacy of slavery and segregation: overwhelming poverty, family and community structures unnurtured by society, physical and cultural isolation from the mainstream, and the absence of reasons for optimism and motivation. They believed that these liabilities so exceeded in depth and duration the related hardships faced by white immigrants as to constitute a unique pathology of the ghetto.

Among many blacks hope faded into frustration and pacific appeals for justice gave way to militant demands for equality. Between 1964 and 1968 the angriest and most desperate engaged in self-destructive sprees of violence that gutted black areas of New York, Los Angeles, Cleveland, Detroit, and other major cities. A new breed of leaders like Stokely

Carmichael, H. Rap Brown, and Malcolm X called for black pride and black power, talked of the creation of a separate black nation within the United States, and spoke in terms of a worldwide struggle by peoples of other colors against the white race. After his death in Ghana in 1963 the historian William E. B. Du Bois, the first black to receive a Harvard Ph.D., emerged as a patron saint for militants and intellectuals. Du Bois's consistently firm assertion of black rights and his increasing sympathy for the left-wing revolutions of the twentieth century seemed to them more manly and respectable than the temporizing tactics of his early rival, Booker T. Washington. A new generation of scholars discovered that blacks, too, had a valuable past, and popular interest grew both in the elements of African heritage that had survived slavery and in the Afro-American culture created under the conditions of the New World. Even moderate leaders perceived a need for blacks to take control of the schools and other institutions that most directly affected their lives. Most important, blacks successfully sought social legislation to help them overcome the structural deficiencies of their environment and affirmative action programs to insure that they would quickly achieve economic, educational, and occupational parity with the white population.

By the late 1960s both militant and moderate black leaders had reached an unprecedented consensus that they must make the general society conscious rather than unconscious of color. For the most part black leaders had not rejected the goal of integration, but they had accepted the belief that for an indefinite time to come race would have a negative impact on the lives of blacks and must be made to have a positive one as well. In adopting this approach, blacks established a model for the efforts of two other distressed minorities, Indians and Spanish-Americans, to improve their own conditions. Despite important differences between their situations and that of American blacks, the latter groups became increasingly convinced that the most direct road to progress lay in heightening their senses of group identity, flexing political muscles wherever feasible, and winning official recognition of their separate stations.

Emulating their black peers, educated and articulate members of the National Indian Youth Council, including Melvin Thom, condemned "Uncle Tomahawks" and called for red power. Many Indians, like those who occupied Alcatraz Island between 1969 and 1971 in the vain hope of establishing a cultural center there, set out to revive the old ways and instill them in the young. Adherents of the American Indian Movement, led by Dennis Banks and Russell Means, occupied Wounded Knee, South Dakota, in 1973 in an unsuccessful effort to overthrow the moderate leadership of the Pine Ridge Reservation and to win the government's recognition of the tribes as sovereign nations. Other Indians strove to revive the Wheeler-Howard, or Indian Reorganization, Act of 1934, through which the New Deal had sought to restore tribal and reservation life. Rejecting the policy of rapid termination of federal responsibilities instituted in 1950 by Commissioner of Indian Affairs Dillon S. Myer, several tribes, including the Menominee of Wisconsin, actually returned to the reservation and federal protection.

Hispanics, like blacks and unlike Indians, are numerous and geographically concentrated. At present, persons of Spanish and especially Mexican origin account for 36.6 percent of the population in New Mexico, 21.0 percent in Texas, 19.2 percent in California, 16.2 percent in Arizona, and 11.7 percent in Colorado. Persons with roots in Puerto Rico, the island commonwealth whose inhabitants are born American citizens with unrestricted rights to enter the United States, comprise 5.6 percent of the population in New York, 3.3 percent in New Jersey, and 2.8 percent in Connecticut. Cubans amount to 4.8 percent of the population of Florida, and sizable groups of Spanish-Americans from various other Western Hemisphere nations are also found across the country. Hispanics, therefore, have become a force in conventional politics, and especially in movements based on ethnic Mexican, or Chicano, nationalism. In 1963 Reies López Tijerina founded the Alianza Federal de Mercedes in New Mexico with the hope of forming a separatist state; he eventually was jailed for confrontations with the authorities, including the brief seizure of a courthouse in Tierra Amarilla in 1967. The Crusade for Justice, established in 1965 in Denver by Rodolfo "Corky" Gonzales, envisioned the establishment of an independent nation, Aztlán, and José Angel Gutiérrez's La Raza Unida party, which enjoyed local electoral successes in Texas after its birth in 1970, emphasized the fostering of Mexican-American culture. Groups like the Movimiento Estudiantil Chicano de Aztlán (MECHA) and the Mexican American Youth Organization encouraged the development of Chicano consciousness and cultural studies at the college and high school levels, respectively. Even a fairly traditional group like César Chávez's United Farm Workers Organizing Committee, which won national recognition during the five-year Delano grape strike of the late 1960s, made use of such powerful Mexican symbols as the Virgin of Guadalupe.

The blacks' claim to be—like white Catholics, Jews, and Protestants—a fundamental building block of the American population, was reasonable. Conceding this point, however, attenuated the descriptive power of the triple melting pot metaphor. The addition of a demographic category based on race destroyed the logical purity of a classification system originally rooted in religious identities. Moreover, the inclusion of blacks and perhaps of Indians and Spanish speakers as separate, more or less permanent entities doubled the number of recognizable substantial divisions in the society. Whereas proponents of the triple melting pot concept had appreciated the amplitude of acculturation, as well as the strength of primal ties found in the United States, later observers seemed more impressed by the amount of heterogeneity remaining than by the level of homogeneity achieved. Many Americans were distressed by a situation that seemed increasingly contrary to their nation's ideals, but scholarly analysts of these trends were more sanguine. The latter were more aware than the general public of the existence of diversity in the past and, given the relatively liberal intellectual atmosphere of the 1960s, some were willing to embrace such a state of affairs in the present. Those optimists rekindled the vision of cultural pluralism offered fifty years earlier, in 1915, by Horace Kallen, a Harvard educated philosopher of American Jewish descent. He and they thought that cultures, coexisting competitively in a democracy, could enrich each other, reach new heights of refinement, and benefit the entire society. Other academic commentators were more cautious. In a remarkably temperate study entitled *Assimilation in American Life*, Milton M. Gordon noted that pluralism in the United States was based not on a multiplicity of cultures, in the proper sense of the word, but on members of different races and religions living the most important parts of their lives within their own groups. Although hardly an alarmist in regard to the immediate prospects of the United States, Gordon warned that such "structural pluralism" could lead to the serious "compartmentalization" of a nation and a loss of popular concern with the common good.

The incorporation of America's most unassimilated minorities into the framework of the ideology of cultural pluralism that emerged in the 1960s had varying impacts on these groups and on the charter members of the somewhat discredited triple melting pot. Blacks, Indians, and persons of Spanish origin made a historic breakthrough in finally gaining legitimation of their aspirations to participate as equals in the society. White Protestants, with the possible exception of southerners, experienced almost no change in their status; their culture continued to be norm. Jews, especially middle-class ones, continued to enjoy an unprecedented level of acceptance in the United States. They were safe from most racial slurs and even from sharp criticism as long as memories of nazism and the Holocaust lingered, and they were, thus, relatively secure in their dually based ethnic and religious identity. Catholics, however, found their position deteriorating. Success seemed to escape them; to many they came to symbolize the backward aspects of life in urban America; and their religion's cohesive force was waning. For certain Catholics, therefore, real threats lay in the new emphasis on economic and occupational mobility as the main measure of the extent of assimilation and in the addition of the nation's racial minorities to the quest for these prizes.

By the 1960s the economic and occupational inferiority of American Catholics to the general Protestant population was a truism demonstrated by almost a score of studies done in the previous generation. As early as 1943, Hadley Cantril had found, through data in public opinion polls, that the ratio of Protestants to Catholics increased at each plateau of education and income beyond the lowest, at which many southern Protestants were trapped. As late as 1965 the Gallup poll showed that Protestants were noticeably more well-to-do than Catholics past the $7,000 level of annual income. The persistence of the pattern became distressing in light both of the apparent assimilation of the Catholic population in other respects and of the discovery that American Jews had equaled and perhaps surpassed the achievements of their Protestant neighbors.

Commentators offered various explanations for the Catholics' poor performance but the one that stirred the most interest applied to America a modified version of a thesis first proposed by the German sociologist Max Weber. In 1920 Weber had suggested that general Protestant asceticism and the specific Calvinist doctrines of worldly vocation and of predestination, which created a longing for signs of God's grace, proved more hospitable than Catholic values and beliefs to the rise of capitalism in Europe. After studying Detroit in the late 1950s, Gerhard Lenski reached a set of analogous conclusions. Compared with their more successful white Protestant and Jewish fellow residents, Detroit's Catholics had less positive attitudes toward work, were less likely to seek self-employment, and were more inclined to believe that connections, rather than ability, were the key to promotion. Moreover, Catholics often bore the costly burden of large families and had strong kinship ties of a kind that discouraged the geographic mobility frequently necessary for advancement. Catholics most resembled black Protestants, but the latter at least had the excuse that their outlook was the product of an oppressive environment rather than a cherished religious tradition. Indeed, although Lenski did not forecast the imminent civil rights revolution and its positive effects, the logic of his argument implied that a fully assimilated black population might overtake the Catholic group.

Lenski's thesis had implications for realms beyond economics. His argument that Catholics lacked intellectual autonomy and were passive in the face of the teaching authority claimed by the church offered a plausible explanation for their marked underrepresentation in the intellectual life of the nation. In an important study published in 1953, for example, R. H. Knapp and H. B. Goodrich had found that non-Catholic men's colleges were producing scientists at more than five times the rate of Catholic ones. In the humanistic disciplines Catholic schools were even less productive. The church's exaltation of authority and tradition also seemed to explain an apparent drift of Catholics to the political right. Lenski found that Detroiters with parochial educations

inclined toward Republicanism and that although church schools did
not encourage racism Catholics tended to be hostile to blacks. Throughout the 1960s the popular media advanced the theme of Catholic conservatism, pointing to evidence that concerned civil rights, the Vietnam
War, student and urban unrest, and the rise of Governor George Wallace to national prominence.

Catholic response to this ground swell of criticism was mixed. To a
surprising extent, both the clergy and the laity admitted the charges.
Monsignor John J. Kane conceded that Catholics suffered from a kind
of orientation to lower-class or to lower middle-class educations and occupations. And a number of Catholic intellectuals realized that some
faculty members and administrators at the church's universities were
hostile to empirical research and convinced that the core of education
lay in the inculcation of revealed and traditionally known truths about
human nature. But unlike some non-Catholic critics, men like John
Tracy Ellis, Gustave Weigel, and Thomas F. O'Dea did not find any inherent conflict between their religion and broadly or narrowly construed
scientific pursuits. They saw, instead, a situation produced by specific
conditions, including the relatively late development of the church in the
United States and the hostility it had met here for many years. The need
for Catholics to achieve minimal material security, to build their institutions, and to protect their theological integrity in a hostile environment
was held responsible for what they hoped was only a temporary neglect
of the intellectual life.

The willingness of Catholics to be self-critical was evidence that they
were assimilated enough both to be secure about past progress and to
understand that the journey toward full integration was not complete.
This reaction also revealed a desire to conform to American norms that
was eroding the religion's very ability to provide a strong cultural identity for its adherents. Worldwide in the 1960s Catholicism and Protestantism were experiencing a rapprochement made possible by the good
will of both sides and by the clear liberalization of the former's attitudes
and practices. In the United States, Catholics quickly embraced
ecumenical cooperation, interfaith dialogue, and the reforms adopted
by the Second Vatican Council. Indeed, many Catholics changed more
quickly than did their church on the issues of priestly celibacy and the
ordination of women, and Rome's refusal to soften its opposition to
forms of contraception other than rhythm led to unprecedented declines
in sacramental participation. Perhaps the most important development
was the increase in the number of "communal Catholics," as Andrew
M. Greeley, priest and sociologist, described them. These people, a
large proportion of whom were educated and articulate, remained Catholic in their personal identity and, in many cases, even in their ordinary
religious practices but ceased to think of the institutional church as rele-

vant to their daily lives. Whatever the long-term implications of these changes for religious life in general, they could, in the short run, only lessen the sociological utility of the adjective "Catholic" and blur both popular and official comprehension of the remaining problems facing a group that had achieved a remarkable degree of acculturation but not full assimilation into the American mainstream.

As the new vulnerability of the Catholic position in the United States became evident, researchers inside and outside the religion began to reevaluate assumptions about the church and its members. They found that many stereotypes were outdated or unsubstantiated. Historians and economists had begun dismantling the original Weberian thesis even before its Americanized version took hold in academic circles and, not surprisingly, Lenski's work soon fell under sharp attack. The fresh examination of religion's relationship to economic achievement and mobility, an analysis carried out largely by non-Catholic scholars, was remarkably sophisticated in its statistical argumentation. The conclusions reached were by no means uniform, but they tended to dismiss Catholic theology and attitudes as causes of the worldly fortunes of the faithful. Most investigators decided that Catholics had been catching up with Protestants economically and occupationally since World War II. They explained the differences that remained as a product of the relatively recent immigrant background of a sizable portion of the Catholic population. The underrepresentation of Catholics at the highest level of income, for example, reflected their lack of education a generation earlier. By the mid-1960s, however, the situation had turned around and Catholics, in keeping with their concentration in the prosperous urban areas of the country, were actually attending college at a higher rate than were Protestants. This trend boded well not only for Catholics' financial hopes but also for their intellectual emergence. Research based on a survey by the Carnegie Commission on Higher Education showed that Catholics were increasingly represented on college faculties. Whereas they accounted for only 15 percent of the nation's professors who were fifty-five years of age or older, they amounted to 20 percent of the total aged thirty-four years or younger. The comparable figures at seventeen top-ranked universities were only 10 percent and 16 percent, but even there Catholics were making progress toward the 26 percent that equaled their share of the overall population.

Data gathered in 1977, 1978, and 1980 by the National Opinion Research Center (NORC) of Chicago confirmed the findings of contemporary studies of educational and economic stratification. According to those surveys, Jews formed the most successful element of the white population: approximately 44 percent of America's Jews had schooling beyond the secondary level and 35 percent had personal incomes of at least $25,000 annually. Within the remainder of the white population no major discrepancies existed in the distribution of education and wealth between Catholics and Protestants; however, some differences could be seen in the accomplishments of specific denominations and ethnic groups. For the most part, such variations were rooted in historical circumstances. With their concentration in the urban centers of the North, for example, Catholic Irish had a better base for taking advantage of the economic opportunities available in modern America than their Protestant counterparts enjoyed. Likewise, some groups associated with the new immigration had not yet achieved complete parity with the descendants of earlier arrivals, and very recent additions to the country, such as the Mexicans, had few educational or occupational advantages. Tantalizing evidence exists, however, that Catholic blacks have fared better than Protestant ones. While almost two-thirds of all blacks had individual incomes below $10,000 and just over 10 percent of them had more than a secondary education, among Catholic members of the race only 56 percent had incomes under $10,000; 30 percent had training beyond high school; and 25 percent had incomes over $15,000 (Tables VIII–1 and VIII–2).

Various studies conducted in the same period revealed that Catholics were not steadfastly conservative. According to the NORC surveys for 1977, 1978, and 1980, 28.3 percent of American Catholics considered themselves liberal and 29.9 percent identified themselves as conservative; the comparable figures for Protestants were 22.1 percent and 38.0 percent. Indeed, throughout the 1960s and 1970s, Catholics proved at least as liberal as Protestants on a variety of controversial social questions. As early as 1967, approximately 24 percent of the Catholic population took a dovish stance on Vietnam, while only 16.5 percent of American Protestants assumed a similar position. Both Catholics and Protestants were overwhelmingly and equally opposed to the use of busing for the purpose of integrating schools; yet, according to data reported in 1972, 78 percent of Catholic and 72 percent of Protestant blue-collar workers claimed to be willing to vote for a black presidential candidate. Even on the explosive issue of abortion, the Catholic laity was more like the general population than different from it. Responses from the NORC surveys for 1977, 1978, and 1980 showed that Protestants and Catholics accepted legalized abortion by margins of 92 percent and 86 percent, respectively, in situations of danger to the mother's health; 85 percent and 79 percent, respectively, in cases involving defective fetuses; and 84 percent and 80 percent, respectively, in pregnancies resulting from rape. Majorities in both religions rejected abortions for couples who simply wanted no more children and for single women. Protestants and Catholics disagreed only on the propriety of abortions to prevent the addition of new mouths in poor families: 51 percent of the former accepted the practice, and 54 percent of the latter rejected it.

TABLE VIII-1

Race, Religion, Ethnicity, and Educational Level, 1977, 1978, 1980

| Population Category | Less Than High School (%) | High School (%) | Junior College (%) | Four-Year College (%) | Graduate School (%) |
|---|---|---|---|---|---|
| Race | | | | | |
| White (4005)[1] | 30.7 | 51.6 | 2.6 | 10.3 | 4.8 |
| Black (471) | 45.4 | 43.7 | 3.0 | 5.7 | 2.1 |
| Religion (whites only) | | | | | |
| Protestant (2487) | 32.3 | 51.5 | 2.5 | 9.2 | 4.4 |
| Catholic (1076) | 30.9 | 53.1 | 2.8 | 9.6 | 3.6 |
| Jewish (95) | 15.8 | 40.0 | 2.1 | 22.1 | 20.0 |
| Protestant denomination (whites only) | | | | | |
| Baptist (657) | 42.2 | 48.5 | 1.8 | 5.5 | 2.0 |
| Methodist (493) | 26.2 | 53.1 | 3.0 | 11.8 | 5.5 |
| Lutheran (343) | 26.2 | 60.6 | 1.7 | 6.4 | 5.0 |
| Presbyterian (203) | 23.6 | 51.2 | 3.9 | 15.3 | 5.9 |
| Episcopalian (108) | 13.9 | 43.5 | 6.5 | 24.1 | 12.0 |
| Nondenominational (152) | 32.2 | 50.0 | 2.6 | 9.9 | 5.3 |
| Ethnic group | | | | | |
| Czechoslovak (61) | 23.0 | 65.5 | 3.3 | 8.2 | 0.0 |
| English, Scot, Welsh (638) | 20.4 | 49.4 | 3.9 | 19.1 | 7.2 |
| German (731) | 26.1 | 57.0 | 3.4 | 8.3 | 5.1 |
| Irish Protestant (228) | 32.0 | 57.0 | 1.3 | 7.0 | 2.6 |
| Irish Catholic (156) | 19.2 | 55.1 | 3.2 | 17.9 | 4.5 |
| Italian (199) | 35.2 | 47.2 | 5.5 | 9.5 | 2.5 |
| Mexican (62) | 51.6 | 41.9 | 1.6 | 4.8 | 0.0 |
| Polish (126) | 31.7 | 52.4 | 0.8 | 9.5 | 5.6 |
| Scandinavian (164) | 20.7 | 54.2 | 4.3 | 14.0 | 6.1 |
| American Indian (129) | 40.3 | 54.2 | 1.6 | 2.3 | 1.6 |
| Overall (4517) | 32.1 | 50.7 | 2.7 | 9.9 | 4.6 |

Source: *General Social Survey Cumulative File, 1972–1980* [machine-readable data file]. Principal Investigator, James A. Davis, NORC ed. (Chicago: National Opinion Research Center [producer], 1980). (Ann Arbor: Inter–University Consortium for Political and Social Research [distributor]). Data extraction and computations done by Thomas J. Archdeacon.

[1] Some percentages may not add 100.0 because of decimal rounding effects.

In politics, despite fears expressed by popular commentators that black protest and antiwar demonstrations would provoke an ethnic backlash, Catholics did not turn decisively in the 1960s and 1970s to conservative Republicanism. The NORC data from the late 1970s showed that a sizable majority of Catholics still called themselves Democrats. They did not equal blacks or Jews in loyalty to the party, but they far exceeded Protestants in allegiance, particularly outside Baptist strongholds in the South. Predominantly Catholic ethnic groups tended still to be Democratic in orientation. Protestant dominated nationalities, although sharing in the general post–New Deal predisposi-

TABLE VIII-2

Race, Religion, Ethnicity, and Income Distribution, 1977, 1978, 1980

| POPULATION CATEGORY | LESS THAN $5,000 (%) | $5,000– $9,999 (%) | $10,000– $14,999 (%) | $15,000– $19,999 (%) | $20,000– $24,999 (%) | $25,000– $49,999 (%) | $50,000 + (%) |
|---|---|---|---|---|---|---|---|
| Race | | | | | | | |
| White (2537) | 24.6 | 24.1 | 20.6 | 13.8 | 6.8 | 6.3 | 1.5 |
| Black (275) | 35.6 | 29.1 | 22.2 | 6.5 | 2.2 | 1.5 | 0.4 |
| Religion (whites only) | | | | | | | |
| Protestant (1520) | 25.2 | 25.1 | 20.5 | 14.5 | 6.3 | 5.1 | 1.3 |
| Catholic (683) | 26.2 | 24.0 | 20.5 | 12.2 | 7.5 | 6.4 | 1.2 |
| Jewish (62) | 11.3 | 21.0 | 16.1 | 11.3 | 4.8 | 16.1 | 11.3 |
| Protestant denomination (whites only) | | | | | | | |
| Baptist (404) | 30.7 | 27.5 | 19.1 | 13.1 | 3.7 | 4.0 | 0.2 |
| Methodist (304) | 19.4 | 21.4 | 23.4 | 17.4 | 7.2 | 5.9 | 2.0 |
| Lutheran (216) | 23.1 | 28.7 | 17.1 | 14.4 | 8.8 | 4.2 | 1.4 |
| Presbyterian (113) | 23.9 | 23.9 | 27.4 | 8.0 | 5.3 | 8.0 | 2.7 |
| Episcopalian (65) | 18.5 | 24.6 | 18.5 | 16.9 | 7.7 | 6.2 | 6.2 |
| Nondenominational (98) | 25.5 | 19.4 | 23.5 | 12.2 | 4.1 | 10.2 | 0.0 |
| Ethnic Group | | | | | | | |
| Czechoslovak (50) | 24.0 | 28.0 | 22.0 | 12.0 | 6.0 | 6.0 | 2.0 |
| English, Scot, Welsh (399) | 22.3 | 21.8 | 22.3 | 14.5 | 9.5 | 6.3 | 2.5 |
| German (479) | 23.4 | 23.6 | 21.1 | 15.0 | 7.3 | 6.5 | 1.3 |
| Irish Protestant (147) | 26.5 | 32.0 | 15.6 | 12.2 | 3.4 | 7.5 | 1.4 |
| Irish Catholic (95) | 28.4 | 18.9 | 17.9 | 13.7 | 6.3 | 9.5 | 1.0 |
| Italian (126) | 23.0 | 25.4 | 20.6 | 10.3 | 8.7 | 7.1 | 0.0 |
| Mexican (44) | 31.8 | 25.0 | 25.0 | 11.4 | 6.8 | 0.0 | 0.0 |
| Polish (81) | 27.2 | 22.2 | 18.5 | 13.6 | 7.4 | 7.4 | 0.0 |
| Scandinavian (111) | 21.6 | 23.4 | 21.6 | 15.3 | 9.0 | 5.4 | 1.8 |
| American Indian (76) | 30.3 | 25.0 | 17.1 | 17.1 | 6.6 | 2.6 | 0.0 |
| Overall (2774) | 26.3 | 25.3 | 21.2 | 13.3 | 6.5 | 5.9 | 1.5 |

SOURCE: *General Social Survey Cumulative File, 1972–1980* [machine–readable data file]. Principal Investigator, James A. Davis. NORC ed. (Chicago: National Opinion Research Center [producer], 1980). (Ann Arbor: Inter–University Consortium for Political and Social Research [distributor]). Data extraction and computations done by Thomas J. Archdeacon.

[1] The percentages may not always add to 100.0 because a few people refused to divulge information about their incomes.

tion toward the Democrats, were above the overall average in their support for the Republican party. The Irish were perhaps the most notable exception to their generalization. Irish Protestants, probably because of their identification with the traditional Democratic stronghold in the South, exceeded their Catholic counterparts in their allegiance to the party of Jefferson and Jackson, but Irish Catholics also scored above the national mean in this regard. Germans, however, strikingly confirm the rule of thumb: Catholic Germans far exceeded Protestant ones both in strength of their liberal leanings and in their identity with the Democrats (Table VIII–3).

Although Republican presidential candidates fared much better since the late 1960s than an observer might have predicted on the basis of the pattern of nominal party affiliations, the popular self-assessments of political attitudes and allegiances have translated well as relative measures of group electoral behavior at the critically important national level. Race has had a clear impact on voting. Black Americans, who disproportionately endure the sting of low income and discrimination, were the most persistent supporters of liberal and Democratic candidates. Of all groups blacks were the most loyal in 1980 to President Jimmy Carter, who benefited among them both by virtue of his southern and religious ties and because of the troubling forces gathered in support of his opponent. Among whites, Protestants, especially outside the South, maintained their traditional position as the most Republican-leaning religious group; Jews remained remarkably strong Democrats; and Catholics fell into an intermediate position. Catholics seemed inclined to continue their historic ties with the Democratic party except during years, such as 1972 and 1980, in which it put forward a grossly unpopular nominee; even then, however, they showed no real enthusiasm for the Republican alternative (Table VIII–4).

To a number of commentators, the resilience, despite this mass of evidence, of inaccurate and unsympathetic stereotypes about Catholics indicated the presence of residual nativism and a general indifference about this group's remaining problems and legitimate interests. The knowledgeable realized that contrary to media reports, religious prejudice had tainted even the most important symbol of Catholic integration, John F. Kennedy's presidential election. The best academic study of the results showed that while the senator had gained the votes of some Catholic Republicans, he had lost more support among Protestant Democrats and independents. Kennedy lost at least 2 percent of the ballots a Democrat could have expected had traditional voting patterns held; he probably fell short by a larger margin, inasmuch as economic factors strongly favored his party in 1960. Furthermore, for some Catholic spokesmen prejudice and discrimination were matters of personal experience. They were stung by government officials and foundation directors who openly said that Catholics were politically and socially unimportant and by professors at elite private universities who doubted that they would display enough intellectual vigor to deserve faculty posts. At the same time, Catholic leaders knew that Italians, Poles, and other ethnic co-religionists were badly underrepresented in some desirable occupations. Indeed, at one point in the 1970s, out of the

TABLE VIII-3

Race, Religion, Ethnicity, and Political Attitude and Affiliation,
1977, 1978, 1980

| | POLITICAL ATTITUDE | | | POLITICAL AFFILIATION | | |
| POPULATION CATEGORY | Liberal (%) | Moderate (%) | Conservative (%) | Democrat (%) | Independent (%) | Republican (%) |
|---|---|---|---|---|---|---|
| Race | | | | | | |
| White (3849, 3998)[1] | 26.5 | 39.4 | 34.0 | 51.3 | 14.3 | 34.0 |
| Black (432, 471) | 35.4 | 38.9 | 25.6 | 77.6 | 13.0 | 9.1 |
| Religion (whites only) | | | | | | |
| Protestant (2395, 2485) | 22.1 | 39.9 | 38.0 | 46.2 | 13.1 | 40.5 |
| Catholic (1035, 1074) | 28.3 | 41.8 | 29.9 | 61.4 | 14.0 | 23.8 |
| Jewish (92, 95) | 42.4 | 40.2 | 17.4 | 65.2 | 16.8 | 16.9 |
| Protestant denomination (whites only) | | | | | | |
| Baptist (628, 659) | 22.1 | 40.4 | 37.5 | 53.7 | 13.4 | 32.5 |
| Methodist (481, 492) | 23.7 | 41.4 | 34.9 | 43.1 | 11.8 | 45.0 |
| Lutheran (336, 342) | 20.3 | 42.8 | 36.9 | 45.4 | 11.1 | 43.2 |
| Presbyterian (198, 203) | 21.3 | 34.8 | 43.9 | 38.8 | 10.3 | 50.7 |
| Episcopalian (108, 107) | 28.7 | 38.0 | 33.3 | 26.2 | 13.1 | 57.9 |
| Nondenominational (147,152) | 25.2 | 37.4 | 37.4 | 50.0 | 19.1 | 30.9 |

| Ethnic group | | | | | | |
|---|---|---|---|---|---|---|
| Czechoslovak (61, 61) | 24.6 | 47.5 | 27.9 | 59.0 | 18.0 | 23.0 |
| English, Scot, Welsh (626, 636) | 24.6 | 34.0 | 41.3 | 44.5 | 10.4 | 44.6 |
| German Protestant (498, 512) | 20.5 | 37.3 | 42.2 | 40.4 | 10.9 | 48.2 |
| German Catholic (147, 150) | 29.9 | 45.6 | 24.5 | 62.7 | 14.6 | 22.7 |
| Irish Protestant (219,226) | 26.9 | 40.2 | 32.9 | 63.7 | 8.4 | 27.9 |
| Irish Catholic (155, 156) | 26.4 | 39.4 | 34.2 | 56.4 | 7.7 | 32.7 |
| Italian (188, 198) | 26.6 | 43.6 | 29.8 | 57.6 | 18.7 | 21.7 |
| Mexican (57, 62) | 45.6 | 38.6 | 15.8 | 71.0 | 11.3 | 17.7 |
| Polish (120, 126) | 23.3 | 46.7 | 30.0 | 61.9 | 17.5 | 20.6 |
| Scandinavian (164, 164) | 24.4 | 39.6 | 36.0 | 49.4 | 14.0 | 36.6 |
| American Indian (128, 129) | 32.0 | 34.4 | 33.6 | 58.9 | 13.2 | 27.9 |
| Overall (4317, 4510) | 27.5 | 39.3 | 33.2 | 53.9 | 14.2 | 31.3 |

SOURCE: General Social Survey Cumulative File, 1972–1980 [machine-readable data file]. Principal investigator, James A. Davis, NORC ed. (Chicago: National Opinion Research Center [producer], 1980). (Ann Arbor: Inter-University Consortium for Political and Social Research [distributor]). Data extraction and computations done by Thomas J. Archdeacon.

[1] The numbers in parentheses are, respectively, the numbers of cases for which there was information on political attitude and political affiliation. The percentages for the latter may not always add to 100.0 because a few people identified themselves as belonging to minor parties or declined to divulge information about their attitudes.

TABLE VIII-4
Race, Religion, Ethnicity, and Presidential Voting, 1972, 1976, 1980

| | 1972 | | 1976 | | 1980[1] | | |
|---|---|---|---|---|---|---|---|
| POPULATION CATEGORY | Nixon (%) | McGovern (%) | Ford (%) | Carter (%) | Reagan (%) | Carter (%) | Anderson (%) |
| Race | | | | | | | |
| White (807, 2516, 856)[2] | 64.8 | 32.7 | 47.2 | 50.6 | 56.4 | 32.9 | 9.1 |
| Black (77, 258, 106) | 16.9 | 83.1 | 6.6 | 93.0 | 6.6 | 92.5 | 0.9 |
| Religion (whites only) | | | | | | | |
| Protestant (500, 1560, 537) | 74.0 | 23.0 | 52.3 | 45.6 | 60.5 | 30.7 | 7.3 |
| Catholic (230, 702, 207) | 53.9 | 43.9 | 40.7 | 57.3 | 50.7 | 40.1 | 9.2 |
| Jewish (27, 68, 30) | 25.9 | 74.1 | 33.8 | 63.2 | 36.7 | 46.7 | 13.3 |
| Protestant denomination (whites only)[3] | | | | | | | |
| Baptist (109, 368, 115) | 74.3 | 20.2 | 45.1 | 53.5 | 64.3 | 30.4 | 5.2 |
| Methodist (123, 345, 97) | 74.0 | 23.6 | 57.4 | 40.6 | 59.8 | 33.0 | 5.2 |
| Lutheran (96, 225, 66) | 75.0 | 25.0 | 46.2 | 51.6 | 57.7 | 30.2 | 12.1 |
| Presbyterian (41, 137, 54) | 78.0 | 22.0 | 59.9 | 39.4 | 66.7 | 24.1 | 7.4 |
| Episcopalian (25, 89, 29) | 60.0 | 36.0 | 60.7 | 37.1 | 72.4 | 20.7 | 6.9 |
| Nondenominational (25, 87, 35) | 72.0 | 20.0 | 48.3 | 48.3 | 68.6 | 25.7 | 5.7 |
| Ethnic group[3] | | | | | | | |
| Czechoslovak (12, 40, 9) | 75.0 | 25.0 | 37.5 | 60.0 | 66.7 | 22.2 | 11.1 |
| English, Scot, Welsh (140, 473, 101) | 72.1 | 24.3 | 55.6 | 41.2 | 52.5 | 35.6 | 11.9 |

| German Protestant | | | | | | | |
|---|---|---|---|---|---|---|---|
| (111, 336, 96) | 73.9 | 23.4 | 55.7 | 43.2 | 71.9 | 17.7 | 10.4 |
| German Catholic (30, 99, 33) | 43.3 | 53.3 | 44.3 | 53.5 | 36.4 | 48.5 | 15.1 |
| Irish Protestant (43, 141, 42) | 72.1 | 23.3 | 45.4 | 53.2 | 59.2 | 35.1 | 5.7 |
| Irish Catholic (33, 122, 42) | 60.6 | 36.4 | 49.2 | 47.5 | 47.6 | 35.7 | 16.7 |
| Italian (48, 116, 25) | 58.3 | 39.6 | 36.2 | 62.1 | 56.0 | 28.0 | 16.0 |
| Mexican (7, 25, 8) | 42.9 | 57.1 | 16.0 | 84.0 | 25.0 | 62.5 | 12.5 |
| Polish (23, 86, 14) | 52.2 | 47.8 | 32.6 | 64.0 | 42.9 | 50.0 | 7.1 |
| Scandinavian (40, 111, 35) | 70.0 | 27.5 | 48.6 | 48.6 | 51.4 | 31.4 | 11.4 |
| American Indian (10, 65, 10) | 60.0 | 40.0 | 32.3 | 67.7 | 60.0 | 30.0 | 10.0 |
| Overall (883, 2766, 972) | 61.2 | 37.3 | 43.8 | 55.0 | 50.8 | 39.4 | 8.3 |

SOURCE: For the 1972 and 1976 data: *General Social Survey Cumulative File, 1972–1980* [machine-readable data file]. Principal investigator, James A. Davis. NORC ed. (Chicago: National Opinion Research Center [producer], 1980). (Ann Arbor: Inter–University Consortium for Political and Social Research [distributor]); for the 1980 data: *American National Election Study, 1980: Pre- and-Post-Election Surveys* [machine-readable data file]. Principal investigator, Warren E. Miller. 1982 ed. (Ann Arbor: Center for Political Studies, Institute for Social Research, University of Michigan [producer]. (Ann Arbor: Inter–University Consortium for Political and Social Research [distributor]). Data extraction and computations done by Thomas J. Archdeacon.

[1] This study involved pre-election interviews with 1,614 persons and post-election interviews with 1,408 of the same respondents.

[2] The numbers in parentheses represent the number of voters in the particular group for the 1972, 1976, and 1980 elections, respectively. The percentages for the vote in each election may not add to 100.0 because a few people cast ballots for candidates from minor parties or declined to divulge for whom they voted.

[3] Unfortunately, some of the population categories used by the Center for Political Studies do not or may not exactly coincide with those used by the National Opinion Research Center in its surveys. For the 1980 figures in this table Baptist includes both Baptist and southern Baptist; Lutheran joins Lutheran and Missouri Synod Lutheran; and nondenominational Protestant combines persons without specific Protestant affiliations and members of avowedly nondenominational congregations. Likewise, some adjustments were made to fit the Center for Political Studies ethnic data to this table. Most notably, Irish Protestant means either Irish or Scotch-Irish.

4 million Italo-Americans in the New York region, only fifteen were among 912 lawyers associated with the twenty largest law firms in the city. But what rankled Catholics most was the widespread assumption that the absence of women or of members of racial minorities in socially desirable positions was prima facie evidence of discrimination whereas the similar absence of white Catholics was proof of the latter's inferiority. Whatever the patterns actually meant about job discrimination, the attitude revealed the existence of a "respectable bigotry" against Catholic ethnics.

Irritated and frustrated spokesmen for the national groups associated with the new immigration hoped that a revitalization of ethnicity would help their constituencies find a full and equal place in America. In the worst cases the call for a new ethnicity fostered a new set of inaccurate stereotypes that pitted the loving families and warm neighborhoods of southern and eastern Europeans against the emotional coldness and rigid moralism of white, Anglo-Saxon Protestants, or WASPS, as the dôminant group was tautologically called. In the best, this appeal reminded people under pressure to respect themselves as they had been taught to respect others. The declaration of the new ethnicity echoed and resembled the cry of black power, but the differences between these movements were substantial. Whereas the latter celebrated a color that could not be escaped and a culture formed and kept alive by segregation, the former sought to recapture what no longer had the institutional or social base to sustain itself. Books like Michael Novak's *Rise of the Unmeltable Ethnic,* which poignantly recounted the struggles of America's Poles, Italians, Greeks, and Slavs, were the products of writers intelligent and introspective enough to recognize fundamental changes and to understand that they brought losses, as well as gains. But such works came a generation too late to affect profoundly people who were making progress, however halting, by suppressing their pasts. For this reason, much of the ethnic revival never got beyond the stage of wistful recollections.

A politically potent new ethnicity was not born in the 1960s and 1970s, but observers became aware that Americans from all kinds of backgrounds were conscious of their heritages. The social surveys taken by NORC in 1977, 1978, and 1980 revealed that only 12.5 percent of the persons polled could not or, for some reason, did not answer the following question: "From what countries or part of the world did your ancestors come?" Just 2.4 percent named America as the only or primary country of origin. Thus, a mere 14.9 percent of the population did not acknowledge affiliation with at least one of the ethnic subgroups present in the society. Even this number might have been an overestimation rooted in a misunderstanding of the question. Blacks were overrepresented among those who could not name a place of origin; they constituted 10.4 percent of the 4,493 persons in the sample who provided some kind of answer to the questions on race and ethnic background but accounted for 23.8 percent of the 529 men and women who could not identify a homeland. Moreover, of the 107 persons who described themselves simply as American, 50.5 percent were black. If the 194 blacks who could not choose a country of ancestry or who identified themselves as exclusively American are recognized on the basis or prima facie evidence as having obvious, albeit remote, African backgrounds, then only 10.6 percent of all the men and women in the sample could not be clustered in a non-American ethnic subgroup.

Examined from another perspective, the NORC data showed that three-quarters of all Americans could name a familial point of origin that either was outside the continental bounds of the United States or, in the case of American Indians, predated European settlement of the nation. About 50 percent of the men and women in the total sample selected a single answer other than "America only" to the question "From what countries or part of the world did your ancestors come?" Another 24.4 percent chose a response other than "America only" when asked to pick between the two answers they initially had offered. Members of a third group, which included approximately 10.8 percent of the 4,530 persons polled, also claimed dual identities, at least one of which, by the construction of the question, had to be that of an ethnic minority. These people, unlike those in the second category, were unable to choose between their two perceived affiliations. The vast majority of respondents in all three groups were American born; among those able to choose a primary identity the percentage of natives amounted to 91.5; and among those unable to select between two affiliations the figure reached 98.4. Unfortunately, the data did not include the kinds of additional information needed to uncover some basic characteristics of the men and women with multiple ties. Most notably, the surveys did not reveal how many in this group traced their roots to two minority peoples or how many combined an ethnic identity with a strictly American one. Common sense suggests that a good portion of the respondents in the second and third groups were hyphenates claiming backgrounds such as German-American or Italian-American.

As evidence of widespread ethnic consciousness mounted in the 1960s and 1970s, scholars discerned the need for research that included an ethnic dimension and monitored its interactions with religion, economics, and other factors. This approach, which worries less about the amorphous concept of ethnic culture than about the behavior of ethnic blocs under varying political and social conditions, had a broad appeal among academics and an apparently special fascination for the Irish-Americans in their ranks. Indeed, as far back as 1963, in an influential book entitled *Beyond the Melting Pot*, Daniel Patrick Moynihan had joined the Jewish sociologist Nathan Glazer in applying such an approach to the study of New York City. The reasons for this appeal are problematic, but some conjectures may be in order. The Irish-Americans were never impressed by the new ethnicity. They recognized, sadly but realistically, that almost all the visible and usable elements of their Celtic past were long gone, and they saw no hope for others or benefit to themselves in efforts to resuscitate the moribund heritages of Americans from southern and eastern Europe. They may have intuitively realized that findings drawn from a multifaceted approach would keep them in the prominent position they had held among the ethnic groups as leaders of the Roman Catholic church. Finally, the traditional Irish status and function as an intermediary group between the Anglo-Saxons and the new immigrants may have given Irish-Americans a valuable sense of the complexity of U.S. social patterns and of the need for subtlety in explaining them.

Ethnic background, it seems clear, can affect actions and attitudes whether the person involved is unconscious of his or her heritage, publicly rejects it, or chauvinistically flaunts it. For the most part ethnicity is a clue to the historical experiences of recognizable subgroups of Americans—why they came to the United States, when they arrived, where they lived, how they were welcomed, and what they have achieved. Ethnicity can also call attention to deeply rooted cultural and psychological patterns, but scholars have probably had much more success dispelling rather than sustaining traditional assumptions about the independent importance of such almost mystical factors. The modern, multivariate techniques that make it possible statistically to distinguish the effects of various kinds of social attributes indicate that ethnicity's individual impact is real but limited. Ethnic background almost always works interdependently with several other factors, including age, generation, education, income, occupation, and place of residence. The effect of a particular ethnic heritage is neither universal nor immutable: the Irish in Boston have an American history that is different from that of those in Chicago; poor Jews and rich ones do not necessarily think alike; Italian-Americans of the second generation do not automatically share the world view of their offspring in the third. Hence, although communication and comprehension require simplification, generalizations related to ethnicity must be made with proper caution and qualification.

The almost symbiotic relationship between ethnicity and religion remains obvious. Nevertheless, the two factors are conceptually, if not always practically, separate and deserve to be analyzed individually. Religion can build bridges between members of different nationalities and create gulfs between persons of the same origin. Yet each ethnic group tends to have an individualized interpretation and practice of the religious tradition it shares with other nationalities. There undoubtedly has been a common Catholic experience in the United States born of the interactions of the various Catholic minorities with each other and with the host society. But the habits and perhaps even some of the central attitudes of the Irish, Germans, Italians, and others who constitute the Catholic population have not melted into equivalence. In an analogous, though substantially different, fashion, the presence of Sephardim from Iberia, Westernized Germans, and the main body of Ashkenazim from central and eastern Europe has imparted to American Judaism not only a heritage of three centuries in the Western Hemisphere but also a measure of ethnic diversity. Furthermore, the emergence of Reform, Conservative, and Orthodox versions of Judaism has given formal recognition to variations of religious attitudes and experiences akin to those informally present in Catholicism. It must be recognized, however, that the small size of the Jewish population in the United States, the overwhelming proportion of central and eastern Europeans in it, and the absence of publicly gathered information on the fine points of Jewish religious practice make careful consideration of these ethnic and affiliational divisions almost impossible, except in certain large-scale, tightly focused studies. Finally, scholars have come to recognize the importance of the denominational divisions among American Protestants. Although these affiliations sometimes reflect nominal, rather than substantive, differences, they can reveal variations in doctrine and emphasis. Equally important, they can, given the historic connections between certain Protestant churches and particular ethnic groups, provide something like a key to the undocumentable national origins of old-stock Americans.

Reaching an understanding of the relationship between ethnicity and race and of their relative impacts on American history continues to be an intellectually difficult and politically sensitive task. Many students of white ethnic peoples resist treating race as a distinct concept dealing with a unique set of experiences. They recognize that undeserved suffering has played a crucial role in the histories of most groups that came to the United States. They are conscious that white ethnics, albeit to a significantly lesser degree than blacks, have had their assimilation impeded and their self-respect damaged both by ostracism and by economic deprivation. Moreover, they believe that changing popular attitudes and positive government programs have recently allowed blacks to achieve political influence on a par with that exercised at some times and in some places by European ethnics. On the other hand, many white and nonwhite observers of the black experience oppose the melding of race and ethnicity. They see the United States as responsible for the ills of the black population in a way that it cannot be held guilty for the pre-American pasts of the Irish, Jews, Poles, and others. And they resent arguments that cavalierly dismiss the blacks' long history in the United States by defining their legitimate expectations for success and acceptance in terms of the experiences of the latest, rather than the earliest, white immigrants.

Both sides exaggerate their legitimate arguments. The former, on the one hand, tend through their descriptions of white ethnics as late arrivals and as targets of prejudice themselves to free them of responsibility for the original wrongs done to Africans and others and to weaken the claims of racial minorities to special consideration in today's social competition. The latter, on the other, drift toward the questionable principle of white collective guilt for the past when they tar as racism the unwillingness of the ethnics to endanger hard-won gains. The first group forgets how all whites have profited indirectly from racism and the second how few disadvantages some mobile blacks have personally endured.

Neither ethnicity nor race has been a constant either in its conceptual content or in its practical impact. As abstractions each is a scientifically imprecise system for classifying peoples by their cultural, physical, and supposedly innate traits; in that sense, the latter seems primarily an extension of the former. In practice, race has been a much more fundamental factor than ethnicity for most of America's history. Race has pointed to more striking and immutable differences; racism has had a more fixed, focused target than the changing collection of ethnic prejudices has had; and the existence of a strong color line has provided a reliable criterion for the implementation of institutionalized discrimination. In recent years, however, the official proscription of racism and the effort to extend social benefits to dark-skinned Americans have signaled significant change. Among the racial minorities current reforms have created a new order divided between those persons for whom color has become a badge of historical experience, rather than of current liability, and those who are so socially disadvantaged by the past as not to be able to participate in the improvements of the present. For the former, the difference between race and ethnicity has become quantitative—a matter of degree; for the latter, the difference continues to be qualitative—a matter of kind.

Immigration, ethnicity, religion, and race have been and continue to be integral parts of American history. All of these elements undoubtedly have caused great torment to the country and its people, but they have also made contributions of fundamental political and social importance. Time and again, the presence of alien peoples, in both the specific and the general meanings of that term, has forced the nation to confront its founding principle of human equality and its self-proclaimed mission to be a refuge of liberty. The responses have been fitful and reluctant and the implementation of the vows imperfect, but

Americans more often than not have reaffirmed their ideals and with each repetition have gained a broader understanding of their destiny. Moreover, ethnic, religious, and racial divisions have paradoxically been important sources of communal identity counterbalancing the atomizing tendencies inherent in America's rapid growth and in its mystique of geographic mobility. Finally, as the society has increasingly emphasized the central position of economic success in the self-image of the United States, immigration and these divisions have helped perpetuate the vision of America as the land of unlimited opportunity. The nation's unfailing ability to capture the imaginations of the world's poor has been the best evidence of the promise here of a better life. And even more important, the availability of foreigners, unassimilated ethnics, and supposedly unabsorbable minorities to fill many of the lowliest occupational ranks has allowed Americans to avoid thinking of failure as a phenomenon affecting natives and, to the dismay of the left, to reject the idea of permanent class divisions that has revolutionized modern politics elsewhere. Of course, it is not clear that such opportune reinforcements of the nation's ideals and myths will continue to be available, and how the absence of these artificial supports may affect the course of politics and of domestic socioeconomic relationships remains the great question for the future.

# Epilogue:
# America, 1980

MEASUREMENTS OF CHANGE necessarily involve comparison, and evaluation of future developments in America's ethnic structure and its related social and economic patterns will have to be made in terms of an earlier base. It seems proper, therefore, to conclude this study with some observations pertinent to current conditions in the United States. The task is not easy, given the absence from the federal decennial census of questions relating either to religion or to the remote foreign origins of persons with at least one generation of ancestors born in this country. Even producing overall estimates of the ethnoreligious composition of the general population is difficult. In 1969, for example, the Census Bureau, in a Current Population Report, asked a representative sample of non-Spanish-Americans to identify their "origin or descent" according to the following categories: German, Irish, Italian, Polish, Russian, English, Negro, American Indian, other, or don't know. Three years later, another Current Population Report asked the same question but listed French as an additional response, added Scots and Welsh to the English category, and instructed questioners to probe more deeply into the backgrounds of people who initially had trouble specifying a non-U.S. point of family origin. The "don't know" rate remained stable, registering 8.9 percent in 1969 and 8.6 percent in 1972, but the reformulation of the question produced changes in other categories. The "other" classification, which incorporated black respondents in its final form, decreased from 53.3 to 41.1 percent and several European nationalities made sizable gains.

Information available from the General Social Surveys conducted in 1977, 1978, and 1980 by the National Opinion Research Center (NORC) of Chicago helps compensate for the shortcomings of the Census Bureau's data and for questions unasked in the Current Population Reports. Each of these three studies was based on the responses of approximately 1,500 adult residents of the continental United States to more than 200 questions about their demographic characteristics, personal and family histories, socioeconomic situations, and attitudes on a host of political issues and cultural phenomena. Each survey uncovered, within a reasonable margin of error, the pattern of answers that would have been found had every American adult been polled. Together the studies reported on enough cases to make feasible discussion of the particular attributes of the nation's ethnic and religious subpopulations. Estimates based on these NORC surveys indicate that whites constituted 88.6 percent of the American population; blacks, 10.5 percent; and members of other races, .9 percent. Not surprisingly, the third category included Asian men and women such as Chinese, Japanese, and Filipinos, but it also incorporated about 5 percent of the American Indians in the sample. Of the blacks counted, 48.7 percent claimed African as their ethnic background, 26.6 percent could not name a people or place of origin, 11.4 percent identified themselves as "American only," and 3.6 percent classified themselves as American Indian. This last choice might seem unusual, but it is plausible given the high frequency of black and Indian intermarriage in some areas of the country. Most other blacks assigned themselves to ethnic groups, such as West Indian, that are known to share in African culture. A tiny remainder, who were possibly of mixed racial origin, claimed basically European heritages.

Using the NORC data to establish the distribution of ethnic backgrounds within the white population poses some methodological problems. The 473 whites who declined to choose between two perceived ethnic heritages may have been people, like German-Scandinavians, with deeply felt dual non-American identities; such respondents should perhaps be represented as half persons in the tallies of each of the appropriate groups. Or they may have been persons, like Italian-Americans, whom a disinterested observer might readily assign, on the basis of historical common knowledge, to a single, non-American ethnic group. The most prudent course of action may be to assume that the unspecified nationalities associated with this group reflected the general pattern of nationalities claimed by the 4,015 whites able to settle on a single identity. Consequently, these respondents can be omitted from subsequent consideration. Dealing with the 403 men and women who could not name any people or place of origin and the 29 for whom information is completely missing is more difficult. Should these seemingly rootless people be classified as completely assimilated American only? In the following analysis, these 432 persons are handled in three different ways: all are omitted; half are omitted and half are counted as American only; and all are counted as American only. Computations based on these three approaches lead, respectively, to high, medium, and low estimates of the contributions of various national and ethnic groups to the present American population (Table E–1).

Estimates thus calculated are informative but must be used with caution. For the most part they are consistent in their rankings of the representation of various ethnic subcommunities in the American population, and the percentages they present can serve as a rough guide to the relative size of these groups. The estimates, however, are dependent on the efforts of respondents to classify themselves; they are not the product of scientifically rigorous projections based on the application of genealogical and demographic theories to indisputably accurate data. The range of the estimates reveals that the methods used are imprecise and the results achieved are prone to substantial revision in the context of reworded questions and newly permissible answers. Moreover, the reliance on self-description may lead to an undercount of those nationalities for which the main periods of immigration are most remote from the present. Of course, this argument must be tempered by the realization that the method of self-description has the advantages of documenting the possible growth of an American nationality and of not perpetuating the attribution of foreign ethnic identities to people who no longer deem these categories important in their lives.

Examination of the NORC data on the religious composition of the American population indicated that about 64 percent of the people surveyed were Protestant. Among these men and women 33 percent were Baptist; 19 percent, Methodist; 12 percent, Lutheran; 7 percent, Presbyterian; 5 percent, nondenominational; and 4 percent, Episcopalian. Approximately 25 percent of Americans were Catholics, 2 percent were Jews, over 1 percent belonged to other religions, and 7 percent had no church ties. As might be expected, ethnic and racial backgrounds and religion were strongly related. About 88 percent of the black population was Protestant, and among these men and women 69 percent belonged to the Baptist denomination. Germans, Scandinavians, and Finns accounted for almost three-quarters of the Lutherans in the United States. People of British descent constituted almost half of the Episcopalians. About 34 percent of America's Jews identified their ethnic heritage as Russian; conversely, Jews accounted for 70 percent of that nationality's representation in this country. Another 16 percent of the Jews called themselves Poles, 7 percent stated they were Germans, and almost 22 percent could not or would not claim a single identity. These figures not only testified to the prudence of recognizing the

TABLE E-1
Proportional Representation of America's Largest Ethnic Groups, 1969–1980

| NATIONAL ORIGIN | CPR 1969 (%) | CPR 1972 (%) | NORC 1977, 1978, 1980 | | |
|---|---|---|---|---|---|
| | | | A (%) | B (%) | C (%) |
| Germany | 10.1 | 12.5 | 18.0 | 19.0 | 20.1 |
| England, Scotland, Wales[1] | 9.6 | 14.4 | 15.8 | 16.7 | 17.7 |
| Ireland | 6.7 | 8.0 | 10.3 | 10.9 | 11.5 |
| Italy | 3.7 | 4.3 | 4.9 | 5.2 | 5.5 |
| Poland | 2.0 | 2.5 | 3.1 | 3.3 | 3.5 |
| Russia | 1.1 | 1.1 | 3.0 | 3.2 | 3.4 |
| American Indian | — | — | 2.6 | 2.7 | 2.9 |
| France | — | 2.6 | 2.0 | 2.1 | 2.2 |
| Scandinavia | — | — | 4.1 | 4.2 | 4.5 |
| Sweden | | | 1.8 | 1.9 | 2.0 |
| Norway | | | 1.5 | 1.5 | 1.6 |
| Denmark | | | 0.8 | 0.8 | 0.9 |
| Canada | — | — | 1.6 | 1.7 | 1.8 |
| French Canada | | | 0.9 | 0.9 | 1.0 |
| Other Canada | | | 0.7 | 0.8 | 0.8 |
| Spanish | 4.7 | 4.5 | 3.2 | 3.4 | 3.7 |
| Mexico | | | 1.5 | 1.6 | 1.7 |
| Puerto Rico | | | 0.7 | 0.8 | 0.8 |
| Spain | | | 0.6 | 0.6 | 0.7 |
| Other Spanish | | | 0.4 | 0.4 | 0.5 |
| Netherlands | — | — | 1.6 | 1.7 | 1.8 |
| Czechoslovakia | — | — | 1.5 | 1.6 | 1.7 |
| America only | — | — | 11.9 | 7.0 | 1.4 |
| Africa[2] | — | — | 10.5 | 10.5 | 10.5 |
| Other[3] | 53.3 | 41.6 | 5.9 | 6.6 | 7.8 |
| Not reported[4] | 8.9 | 8.6 | — | — | — |

SOURCE: U.S. Bureau of the Census, *Current Population Reports,* P20 (CPR), No. 221, "Characteristics of the Population by Ethnic Origin: November 1969 (Washington, D.C.: Government Printing Office, 1971); and No. 249, "Characteristics of the Population by Ethnic Origin: March 1972 and 1971" (Washington, D.C.: Government Printing Office, 1973); and *General Social Survey Cumulative File, 1972–1980* [machine-readable data file]. Principal investigator, James A. Davis. NORC ed. (Chicago: National Opinion Research Center [producer], 1980). (Ann Arbor: The Inter-University Consortium for Political and Social Research [distributor]). Data extraction and computation done by Thomas J. Archdeacon.

LEGEND A: assigning all whites without specified origin to the "America only" category; total population = 4,057.

B: assigning half of the whites without specified origin to the "America only" category and omitting the other half; total population = 3,841.

C: omitting all whites without specified origin; total population = 3,625.

[1] Scots and Welsh were counted in the "other" category in 1969.

[2] All blacks were arbitrarily assigned to this category for purposes of this table and the percentage of blacks in the population was fixed at that known to be in the whole sample of 4,530.

[3] All blacks were counted in the "other" category in 1969 and 1972.

[4] Percentages may not add to 100.0 because of decimal rounding effects.

special status of the Jewish subcommunity but also reaffirmed the wisdom of loosely equating the Russian ethnic group in the United States with descendants of the Jewish immigrants from the early years of the twentieth century.

An analysis of the intersection of ethnic background and religion also contradicted familiar stereotypes to reveal that 55 percent of the Irish in the survey were Protestant, while only 34 percent were Catholic and 7 percent professed no religion. No other major ethnic component of the population was so internally split and in no other did religious divisions reflect such fundamentally different historical experiences. America's Protestant Irish are the descendants of the Scotch-Irish pioneers and other Irish settlers from the colonial era, while the Catholic Irish in the United States have their roots in the great migrations of the nineteenth and twentieth centuries. Just under 47 percent of Irish-American Protestants interviewed lived in the southern states, where their ancestors made their homes, and almost a third of this group resided in the smallest villages and most rural areas of the country. By contrast, almost 73 percent of Irish-American Catholics lived in the northeastern quadrant of the nation, where this group has traditionally been found, and almost two-thirds of them resided in or immediately around cities with populations in excess of 50,000 people. It seems, in effect, that there are really two Irelands in the United States (Table E-2).

Children usually adopted the religious identity of their parents, but young people may have also changed or dropped their church ties as they matured. Such alterations weakened the connection between eth-

TABLE E-2
Religious Composition of America's Largest Ethnic Groups, 1977, 1978, 1980

| NATIONAL ORIGIN | PROTESTANT (%) | CATHOLIC (%) | JEWISH (%) | NO RELIGION (%) | OTHER (%) |
|---|---|---|---|---|---|
| Africa (230)[1] | 89.6 | 3.9 | 0.0 | 5.2 | 1.3 |
| England, Scotland, Wales (637) | 82.7 | 8.0 | 0.3 | 7.7 | 1.3 |
| Germany (730) | 70.1 | 20.7 | 1.0 | 7.7 | 0.5 |
| Ireland (417) | 54.7 | 37.4 | 0.5 | 7.2 | 0.2 |
| Italy (198) | 9.6 | 80.3 | 0.5 | 7.1 | 2.5 |
| Poland (124) | 12.1 | 71.8 | 12.1 | 4.0 | 0.0 |
| Scandinavia (163) | 85.3 | 10.4 | 0.0 | 4.3 | 0.0 |

SOURCE: General Social Survey Cumulative File, 1972–1980 [machine–readable data file]. Principal investigator, James A. Davis, NORC ed. (Chicago: National Opinion Research Center [producer], 1980). (Ann Arbor: The Inter–University Consortium for Political and Social Research [distributor]). Data extraction and computations done by Thomas J. Archdeacon.

[1] The numbers in parentheses represent the number of cases for which information on religious affiliation was available.

nicity and religion in the United States, and estimating the frequency with which this process occurred was an important but difficult task. Fortunately, the NORC surveys reported religious affiliations at age sixteen, as well as present religious ties, for 4,509 of the persons in the samples under scrutiny. The data revealed that in the interim between the teen and the adult years, the numbers of persons identifying themselves as Protestants or as Jews fell 4 percent, the Catholic total decreased by 6 percent, and the ranks of the uncommitted grew 138 percent. More specifically, over 83 percent of the Catholics remained in their church, over 8 percent became Protestants, and 7 percent dropped all religious ties. Among Jews about 87 pecent remained faithful, 2 percent became Protestants, 3 percent converted to Catholicism, and 6 percent abandoned religion. Among Protestants, about 90 percent remained in that category, over 3 percent became Catholics, and almost 6 percent lost all religious identity. Moreover, although the pattern of answers cannot prove this point, the data hinted strongly that the phenomenon of conversion in the United States is closely related to the occurrence of interfaith marriages: of married Protestants who had been raised as Catholics, 87 percent had Protestant spouses at the time of the survey; of married Catholics who had been raised as Protestants, almost 98 percent had Catholic mates.

Intrafaith marriage remained strong, however, especially among minority religions. According to the NORC surveys, 83.2 percent of the married respondents who were Protestant at age sixteen took spouses who were also Protestant in their teen years; about 13.7 percent married Catholics; and .2 percent wedded Jews. Among Catholics, 63.9 percent married people of their own faith; 32.6 percent, Protestants; and .8 percent, Jews. Among Jews, 69.4 percent took mates from the same background, 17.7 percent wed Protestants, and 8.1 percent married Catholics. If marriages had occurred at random, the intrafaith marriage rates would have been only 46 percent for Protestants, 6.76 percent for Catholics, and less than .5 percent for Jews. It ought to be noted, however, that while the patterns observed undoubtedly reflected conscious choices to preserve specific heritages by intragroup marriage or selective intermarriage, they also were the product of factors of geographic, social, or economic isolation, which lessen the opportunity for persons to meet potential spouses outside their immediate ethnic or religious circles.

The NORC data also uncovered a strong tendency for interfaith courtships to generate homogamous unions either upon marriage or thereafter. Rates of religious intrafaith marriage became noticeably higher when respondents answered in terms of the current church affiliations of themselves and their spouses. Among Protestants, the percentage of endogamy reached 89.2; among Catholics, it rose to 81.4;

and among Jews, it increased to 78.0. A close examination of differences in marriage patterns among various age groups, however, suggests that both the practice of marriage-related conversion and the traditional tendency of men and women to wed co-religionists may be weakening among Catholics and especially among Jews. Members of these minority groups who reached maturity in the recent era of general denominational rapprochment and of declining respect for institutional faith were less concerned than their elders with marrying co-religionists or converting their spouses. Among Catholics in their twenties when the surveys were taken only 70.8 percent were endogamously married and just 53.8 percent had wed co-religionists. The parallel figures were even lower among Jews in the same age group—50.0 and 37.5 percent, respectively.

Taken collectively, these findings seem to describe ethnicity in contemporary America. In fact, they are like a single frame from a motion picture. Ethnicity is a dynamic force that keeps America's national, racial, and religious groups in constant flux. And immigration continues to complicate the mix. Indeed, the importance of immigration for the United States has begun perhaps to increase again. Since the demise of the national origin quota law and the revision of the preference system, the United States has been admitting a greater and more ethnically diverse number of newcomers. Between July 1, 1960, and June 30, 1968, approximately 259,000 immigrants entered the country annually; from July 1, 1968, when the new law went fully into effect, until June 30, 1976, the figure rose to 391,000. These estimates, of course, include both quota and nonquota arrivals. During the same two periods the proportions of Europeans and Canadians in the totals fell, respectively, from 35.2 to 24.9 percent and from 16.5 to 3.3 percent; the share from other countries of the Western Hemisphere increased slightly, from 37.7 to 38.8 percent; and the portions from Africa and Asia rose, respectively, from .5 to 1.8 percent and from 9.2 to 28.1 percent. Both the Far and Middle East have been producing sizable numbers of emigrants, who create notable ethnic and racial diversity even within the strikingly large Asian component of this newest immigration. In the fiscal year of 1977, for example, the Philippines sent 39,111 people; Korea, 30,917; China, Taiwan, and Hong Kong, 25,396; India, 10,613; Vietnam and Thailand, 8,574; and Japan, 4,178. At the same time, Israel sent 3,008; Iran, Iraq, Jordan, Lebanon, and Syria contributed a total of 17,308. Finally, much of the current European immigration to the United States originates in nations that were formerly out of favor. Among the nations contributing more than 1,000 newcomers in 1977, for example, England sent 12,579; Portugal, 9,977; Italy, 7,369; Spain, 5,568; Russia, 5,443; Poland, 3,331; France, 2,651; Yugoslavia, 2,315; Rumania, 1,506; and the Netherlands, 1,039.

Most Americans are only dimly aware of the demographic impact of the nation's revised immigration laws and have reacted more to the particular applications rather than to the general principles of current U.S. refugee policies. But an increasing number have perceived disturbing implications in recent developments. Many Americans are especially concerned by sizable increases in the influx to the United States of legal and undocumented immigrants from the southern regions of the Western Hemisphere. According to the 1980 census, the number of persons of Spanish origin resident in the United States had reached 14,608,673 and accounted for 6.4 percent of the nation's total population. In 1980 Mexicans constituted an estimated 59.8 percent of the Spanish group; Puerto Ricans, 13.8 percent; and Cubans, 5.5 percent. Persons of Spanish origin form, after the black population, the largest identifiable ethnic minority in the United States. To some extent this statistic is an artifact of a tally that did not concern itself with the ethnic background of people whose forebears immigrated from Europe more than one generation ago. But it also reflects a real increase in the volume of immigration from Latin America, and it hints at the potential for an even greater flow of arrivals, especially from nearby Mexico. In 1979 the per capita gross national product of Mexico was $1,590, whereas that of the United States was $11,360, and the gap may grow. Nearly half of the Mexican population is under fifteen years of age, while the median age of non-Spanish-Americans is roughly thirty. The crude death rates for the two countries are approximately equal, but the Mexican crude birth rate, which has fluctuated between 37 and 45 per 1,000, is two to three times as large as the American, which was 15.4 in 1977. In 1978 Mexico had some 67 million people and the United States over 218 million, but, if natural increases were the only factor in growth, the former could surpass the latter in population sometime early in the next century. Overall, Mexico shows strong signs of a population crisis, and the lengthy border attaching that nation to the prosperous states of the American Southwest seems the most likely object against which the explosive force of the boom will be spent.

The Bureau of the Census reports that over 8.7 million persons of Mexican origin live in the United States, and the Immigration and Naturalization Service reports that an average of almost 63,000 Mexicans entered the country on permanent visas in each year from 1971 to 1976. This population, however, is constantly in flux. Many Mexicans use the alien registration receipt cards that identify them as legal immigrants as passes to get from their homes south of the border to jobs north of it. Approximately 64,000 of these "green carders" commute daily and a much smaller number enter the country periodically to take seasonal employment. Remigration is common, and a study has found that legal immigrants from the state of Michoacán spend an average of roughly nine months in the United States. The presence of a large contingent of migrants who cross the border surreptitiously and take pains to avoid subsequent capture or enumeration makes the task of accurately determining the size of the Mexican population in the United States even more difficult. The border patrol believes that its officers catch only one out of every three persons who try to enter the country illegally; this agency estimates that each year about 1.4 million Mexicans successfully cross into the United States without proper documentation. But the numbers of arrests and repatriations, on which these projections are based, reflect changes in enforcement efforts, as well as real ebbs and flows in undocumented immigration. In any case, these figures do not take into account the high remigration rate that leads the typical illegal Mexican entrant home after little more than a year. The best estimate of the impact of undocumented immigration suggests that the hidden traffic added between 425,000 and 1.2 million permanent Mexican residents to the American population between 1970 and 1975.

Latin American immigration, especially the illegal variety, is likely to become an increasingly prominent political issue in the United States. Just as previous generations of native-stock Americans feared the arrival of waves of European and Asian newcomers, members of the present population and their offspring will recoil from a major influx of predominantly Spanish-speaking *mestizos* and mulattoes. The ongoing battles in many school districts over the wisdom, goals, and methods of bilingual education are a harbinger of a potentially high level of cultural conflict. Reformers and less skilled workers, including legal Mexican immigrants, have begun to complain that unscrupulous employers exploit undocumented aliens, who dare not go to the authorities, and use them to undermine the position of the American labor force. Some taxpayers lay the additional charge that illegal immigrants are bankrupting the nation's social welfare system, but this allegation seems incorrect; investigations have shown that undocumented aliens, in order to avoid detection, neither dodge taxes nor seek many of the services to which registered residents are entitled. A number of communities, however, may be strained by judicial decisions obligating them to provide services, such as schooling, for the children of undocumented residents. Perceptions and problems like these will probably lead to popular pressure for effective programs to bring back under control the tide of immigration from Mexico and other Latin American states. In 1976 the United States amended its immigration law to impose on the nations of the Western Hemisphere the same individual annual limit of 20,000 visas placed on the countries in the rest of the world in 1965. The Congress also ordered that applicants for admission from other countries in the Americas no longer be issued entry permits on a first-come-first-served basis but instead be subjected to the general seven-point preference system. These two measures could substantially reduce the volume of legal Mexican arrivals and act as a barrier to immigration by the unskilled, but their long-term efficacy is doubtful. Documented and undocumented immigration are two facets of the same phenomenon; the latter will exist as long as the demand for permanent visas exceeds the supply of them, and the number of persons seeking admission to the United States will increase as long as rampant poverty and excessively rapid population growth plague America's southern neighbors and the island countries of the Caribbean.

Most observers agree that the first step in dealing with the problem of undocumented immigration is to make legal the status of aliens who have been living illegally in the country for a considerable time. That action would emancipate them from the exploitable situation in which they now exist and free the government from the thankless task of pursuing those elusive men and women. President Ronald Reagan has proposed that illegal aliens living in the United States before January 1, 1980, be declared "renewable term temporary residents." They would be ineligible for most forms of public assistance, but after ten years of continuous residence a person in this category could apply for permanent residency status provided he or she had learned to communicate in English. This proposal seems unworkable both in its restriction on social services and in its emphasis on acculturation of the first generation. It seems likely that at the end of a decade the government would have to abandon its avowed requirement of English competency, or bring down the passing standard for communication skills to a meaningless level, or embark upon a massive eviction of long-term legal residents. Overall, a provision of the comprehensive immigration bill being advocated by Senator Alan K. Simpson of Wyoming and Representative Romano L. Mazzoli of Kentucky seems more practical. As passed by the Senate, their measure made undocumented immigrants who entered the country by January 1, 1977 permanent resident aliens with access to most social services and accorded temporary resident status to those who entered illegally between that date and January 1, 1980.

Legalizing the status of resident undocumented aliens is tantamount to defining a problem out of existence. The approach is humanitarian and can work but only if the government can effectively close the border to further unauthorized penetration. Congress is currently considering a variety of familiar and fresh proposals to achieve this goal but most, even if enacted, seem doomed to failure. The Reagan administration has substantially increased the budget of the border patrol, but American land and water frontiers are so gigantic and porous that the rate of detection and apprehension is not likely ever to reach a level high enough to discourage would-be illegal entrants. Proposals both by the White House and in the Simpson-Mazzoli bill to provide penalties for employers who hire undocumented aliens seem more innovative, but these, too, have shortcomings. Civil libertarians fear that congressional suggestions that the executive branch devise a secure system of documentation to prove eligibility for employment will lead to the introduction of a national identity card, and many commentators doubt that even such an internal passport would be safe from counterfeiting. Businessmen are complaining that they are being saddled with the responsibilities of the Immigration and Naturalization Service and with an unmanageable burden of paperwork. Spokesmen for the League of United Latin American Citizens (LULAC) and other interested organizations worriedly predict that employers, in order to avoid trouble, will simply shun hiring all Hispanics. And, finally, the likely economic impact of this approach is far from clear. The administration's highly publicized raids in the spring of 1982 on establishments employing undocumented aliens did not convincingly indicate that legal residents are willing to come forward to fill the low-paying jobs vacated by the apprehensions or that employers will raise the level of compensation in order to entice citizens or properly documented aliens to replace arrested workers.

Adoption of a European style guest workers program has the marks of a reasonable compromise, but this approach is less attractive on closer inspection. Many Mexicans and Americans unhappily associate this initiative with the *bracero* program terminated by Congress in 1964 after protests that recruited workers had been systematically exploited. Opponents of the plan argue that the addition of temporary workers to the population will undermine the position of permanent residents. They note that *bracero* programs have in the past increased illegal immigration by drawing large numbers of people to points along the American border at which those who fail to obtain contracts as temporary workers easily fall prey to the temptation to enter the country secretly. For example, American authorities captured more than 5 million undocumented Mexicans in the years between 1951 and 1964, when the last *bracero* agreement was legally recruiting 4.8 million of their compatriots. This fact makes the Reagan administration's current call for the entry of 50,000 workers for stays of nine to twelve months seem a remarkably inadequate response to a problem that may now involve as many as 1 million or more illegal entries each year.

Probably the only effective way to control undocumented immigration is to make it unnecessary by actively encouraging the quick development of nearby donor nations. The United States will have to do much to improve the level of general education and of medical knowledge in neighboring countries. Humanitarian considerations demand this course of action, but so too does the recognition that in other societies such progress has encouraged and enabled the people to limit their families to a size in keeping with the demographic consequences of lower mortality rates and the demands of postagricultural economies. America will also have to provide adequate temporary aid to relieve the urge to panicked flight among the hard-pressed. Most important, the United States will have to encourage by public and private investments and by tariff policies the emergence of productive economies in these nations. This program may entail economic dislocation in the United States inasmuch as Washington, in assisting neighboring economies, will inevitably underwrite competition for already marginal American industries such as shoe manufacturing. Justice will demand that entrepreneurs and employees hurt by the restructuring receive compensation and retraining.

Americans are not likely to accept voluntarily a comprehensive assistance plan that would obviously entail enormous expenditures. They will probably find greater appeal in programs that combine rigorous border enforcement with minor efforts to accommodate some aliens. This response, however, may prove unfortunately shortsighted. The United States is on the geographic edge of an area of impending demographic, economic, and political revolutions. Change is coming, and great costs cannot be escaped. The United States can pay the price in ineffective efforts both to isolate itself from a world of which it is inextricably part and to compensate for the problems that may be engendered by the potential, precipitate introduction of a large alien subculture into American society. Or the United States can pay to channel the currents of change along beneficial paths by building a strong regional economy. The latter alternative would foster America's political influence and would ultimately improve its capability for self-defense by bringing both the major sources of supply and the main markets for the nation closer to home. But, perhaps most important, this approach would create a situation in which cultural exchange could occur without acrimony and in which suffering was no longer a prime factor in the movement of people from their native lands.

# Essay on Sources

For other treatments of immigration and assimilation in American history see: Leonard Dinnerstein, Roger L. Nichols, and David M. Reimers, *Natives and Strangers: Ethnic Groups and the Building of America* (New York: Oxford University Press, 1979); Maldwyn A. Jones, *American Immigration* (Chicago: University of Chicago Press, 1960); and Maxine Seller, *To Seek America: A History of Ethnic Life in the United States* (Englewood: Ozer, 1977). For larger bibliographies on these subjects see John D. Buenker and Nicholas C. Burckel, eds., *Immigration and Ethnicity: A Guide to Information Sources* (Detroit: Gale, 1977); and Wayne C. Miller, *A Comprehensive Bibliography for the Study of American Minorities,* 2 vols. (New York: New York University Press, 1976). Stephan Thernstrom, ed., *Harvard Encyclopedia of American Ethnic Groups* (Cambridge: Harvard University Press, 1980), has established itself as the standard reference work in its field.

## CHAPTER I: THE FORMATIVE PERIOD, 1607–1790

For demographic information about the aboriginal settlers of the New World consult the essays in William M. Denevan, ed., *The Native Population of the Americas in 1492* (Madison: University of Wisconsin Press, 1976). Gary B. Nash includes useful background information about Indian settlements, along with a discussion of the interrelationships among the aborigines and European and African settlers in *Red,*

*White, and Black: The Peoples of Early America* (Englewood Cliffs: Prentice-Hall, 1974). Nancy O. Lurie discusses "Indian Cultural Adjustment to European Civilization," in James M. Smith, ed., *Seventeenth-Century America: Essays on Colonial History* (Chapel Hill: University of North Carolina Press, 1959).

David B. Quinn, *The Elizabethans and the Irish* (Ithaca: Cornell University Press, 1966), examines the parallels in the positions of the Irish and the Indians. Francis Jennings's *Invasion of America* (Chapel Hill: University of North Carolina Press, 1975) is more condemnatory of white behavior toward the natives than is Alden Vaughan's *New England Frontier: Puritans and Indians, 1620-1675* (Boston: Little, Brown, 1965). On the subject of Indian–white conflict see also the following works by Wilcomb E. Washburn: *The Indian in America* (New York: Harper & Row, 1975); and "The Moral and Legal Justification for Dispossessing the Indians," in James M. Smith, *Seventeenth-Century America.*

Carl Bridenbaugh's *Vexed and Troubled Englishmen, 1590-1642* (New York: Oxford University Press, 1968) discusses the preconditions of migration to America. Sigmund Diamond makes it clear why the English eventually chose large-scale settlement in "From Organization to Society: Virginia in the Seventeenth Century," *American Journal of Sociology 63* (1958):457-475; he offers an interesting comparison with French attitudes in "An Experiment in 'Feudalism': French Canada in the Seventeenth Century," *William and Mary Quarterly 18* (1961):3-34. (This and all other citations to the *William and Mary Quarterly* are to the volumes in the third series.) Samuel G. Nissenson, *The Patroon's Domain* (New York: Columbia University Press, 1937), is the standard treatment of Dutch settlement efforts in the Hudson Valley.

Timothy H. Breen and Stephen Foster, in "Moving to the New World: The Character of Early Massachusetts Immigration," *William and Mary Quarterly 30* (1973):189-223, discuss important aspects of the Great Migration to New England. Edmund S. Morgan examines the local conditions of labor in "The First American Boom: Virginia, 1618-1630," *William and Mary Quarterly 28* (1971):169-198. Richard S. Dunn, *Sugar and Slaves: The Rise of the Planter Class in the English West Indies, 1624-1713* (Chapel Hill: University of North Carolina Press, 1972), illustrates a number of important contrasts between life in Caribbean and mainland colonies.

Richard B. Morris, *Government and Labor in Early America* (New York: Columbia University Press, 1946), remains the best general treatment of the status of both free and bound workers. Abbot Emerson Smith, *Colonists in Bondage: White Servitude and Convict Labor in America, 1607-1776* (Chapel Hill: University of North Carolina Press, 1947), is also a standard for this topic. Among the recent scholarly efforts to understand the condition of labor and the eventual fate of America's indentured servants are Russell Menard, "From Servant to Freeholder," *William and Mary Quarterly 30* (1973):37–64; and Robert O. Heavner, *Economic Aspects of Indentured Servitude in Colonial Philadelphia* (New York: Arno, 1978).

Much of the modern literature on American slavery dates from a debate between Oscar Handlin and Mary F. Handlin and Carl N. Degler on the relationship between prejudice and the origins of the institution. Handlin and Handlin, in "Origins of the Southern Labor System," *William and Mary Quarterly 7* (1950):199–222, emphasize the colonies' hunger for labor and see antiblack attitudes as a consequence, rather than a cause, of slavery; Degler reverses the relationship in "Slavery and the Genesis of American Race Prejudice," *Comparative Studies in History and Society 2* (1959):49–66. David Brion Davis, *The Problem of Slavery in Western Culture* (Ithaca: Cornell University Press, 1964); and Winthrop Jordan, *White over Black: American Attitudes toward the Negro, 1550–1812* (Chapel Hill: University of North Carolina Press, 1968), have documented the existence of precolonial racism.

Philip Curtin, *The Atlantic Slave Trade: A Census* (Madison: University of Wisconsin Press, 1969), offers the best estimates of the number of Africans imported to various places in the New World between the fifteenth and the nineteenth century. John Blassingame discusses the African cultural background of America's blacks in *The Slave Community: Plantation Life in the Antebellum South* (New York: Oxford University Press, 1972). For some examples of how local economic conditions shaped the conditions of slavery and how the presence of bondsmen affected white society see Dunn, *Sugar and Slaves;* and Edgar J. McManus, *A History of Negro Slavery in New York* (Syracuse: Syracuse University Press, 1966).

For an overview of New Netherland–New York see Thomas Condon, *New York Beginnings: The Commercial Origins of New Netherland* (New York: New York University Press, 1968); and Henry Kessler and Peter Rachlis, *Peter Stuyvesant and His New York* (New York: Random House, 1959). George L. Smith, *Religion and Trade in New Netherland: Dutch Origins and American Development* (Ithaca: Cornell University Press 1973), examines the failure of the Dutch Reformed church to establish religious orthodoxy along the Hudson. Thomas J. Archdeacon discusses the long-range consequences of the English victory over the Dutch in *New York City, 1664–1710: Conquest and Change* (Ithaca: Cornell University Press, 1976). For more on William Penn see Mary M. Dunn, *William Penn: Politics and Conscience* (Princeton: Princeton University Press, 1967). For a history of the settlement of Pennsylvania see Edwin B. Bronner, *William Penn's "Holy Experiment:" The Founding of Pennsylvania, 1681–1701* (New York: Columbia University Press, 1962). James T.

Lemon, *The Best Poor Man's Country: A Geographical Study of Early Southeastern Pennsylvania* (Baltimore: John Hopkins Press, 1972), explains the colony's economic attractions.

Albert Bernhardt Faust, *The German Element in the United States,* 2 vols. (Boston: Houghton Mifflin, 1909), is badly outdated in its interpretations but remains the best general source for the subject. Charles W. Baird, *History of the Huguenot Emigration* (New York: Dodd, Mead, 1885), is another old but useful study. Walter Allen Knittle, *Early Eighteenth Century Palatine Emigration* (Philadelphia: Dorrance, 1937), focuses on an interesting episode in the history of refugee migrations. Richard H. Shryock, "British versus German Tradition in Colonial Agriculture," *Mississippi Valley Historical Review 26* (1939):39–54, judiciously treats this important topic. R. J. Dickson, *Ulster Emigration to Colonial America, 1718-1775* (London: Routledge & Kegan Paul, 1966); and Ian Charles Cargill Graham, *Colonists from Scotland: Emigration to North America, 1707-1783* (Ithaca: Cornell University Press, 1956), offer broad accounts of these related movements.

Gary B. Nash, "Slaves and Slaveowners in Colonial Philadelphia," *William and Mary Quarterly 30* (1973):223–256, examines urban slavery in early America. Peter H. Wood, *Black Majority* (New York: Knopf, 1974), examines the slaves' impact on the one colony in which they temporarily formed a majority; see especially his treatment of the Stono rebellion. Kenneth Scott, "The Slave Insurrection in New York in 1712," *New York Historical Society Quarterly 45* (1961):43–74; and Ferenc M. Szasz, "The New York Slave Revolt of 1741: A Re-examination," *New York History 48* (1967):215–230, analyze those important uprisings.

Emberson E. Proper, *Colonial Immigration Laws* (New York: Columbia University Press, 1900), remains a standard source for its topic; as does Glenn Weaver's "Benjamin Franklin and the Pennsylvania Germans," *William and Mary Quarterly 14* (1957):536–559. For a discussion of convict migrations see Morris, *Government and Labor;* and Abbott Smith, *Colonists in Bondage.* On the subject of anti-Catholicism in the Glorious Revolution see Archdeacon, *New York City;* and Lois Green Carr and David William Jordan, *Maryland's Revolution of Government, 1689-1692* (Ithaca: Cornell University Press, 1974). Timothy Bosworth's "Anti-Catholicism as a Political Tool in Mid-Eighteenth Century Maryland," *Catholic Historical Review 61* (1975):539–563; and Charles H. Metzger, *Catholics and the American Revolution: A Study in Religious Climate* (Chicago: Loyola University Press, 1962), are useful. John T. Ellis, *Catholics in Colonial America* (Baltimore: Helicon, 1965), is the best general history of that group before the Revolution.

Wallace Brown, *The King's Friends: The Composition and Motives of the American Loyalist Claimants* (Providence: Brown University Press, 1965); and Mary Beth Norton, *The British Americans: The Loyalist Exiles in En-*

*gland, 1774–1789* (Boston: Little, Brown, 1972), touch on the issue of emigration from the newly formed United States. For the Revolution's connection with Canadian history see Marcus Lee Hansen, *The Mingling of the Canadian and American Peoples* (New Haven: Yale University Press, 1940); and George M. Wrong, *Canada and the American Revolution* (New York: Macmillan, 1935).

Everts B. Greene and Virginia D. Harrington, *American Population before the Federal Census of 1790* (New York: Columbia University Press, 1932); and Stella H. Sutherland, *Population Distribution in Colonial America* (New York: Columbia University Press, 1936), are older, standard studies of colonial demography. Robert V. Wells, *The Population of the British Colonies in America before 1776* (Princeton: Princeton University Press, 1975), presents a more recent approach to this topic. The discussion of the ethnic origins of the American people at the first federal census is based on the American Council of Learned Societies, "Report of the Committee on Linguistic and National Stocks in the Population of the United States," *Annual Report of the American Historical Association for the Year 1931* (Washington D.C.: Government Printing Office, 1932), I:103–441.

## CHAPTER II: THE OLD IMMIGRATION, 1790–1890

E. P. Hutchinson provides an overview of the statistical sources available for the study of American immigration and supplies important supplementary information in "Notes on Immigration Statistics of the United States," *Journal of the American Statistical Association 53* (1958): 963–1025. For discussions of Britain's emigration policy see Maldwyn A. Jones, "The Background to Emigration from Great Britain in the Nineteenth Century," *Perspectives in American History 7* (1973):3–92; and Kathleen Walpole, "Emigration to North America under the early Passenger Acts, 1803–1842," *Transactions of the Historic Society of Lancashire and Cheshire for the Year 1929 81* (1930):110–214.

Frances S. Childs, *French Refugee Life in the United States, 1790–1800* (Baltimore: Johns Hopkins Press, 1940), carefully examines the most obvious impact of the French Revolution on American immigration. E. P. Thomson, *The Making of the English Working Class* (New York: Pantheon, 1963), provides useful background on the French uprising's influence in England. And Maldwyn A. Jones's "Ulster Emigration, 1783–1815," in Edward R. R. Green, ed., *Essays in Scotch-Irish History* (New York: Humanities, 1969), discusses emigration from Ireland in this era.

The best general treatment of European immigration to the United States during the first half of the nineteenth century remains Marcus

Lee Hansen's *Atlantic Migration, 1607–1860* (Cambridge: Harvard University Press, 1940). William Forbes Adams's *Ireland and Irish Emigration to the New World from 1815 to the Famine* (New Haven: Yale University Press, 1942), ably lives up to its title. Mack Walker, *Germany and the Emigration, 1816–1885* (Cambridge: Harvard University Press, 1964), is one of the few valuable sources on its subject for this period.

Frank Thistlethwaite, "Migration from Europe Overseas in the Nineteenth and Twentieth Centuries," in Herbert Moller, ed., *Population Movements in Modern European History* (New York: Macmillan, 1969), offers an excellent, succinct analysis of migration's function as a response to social and economic changes in the migrant's country of origin. For additional readings on the intersection between demographic developments and population movement consult D. V. Glass and D. E. C. Eversley, eds., *Population in History: Essays in Historical Demography* (London: Arnold, 1965). D. V. Glass and P. A. M. Taylor, *Population and Emigration* (New York: Academic, 1976), is also useful; as is D. V. Glass, ed., *Introduction to Malthus* (New York: Wiley, 1953).

Adna F. Weber, *The Growth of Cities* (Ithaca: Cornell University Press, 1899), discusses the impact of immigration on the development of many of the world's major cities in the nineteenth century. Sune Akerman, "Theories and Methods of Migration Research," in Harald Runblom and Hans Norman, eds., *From Sweden to America* (Minneapolis: University of Minnesota Press, 1976), examines the connection between local and international movements. For important analyses of emigration policies in Europe see H. J. M. Johnston, *British Emigration Policy, 1815–1830* (New York: Oxford University Press, 1972); and Ann-Sofie Kälvemark, "Swedish Emigration Policy in an International Perspective," in Runblom and Norman, *From Sweden to America.*

Adams, *Ireland and Irish Emigration;* Hansen, *Atlantic Migration;* and Walker, *Germany and the Emigration* describe the flow of immigrants in the 1820s and 1830s. Norman Macdonald, *Canada, 1763–1841, Immigration and Settlement: The Administration of the Imperial Land Regulations* (London: Longmans, Green, 1939), introduces the subject of immigration to that country. Hansen's *Mingling of the Canadian and American Peoples* is another excellent work.

Oliver C. MacDonagh, *A Pattern of Government Growth: The Passenger Acts and Their Enforcement* (London: Macgibbon & Kee, 1961), approaches the subject from the British perspective. E. P. Hutchinson, *The Legislative History of American Immigration Policy, 1798–1965* (Philadelphia: University of Pennsylvania Press, 1981), has occasional references to regulatory efforts by the United States. The standard work on ocean travel in the pre–Civil War era is Edwin C. Guillet, *The Great Migration: The Atlantic Crossing by Sailing-Ship since 1770* (New York: Nelson, 1937).

Philip A. M. Taylor, *The Distant Magnet: European Migration to the U.S.A.* (New York: Harper & Row, 1971), provides important information on the ships of the late nineteenth century. The data on sailing vessels and steamships in the port of New York are from the appendixes of Frederick Kapp's *Immigration and the Commissioners of Emigration of the State of New York* (New York: Nation, 1875).

Berit Brattne and Sune Åkerman, "The Importance of the Transportation Sector for Mass Emigration," in Runblom and Norman, *From Sweden to America,* discusses the role of the steamship agent. Theodore C. Blegen, "The Competition of the Northwestern States for Immigrants," *Wisconsin Magazine of History 3* (1919):3-29, is a pioneering effort at studying the recruitment of settlers. Lars Ljungmark, *For Sale—Minnesota: Organized Promotion of Scandinavian Immigration, 1866–1873* (Stockholm: Scandinavian University Books, 1971), examines the policies of both the state governments and the railroads.

Hans Norman, "Swedes in North America," in Runblom and Norman, *From Sweden to America,* reveals how the migrants' practice of seeking reunion with friends and families could lead to the virtual reconstitution of European communities in the United States. Arnold Schrier, *Ireland and the American Emigration, 1850–1900* (Minneapolis: University of Minnesota Press, 1958), discusses the subject of remittances to the parent country. The data on money orders are from U.S. Postmaster General, *Annual Reports* (Washington, D.C.: Government Printing Office, 1877–1890).

American immigration statistics for this period can be found in U.S. Bureau of the Census, *Historical Statistics of the United States: Colonial Times to 1970* (Washington, D.C.: Government Printing Office, 1975), series C89-119. For general information on Irish and German immigration see Hansen's *Atlantic Migration;* Adams, *Ireland and the Irish Emigration;* Schrier, *Ireland and the American Emigration;* and Walker, *Germany and the Emigration.* R. D. Edwards and T. D. Williams, eds., *The Great Famine: Studies in Irish History, 1845–1852* (New York: New York University Press, 1957), is excellent; see especially Oliver MacDonagh's chapter on "Irish Emigration to the United States and the British Colonies during the Famine." Cecil Woodham-Smith's *Great Hunger: Ireland, 1845–1849* (New York: Harper & Row, 1962), is a moving account of that tragic time. Wolfgang Köllman and Peter Marschalck's "German Emigration to the United States," which Thomas C. Childers translated for *Perspectives in American History 7* (1973):499-554, is a sharply analytic essay. Marcus Lee Hansen, "The Revolutions of 1848 and German Emigration," *Journal of Economic and Business History 2* (1930):630-658, deemphasizes political yearnings as a cause of German immigration to the United States; while Adolf E. Zucker, ed., *The Forty-eighters: Political Refugees of the German Revolution of 1848* (New York: Columbia University Press, 1950), discusses the fate of those rebels who actually came.

*International Migrations,* a two-volume study prepared for the National Bureau of Economic Research (New York: National Bureau of Economic Research, 1929), is the best general source of statistics on worldwide migration. Imre Ferenczi compiled the first volume, entitled *Statistics,* and Walter F. Willcox edited the second, entitled *Interpretations.* The data on New York's role as the major immigrant port are derived from U.S. Treasury Department, *Arrivals of Alien Passengers and Immigrants in the United States from 1820 and 1892,* prepared by the Bureau of Statistics (Washington, D.C.: Government Printing Office, 1893). The figures on the ethnic composition of the arrivals at the various ports have been compiled from reports of the secretary of state that were presented as congressional documents; for a list of these reports see the U.S. Serial Set Index for the First through the Thirty-fourth Congress (1789–1857), p. 117.

On the immigrants' often harsh early experiences in the major cities see Robert Ernst, *Immigrant Life in New York City, 1825–1863* (New York: King's Crown, 1949); and Oscar Handlin, *Boston's Immigrants, 1790–1880: A Study in Acculturation,* rev. and enl. ed. (New York: Atheneum, 1970). David Ward's *Cities and Immigrants* (New York: Oxford University Press, 1973), views developments from a geographer's perspective.

Statistical evidence on the distribution of the foreign born in the United States can be found in U.S. Census Office. Eighth Census, 1860, *Statistics of the United States in 1860* (1866; reprint ed. New York: Arno, 1976), tables LL and NN in the introduction; and in U.S. Census Office. Ninth Census, 1870; *Statistics of the Population of the United States* (Washington, D.C.: Government Printing Office, 1872), I:table 4. See also U.S. Treasury, *Arrivals,* table 14. M. Justille McDonald, *History of the Irish in Wisconsin in the Nineteenth Century* (Washington, D.C.: Catholic University Press, 1954), examines the slow westward trek of the Irish. The arrival of Irishmen and Germans after 1860, as well as of persons from other places both before and after the Civil War, are recorded in U.S. Bureau of the Census, *Historical Statistics of the United States,* series C89–119. Clifford H. Bissell, "The French Language Press in California," *California Historical Society Quarterly* 39 (1960):1–353, offers an interesting analysis of the often forgotten French immigration of the 1850s.

Scholars have for a long time been interested in Scandinavian immigration to the United States. See, for example, Amandus Johnson, *The Swedish Settlements on the Delaware, 1638–1664,* 2 vols. (New York: Appleton, 1911); Theodore C. Blegen, *Norwegian Migration to America, 1825–1860* (Northfield: Norwegian-American Historical Association,

1931); and Carlton C. Qualey, *Norwegian Settlement in the United States* (Northfield: Norwegian-American Historical Society, 1938). Blessed by a wealth of demographic records kept by its governments and churches, Scandinavia has emerged as perhaps the liveliest European center for emigration studies. Ingrid Gaustad Semmingsen's "Norwegian Emigration in the Nineteenth Century," *Scandinavian Economic History Review 8* (1960):150–160, is an early example of the fine work done in recent years. Frequent mention has already been made to Runblom and Norman, *From Sweden to America,* which includes Sten Carlsson's essay on the "Chronology and Composition of Swedish Emigration to America." Kristian Hvidt's *Flight to America: The Social Background of 300,000 Danish Emigrants* (New York: Academic, 1975), has quickly become the standard work in its field.

Britain's non-Irish emigrants to the United States are too easily forgotten. Rowland T. Berthoff, *British Immigrants in Industrial America, 1790–1950* (Cambridge: Harvard University Press, 1953), offers the best overview of their coming. Three essays in *Perspectives in American History 9* (1973) are also of interest: Jones's "Background" has already been cited; see also Malcolm Gray, "Scottish Emigration: The Social Impact of Agrarian Change in the Rural Lowlands, 1775–1875" (pp. 95–174); and Alan Conway, "Welsh Emigration to the United States" (pp. 177–271). Brinley Thomas discusses the complementary functions of the American and British economies in *Migration and Economic Growth: A Study of Great Britian and the Atlantic Economy* (New York: Cambridge University Press, 1973). The best data on the employment of British and other immigrants can be found in U.S. Senate, *Reports of the Immigration Commission* (1911; reprint ed., New York: Arno, 1970), vols. VI–XX; vol. I of this forty-two-volume series contains a valuable abstract of the information (pp. 285–541). On the related subject of Canadian immigration consult Hansen, *Mingling of the Canadian and American Peoples.*

U.S. Senate, *Immigration Commission,* vol. III:*Statistical Review of Immigration, 1819–1910—Distribution of Immigrants, 1850–1900,* is an invaluable source of information; see especially tables 1–9, pp. 444–87; table 21, p. 554; and table 25, pp. 572–83 for data on 1890.

Chapter III: Natives and Newcomers: Confrontation

On the design of the Great Seal read John Adams's letter to his wife, August 14, 1776, in Edward C. Burnett, ed., *Letters of Members of the Continental Congress* (Washington, D.C.: Carnegie Institution, 1923), II:49–50. The best discussion of attitudes toward naturalization and constitutional provisions affecting it can be found in James H. Kettner, *The*

*Development of American Citizenship, 1608–1970* (Chapel Hill: University of North Carolina Press, 1978). Hutchinson's *Legislative History of American Immigration Policy* is also of great value.

For an introduction to the conflicts between the Jeffersonian Republicans and the Federalists see Noble E. Cunningham, Jr., *Jeffersonian Republicans: The Formation of a Party Organization, 1789–1801* (Chapel Hill: University of North Carolina Press, 1957); and Richard Hofstadter, *The Idea of a Party System: The Rise of Legitimate Opposition in the United States, 1780–1840* (Berkeley: University of California Press, 1969). Richard Buel, Jr., *Securing the Revolution: Ideology in American Politics, 1789–1915* (Ithaca: Cornell University Press, 1972); and David H. Fischer, *Revolution of American Conservatism: Federalist Party in the Era of Jeffersonian Democracy* (New York: Harper & Row, 1965), provide insights into the competing ideologies of the early republic. Harry Ammon, "The Genêt Mission and the Development of American Political Parties," *Journal of American History 52* (1966):725–741, demonstrates how foreign policy and domestic politics intermingled. James Morton Smith's *Freedom's Fetters: The Alien and Sedition Laws and American Civil Liberties* (Ithaca: Cornell University Press, 1956) is of fundamental importance.

Several studies provide information about the Americanization that occurred after the Revolution. See, for example, William H. Gehrke's "Transition from the German to the English Language in North Carolina," *North Carolina Historical Review 12* (1935):1–19. Adolph Burnett Benson has provided an edition of Peter Kalm's *The America of 1750: Peter Kalm's Travels in North America—the English Version of 1770*, 2 vols. (New York: Wilson-Erickson, 1937). Adrian C. Leiby, *The Early Dutch and Swedish Settlers of New Jersey* (Princeton: Van Nostrand, 1964), is also informative. Sydney E. Ahlstrom, *A Religious History of the American People* (New Haven: Yale University Press, 1972), is an excellent starting point for the study of American religious history.

Residents of the United States are poorly informed about the history of their northern neighbor. Mason Wade, *The French Canadians*, 2 vols. (New York: Macmillan, 1968), is probably the most thorough available account of the Quebecers. Aileen Dunham treats *Political Unrest in Upper Canada, 1815–36* (London: Longmans, Green, 1927). Charles W. New recounts the career of *Lord Durham* (Oxford: Clarendon, 1929).

John A. Krout and Dixon Ryan Fox, *The Completion of Independence* (New York: Macmillan, 1944); and George Dangerfield, *The Awakening of American Nationalism, 1815–1828* (New York: Harper & Row, 1965), examine the development of a distinct American identity. Robert T. Handy, *The Protestant Quest for a Christian America, 1830–1930* (Philadelphia: Fortress, 1967), shows how closely that identity meshed with a Protestant world view. Several works reveal the strong religious impulse in the varied reform movements of the pre–Civil War era. Among the best are Whitney R. Cross, *The Burned-Over District, 1800–1850* (Ithaca: Cornell University Press, 1950); and Timothy L. Smith, *Revivalism and Social Reform in Mid-Nineteenth-Century America* (New York: Abingdon, 1957). Frederick Merk's *Manifest Destiny and Mission in American History* (New York: Knopf, 1963) captures the varied meanings of that slogan.

Curtin, *The Atlantic Slave Trade,* is the broadest, most balanced study of the subject. George Frederickson, *Black Image in the White Mind: The Debate on Afro-American Character and Destiny, 1817–1914* (New York: Harper & Row, 1972); and Leon Litwack, *North of Slavery: The Negro in the Free States, 1790–1860* (Chicago: University of Chicago Press, 1961), reveal much about the position of Afro-Americans in the mid-nineteenth century. Among other works that examine major components of the antislavery movement are P. J. Staudenraus, *The African Colonization Movement, 1816–1865* (New York: Columbia University Press, 1961); William H. Pease and Jane H. Pease, "Antislavery Ambivalence: Immediatism, Expediency, Race," *American Quarterly 17* (1965):682–695; Martin Duberman, ed., *The Antislavery Vanguard: New Essays on the Abolitionists* (Princeton: Princeton University Press, 1965); and Eric Foner, *Free Soil, Free Labor, Free Men: Ideology of the Republican Party before the Civil War* (New York: Oxford University Press, 1970).

William T. Hagan, *American Indians* (Chicago: University of Chicago Press, 1961), and Wilcomb E. Washburn, *The Indian in America* (New York: Harper, 1975), offer important overviews. Bernard W. Sheehan, *Seeds of Extinction: Jeffersonian Philanthropy and the American Indian* (Chapel Hill: University of North Carolina Press, 1973), examines changing attitudes in the early nineteenth century. Robert F. Berkhofer, Jr., *Salvation and the Savage: An Analysis of Protestant Missions and American Indian Response, 1787–1862* (Lexington: University of Kentucky Press, 1965), is also useful. Angie Debo, *And Still the Waters Run* (Princeton: Princeton University Press, 1940), deals with the removal of the five so-called civilized tribes; and Francis Paul Prucha, *Broadax and Bayonet* (Lincoln: University of Nebraska Press, 1967), analyzes the role of the army on the northwestern frontier between 1815 and 1860. Matt S. Meier and Feliciano Rivera, *The Chicanos: A History of Mexican Americans* (New York: Hill and Wang, 1972), discusses the conquest of the Southwest. Richard O. Ulibarri, "American Interest in the Spanish Southwest, 1803–1848" (Ph.D. diss., University of Utah, 1963), treats that development in relation to Manifest Destiny and racism.

Robert L. Heilbroner and Aaron Singer's *Economic Transformation of America* (New York: Harcourt Brace Jovanovich, 1977), helps place the coming of the immigrants in the proper context. Robert Ernst, *Immigrant Life in New York City;* and Michael Feldberg, *The Philadelphia*

*Riots of 1844: A Study in Ethnic Conflict* (Westport: Greenwood, 1975), examine competition between the natives and the newcomers. Sam Bass Warner, *Streetcar Suburbs: The Process of Growth in Boston, 1870–1900* (Cambridge: Harvard University Press, 1962), discusses changing residential patterns in the mid-nineteenth-century city. David Ward, "The Emergence of Central Immigrant Ghettoes in American Cities, 1840–1920," *Annals of the Association of American Geographers 58* (1968): 343–359, illustrates how the foreign arrivals fit in the new arrangement.

Charles Rosenberg, *The Cholera Years: 1832, 1849, and 1866* (Chicago: University of Chicago Press, 1962); and John Duffy, *History of Public Health in New York City, 1625–1866* (New York: Russell Sage, 1968), are important for an understanding of the immigrants' milieu. Herbert Asbury, *The Gangs of New York* (New York: Knopf, 1922); and Joel Tyler Headley, *Great Riots of New York, 1712–1873* (1873; reprint ed., Indianapolis: Bobbs-Merrill, 1970), are dated and distorted but have yet to be replaced. David J. Rothman's *Discovery of the Asylum: Social Order and Disorder in the New Republic* (Boston: Little, Brown, 1971) examines American efforts to correct social ills through an institutional approach. Carroll Smith Rosenberg, *Religion and the Rise of the American City: The New York City Mission Movement, 1812–1870* (Ithaca: Cornell University Press, 1971), treats Protestant efforts to reach the slum dwellers.

On the development of Roman Catholicism in the United States see Ahlstrom, *Religious History of the American People;* and Thomas T. McAvoy, *A History of the Catholic Church in the United States* (South Bend: University of Notre Dame Press, 1969). The standard study of anti-Catholicism in pre–Civil War America is Ray A. Billington, *Protestant Crusade, 1800–60: A Study of the Origins of American Nativism* (New York: Macmillan, 1938). See also Richard Hofstader, "The Paranoid Style in American Politics," in his *Paranoid Style in American Politics and Other Essays* (New York: Knopf, 1965). Joseph R. Gusfield, *Symbolic Crusade: Status Politics and the American Temperance Movement* (Urbana: University of Illinois Press, 1963); and Feldberg, *The Philadelphia Riots of 1844,* show how reform movements served natives in the social competition against the newcomers. Vincent P. Lannie, *Public Money and Parochial Education: Bishop Hughes, Governor Seward, and the New York School Controversy* (Cleveland: Press of Case Western Reserve University, 1968), is the best work on the issue.

Albon P. Man, Jr., "Labor Competition and the New York Draft Riots of 1863," *Journal of Negro History 36* (1951):375–405, discusses tensions between blacks and Irishmen. On German attitudes see Andreas Dorpalen, "The German Element and the Issues of the Civil War," *Mississippi Valley Historical Review 29* (1942):55–76. William G. Bean, "An Aspect of Know-Nothingism: The Immigrant and Slavery," *South*

*Atlantic Quarterly 23* (1924):319-334; and Harry J. Carman and Reinhard H. Luthin, "Some Aspects of the Know-Nothing Movement Reconsidered," *South Atlantic Quarterly 39* (1940):213-234, examine the connection between nativism and reform. M. Evangeline Thomas, *Nativism in the Old Northwest, 1850-1860* (Washington, D.C.: Catholic University Press, 1936); and W. Darrell Overdyke, *The Know-Nothing Party in the South* (Baton Rouge: Louisiana State University, 1950), provide information on the political climate of the 1850s. See also Billington, *Protestant Crusade.*

Ella Lonn has written the standard histories of the immigrants' participation in the Civil War: *Foreigners in the Confederacy* (Chapel Hill: University of North Carolina Press, 1940) and *Foreigners in the Union Army and Navy* (Baton Rouge: Louisiana State University Press, 1969). On the Draft Riots see Adrian Cook, *The Armies of the Streets* (Lexington: University of Kentucky Press, 1974).

CHAPTER IV: NATIVES AND NEWCOMERS: ACCOMMODATION

Donald G. Creighton offers some of the best accounts of the creation of modern Canada: *John A. Macdonald,* 2 vols. (New York: Macmillan, 1952, 1955); and *British North America at Confederation* (Ottawa: Patenaude, 1939). George Stanley examines resistance to confederation in *The Birth of Western Canada: A History of the Riel Rebellion* (London: Longmans, Green, 1936). See also Wade, *The French Canadians.*

For a general review of the situation of the Indians see Hagan, *American Indians.* Many books deal with the Indian campaigns of the second half of the nineteenth century. See Robert Marshall Utley's *Frontiersmen in Blue: The United States Army and the Indian, 1848-1865* (New York: Macmillan, 1967) and his *Frontier Regulars: The United States Army and the Indian, 1866-1891* (New York: Macmillan, 1974). An account from the Indians' perspective is Dee Brown, *Bury My Heart at Wounded Knee: An Indian History of the American West* (New York: Holt, Rinehart & Winston, 1970).

Henry E. Fritz discusses President Ulysses S. Grant's so-called peace policy and its aftermath in *The Movement for Indian Assimilation, 1860-1890* (Philadelphia: University of Pennyslvania Press, 1963). Elaine G. Eastman, *Pratt: The Red Man's Moses* (Norman: University of Oklahoma Press, 1935), traces the activities of the founder of Carlisle Institute. William T. Hagan, *Indian Police and Judges: Experiments in Acculturation and Control* (New Haven: Yale University Press, 1966), examines assimilative efforts on the reservation. Helen Hunt Jackson, *A Century of Dishonor: The Early Crusade for Indian Reform* (New York: Harper, 1881), is the classic indictment of American policy; while

Robert W. Mardock's *Reformers and the American Indian* (Columbia: University of Missouri Press, 1971), evaluates the milieu in which Jackson operated. For information about the government's changing programs see Loring Benson Priest, *Uncle Sam's Stepchildren: The Reformation of United States Indian Policy, 1865-1867* (New Brunswick: Rutgers University Press, 1942); and D. S. Otis, *The Dawes Act and the Allotment of Indian Land,* ed. Francis P. Prucha (Norman: University of Oklahoma Press, 1972).

Willie Lee Nichols Rose, *Rehearsal for Reconstruction: The Port Royal Experiment* (Indianapolis: Bobbs-Merrill, 1964), investigates a short-lived effort to provide former slaves with economic and social self-determination. William S. McFeely, *Yankee Stepfather: General O. O. Howard and the Freedmen* (New Haven: Yale University Press, 1968), shows how the Freedmen's Bureau served as a means of control. C. Vann Woodward presents two superb studies in the *Origins of the New South, 1877-1913* (Baton Rouge: Louisiana State University Press, 1951); and *The Strange Career of Jim Crow,* 3d rev. ed. (New York: Oxford University Press, 1974). Rayford W. Logan, *The Negro in American Life and Thought: The Nadir, 1877-1901* (New York: Dial, 1954), traces the North's abandonment of the blacks. Black responses to their changing circumstances are examined in August Meier and Elliott Rudwick, ed., *Negro Thought in America, 1880-1915: Racial Ideologies in the Age of Booker T. Washington* (Ann Arbor: University of Michigan Press, 1964).

Data on the arrival of immigrants at American ports are conveniently available in U.S. Treasury, *Arrivals,* table 8. The ethnic composition of those arriving at particular ports has been determined from a variety of House and Senate documents on commerce and immigration, which can be traced through the Serial Set Indexes for the Thirty-fifth through the Forty-fifth Congress (1857-1879), pp. 79-80, and for the Forty-sixth through the Fiftieth Congress (1879-1889), pp. 460-461. Information on the distribution of the foreign stock in America's cities comes from U.S. Census Office, Eleventh Census, 1890, *Report on Population of the United States* (Washington, D.C.: Government Printing Office, 1895), part 1, tables 35-62. Useful data on the dispersion of the foreign born and their children among the various states in 1890 can also be found in U.S. Senate, *Statistical Review of Immigration,* table 15, pp. 522-29.

The conditions of Irish life in this period are treated in Stephan Thernstrom, *Poverty and Progress: Social Mobility in a Nineteenth Century City* (Cambridge: Harvard University Press, 1964), and in Bruce Laurie, Theodore Hershberg, and George Alter, "Immigrants and Industry: The Philadelphia Experience," in Richard L. Ehrlich, ed., *Immigrants in Industrial America, 1850-1920* (Charlottesville: University of Virginia Press, 1977). See also Howard M. Gitelman, "No Irish Need Apply:

Patterns of and Responses to Ethnic Discrimination in the Labor Market,'' *Labor History 14* (1973):56–68.

Joel Tyler Headley's *Great Riots of New York, 1712–1873* offers a biased contemporary account of urban violence involving the Irish. Thomas N. Brown, *Irish American Nationalism, 1870–1890* (Philadelphia: Lippincott, 1966), discusses Fenianism. Wayne G. Broehl, Jr., *The Molly Maguires* (Cambridge: Harvard University Press, 1965), places these labor activists in a broader context.

For an example of the practice of ethnic politics in the seventeenth century see Archdeacon, *New York City*. Gary B. Nash, ''The Transformation of Urban Politics, 1700–1765,'' *Journal of American History 60* (1973):605–632; and Owen S. Ireland, ''The Ethnic–Religious Dimensions of Pennsylvania Politics, 1778–1779,'' *William and Mary Quarterly 30* (1973):423–448, offer more illustrations of ethnicity in politics from the eighteenth century. Lee Benson's *Concept of Jacksonian Democracy: New York as a Test Case* (Princeton: Princeton University Press, 1961), is a seminal work in the ethnocultural interpretation of American politics.

Edward M. Levine, *The Irish and Irish Politicians: A Study of Cultural and Social Alienation* (South Bend: University of Notre Dame Press, 1966), is an insightful study of the Irish political style. Florence Elizabeth Gibson, *The Attitudes of the New York Irish toward State and National Affairs, 1848–1892* (New York: Columbia University Press, 1951), examines Irish influence in a critical state. Robert K. Merton, ''Latent Functions of the Machine,'' in Alexander Callow, comp., *American Urban History* (New York: Oxford University Press, 1969), explains the appeal of the machine to the disadvantaged. Douglas V. Shaw, ''Political Leadership in the Industrial City: Irish Development and Nativist Response in Jersey City,'' in Ehrlich, *Immigrants in Industrial America* discusses the particulars of the rise of the Irish in Jersey City. Albert Bigelow Paine, *Thomas Nast: His Period and His Pictures* (New York: Harper, 1909), is excessively sympathetic to the cartoonist, but the sensitive reader can find numerous examples of the artist's attitude toward the Irish. Lewis Perry Curtis, Jr., *Apes and Angels: The Irishman in Victorian Caricature* (Washington, D.C.: Smithsonian Institution Press, 1971), brilliantly illustrates the intellectual climate in which Nast worked.

James A. Burns, *The Growth and Development of the Catholic School System in the United States* (New York: Benziger, 1912), ought to be supplemented by a more recent look at the origins of parochial education; see James W. Sanders, *The Education of an Urban Minority: Catholics in Chicago, 1833–1965* (New York: Oxford University Press, 1977). The best work on the Catholic Americanizers is Robert D. Cross, *The Emergence of Liberal Catholicism in America* (Cambridge: Harvard University Press, 1958). Daniel F. Reilly, *The School Controversy, 1891–1893*

(Washington, D.C.: Catholic University Press, 1943), discusses the relevant issues.

The figures on population dispersion are derived from U.S. Senate, *Statistical Review of Immigration,* table 15, pp. 522-529. See also State of Wisconsin, *Tabular Statements of the Census Enumeration* (Madison: Democrat Printing Company, 1895), pp. 110-111. On the German reformers read Zucker, *The Forty-eighters.* Frederick C. Luebke, ed., *Ethnic Voters and the Election of Lincoln* (Lincoln: University of Nebraska Press, 1971), introduces the historical controversies over German voting behavior. Laurie, Hershberg, and Alter, "Immigrants and Industry," examine the relative economic position of the Germans and Irish. John Arkan Hawgood, *The Tragedy of German-America: The Germans in the United States of America during the Nineteenth Century—and After* (New York: Putnam, 1940), is important.

Jay P. Dolan, *Immigrant Church: New York's Irish and German Catholics, 1815-1865* (Baltimore: John Hopkins Press, 1975), discusses conditions before the Civil War in an eastern city. Colman J. Barry, *The Catholic Church and German Americans* (Milwaukee: Bruce, 1954), has a midwestern, postwar orientation. On the Cahensly affair consult Barry, *The Catholic Church;* Cross, *Emergence of Liberal Catholicism in America;* and two articles by John J. Meng—"Cahenslyism: The First Stage, 1883-1891," *Catholic Historical Review 31* (1946):389-413; and "Cahenslyism: The Second Chapter," *Catholic Historical Review 32* (1947):302-340. Paul Kleppner, *The Cross of Culture: A Social Analysis of Midwestern Politics, 1850-1900* (New York: Free Press, 1970), discusses the divisions among German Protestants. Walter H. Beck, *Lutheran Elementary Schools in the United States* (St. Louis: Concordia, 1939), examines parochial education among Lutherans.

Charlotte Erickson, *Invisible Immigrants: The Adaptation of British and Scottish Immigrants in Nineteenth-Century America* (Coral Gables: University of Miami Press, 1972), argues that these newcomers did not easily assimilate. The data on the geographic dispersion of the Scandinavians are derived from the census of 1890. On Swedes in cities see Ulf Beijbom, *Swedes in Chicago: A Demographic and Social Study of the 1846-1880 Immigration* (Chicago: Chicago Historical Society and Studia Historia Upsaliensia, 1973). On Mormon Immigrants see John A. Olson, "Proselytism, Immigration and Settlement of Foreign Converts to the Mormon Culture in Zion," *Journal of the West 6* (1967):189-204.

CHAPTER V: THE NEW IMMIGRATION, 1890-1930

The most readily available summary of American immigration statistics for this period is found in U.S. Bureau of the Census, *Historical*

*Statistics of the United States,* series C89–119. American immigration in the late nineteenth and early twentieth centuries must be seen in an international context. For the basic comparative statistics see Ferenczi, *Statistics;* and Willcox, *Interpretations.* For data on immigration to Argentina, Australia, Brazil, Canada, Chile, the United States, and other countries see Ferenczi, *Statistics,* table 13 of the international tables. The analysis of immigration's changing impact across the decades is based on information in U.S. Bureau of the Census, *Historical Statistics of the United States,* series C89–90 and A6–8.

Little is known about the phenomenon of remigration. The government began keeping records on alien departures in 1908 but has not kept them since 1958. See Hutchinson, "Notes on Immigration Statistics of the United States," especially pp. 992–993; and Charles B. Keely, "Immigration Composition and Population Policy," *Science 185* (1979): 587–593. Among the few works on the subject of remigration are Betty Boyd Caroli, *Italian Repatriation from the United States, 1900–1914* (New York: Center for Migration Studies, 1974); Francesco P. Cerase, "A Study of Italian Migrants Returning from the U.S.A.," *International Migration Review 1* (1966–67):67–74; George R. Gilkey, "The United States and Italy: Migration and Repatriation," *Journal of Developing Areas 2* (1967):23–36; and Theodore Saloutos, *They Remember America: The Story of Repatriated Greek-Americans* (Berkeley: University of California Press, 1956). The statistics on remigration are derived from Ferenczi, *Statistics,* table 15 in the section on the United States and tables 1, 4, and 5 in the section on Argentina; for information about the ethnic makeup of the immigrant population in other receiving nations see especially table 13 of the international tables.

U.S. Senate, *Immigration Commission,* vol. XL: *The Immigration Situation in Other Countries: Canada, Australia, New Zealand, Argentina, Brazil,* is a starting point for the study of immigration outside the United States. For detailed information on Canadian immigration see Norman Macdonald, *Canada Immigration and Colonization, 1841–1903* (New York: Macmillan, 1968); Warren E. Kalbach, *The Impact of Immigration on Canada's Population* (Ottawa: Dominion Bureau of Statistics, 1970); and Carl A. Dawson, *Group Settlement: Ethnic Communities in Western Canada* (New York: Macmillan, 1936). For a succinct review of Australian immigration in this era see H. Burton, "Historical Survey of Immigration and Immigration Policy," in F. W. Eggleston, P. D. Phillips, G. Packer, E. Scott, S. S. Addison, eds., *The Peopling of Australia* (Melbourne: Melbourne University Press, 1933).

For brief but excellent summaries of the spread of the population explosion see Colin McEvedy and Richard Jones, *Atlas of World Population History* (Baltimore: Penguin, 1978). Taylor's *Distant Magnet* discusses the changing technology of oceanic travel. U.S. Senate, *Immigration*

*Commission,* vol. XXXIX: *Federal Immigration Legislation,* discusses national and international laws affecting steerage conditions.

Chinese immigration to the United States has not been studied with the sophistication this topic deserves. Despite its antiquity, Mary Roberts Coolidge's *Chinese Immigration* (New York: Holt, 1909), is still a standard source of information. Gunther Barth, *Bitter Strength: A History of the Chinese in the United States, 1850–1870* (Cambridge: Harvard University Press, 1964), provides a useful overview of conditions in China; and Kil Young Zo, "Chinese Emigration to the United States, 1850–1880" (Ph.D. diss., Columbia University, 1971), looks more closely at the origins of the emigration from the Sze-yap district. The statistical estimates cited in the chapter are from U.S. Bureau of the Census, *Historical Statistics of the United States,* series C104.

Japanese immigration is another understudied subject. Once again, a relatively old source is still a standard: see Yamato Ichihashi, *Japanese in the United States: A Critical Study of the Problems of the Japanese Immigrants and Their Children* (Stanford: Stanford University Press, 1932). The early chapters of William Petersen's *Japanese Americans: Oppression and Success* (New York: Random House, 1971) offer a useful description of conditions in Japan, the composition of the immigrant population, and the extension of immigration from Hawaii to the American mainland. Yasuo Wakatsuki offers a needed look at the phenomenon from a Japanese perspective in "Japanese Emigration to the United States, 1866–1924: A Monograph," *Perspectives in American History 12* (1979): 387–516. The estimates of annual Japanese immigration are from U.S. Bureau of the Census, *Historico! Statistics of the United States,* series C106.

Robert F. Foerster, *The Italian Emigration of Our Times* (Cambridge: Harvard University Press, 1919), offers an account of the domestic conditions that led to a worldwide dispersal of people from Italy and Sicily. The initial chapters of Joseph Lopreato's *Italian Americans* (New York: Random House, 1970) discuss the extreme impoverishment of southern Italy. John S. MacDonald, "Some Socio-economic Emigration Differentials in Rural Italy, 1902–1913," *Economic Development and Cultural Change 7* (1958):55–72, offers interesting insights into regional variations in the willingness of Italians to emigrate. For the pertinent figures on Italian immigration to the United States and other nations see Ferenczi, *Statistics,* table 13 of the international tables and table 11 in the section on Italy. See also U.S. Bureau of the Census, *Historical Statistics of the United States,* series C100.

Jewish immigration has deservedly received substantial attention. Irving Howe's *World of Our Fathers* (New York: Simon & Schuster, 1976) is a monumental account of the transfer of eastern European Jewry to the United States and of the development of a Jewish American culture there; the opening chapters of this book examine the conditions of the

Jews in Europe. Moses Rischin's *Promised City: New York Jews, 1870–1914* (Cambridge: Harvard University Press) likewise begins with a succinct history of European Jewry. For an excellent account of the impact of socioeconomic structures on decisions to migrate see Simon Kuznets, ''Immigration of Russian Jews to the United States: Background and Structure,'' *Perspectives in American History 9* (1975):35–124. Ferenczi, *Statistics,* reports that the United States began in 1899 to record the ''race or people'' to which immigrants belonged (p. 376); the data on Jewish, or ''Hebrew,'' migration are drawn from his book.

Slavic immigration is just beginning to receive proper attention from scholars. The classic study in the field, William I. Thomas and Florian Znaniecki, *The Polish Peasant in Europe and America,* 5 vols. (Chicago: University of Chicago Press, 1920), is outdated and exaggerates the amount of social disorganization in the Polish-American community. Joseph A. Wytrwal's *Social History of the Poles in America* (Detroit: Endurance, 1961) offers some useful background information but is far from a complete treatment of the causes and course of the immigration. The initial chapters of George J. Prpic's *South Slavic Immigration in America* (Boston: Twayne, 1978) provide a useful introduction to the complicated arrangement of ethnic groups in the Balkans, and later chapters discuss the exodus of these peoples at the turn of the century. Probably the best piece of analysis dealing with Slavic immigration is Johann Chemelar, ''The Austrian Emigration, 1900–1914,'' *Perspectives in American History 7* (1973):273–378. For figures on immigration, U.S. Bureau of the Census, *Historical Statistics of the United States,* series C96–99, is not as useful as Ferenczi, *Statistics,* especially table 13 of the international tables.

Theodore Saloutos was the dean of historians studying Greek immigration. Among his works see ''Causes and Patterns of Greek Emigration to the United States,'' *Perspectives in American History 7* (1973): 379–437; and *The Greeks in the United States* (Cambridge: Harvard University Press, 1964). Also useful are Thomas Capek, *The Czechs in America* (Boston: Houghton Mifflin, 1920); Wasyl Halich, *Ukrainians in the United States* (Chicago: University of Chicago Press, 1937); and Emil Lengyel, *Americans from Hungary* (Philadelphia: Lippincott, 1948). A. William Hoglund's *Finnish Immigrants in America, 1880–1920* (Madison: University of Wisconsin Press, 1960) is excellent.

For data on the Mexican population see McEvedy and Jones, *Atlas.* Arthur F. Corwin, ''Causes of Mexican Emigration to the United States: A Summary View,'' *Perspectives in American History 7* (1973): 557–635, offers a concise and perceptive analysis. The early chapters of Meier and Rivera, *The Chicanos,* are useful; and Carey McWilliams's *North from Mexico: The Spanish-Speaking People in the United States* (Philadelphia: Lippincott, 1948) is still of value. The statistics cited on Mexican immigration are derived from U.S. Bureau of the Census, *Historical Statistics of the United States,* series C112.

Hansen's *Mingling of the Canadian and American Peoples* is useful in the study of the new, as well as the old, immigration and for learning about American-Canadian population movements. But his work can be supplemented for the special topic of French Canadian immigration by Iris S. Pedea's "Quebec to 'Little Canada': The Coming of the French Canadians to New England in the Nineteenth Century," *New England Quarterly 23* (1950):365–380; and by Karel Bicha, *The American Farmer and the Canadian West* (Lawrence: Coronado, 1972). The data on Canadian immigration are spotty. U.S. Bureau of the Census, *Historical Statistics of the United States,* series C111, has some general figures, but for differentiating between the French and English Canadian streams see Ferenczi, *Statistics,* table 6 in the section on Canada and table 38 in the section on the United States.

C. Horace Hamilton, "The Negro Leaves the South," *Demography 1* (1964):273–295, provides a succinct summary of basic information on the movement of blacks to the North. For a more detailed review see Florette Henri, *Black Migration: Movement North, 1900–1920* (New York: Doubleday Anchor, 1975). Nell Irvin Painter, *Exodusters: Black Migration to Kansas after Reconstruction* (New York: Knopf, 1977), examines an early episode in the story of dispersion from the South. Gilbert Osofsky, *Harlem: The Making of a Ghetto* (New York: Harper & Row, 1966), discusses the migration of blacks to New York City from the 1890s through the 1920s. Allan H. Spear, *Black Chicago: The Making of a Negro Ghetto* (Chicago: University of Chicago Press, 1967), treats this episode in intranational migration from the perspective of the Middle West's largest city.

An analysis of U.S. Bureau of the Census, *Historical Statistics of the United States,* series C120–137, is the basis for the discussion of the changing importance of farmers, skilled workers, and laborers in the immigrant population. An examination of U.S. Senate, *Statistical Review of Immigration,* table 22, pp 98–178, underlies the comments on the occupational structure of the main immigrant groups. The data on the age structure among the immigrants are also derived from U.S. Bureau of the Census, *Historical Statistics of the United States,* series C138–142. Ferenczi, *Statistics,* is the best source of information on the sexual composition of the immigrant groups; see especially table 10 in the section on the United States.

Cecyle S. Neidle's *America's Immigrant Women* (Boston: Twayne, 1975) and Charlotte Baum, Paula Hyman, and Sonya Michel, *The Jewish Woman in America* (New York: New American Library, 1975) come to grips with an important topic, but much work remains to be done on the intersection of gender and ethnicity in the immigrant experience. Four contributions relevant to the area can be found in Ehrlich, *Immigrants in Industrial America:* Caroline Golab, "The Impact of the Industrial Experience on the Immigrant Family: The Huddled Masses Reconsidered," focuses on Poles in Pennsylvania; Carol Groneman, "She Earns as a Child—She Pays as a Man: Women Workers in a Mid-Nineteenth Century New York City Community," deals primarily with the Irish in and around the Five Points slum in Lower Manhattan; Tamara K. Hareven, "Family and Work Patterns of Immigrant Laborers in a Planned Industrial Town, 1900–1930," concentrates on the French Canadians of the Amoskeag Mills in Manchester, New Hampshire; and Virginia Yans McLaughlin, "A Flexible Tradition: South Italian Immigrants Confront New Work Experience," concerns newcomers in the region around Buffalo, New York.

The discussion of remigration is based on data drawn from Ferenczi, *Statistics,* tables 10, 15, and 19 in the section on the United States. Caroli, *Italian Remigration;* Cerase, "Study of Italian Migrants," Gilkey, "United States and Italy;" and Saloutos, *They Remember America* are also pertinent at this point. In addition, there is useful information in Barth, *Bitter Strength;* and in Rose Hum Lee, *The Chinese in the United States* (Hong Kong: Hong Kong University Press, 1960), on Chinese attitudes toward repatriation. Virginia Yans-McLaughlin's *Family and Community: Italian Immigrants in Buffalo, 1880–1930* (Ithaca: Cornell University Press, 1977) touches on the topic of the international market for migrant labor at the beginning of the twentieth century. For the sources used in assessing the geographic distribution of foreign-stock Americans and their demographic impact on the nation's population see U.S. Bureau of the Census. *Abstract of the Fourteenth Census of the United States, 1920* (1923; reprinted. New York: Arno, 1976), tables 3, 69–77, and 101–108.

CHAPTER VI: THE MOVEMENT TOWARD RESTRICTION, 1865–1924

A summary of court decisions affecting state efforts to regulate immigration can be found in U.S. Senate, *Immigration Commission, Federal Immigration Legislation.* Hutchinson, *Legislative History of American Immigration Policy,* provides comprehensive coverage of legislative action concerning immigration. Charlotte Erickson, *American Industry and the European Immigrant, 1860–1885* (Cambridge: Harvard University Press, 1957), examines the contract labor issue. Thomas Monroe Pitkin, *Keepers of the Gate: A History of Ellis Island* (New York: New York University Press, 1975); and Willard A. Heaps, *The Story of Ellis Island* (New York: Seabury, 1967), tell the story of the main immigrant reception center.

Gunther Barth discusses the Six Companies in *Bitter Strength*. Stuart C. Miller, *The Unwelcome Immigrant: The American Image of the Chinese, 1785-1882* (Berkeley: University of California Press, 1969), argues that unfavorable stereotypes of the Chinese predated their arrival in the United States. Alexander Saxton, *The Indispensable Enemy: Labor and the Anti-Chinese Movement in California* (Berkeley: University of California Press, 1971), focuses on the conflicts preceding exclusion.

John Higham, *Strangers in the Land: Problems of American Nativism, 1860-1925* (New Brunswick: Rutgers University Press, 1955), a recognized classic, is undoubtedly the best overview of its subject. On the development of the American economy after the Civil War see Edward C. Kirkland, *Industry Comes of Age: Business, Labor, and Public Policy, 1860-1897* (New York: Holt, Rinehart, 1961). Robert V. Bruce, *1877: Year of Violence* (Indianapolis: Bobbs-Merrill, 1959); and Henry David, *The History of the Haymarket Affair* (New York: Farrar & Rinehart, 1936), discuss major episodes of labor strife. Donald L. Kinzer, *An Episode in Anti-Catholicism: The American Protective Association* (Seattle: University of Washington Press, 1964), examines the foremost anti-Catholic organization of the 1890s. For information on the growing tolerance toward Catholics among some leading Protestants consult Cross, *Emergence of Liberal Catholicism in America*.

The literature on the economic position of the immigrants in America during the late nineteenth century is complex. Insights can be gained from Robert Higgs, "Race, Skills, and Earnings: American Immigrants in 1909," *Journal of Economic History 31* (1971):420-428; Peter J. Hill, "Relative Skill and Income Levels of Native and Foreign-Born Workers in the United States," *Explorations in Economic History 12* (1975):47-60; and Paul F. McGouldrick and Michael B. Tanner, "Did American Manufacturers Discriminate against Immigrants before 1914," *Journal of Economic History 37* (1977):723-746. The comparative data on literacy and on income are derived from *U.S. Senate, Immigration Commission;* vol. IV examines emigrant conditions in Europe, including literacy, and vols. VI-XX provide abundant material on immigrants in manufacturing and mining; for quick reference see vol. I: *Abstracts of Reports of the Immigration Commission*, especially table 1, p. 175 and tables 54-56, pp. 407-10.

Rischin, *The Promised City*, examines some of the internal divisions in the Jewish community. See also Myron Berman, "The Attitude of American Jewry towards East European Jewish Immigration, 1881-1914" (Ph.D. diss., Columbia University, 1963). Theodore Saloutos, "The Greek Orthodox Church in the United States and Assimilation," *International Migration Review 7* (1973):395-407, examines the path taken by a major Orthodox denomination.

Cross, *Emergence of Liberal Catholicism in America* is important to an understanding of the Americanization of Catholicism. Donna Merwick, *Boston's Priests, 1848–1910: A Study of Social and Intellectual Change* (Cambridge: Harvard University Press, 1973), traces the development of a native American but defensive Catholic clergy. Thomas T. McAvoy, *The Great Crisis in American Catholic History* (Chicago: Regnery, 1957), examines the Americanist controversy. Richard M. Linkh, *American Catholicism and European Immigrants, 1900–1924* (New York: Center for Migration Studies, 1975), analyzes the church's attitudes toward the new immigration. Silvano M. Tomasi, *Piety and Power: The Role of Italian Parishes in the New York Metropolitan Area, 1880–1930* (New York: Center for Migration Studies, 1975), discusses the role of the Italian national parish. Victor R. Greene, *For God and Country: The Rise of Polish and Lithuanian National Consciousness in America* (Madison: State Historical Society of Wisconsin, 1976), deals with, among other things, the Polish National Catholic church.

Caroline Golab, *Immigrant Destinations* (Philadelphia: Temple University Press, 1977), analyzes Philadelphia's Polish neighborhoods. Humbert S. Nelli, *Italians in Chicago, 1880–1930: A Study in Ethnic Mobility* (New York: Oxford University Press, 1970), discusses Italian neighborhoods in Chicago. Merton, "Latent Functions of the Machine," in Callow, *American Urban History* explains the appeal of the machine to the disadvantaged. On rates of naturalization see the abstract of the U.S. census for 1920, table 89. Milton L. Barron, "Intermediacy: Conceptualization of Irish Status in America," *Social Forces* 27 (1949):256–263, suggests reasons for the success of the Irish as ethnic politicians. Edward Kantowicz, *Polish-American Politics in Chicago, 1888–1940* (Chicago: University of Chicago Press, 1975), follows the growth of Polish influence in Chicago; and Howe, *World of Our Fathers,* traces the development of New York's Jewish community.

Barbara M. Solomon, *Ancestors and Immigrants: A Changing New England Tradition* (Cambridge: Harvard University Press, 1956), ably discusses old-stock Americans' inversely changing attitudes toward the old and new immigrants. Humbert S. Nelli, "The Padrone System in the United States," *Labor History 5* (1964):153–167, sensitively deals with a difficult subject; in his *Business of Crime: Italian and Syndicate Crime in the United States* (New York: Oxford University Press, 1976), Nelli discusses the role of criminal groups in late nineteenth-century Italy. Edwin Fenton, *Immigrants and Unions, A Case Study: Italians and American Labor, 1870–1920* (New York: Arno, 1975), presents a positive view of the Italians as union members.

George Mosse's *Toward the Final Solution: A History of European Racism* (New York: Fertig, 1978) is a brilliant exposition of the growth of modern anti-Semitism. Parts of Leonard Dinnerstein, ed., *Antisemitism in the United States* (New York: Holt, Rinehart & Winston, 1971), examine the roots of American anti-Semitism. Read also John Higham's "Anti-Semitism in the Gilded Age: A Reinterpretation," *Mississippi Valley Historical Review 43* (1957):559–578; and Solomon, *Ancestors and Immigrants.*

Richard Gambino retells the story of the New Orleans lynching in *Vendetta* (New York: Doubleday, 1977). See also Leonard Dinnerstein, *The Leo Frank Case* (New York: Columbia University Press, 1970). Early in 1982 a elderly witness to the killing came forward with evidence of Frank's innocence; see the *New York Times,* 8 March 1982.

Mosse, *Toward the Final Solution,* subtly points to disturbingly common roots to the thinking behind the American movement to restrict immigration and what ultimately took the heinous form of Nazi racial theory in Europe. Richard Hofstadter, *Social Darwinism in American Thought, 1860–1915* (Philadelphia: University of Pennsylvania Press, 1944), offers an excellent account of the spread of this intellectual school in the United States. Sidney Fine, *Laissez Faire and the General-Welfare State: A Study of Conflict in American Thought, 1865–1901* (Ann Arbor: University of Michigan Press, 1956), analyzes the conflict between the Social Darwinists and the Social Gospelers. On one of the most important of the new sciences see George W. Stocking, Jr., *Race, Culture, and Evolution: Essays in the History of Anthropology* (New York: Free Press, 1968). And on all these subjects, including the Immigration Restriction League, consult Solomon, *Ancestors and Immigrants;* and Higham, *Strangers in the Land.*

This Essay on Sources has frequently cited portions of the forty-two-volume report by the Immigration Commission. First published in 1911, these volumes were reprinted in 1970 by Arno Press and the *New York Times.* The new edition contains an incisive introduction by Oscar Handlin, who originally published the piece in his *Race and Nationality in American Life* (Boston: Little, Brown, 1948).

Ichihashi, *Japanese in the United States;* and Roger Daniels, *The Politics of Prejudice: The Anti-Japanese Movement in California and the Struggle for Japanese Exclusion* (Berkeley: University of California Press, 1962), examine the Gentlemen's Agreement. On Canadian immigration see Kalbach, *Impact of Immigration on Canada's Population.*

For information on Australia's programs consult Alexander T. Yarwood, "The Dictation Test: Historical Survey," *Australian Quarterly 30* (1958): 19–29; and A. C. Palfreeman, *The Administration of the White Australia Policy* (Melbourne: Melbourne University Press, 1967). John A. Garrard, *The English and Immigration, 1880–1910* (New York: Oxford University Press, 1971); and Lloyd P. Gartner, *The Jewish Immigrant in England, 1870–1914* (Detroit: Wayne State University Press, 1960), cover Great Britain's policies in this era. Carl E. Solberg, *Immigration and Nationalism: Argentina and Chile, 1890–1914* (Austin: University of

Texas Press, 1970), examines attitudes toward immigration in those nations.

Edward Cuddy, "Irish-American Propagandists and American
Neutrality," *Mid-America 49* (1967):252–275; and George M. Stephen-
son, "The Attitude of Swedish Americans towards the World War,"
*Proceedings of the Mississippi Valley Historical Association 10* (1918-19):
79–94, examine the responses of two groups to the international scene.
Edward G. Hartmann, *The Movement to Americanize the Immigrant* (New
York: Columbia University Press, 1948), recounts the drive for acculturation before, during, and after the war. Frederick C. Luebke's
*Bonds of Loyalty: German Americans during World War I* (DeKalb: Northern
Illinois University Press, 1974) is essential for an understanding of the
plight of these people. Joseph P. O'Grady, ed., *The Immigrants' Influence
on Wilson's Peace Policies* (Lexington: University of Kentucky Press,
1967), concludes that only the Jews and Poles made any impact.

For general information about the nativist movement after World
War I consult Higham, *Strangers in the Land.* David Brody, *Labor in Crisis:
The Steel Strike of 1919* (Philadelphia: Lippincott, 1965), provides useful
background about contemporary labor strife involving large numbers of
immigrants. Stanley Coben, "A Study in Nativism: The American Red
Scare of 1919-20," *Political Science Quarterly 79* (1964):52–75; and Robert
K. Murray, *Red Scare: A Study in National Hysteria, 1919-1920* (Minneapolis: University of Minnesota Press, 1955), discuss the roots of that
unhappy phenomenon. Francis Russell, *Tragedy in Dedham: The Story of
the Sacco-Vanzetti Case* (New York: McGraw-Hill, 1962), offers a lengthy
treatment of the still controversial episode.

Paul L. Murphy, "Intolerance in the 1920s," *Journal of American
History 51* (1964):60–76, presents a brief overview of the 1920s.
Gusfield, *Symbolic Crusade,* points out the social implications of the prohibition drive. Kenneth T. Jackson, *The Ku Klux Klan in the Cities, 1915–
1930* (New York: Oxford University Press, 1967), emphasizes the anti-
Catholic and anti-Semitic aspects of the Klan. Robert Divine, *American
Immigration Policy, 1924-1952* (New Haven: Yale University Press,
1957); and Hutchinson, *Legislative History of American Immigration Policy,*
provide excellent analyses of the legislation passed in the 1920s.

CHAPTER VII: FROM IMMIGRANTS TO ETHNICS

Divine, *American Immigration Policy;* and Hutchinson, *Legislative History of American Immigration Policy,* offer the best reviews of the pertinent
debates and laws. On labor's attitudes see Robert D. Parmet, *Labor and
Immigration in Industrial America* (Boston: Twayne, 1981). For a background on the stance taken by business consult James Weinstein, *The
Corporate Ideal in the Liberal State, 1900-1918* (Boston: Beacon, 1968).

The Quota Board's report can be found in the American Council of Learned Societies, "Report of the Committee on Linguistic and National Stocks." The quotas in effect in 1921–1924, in 1924–1929, and after July 1, 1929, are reported in U.S. Senate, Committee on the Judiciary, *The Immigration and Naturalization Systems of the United States* (Washington, D.C.: Government Printing Office, 1950), table 2; this source also contains a useful summary of the preference categories in the Reed-Johnson Act. Divine, *American Immigration Policy;* Hutchinson, *Legislative History of American Immigration Policy;* and Abraham Hoffman, *Unwanted Mexican Americans in the Great Depression: Repatriation Pressures, 1929–39* (Tucson: University of Arizona Press, 1974), examine the special situation of Latin American immigration.

Several works have examined America's response to Hitler's ethnic policies. The most notable and balanced are Saul Friedman, *No Haven for the Oppressed: United States Policy toward Jewish Refugees, 1938–1945* (Detroit: Wayne State University Press, 1973); and David S. Wyman, *Paper Walls: America and the Refugee Crisis, 1938–1941* (Amherst: University of Massachusetts Press, 1968). For accounts of those fortunate enough to escape consult Laura Fermi, *Illustrious Immigrants: The Intellectual Migration from Europe, 1930–1941* (Chicago: University of Chicago Press, 1958); and Donald Fleming and Bernard Bailyn, eds., "The Intellectual Migration: Europe and America, 1930–1960," published as *Perspectives in American History 2* (1969).

Ernesto Galarza, *Merchants of Labor: The Mexican Bracero Story* (San Jose: Rosicrucian Press, 1964), puts in historical perspective the problems of the Mexican agricultural laborer in the United States. Richard B. Craig, *The Bracero Program: Interest Groups and Foreign Policy* (Austin: University of Texas Press, 1971), carries the study of the *bracero* program through to its conclusion. See also James F. Creagan, "Public Law 78: A Tangle of Domestic and International Relations," *Journal of Inter-American Studies 7* (1965): 541–556.

Divine, *American Immigration Policy;* Hutchinson, *Legislative History of American Immigration Policy;* and U.S. Senate, *Immigration and Naturalization Systems,* are all useful for an understanding of America's postwar policies. See also Leonard Dinnerstein, *America and the Survivors of the Holocaust* (New York: Columbia University Press, 1982). M. Madeline Lorimer, "America's Response to Europe's Displaced Persons, 1945–1962: A Preliminary Report" (Ph.D. diss., St. Louis University, 1964), examines the Displaced Persons Act of 1948. An entire issue of *Law and Contemporary Problems 21* (1956) is devoted to immigration restriction and the McCarran-Walter Act.

David Johanson discusses the "History of the White Australia Policy," in Kenneth Rivett, ed., *Immigration: Control or Colour Barrier* (Melbourne: Melbourne University Press, 1962). See also Kenneth Rivett, ed., *Australia and the Non-white Migrant* (Melbourne: Melbourne

University Press, 1975). U.S. Senate, *Immigration and Naturalization Systems,* summarizes policies in Latin America and other areas of the world. Kalbach, *Impact of Immigration on Canada's Population,* examines attitudes north of the United States.

For information on the flow of immigrants from the mid-1920s through the late 1940s consult U.S. Senate, *Immigration and Naturalization Systems,* especially tables 4–9B. Helen F. Eckerson, "Immigration and National Origins," *Annals of the American Academy of Political and Social Science 367* (1966):4–14, contrasts the expected and actual demographic results of the immigration restriction laws.

Hartmann, *Movement to Americanize the Immigrant,* discusses various aspects of the Americanization effort. See also Higham, *Strangers in the Land.* Robert A. Carlson, *The Quest for Conformity: Americanization through Education* (New York: Wiley, 1975), analyzes the role of the schools in this drive. Selma Berrol, "Public Schools and Immigrants: The New York City Experience"; and John F. McClymer, "The Americanization Movement and the Education of the Foreign Born Adult, 1914–25," which appear in Bernard J. Weiss, ed., *American Education and the European Immigrant, 1840–1940* (Urbana: University of Illinois Press, 1982), are valuable. See also A. Gerd Korman, *Industrialization, Immigrants, and Americanizers: The View from Milwaukee, 1865–1925* (Madison: State Historical Society of Wisconsin, 1967).

Data on the demographic changes in the foreign-stock population are available in U.S. Bureau of the Census, *Summary of the Sixteenth Census of the United States, 1940* (1943; reprint ed., New York: Arno, 1976), tables 10, 14, 15, 36, and 64; U.S. Bureau of the Census, *Summary of the Seventeenth Census, 1950* (1953; reprint ed., New York: Arno, 1976), table 49; and U.S. Bureau of the Census, *Summary of the Eighteenth Census, 1960* (1961; reprint ed., New York: Arno, 1976), table 70. Joshua Fishman, Vladimir C. Nahirny, John E. Hofman, and Robert G. Hayden, *Language Loyalty in the United States: The Maintenance and Perpetuation of Non-English Mother Tongues by American Ethnic and Religious Groups* (The Hague: Mouton, 1966), is the standard work on its subject. Irvin L. Child, *Italian or American: The Second Generation in Conflict* (New York: Russell and Russell, 1943), is a sensitive study of acculturation across generations.

Nathan Glazer, *American Judaism* (Chicago: University of Chicago Press, 1960), is a fine, brief account. Marshall Sklare, *Conservative Judaism: An American Religious Movement* (New York: Free Press, 1955), examines the emergence of this middle tradition. Judith R. Kramer and Seymour Leventman, *Children of the Gilded Ghetto: Conflict Resolution of Three Generations of American Jews* (New Haven: Yale University Press, 1961), analyzes various paths of acculturation.

Data on naturalization have been taken from table 10 of the subsection of the U.S. census for 1940 entitled "Country of Origin of the Foreign Stock." table 10. Arthur Mann's *La Guardia: A Fighter against His Times, 1882–1933* (Philadelphia: Lippincott, 1959) and *La Guardia Comes to Power, 1933* (Philadelphia: Lippincott, 1965) are the standard works on the "Little Flower." On New York politics see Ronald H. Bayor, *Neighbors in Conflict: The Irish, Germans, Jews and Italians of New York City, 1929–1941* (Baltimore: Johns Hopkins University Press, 1978). Alex Gottfried, *Boss Cermak of Chicago: A Study of Political Leadership* (Seattle: University of Washington Press, 1962), is solid and informative. Oscar Handlin, *Al Smith and His America* (Boston: Little Brown, 1958), is brief but valuable. Ruth C. Silva, *Rum, Religion, and Votes: 1928 Reexamined* (University Park: Pennsylvania State University Press, 1962), investigates the impact of Smith's Catholicism on the election. For varying views of the long-term effects of Smith's candidacy consult Samuel Lubell, *The Future of American Politics,* 2d. rev. ed. (New York: Doubleday, 1956); and Jerome M. Clubb and Howard W. Allen, "The Cities and the Election of 1928: Partisan Realignment," *American Historical Review* 74 (1969):1205–1220. John Allswang, *A House for All Peoples: Ethnic Politics in Chicago, 1890–1936* (Lexington: University of Kentucky Press, 1971), focuses on the growth of the Democratic party among ethnics in these years.

Sander A. Diamond, *The Nazi Movement in the United States, 1924–1941* (Ithaca: Cornell University Press, 1974), emphasizes the role of recent immigrants. John P. Diggins, in *Mussolini and Fascism: The View from America* (Princeton: Princeton University Press, 1972); and in "The Italo-American Anti-Fascist Opposition," *Journal of American History* 54 (1967):579–598, discusses both sympathy with Mussolini and opposition to him among Italian-Americans. Roger Daniels, *Concentration Camps U.S.A.: Japanese Americans and World War II* (New York: Holt, Rinehart & Winston, 1971); and Morton Grodzin, *Americans Betrayed: Politics and the Japanese Evacuation* (Chicago: University of Chicago Press, 1949), examine the causes and consequences of the detention of Japanese Americans.

Meier and Rivera, *The Chicanos,* includes some information on the zoot suit riots and on the Sleepy Lagoon case, a 1942 murder trial in which twenty-three Mexican-Americans were defendants. Harvard Sitkoff examines "The Detroit Race Riot of 1943," *Michigan History* 53 (1969):183–194. Dominic J. Capeci, Jr., *The Harlem Riot of 1943* (Philadelphia: Temple University Press, 1977), puts this event in a broader context. Hamilton, "The Negro Leaves the South," provides basic statistics on the black exodus of the 1930s and 1940s.

Louis L. Gerson, *The Hyphenate in Recent American Politics and Diplomacy* (Lawrence: University of Kansas Press, 1964), has useful information on the Cold War period. Everett C. Ladd, Jr., and Charles

D. Hadley, *Transformation of the American Party System: Political Coalitions from the New Deal to the 1970s* (New York: Norton, 1975), is also pertinent. William M. Halsey, *The Survival of American Innocence: Catholicism in an Era of Disillusionment, 1920–1940* (Notre Dame: University of Notre Dame Press, 1980), examines a little-known phase of the church's development. Vincent P. De Santis, "American Catholics and McCarthyism," *Catholic Historical Review 51* (1965):1–30; and Donald F. Crosby, *God, Church, and Flag: Senator Joseph R. McCarthy and the Catholic Church, 1950–57* (Chapel Hill: University of North Carolina Press, 1978), take balanced views of a controversial subject.

CHAPTER VIII: THE TRIPLE MELTING POT AND BEYOND

Data on demographic changes have been derived from the U.S. Bureau of Census, *Summary of the Eighteenth Census, 1960,* especially tables 162–163. The best study of the demise of an immigrant neighborhood is Herbert Gans, *The Urban Villagers: Group and Class in the Life of Italian-Americans* (New York: Free Press, 1962), which recounts the fate of Boston's West End.

U.S. Bureau of the Census, *Current Population Reports* (Washington, D.C.: Government Printing Office, 1958), Series P-20, No. 79, concerns "Religions Reported by the Civilian Population of the United States: March 1957." Ruby Jo Reeves Kennedy, "Single or Triple Melting Pot: Intermarriage in New Haven, 1870–1950," *American Journal of Sociology 58* (1952):55–66, is one of several groundbreaking studies she made of intermarriage. Will Herberg, *Protestant-Catholic-Jew* (New York: Doubleday, 1955), is of fundamental importance to understanding the 1950s. John Courtenay Murray, *We Hold These Truths: Catholic Reflections on the American Proposition* (New York: Sheed and Ward, 1960), best summarizes his views. Theodore H. White, *The Making of the President, 1960* (New York: Atheneum, 1961), presents a journalist's account of the campaign.

Hutchinson, *Legislative History of American Immigration Policy,* discusses in detail the changes made in American laws in this period. Silvano M. Tomasi and Charles B. Keely, *Whom Have We Welcomed?* (New York: Center for Migration Studies, 1975), focuses on current policy. On recent refugee programs consult Edward M. Kennedy, "Refugee Act of 1980," *International Migration Review 15* (1981):141–156.

For discussions of recent Canadian programs read Freda Hawkins, "Canadian Immigration Policy and Management," *International Migration Review 8* (1974):141–154; and Anthony H. Richmond, "Canadian Immigration: Recent Developments and Future Prospects," *Interna-*

*tional Migration 13* (1975):163–182. Ian A. Macdonald, *The New Immigration Law* (London: Butterworths, 1972), examines changes in Britain's policies. On Australian practices see Rivett, *Australia and the Non-white Migrant;* and *New York Times,* 2 November 1981. Several works discuss the conditions of migrants in Europe. See, for example, W. R. Böhning, *The Migration of Workers in the United Kingdom and the European Community* (New York: Oxford University Press, 1972); Stephen Castles and Godula Kosack, *Immigrant Workers and Class Structure in Western Europe* (New York: Oxford University Press, 1973); and Ronald E. Krane, ed., *International Labor Migration in Europe* (New York: Praeger, 1979).

Statistics on recent immigration to the United States are available in U.S. Department of Justice, *1977 Annual Report of the Immigration and Naturalization Service* (Washington, D.C.: Government Printing Office, 1979). Monica Boyd analyzes ''The Changing Nature of Central and Southeast Asian Immigration to the United States, 1961–1972,'' *International Migration Review 8* (1974):507–520. For related information consult Charles B. Keely, ''Immigration Composition and Population Policy,'' *Science 185* (1974):587–593. On America's importation of foreign talent see Thomas L. Bernard, ''United States Immigration Laws and the Brain Drain,'' *International Migration 8* (1970): 31–38; and Amelendu Guhu, ''Brain Drain Issue and Indicators on Brain Drain,'' *International Migration 15* (1977):3–20.

Arthur A. Markowitz, ''Humanitarianism versus Restrictionism: The United States and the Hungarian Refugees,'' *International Migration Review 7* (1973):46–59, discusses an example, taken from the 1950s, of American ambivalence toward refugees. Darrel Montero, *Vietnamese Americans: Patterns of Resettlement and Economic Adaptation in the United States* (Boulder: Western, 1979), examines the influx of people from Southeast Asia in the 1970s. Rafael J. Prohias and Lourdes Casal, *The Cuban Minority in the U.S.: Preliminary Report on Need Identification and Program Evaluation, Final Report for Fiscal Year 1973,* 2d. ed. rev. (Washington, D.C.: Cuban National Planning Council, 1974); and Robert L. Bach, ''The New Cuban Immigrants: Their Background and Prospects,'' *Monthly Labor Review 103* (1980):39–46, contribute to an understanding of the changing phases of this refugee influx. For measures of public opinion consult the *Gallup Opinion Index* (Princeton: American Institute of Public Opinion), Report No. 170 (Sept. 1979); No. 177 (April–May 1980).

Stanley Elkins, *Slavery: A Problem in American Institutional and Intellectual Life* (Chicago: University of Chicago Press, 1959), is a famous study; however, Elkins's thesis has been seriously challenged in works like Blassingame, *Slave Community,* which itself relfects the changing intellectual climate. Benjamin Muse, *The American Negro Revolution:*

*From Nonviolence to Black Power, 1963–1967* (Bloomington: Indiana University Press, 1968), discusses an important period in the civil rights struggle. August Meier and Elliott Rudwick, eds., *Black Protest in the Sixties* (Chicago: Quadrangle, 1970), is a useful compilation.

Vine Deloria, *Custer Died for Your Sins: An Indian Manifesto* (New York: Macmillan, 1969), exemplifies the new Indian assertiveness. Alvin M. Josephy, Jr., comp., *Red Power: The American Indians' Fight for Freedom* (New York: McGraw-Hill, 1970), is a documentary history of the movement. On recent federal policy toward the Indians, consult Hagan, *American Indians;* and Gary Orfield, *A Study of the Termination Policy* (Chicago: University of Chicago Press, 1966).

The figures on the distribution of the Hispanic population are derived from the U.S. Census for 1980. Joseph P. Fitzpatrick, *Puerto Rican Americans: The Meaning of Migration to the Mainland* (Englewood Cliffs: Prentice-Hall, 1971); and Roy Simon Bryce-Laporte, "New York City and the New Caribbean Immigration: A Contextual Statement," *International Migration Review 13* (1979):214–234, are valuable sources on non-Mexican Hispanics in the United States. Stan Steiner, *La Raza: The Mexican Americans* (New York: Harper & Row, 1968), examines the growing political and cultural awareness of this group.

Horace M. Kallen, *Culture and Democracy in the United States* (New York: Boni and Liveright, 1924), incorporates an essay, "Democracy versus the Melting Pot," that he originally wrote for *The Nation* in 1915. Milton M. Gordon, *Assimilation in American Life: The Role of Race, Religion, and National Origins* (New York: Oxford University Press, 1964), has become a classic study.

Hadley Cantril, "Educational and Economic Composition of Religious Groups: An Analysis of Poll Data," *American Journal of Sociology 48* (1943):574–579, is one of the earliest regularly cited studies of this topic. Gerhard Lenski presents his thesis in *The Religious Factor* (New York: Doubleday, 1961). R. H. Knapp and H. B. Goodrich's "The Origins of American Scientists" can be found in D. C. McClelland, ed., *Studies in Motivation* (New York: Appleton-Century-Crofts, 1955). For views from scholars with Catholic backgrounds consult John J. Kane, *Catholic-Protestant Conflicts in America* (Chicago: Regnery, 1955); Thomas F. O'Dea, *American Catholic Dilemma: An Inquiry into Intellectual Life* (New York: Sheed and Ward, 1958); John Tracy Ellis, "American Catholics and the Intellectual Life," *Thought 30* (1955):351–388; and Gustave Weigel, "American Catholic Intellectualism: A Theologian's Reflections," *Review of Politics 19* (1957):275–307.

For incisive studies of the contemporary Catholic condition consult Andrew M. Greeley's *The American Catholic: A Social Portrait* (New York: Basic Books, 1977) and *Communal Catholic: A Personal Manifesto* (New York: Seabury, 1976). Greeley's *Crisis in the Church: A Study of Religion in*

*America* (Chicago: Thomas More, 1979), among other contributions, brings up to data his longtime interest in Catholic representation in American intellectual life. Norval D. Glenn and Ruth Hyland, "Religious Preference and Worldly Success: Some Evidence from National Surveys," *American Sociological Review 32* (1967):73–85; and Gary D. Bouma, "Beyond Lenski: A Critical Review of Recent 'Protestant Ethic' Research," *Journal for the Scientific Study of Religion 12* (1973): 141–155, examine new findings by economists and sociologists since the 1960s. Stephen Steinberg, *The Ethnic Myth: Race, Ethnicity, and Class in America* (New York: Atheneum, 1981), documents the growing number of Catholics in academics.

Much of the statistical information on ethnic attitudes and behavior in recent years is derived from data extracted for the years 1977, 1978, and 1980 from the *General Social Survey Cumulative File, 1972–1980* [machine-readable data file]. Principal investigator, James A. Davis, NORC ed. (Chicago: National Opinion Research Center [producer], 1980). (Ann Arbor: Inter-University Consortium for Political and Social Research [distributor]). For additional information on the questions asked consult National Opinion Research Center, *General Social Surveys, 1972–1980: Cumulative Codebook* (Storrs: Roper Center, University of Connecticut, 1980). The statistical information on the 1980 election is based on an analysis of the *American National Election Study, 1980: Pre- and Post-Election Surveys* [machine-readable data file]. Principal investigator, Warren E. Miller. 1982 ed. (Ann Arbor: Center for Political Studies, Institute for Social Research, University of Michigan [producer]. (Ann Arbor: Inter-University Consortium for Political and Social Research [distributor]). For additional information on the questions asked consult Warren E. Miller and the National Election Studies Center for Political Studies, University of Michigan, *American National Election Study, 1980* (Ann Arbor: Inter-University Consortium for Political Social Research, 1982): vol. I: *Pre- and Post-Election Surveys.* See also Andrew M. Greeley, *Ethnicity, Denomination, and Inequality* (Beverly Hills: Sage, 1976); Norman H. Nie, Barbara F. Currie, and Andrew M. Greeley, "Political Attitudes among American Ethnics: A Study of Perceptual Distortion," *Ethnicity 1* (1974):317–344; Joan L. Fee, "Party Identification among American Catholics, 1972, 1973," *Ethnicity 3* (1976):53–69; and the epilogue to Mark R. Levy and Michael S. Kramer, *The Ethnic Factor: How America's Minorities Decide Elections* (New York: Simon & Schuster, 1973).

Philip E. Converse, Angus Campbell, Warren E. Miller, and Donald E. Stokes, "Stability and Change in 1960: A Reinstating Election," *American Political Science Review 55* (1961):269–280, discusses the impact of religion on the Kennedy-Nixon contest. Andrew M. Greeley examines the persistence of anti-Catholicism in *An Ugly Little Secret* (New

York: Sheed, Andrews and McMeel, 1978). For an analysis of prejudice against white ethnics, see Michael Lerner, "Respectable Bigotry," *American Scholar 38* (1969):606–617. Michael Novak's angry volume, *The Rise of the Unmeltable Ethnics: Politics and Culture in the Seventies* (New York: Macmillan, 1971), is probably the best-known statement of the new ethnicity. Steinberg, *The Ethnic Myth,* is a sharply critical of the new ethnicity.

Readers should look for Nathan Glazer and Daniel P. Moynihan's *Beyond the Melting Pot: The Negroes, Puerto Ricans, Jews, Italians, and Irish of New York City,* rev. ed. (Cambridge: M.I.T. Press, 1970), which contains an important introduction about developments during the 1960s. See Gordon, *Assimilation in American Life;* and William M. Newman, *American Pluralism: A Study of Minority Groups and Social Theory* (New York: Harper & Row, 1973), for important discussions of the theories of ethnicity. Harry S. Stout examines aspects of the connection between ethnicity and religion in "Ethnicity: The Vital Center of Religion in America," *Ethnicity 2* (1975):204–224. Harold J. Abramson, *Ethnic Diversity in Catholic America* (New York: Wiley, 1973); and Charles H. Anderson, *White Protestant Americans: From National Origins to Religious Group* (Englewood Cliffs: Prentice-Hall, 1970), discuss variations within religious groups.

R. A. Schermerhorn, "Ethnicity in the Perspective of the Sociology of Knowledge," *Ethnicity 1* (1974):1–14, examines the relationship between growing ethnic awareness and rising black consciousness. John Appel, "American Negro and Immigrant Experience: Similarities and Differences," *American Quarterly 18* (1966):95–103, emphasizes the contrasts between the histories of ethnic and racial groups. For an important debate on the relative roles of race and class in black life at present see "The Black Plight: Race or Class? A Debate between Kenneth B. Clark and Carl Gershman," *New York Times Magazine,* October 5, 1980, pp. 22–109. William Julius Wilson, *The Declining Significance of Race: Blacks and Changing American Institutions* (Chicago: University of Chicago Press, 1978), is an important study of changing conditions in the United States.

### EPILOGUE: AMERICA, 1980

Most of the description of ethnic, religious, and racial groups in contemporary America is based on a computer-assisted analysis of the data gathered for General Social Surveys for 1977, 1978, and 1980, See also U.S. Bureau of the Census, *Current Population Reports,* series P-20, nos. 221 (1971) and 249 (1973).

The data on recent immigration to the United States are derived from U.S. Department of Justice, *1977 Annual Report of the Immigration and Naturalization Service.* On Hispanics in the United States see U.S. Bureau of the Census, *Current Population Reports,* series P-20, no. 354. Comparisons between the United States and Mexico can be drawn from U.S. Bureau of the Census, *Country Demographic Profiles: Mexico* (Washington, D.C.: Government Printing Office, 1979), and John Paxton, ed., *Statesman's Yearbook* (New York: St. Martin's Press, 1982).

Julian Samora, *Los Mojados: The Wetback Story* (Notre Dame: University of Notre Dame Press, 1971), offers a good overview of both legal and undocumented Mexican immigration. Additional readings, however, are necessary for recent years. See, for example, Jorge A. Bustamente, "Undocumented Immigration from Mexico: Research Report," *International Migration Review 11* (1977):149–177; Alejandro Portes, "Toward a Structural Analysis of Illegal (Undocumented) Immigration," *International Migration Review 12* (1978):469–484; and Josh Reichert and Douglas S. Massey, "Patterns of U.S. Immigrants from a Mexican Sending Community: A Comparison of Legal and Illegal Immigrants," *International Migration Review 13* (1979):599–623. David M. Heer, "What Is the Annual Net Flow of Undocumented Mexican Immigrants to the United States," *Demography 16* (1979): 417–423, is a balanced effort to estimate the actual number of people involved in this traffic.

Charles B. Keely discusses various aspects of illegal immigration in "Illegal Immigration," *Scientific American 246* (1982):41–47. See also Grant S. McClellan, *Immigrants, Refugees, and U.S. Policy* (New York: Wilson, 1981). Meier and Rivera, *The Chicanos;* and Craig, *The Bracero Program,* are informative about past experiences with undocumented immigration. For recent changes in American immigration law and pending proposals consult the various annual volumes of the *Congressional Quarterly Almanac* and current issues of the *Congressional Quarterly Weekly Report.* In this regard, U.S. Congress, House of Representatives and Senate, Committees on the Judiciary, *U.S. Immigration Policy and the National Interest* (Washington, D.C.: Government Printing Office, 1981); and *Administration's Proposals on Immigration and Refugee Policy* (Washington, D.C.: Government Printing Office, 1982) are also important.

# Index